The Great War

This edition has been printed directly from camera-ready copy.

ISBN 0-7872-1705-0

Library of Congress Catalog Card Number: 95-80659

Printed in the United States of America
10 9 8 7 6 5 4 3 2 1

The Great War

Second Edition

Robert A. Pois

University of Colorado
Boulder, Colorado

KENDALL/HUNT PUBLISHING COMPANY
4050 Westmark Drive Dubuque, Iowa 52002

Contents

Acknowledgments

Picture Credits:

1. Süddeutscher Verlag Bilderdienst
2. Hulton Deutsch Collection (HDC)
3. HDC
4. HDC
5. *Illustrated London News*
6. Libraire Larousse, Paris
7. Imperial War Museum (IMW)
8. HDC
9. IMW
10. IMW
11. Novosti Press Agency
12. *Illustrated London News*
13. IMW
14. IMW
15. Popperfoto
16. Süddeutscher Verlag Bilderdienst
17. IMW
18. IMW
19. IMW
20. Bibliotheque de Documentation Internationale Contemporaine, Paris

21. Women's International League for Peace and Freedom (WILPF) Collection, Archives, University of Colorado–Boulder Libraries
22. IMW
23. IMW
24. IMW
25. IMW
26. Roger Viollet, Paris

Grateful acknowledgment is made to the following:

Little, Brown and Company, Boston, for permission to use maps taken from Basil Liddell Hart, *The Real War, 1914–1918,* Boston, Little, Brown and Company, 1930.

Farrar, Straus & Giroux, Inc., New York, for permission to quote from Philip Larkin, "MCMXIV," originally published in his *Whitsun Weddings,* London, Faber and Faber Limited, 1961.

The Estate of Isaac Rosenberg, Chatto and Windus, for permission to quote from Isaac Rosenberg, "Dead Man's Dump," to be found in Gordon Bottomley and Denys Harding (eds.), *The Collected Poems of Isaac Rosenberg,* London, Chatto and Windus, 1937.

1

An Introduction

WHEN I was an increasingly indifferent student in a Chicago grammar school more years ago than I care to remember, one event in the school year impressed me greatly. On November 11, at 11:00 A.M., the teacher would have her class (all my teachers were female) stand and face east, towards France. At one point, before the seventh grade, this practice ceased. I participated in this ritual often enough, however, so that it made quite an impression on me. Once, a teacher, who must have been somewhat over fifty, wept quietly. One of the class thugs, trying to make light of it, poked me and whispered something to the effect that "Ole Miss Something-or-other lost her boyfriend in 1918. She hasn't had any lovin' in over thirty years. You'd be weeping, too." Despite this effort at what we now call "trivialization," what is variously known as "World War I," "The First World War," or "The Great War," has fascinated me from that time on. In fact, my fascination with it is so great that an acquaintance who believed in reincarnation suggested that I had fought in it, dying, he suspected, in the Somme campaign. I found this explanation, however, to be somewhat unlikely.

While the source for my intense interest in this particular war continues to remain obscure, there is no question in my mind that it was the single most crucial event of this century. Without it, there would have been no Nazis, and hence no Holocaust, Fascism of any kind probably would not have been all that significant, and there would have been no Russian Revolution (or, if radical change had occurred in Russia, it would have assumed a different form), and hence no Soviet Union, with all the terrors associated with it. The Austro-Hungarian and Ottoman Empires, the latter already in sharp decline, might well have fallen apart, but, in ways which might well have spared us the terrible national conflicts which now haunt us. Whether or not the majority of its citizens wished it, the Great War saw the emergence of the United States as a world power.

What World War I, the First World War, or the Great War—whatever one chooses to call it—did that was of the greatest significance was to harden Europeans to mass murder, without which something like the Nazi Holocaust would not have been possible. It did this through engagements such as the Somme and Verdun, where advances measured in yards were paid for in losses of life so stupendous as to be equalled, or, in some cases exceeded, only by casualties sustained by both sides on the Eastern Front in World War II, something in turn made highly probable by the century's first world war. So enormous was the impact of this—for soldiers, probably the worst war ever fought—that I prefer to call it "The Great War." Throughout the text, however, I use all three designations more-or-less interchangeably. The terms "World War I" and "First World War" are used often so that the global nature of the conflict is underscored, as is the fact that it made another such conflict highly likely.

There is another "technical" issue of some importance. Up until the time of the Bolshevik seizure of power, Russia measured time according to what is called the "Julian Calendar." It was thirteen days "behind" the "Gregorian Calendar," which, introduced by Pope Gregory XIII in 1582, had come into use everywhere in the Western World since then. The Bolsheviks switched what would become the Soviet Union over to the Gregorian Calendar soon after they came to power. For purposes of consistency, I follow the Gregorian Calendar, i.e., what has become known as the "new style" one, throughout my consideration of things Russian. Thus, while, according to what is known as the "old style," i.e., Julian, calendar, which was still in use at the time, the Bolsheviks seized power on October 25, 1917, I have this event occurring on November 7. Up to now, anyway, November 7 has been, along with May Day, the most important holiday celebrated in the former Soviet Union.

This book was written during a time of enormous personal stress. Due to this, things haven't moved along as expected. Kevin S. Crossland, associate editor of Kendall/Hunt Publishing Company, has been most understanding, while being a welcome source of encouragement. I am very grateful for this. The work of Ms. Pat Murphy, departmental secretary and literary critic, has been, as always, extraordinary. My thanks go to her. The index was prepared by Natalie Parker. Expressing gratitude towards one's wife is a usage which just about always answers needs often bordering on the ethical. In my case, I can honestly say that, without the encouragement and assistance of Anne Marie (among other things, she taught me how to use a p.c.), this work would never have been completed. Particularly bearing in mind the travails experienced by us in recent days, all that she has done for me is a source not merely of gratitude, but, of wonder. To my dear wife, Anne Marie, thank you.

Robert A. Pois
Boulder, Colorado
April, 1993

2

Diplomatic Adventures and Military Plans

EUROPE RESPONDS TO GERMANY

AFTER years of dreaming and planning by generations of poets, philosophers, and statesmen, Germany became a unified nation-state in January, 1871. While not as the result of divine dispensation, circumstances of power, opportunities, and just plain chance were responsible for Prussia's being the power which achieved the goal of unification and its prime minister, now chancellor of the newly-emerged state, Otto von Bismarck (1815-1898), was determined as much as possible to mold it in his interpretation of the Prussian image.

Bismarck had had to fight three wars in order to unify a country to which he was attached by considerations of power at least as much as he was by sentiment. Denmark, the first victim of his power-political machinations, offered little to fear. Austria-Hungary, the second, while sustaining substantial losses in pride and prestige, and nurturing no small number of grievances against Bismarck in particular and the newly-created Central European power state in general, could not, on its own, undo recent events. And, for the moment, no worthwhile alliance was forthcoming. In any case, nationalistic forces were abroad in the Austro-Hungarian Empire, a crazy-quilt patchwork of Germans, Hungarians, Slavs, and Italians, and, at times, it seemed that all that the ruling Habsburg Dynasty could do to hold things together was to balance off respective national interests and animosities.

France was the country which, in terms of blood, treasure, and prestige, had lost the most during the course of German unification, and Bismarck, who, at one time, had served as Prussian ambassador to the country, was most concerned about a war of revenge, one which, if joined by a power allied with France, might well bring about the demise of his so recently-unified nation. Thus, as Bismarck saw it, an important element of Imperial Germany's foreign policy had to be keeping France isolated diplomatically. Another possible threat to Germany was some sort of falling-out in Eastern Europe, particularly in the volatile Balkans. Austria-Hungary and Russia had conflicting interests there, particularly as regarding territories held by the crumbling Ottoman Empire. If war should break out in this benighted area of the world, Germany might well be drawn into it. Thus, preserving the peace in Eastern Europe was also a cardinal tenet of Bismarck's foreign policy.

Great Britain, traditionally suspicious of France, had watched Germany unify with mixed emotions. Ensconced in her traditional "splendid isolation," she would wait upon events with regard to any foreign policy stance towards this new, powerful, and possibly dangerous, state. In his turn, Bismarck certainly preferred to have some sort of working arrangement with Great Britain, maybe even an alliance. In view of traditional British standoffishness, however, this appeared to be unlikely. All that Germany could do, as Bismarck saw it, was to avoid antagonizing or alienating the island kingdom. Or, perhaps show why it would be a good idea for her to assume a friendly stance to the new nation-state.

Thus, Bismarck's foreign policy revolved around the goals of keeping France isolated, preserving peace in Eastern Europe, and, somehow, assuring that Great Britain would, at the very least, remain benevolently neutral towards Germany. Above all, the "Iron Chancellor" was determined that all foreign policy options be kept open. To this end, he created alliance systems which assured that European diplomacy would revolve around, or be forced to respond to, his own. For all recognized that this new Germany was, in many ways, the nation-of-the-future in Europe. Possessed of the world's most powerful and best-led army, burgeoning human and material resources, and directed by a chancellor of unquestionable genius and determination, Germany was a country which commanded respect, if not admiration. Thus, if the other powers could not construct alliance systems to challenge her, working arrangements with Germany had to be seen as a fact of life.

Austria-Hungary and Russia were both fearful of alienating the powerful new country, and Bismarck was able to play upon this by, at least at first, tying them together in a league of peace and friendship, the Three Emperors' League. Later, when diplomatic troubles were responsible for a falling-out between Austria-Hungary and Russia, Bismarck, in 1879, concluded the "Dual Alliance" between Germany and Austria-Hungary. Yet, in keeping with his practice of keeping all options open, and bearing in mind Russia's fear of isolation, Bismarck was responsible for the revival of the Three Emperors' League in 1881; this, despite increasing evidence that such could not last for very long. Taking advantage of a somewhat temporary falling-out between Italy and France, largely over colonial issues, Bismarck, in 1882, was able to persuade Italy, also recently-unified, to join Austria-Hungary and Germany, and the Dual Alliance became a "Triple" one. This happened even though Italy had long-standing grievances with Austria-Hungary over the latter's possession of the Tyrol, a region with a large Italian-speaking population.

By the mid-1880s, the Three Emperors' League had disappeared, and a nationalistic explosion in France and crises in the Balkans had made it appear as if France might seek out some sort of alliance with Russia. While Bismarck remained firmly committed to the Triple Alliance, he was able to maintain ties with Russia which, as always, fearful of isolation and now facing economic threats from an increasingly powerful Germany, thought it necessary to preserve ties with this country. While Great Britain had been both annoyed and worried by Germany's obtaining of colonies in Africa and Asia, Bismarck had been able to play upon her perennial suspicions of France and Russia (with whom, as we've seen, he'd retained strong ties) in bringing the British to sign treaties with Italy and Austria-Hungary. In these treaties, the three powers declared that they would not tolerate any upsetting of the *status quo* in the Mediterranean. While Germany did not formally sign the treaties, they were gleefully underwritten by Bismarck, delighted at having succeeded in embroiling Great Britain, however temporarily, in continental affairs. In the meantime, France remained as Bismarck wished her to be—diplomatically isolated.

Bismarck had succeeded in his extraordinary juggling game because all of Europe, confronted with a powerful, new state, had been constrained to treat it with respect. In keeping all options open, he had provided room to maneuver while making certain that the other powers had little of their own, and thus few opportunities to form alliances against his country. Germany's maneuver-territory became truncated somewhat in 1890 when Bismarck was dismissed by a new Emperor, Wilhelm II (1888–1918). The latter was determined that the country pursue a course in foreign policy which he, or more importantly, his advisors, saw as more consonant with Germany's long-term interests.

Beginning in 1890, when the so-called "Reinsurance Treaty" with Russia was allowed to lapse, a "new course" in German foreign policy was underway. The most immediate effect of this was, within a few years' time, to drive the Russians and French into an alliance. While most of Germany's colonies had been obtained during Bismarck's tenure in office, the new Emperor, whether or not he chose to recognize it, under the influence of military circles held in check by Bismarck, and ill-served by weaker chancellors, bellowed for a greater German "place in the sun." Thus, whatever new colonial enterprises were underway, they were embarked upon with a bellicose fervor which got on everybody's nerves. Soon, it became plain to those who mattered that, if supply and trade routes to the newly-obtained colonies were to be secured, Germany would have to have a navy, one which, by its very existence, would at least pose a challenge to British naval supremacy. There thus ensued, by the beginning of the Twentieth Century, the first of its ill-starred armaments competitions—the famous "naval race" between Germany and Great Britain. In due course, the immense cost of this "race" became a point of controversy in both of the countries.

As recently as 1898, Great Britain and France seemed close to war over conflicting colonial claims in the Sudan. By the time that the new century was but a few years old, however, the British government had begun to perceive that the primary threat to the country's national interests was posed by Germany. It was decided that, while there would be no formal alliance with France, at the very least, conflicting colonial claims ought to be settled. Thus, in 1904, an *entente* towards that end was arranged between the two powers. Almost immediately tested by Germany, it held firm, even though nobody really knew what it meant in the long run.

Russia, humiliated by Japan in the Russo-Japanese War of 1904–1905—the result of clashing power-political interests in Manchuria—and exhausted by the short-lived but throne-rattling revolution which had followed in its wake, was gratified that Great Britain was eager to settle outsanding colonial issues with her as well. Thus, in 1907, there was concluded an *entente* between these parties. Like the one between Great Britain and France, it was not a formal military alliance, and noone knew for sure what its long-range implications might be.

Germany, due, for the most part, to her own actions (or, at times, lack of them), was now confronted with a kind of "encirclement." It was in response to this situation, a response informed by an admixture of anger and fear, that this country became responsible for most of the "alarums and excursions" which kept tensions high in the decade before the outbreak of the Great War. In the meantime, it had become plain that Italy, whose short-lived grievances against France had been responsible for her joining Germany and Austria-Hungary in the Triple Alliance in the first place, could not be relied upon in case of a general European conflict. In fact, while not formally abandoning the Triple Alliance, Italy, through trade agreements, had grown closer to France while showing increasing interest in the fate of Italians inhabiting the Austro-Hungarian-ruled Tyrol. At the same time, Austria-Hungary and Germany suffered a further setback when, in 1903, a pro-Austrian dynasty in Serbia, after being hacked to pieces by a group of army officers sometimes described as "disaffected" (to put it mildly), was replaced by a pro-Russian one. Considering the proximity of Serbia to the Slav-filled Austro-Hungarian Empire, this change of government proved to be quite disconcerting.

To be sure, Germany, in a process that had commenced during the last few years of Bismarck's tenure in office, was establishing both economic and, to some extent, political ties with the moribund Ottoman Empire. This had resulted in an agreement between the two governments that the construction of what became known as the "Berlin to Baghdad" railway could take place. Such would provide Germany with an important strategic link to the Middle East. Yet, the value of Turkey in any future conflict was uncertain, while construction of the railway, which brought a German presence into areas of British and Russian interest, served to increase further tensions between Germany and these two countries.

Between the time of unification until 1912, Europe had been compelled to react to a country which, by that year, had become the second leading industrial power in the world, as well as the leading military one. Germany and Austria-Hungary, neither quite trusting the other, had been driven ever closer together by a variety of circumstances and, as some in Vienna chose to interpret it, the German government had virtually assured the Empire of its support no matter what measures it might take in response to perceived Slavic threats. While Italy was, for all intents and purposes, outside of the Triple Alliance, France and Russia now maintained a very real one of their own, while *entente* arrangements between Great Britain and those two countries, even though they were still not formal military alliances, had become strengthened.

In the meantime, the naval race between Great Britain and Germany had continued unabated. In 1912–1913, the Balkan Wars, in which a combination of East European powers succeeded in conquering almost all of Turkey's remaining holdings in Europe only to fall out among themselves over the spoils, attracted the worried attention of the rest of Europe. While the great powers had succeeded in mediating the conflict before they could become involved in it, Russia, which had backed Serbia in the war, was compelled to accept a final peace which still left that country without a sea coast (to keep Serbia from gaining one, the independence of Albania was recognized). Between 1904 and 1913, Russia had sustained both a military humiliation and a series of diplomatic ones. This could not go on forever. Austria-Hungary, on the other hand, backed by the threat of German power, had been able to achieve some diplomatic successes. Serbia, however, in her often quite open courting of Slav minorities within the Empire, had become pesky, and Vienna looked forward to a time in the not-too-distant-future when, with German support assured, the south Slav nation could be crushed.

During this time, Germany herself was beset with social problems, most of which were engendered by the sudden industrial growth which provided for her enormous military power while posing threats to British economic interests throughout the world. Increasing domestic tensions seemed to go hand-in-glove with foreign imbroglios. The combination of the two caused many in government circles to think of some sort of relief. At any rate, those military folk who, after Bismarck's downfall, had played a growing role in influencing foreign policy, were warning that German military superiority might well be coming to an end, as the military establishments of France, Great Britain, and Russia strove to modernize. To be sure, while the Franco-Russian alliance seemed firm, *entente* arrangements between Great Britain and these countries were something of an unknown. In case of some sort of conflict with France and Russia, what would the British do? Before the fateful events of summer, 1914, it was highly doubtful that the British themselves knew the answer to this question. All that they were certain of was that Germany had succeeded in getting on national nerves for some time.

While France, like everybody else, had been placed in the position of having to respond to German actions, there can be no question but that the disaster of 1870–1871 had provided plenty of incentive for going to war with its powerhouse neighbor if appropriate pretext or opportunity were provided. German occupation of Alsace and most of Lorraine was reason enough for that, apart from a sense of national shame which had to be expunged.

Writing to his boss, the American president, Woodrow Wilson (1912–1920), from Berlin in the spring of 1914, Colonel E.M. House penned the following lines: "'The whole of Germany is charged with electricity. Everybody's nerves are tense. It only requires a spark to set the whole thing off.'"[1] Perhaps even sooner than anticipated, the spark would be lit. Armies would be waiting for the moment when it would be flamed to conflagration.

THE CULT OF THE OFFENSIVE

In considering the prewar plans of the great powers, one becomes almost immediately aware of an extraordinary clash between mind and heart. On the one hand, general staffs throughout Europe were aware that technological developments were having an immense impact upon what they liked to call "the art of war." The American Civil War already had demonstrated the damage which could be inflicted upon attacking troops by entrenched infantry, even when armed with muzzle-loading rifles. Since that conflict, one that had been assiduously studied by observers from all over Europe, developments in weaponry had proceeded apace and, within a few decades, European armies, engaged in imperial wars, were trying out varieties of breech-loading rifles, and automatic weapons, "machine-guns," as they became known, against more poorly armed native opponents of colonial rule. A sweet little couplet much favored by English school children pretty much captured the situation:

> Whatever happens we have got
> the maxim gun, and they have not.

By the turn of the century, all major armies, and not a few smaller ones, were equipped with breech-loading, quick-firing field artillery, and, in the case of larger varieties, effective ranges were now measured in miles rather than yards or metres. Moreover, there was talk of such exotica as poison gases of one sort or another, armored automobiles, and even projectiles fired from balloons.

To be sure, at peace conferences meeting at the Hague in the Netherlands, in 1899 and 1907 representatives of the world powers signed agreements either banning or limiting the use of at least some new weapons, either already in service or contemplated; but, few took such arrangements very seriously. Everybody knew that, in one way or the other, new varieties of weaponry, some of them already tried out on "lesser breeds" around the world, would be put to use should wars break out between the major powers.

Observers who flocked to witness the land engagements of the Russo-Japanese War saw both sides use machine-guns and the new artillery with great effectiveness. Also demonstrated was the necessity of entrenchments and the difficulties attendant upon controlling the movements of modern mass armies. In the Balkan Wars of 1912–1913, smaller powers, cheerfully armed, of course, by the larger ones, not only demonstrated once again the effectiveness of machine-guns and modern artillery; but also how aircraft could be used for purposes of scouting and observation—and this in just about a decade after the flight at Kitty Hawk. Staff representatives of great power armies took note, hypothesized, and drew the somewhat gloomy conclusion that, in any future major European war, the *traditional* mass assault would be extremely costly. Thus, one would assume that they drew the logical conclusion that, for the foreseeable future, offensive considerations would have to yield to defensive ones. Oddly—at least from our perspective—this did not occur. In a curious way, even as military leaders all over Europe came to recognize that technology had greatly altered battlefield realities, they came to believe, more than ever before, in the *power* of the assault. Such was emphasized in the British Army's *Field Service Regulations* of 1909. According to this manual, a proper battle began with a relatively brief artillery barrage, after which infantry would attack in lines, firing as they advanced. Approximately 200 yards from enemy emplacements, bayonets would be fixed, a charge made and, through the expected gaps created in enemy lines, cavalry would pour through and the foe put to rout.

The French general staff was unique in one very interesting respect. It was probably the only one of the great military powers whose approach to war was informed by philosophy. Around the turn of the century, that of Henri Bergson (1859–1941) was much in vogue. Espousing an approach to life dubbed "vitalism," it emphasized the role of will, of what Bergson called an *"élan vitale,"* in facing and overcoming life's problems. Colonel Grandmaison of the French General Staff was familiar with Bergson's philosophy and, somewhat inclined to the offense to begin with, saw in it a powerful rationalization for emphasizing the assault. What became known as the "Grandmaison Doctrine" came to inform the French approach to war. Thus, emphasis was placed, as in the British case, upon short artillery barrages laid down by light to medium field-pieces. The infantry mass, presumably fired by patriotic enthusiasms, would then, bayonets fixed, rush to the attack, one carried out with an *élan* against which all resistance had to be powerless. When questioned about the desirability of supporting such an assault with heavier varieties of artillery, a leading French military figure replied that heavy artillery was undesirable; it would merely "slow down" the pace of advance and assault.

The prewar French Army was dressed in blue jackets and red trousers, and its almost always recklessly brave young officers wore white gloves, while hats were adorned with waving plumes. Some observers suggested that the colorfully outfitted French troops would make all-too-obvious targets for emplaced infantry firing the new magazine-fed rifles and machine guns. Perhaps uniforms should be of duller hues. So demeaning a suggestion brought the following response from a French general: "Le pantalon rouge, c'est la France!" In any case, those wearing them would be so inflamed by *élan,* that the very sight of ferociously attacking men, clad in uniforms the color of which was both death-defying and life-affirming, would strike terror in the hearts of any enemy. The latter, it was assumed, would be German and "Plan XVII" envisaged immediate, vigorous assaults upon Alsace and Lorraine as soon as war broke out between France and Germany. A break-through would occur almost at once, it was thought, and then, it would be "on to Berlin." All European general staffs knew what "Plan XVII" called for; but, this seemed not to concern the French one all that very much.

The German General Staff, while placing more of an emphasis upon newer forms of fire-power than its British and French equivalents, also emphasized the assault. What it envisaged, however, was a far more sophisticated approach and, because of Germany's geographical position, necessarily, a more far-reaching one than that of the French, to say nothing of the British who, while concerned with battlefield tactics, seemed to have no overall scheme whatsoever.

Between 1891 and 1906, Alfred Count von Schlieffen (1833–1913) was Chief of the German General Staff. As such, he thought it proper that he prepare his country to meet challenges posed by the war of the future, one which, since the conclusion of the Franco-Russian alliance, he assumed would be fought on two fronts. What became known as the "Schlieffen Plan" called for emphasis upon a massive assault in the West while German armies in the East, assisted, of course, by Austro-Hungarian allies, would assume a defensive posture. The Russians, Schlieffen assumed, would mobilize rather slowly in keeping with their antediluvian mobilization and transportation systems. The assault in the West, however, was not to be made all along the line. While a relatively small number of German troops were to contain the expected French attack in Alsace and Lorraine, the main body of the German Army would invade Belgium, the Netherlands, and Luxemburg (later, the attack on the Netherlands was dropped from Schlieffen's scheme) and moving west, and then cutting south, behind Paris, swing north behind the vast mass of the French Army committed to what he assumed would be fruitless assaults in an area ideally suited for the defense. The French Army would be surrounded and either captured or destroyed in a gigantic battle of annihilation. Then, moving on convenient interior lines provided by the best rail network on the continent, the German Army would head east in time to meet and destroy the Russians. The war would be over in a matter of weeks.

Schlieffen knew that Belgium's neutrality in case of war had been assured by the Treaty of London, signed in 1839 by all European powers. An invasion of Belgium, as well as German conquest of the entire Channel coast, directly across from England, certainly would be matters of concern for the British. Furthermore, after 1904, there was that vexing *entente* between Great Britain and France, although, as we have seen, nobody really knew what it meant. Yet, when the Chief of the German General Staff produced a final version of his plan in 1905, it made few concessions to the possibility of British entrance into the war. If France were knocked out quickly, the chances were that the British, with their relatively small army, could do very little to rectify the situation. All would go well, Schlieffen thought, if the German High Command made certain that the overwhelming mass of its army would be on the right flank. In a word, when the French attacked in Alsace and Lorraine, it must not, no matter how threatening the situation in that area might appear, yield to the temptation of weakening the right wing by dispatching reinforcements to the region. It is said that on his death bed Schlieffen raged, "It must come to a fight! Keep the right wing strong! For God's sake keep the right wing strong." Then, he expired.

Like the British and the French, only with much more complicated territorial and logistical considerations in mind, Alfred Count von Schlieffen placed reliance on the offense. However, unlike the cases of British and French military hypothesizing, his plan had a somewhat baleful influence on the foreign policy of his country. From the time of its inception, the Schlieffen plan had the effect of convincing the German government that if war came, it would be a two-front affair. Contingency plans for a different strategic situation were all but non-existent. Thus, foreign policy decision were made bearing in mind the inevitability of a two front war should matter necessitate a clash of arms. In the end, this had to have had the effect of limiting options with regard to decision making in foreign affairs. In any event, if war came, Germany would immediately assume the offensive.

While Schlieffen's approach to this was, as we have seen, neither as quaintly obsolete (or, for that matter, haphazard) as that of the British, nor as dangerously romantic as that of the French, his considerations were informed by the same almost mystical faith in the attack as shown by his future opponents. This mood was captured by General Friedrich von Bernhardi (1849–1932) who, after declaiming on the new conditions of war that had been created by new technologies, came up with the following observation: "Since the tactical efficiency and the morale of the troops are chiefly shown in the offensive, and are then most needful [sic], the necessary conclusion is that safety only lies in offensive warfare."[2]

The Russian Army had undergone substantial improvements since the disastrous Russo-Japanese War. Yet, by any reasonable standard, it was still underequipped, while standards of training and leadership were not as high as they ought to have been. Furthermore, it would be moved and supplied by a road and railway network which barely functioned to any adequate degree in peace-time situations. While it was true that many in the Russian military establishment, and Tsar Nicholas himself, were not in favor of entering a large-scale conflict in the near future, it was thought that if one were to break out, then the army's best course was to take the offensive. The "cult of the offensive," while not adhered to with the tenacious enthusiasm shown further west, prevailed in Russian military circles. In this case, though, it was sustained by the sheer idiocy of the thoroughly incompetent Minister of War Vladimir Sukholminov, who persisted in his belief that the ultimate weapon would always be the bayonet.

While the Russian High Command, aware of the deficiencies of the army, at first had to be nudged somewhat into considering an offensive against Germany, it positively relished the thought of undertaking one against the Austro-Hungarians. Quite correctly, it perceived that the Austro-Hungarian Army, while containing some truly fine units, was, to no small degree, an armed polyglot, the Slavic elements of which were not exactly eager to risk life and limb for an Empire perceived by many as being insensitive to their needs and aspirations. At the same time this army, though not to the degree as the Russian, was, by the reckoning of its own generals, not as well-equipped as it ought to have been. Furthermore, while noble efforts were undertaken to compel German-speaking officers to learn enough of the languages spoken by their men so that some degree of military cohesion could be assured, these had not been as successful as hoped for, and this augured ill for the future. Thus, on the eve of war's outbreak, the German General Staff had little faith in, or respect for, the Austro-Hungarian Army and, in point of fact, it tended to treat the Austro-Hungarian military establishment with contempt. Particularly in view of a situation in which Austria-Hungary was Germany's only true ally, the lack of meaningful contact between the two High Commands was astonishing, even scandalous. Austrian generals voiced occasional complaints about this; but, little was done to improve matters. In fact, it is probable that there were at least as many meaningful contacts between the formally non-allied British and French General Staffs (though, in view of their respective military doctrines what they could learn from one another was highly problematic) as there were between those of formally allied Germany and Austria-Hungary.

To some significant degree ignorant of German plans and preparations, uncertain as to the capabilities of at least a large proportion of its soldiers, numbers of whom were badly equipped, the Austro-Hungarian General Staff planned to hurl them into offensive operations immediately upon the outbreak of war. One Austro-Hungarian army would strike out against the Russians in Poland, while another would be sent south to deal with those pesky Serbs once and for all. As in the Russian case, Austro-Hungarian generals were hardly unaware of glaring deficiencies in the army. Yet, perhaps because they underestimated the abilities of potential Slavic adversaries and, despite little assurance in this regard, assumed that Germany would be of great assistance in whatever operation they chose to undertake, offensive thinking prevailed at the highest command levels.

Thus, as Europe, for the most part unknowing, of course, hovered at the brink, European military establishments, despite the knowledge (Sukholminov can perhaps can be seen as an exception in this regard) of what modern weaponry had done to change the nature of war, adhered to attitudes which have been subsumed under the term "cult of the offensive." Technology had made matters more difficult with regard to the offensive. Very well then, it was now more important than ever before that offensives be sustained by that fervor which could be generated by nationalistic enthusiasm. In the case of non-German units of the Austro-Hungarian Army, it was hoped that loyalty to the Empire would suffice in place of nationalism *per se*. It seems as if, in the case of those military folk who mattered, it was assumed, or at least fervently hoped, that the spiritual aspects attaching to war would allow respective armies to deal with, indeed to overcome, new material circumstances which all knew would make offensive warfare difficult. In military circles usually perceived of as rather cold, heart had conquered mind and this morbid take on sentimentality provided a legacy which would be difficult to overcome even after the most hideous of realities had established its deficiencies for all to see.

Around the turn of the century, a converted Polish Jewish banker, Ivan Bloch (1836–1902), had published a six-volume work entitled *The Future of War*. Bringing to bear information on economic and industrial developments, and applying this to hypothetical military situations, he had come to the conclusion that wars of the future would be of a terribly attritional nature, in which powers with the greatest degree of industrial staying power would win out. Old-style heroism would be rendered obsolete, even absurd. Few military men took the work seriously. After all, Bloch was not one of them and knew little of the "art of war." Also, though a convert to Christianity, he was a born Jew and, to round matters out, a banker to boot. In terms of race and occupation, he represented those elements of degeneracy and materialism to which battlefield heroism would prove to be an antidote. While some in European military establishments recognized that the coming conflict would be a costly one, all seemed to agree that in participating in it, particularly if sustained by high ideals and even higher morale, respective national manhoods would, as of old, redeem themselves, even while casting aside the suffocating raiments of an increasingly materialistic and degenerate civilization.

3

European Society and Culture on the Brink

SOCIAL USAGES AND ASSUMPTIONS UNDER STRESS

WHILE casting occasional, somewhat nervous, glances at the United States, which, by 1914, had become the leading industrial power in the world, European elites and middle classes could take pride in dominating most of the earth's surface. In Africa, Asia, and even portions of Latin America and the Caribbean, European imperial power held sway and, for the foreseeable future, appeared to be unchallengeable. While more socially-advantaged portions of "native populations" sent their offspring to European schools in order to best prepare them for finding the best possible places in a white man's world, European high culture took pride of place (or, in European eyes, certainly seemed to do so) throughout the world. In any event, even allowing for a certain degree of *cultural* relativism, there could be no question of Western technological supremacy.

While there had been depressions as recently as 1893 and 1907, the first of them quite severe, Europeans looked forward to a future of more-or-less continuous economic growth. Capitalism seemed secure, indeed, in demonstrating an ability to overcome severe setbacks, more secure than ever, and it was this ability to surmount difficulties of this nature which caused the German Socialist, Eduard Bernstein (1850–1932), to formulate the doctrine of "Revisionism." According to Bernstein, Marx had been mistaken in assuming that, in the near future, Capitalism would collapse due to contradictions inherent in it. Indeed, whatever one thought of its ethical content, the economic domination of those "moneybags" (as Marx had liked to refer to capitalists) at the top of the heap seemed assured for some time to come. Furthermore, as Bernstein saw it, a growing middle class seemed more and more to be reaping the benefits of a system which admittedly served the interests of a growing number of "moneybags." Also, it was obvious that, rather than viewing them as bloated exploiters of their work and laborers' toil, middle class Europeans seemed, more often than not, to seek to join their ranks, or at least to emulate them.

From a Marxist perspective, working class developments were even more disquieting. While there were grievances aplenty, the governments of more advanced countries, such as Great Britain, France, and Germany, had begun to introduce, however grudgingly at times, various reforms. Laws regulating working conditions—still, by today's standards, quite deplorable—and, in some cases, even pay, had been introduced; while, almost all working men (but no women) had the vote by the turn of the century. While there were still regulatory hurdles which favored big business against them, the trade union movement, particularly in Bernstein's Germany, was growing in membership and effectiveness. The result was that, contrary to Marx's prognostications, while the rich might indeed be getting richer, the poor were not getting poorer. In the final analysis, working class rebellion in any country, to say nothing of some sort of international one, seemed to be an increasingly remote possibility. The best that could be done, according to the tenets of "Revisionism," was for those Socialist parties which represented working class interests to work for meaningful changes within established social, economic, and political orders; if necessary cooperating with progressive elements of the bourgeoisie. Bernstein's "Revisionism" seemed to be a testimonial to the triumph of Capitalism and, as such, was resented by many Socialists, while established Socialist parties went on record as rejecting it. Yet, it simply stated outright what many committed Socialists had come to accept as the prevailing realities of the time.

From a technological perspective, Western Capitalism was a marvel and the heady, prewar years saw an astounding panoply of advances and inventions. By 1900, railroad trains had been pulled by locomotives travelling at over 100 miles per hour, while, in the world of shipping, more romantic sail had almost entirely yielded to grimly efficient steam power. Now, the telephone, while still possessed by relatively few, was hardly a novelty and, within a few years, the sending of messages by the "wireless" would be possible. During the years immediately preceding the Great War, automobiles became a more-or-less accepted (if sometimes grudgingly) aspect of daily life although, to be sure, they were still usually out of reach of the average person. There had even been some experiments with regard to their possible utilization in war. The success of the Wright Brothers at Kitty Hawk, North Carolina in December, 1903 occasioned an interest in heavier-than-air flight so pronounced that it seemed that Western civilization was not only ready but indeed eager to embark on the extraordinary adventures opened up by air travel. An adventure of sorts was the use of aircraft in warfare and, as we have seen, there were examples of this before the outbreak of World War I.

Advances in medicine, agronomy, and the preservation and shipping of food suggested that new advances in technology, and new technologies altogether, would benefit better-fed and healthier peoples. Indeed, as measured by the melioristic, if mundane, standards of middle and upper class life, human progress was occurring at a dizzying rate. Surely, in the end, all Europeans would enjoy the blessings of a material existence so improved as to suggest that the millennium might well be realized in smoothly-functioning urban settings.

It is probable, then, that the average pre-war middle class European—and even more so, the average middle class American—had, by standards of later generations, a somewhat optimistic view of things. optomistc Thus, after the war, and particularly after the second global conflict, there was the tendency for many historians and "lay-people" alike to view pre-Great War folk as naive, even childlike, in their view of the world. When one reflects upon the, by our standards, stultifying formalities which governed relations within families, within and between classes, and between the sexes, and the rules which determined what could be expressed in print and upon the stage, such a viewpoint could receive confirmation. Middle class Western "man" (in every sense of the term) comes across as a self-satisfied, indeed smug, embodiment of bourgeois pieties; a proper microcosm of a civilization in which spiritual and material values had been conflated to the advantage of the latter as, blinded by an infantile belief in progress, it careened to the worst disaster thus far in its history.

Yet, while it is true that the "average" pre-Great War Western human was somewhat less aware than later varieties of the darker aspects of that spiritually-sanctified material advance to which this person had become accustomed, the picture drawn above is certainly an exaggerated one. First of all, as seen earlier, the years before the war had been marked by no small number of diplomatic crises, and there had been wars as well, some of them quite costly. Also, as noted, many in military circles had come to view Western civilization as one which, precisely because of the emphasis upon increased material well-being, had become rather degenerate. This view was shared by no small number of non-military folk, and we will deal with this issue in due course. For now, we must focus upon social unrest, awareness of which was greatly sharpened by the activities of the Anarchists.

While most non-working class Europeans feared Socialism which, "Revisionism" or no, was perceived as a threat to the existing order, it was the activities of idealistic, ruthless, and usually self-motivated fighters for social justice which were primarily responsible for jolting such people into realizing the profound gaps which separated them from those who seemed not to enjoy the benefits of material increase. Between 1894 and 1914, six heads of state (including, in 1901, the American president, William McKinley) scores of less well-known souls, went down before Anarchist guns, bombs, and knives. Anarchism, proclaiming the inherent goodness of humanity, saw the state in any form as the tool of the ruling class. In this regard, their view of the state was similar to that of the Marxists. Unlike the Marxists, however, Anarchists did not place much faith in laws of history to undo social inequities. Also, they thought that working class potential for revolutionary action would never be actualized unless forceful examples of such were provided by men and women utterly and proudly alienated from all elements of bourgeois life, its hypocritical morality in particular. Thus, helped along by an almost hysterical press, a relatively small number of utterly selfless souls went about what they saw as their socially-prescribed role of eliminating representatives of capitalistic parasitism. Almost always, the perpetrators of one or the other assassination or bombing were caught and almost invariably executed. Also, more often than not, the doomed miscreant greeted death upon the gallows with the defiant shout, "Long live anarchy!" or "I will be avenged!" Such indeed often proved to be the case and the Western world—but, Italy, Spain, and, to a lesser degree, France, in particular—became accustomed to a terrible and dreary cycle of terror, counter-terror, and terror again, one which has become all too familiar to more recent generations.

While there can be no doubt but that some Anarchist assassins and bomb-throwers were sustained in their respective tasks mainly by a simple love of killing and mayhem, the primary driving force behind Anarchism, in thought and action, was rage against social injustices. While, as we have seen, even Socialists such as Bernstein had come to see that large numbers of the European working class were benefiting from growing unionization and governmental intervention on their behalf, the gap between rich and poor remained enormous and, in some cases, was growing. For those involved in social and other forms of relief work for the poor, this was hardly startling, and certainly many not involved in such activities took the time to acquaint themselves with the appalling conditions of those who had not benefitted from the prosperity generated by industrialization. For many, perhaps most Europeans, however, the plight of what was often referred to as "the undeserving poor" became a reality only through the actions of those fanatical souls who undertook often atrocious actions in their defense. While theoreticians of Anarchy could be found in a variety of countries, including the United States, the perpetrators of violent deeds came, in disproportionate numbers, from Spain, Italy, and Eastern Europe. It was hardly a coincidence that it was in these lands where rural poverty reigned supreme, while workers in the growing, but still relatively small industrial sectors of the economy—on the whole, benefiting neither from union activities nor government largesse—were grossly underpaid and labored under horrible conditions. At the same time, even as socially-conscious individuals and organizations cried out for social justice, and, in more advanced countries, unions and governmental action won occasional benefits for the under classes, prevailing social attitudes were such that the poorer elements in all countries were perceived of as being something less than human.

This tendency was made plain for all to see by events which transpired in the North Atlantic on the night of April 14–15, 1912. Also made plain was the arrogance both underlying and generated by rapid advances in technology which some saw as leading to mastery over nature. At 11:40 P.M., the giant White Star Line passenger ship, *Titanic*, on a proud maiden voyage, struck an iceberg. At 2:20 in the morning, the vessel foundered. Of 2,235 passengers and crew, only 713 were saved. The number of those perishing in the worst peacetime sea disaster ever was thus 1,522. After an initial gasp of horror, newspapers, clergymen, and public figures of all kinds strove to outdo themselves in praising the courage of first class male passengers who bade wives and children goodbye as they were placed in life boats; the devotion of the two first class women who, rejecting pleas that they take to the boats, chose to remain, and perish with, their husbands; the gallantry of the captain of the *Titanic,* E.J. Smith, who, as some reported, spent his last moments exhorting his crew to "Be British!"; and, quite understandably, the *sang froid* of the ship's orchestra which played ragtime tunes to sustain passenger morale as life-boats were loaded, and then, in a moving gesture to propriety, switched to hymns just before the ship went down.

Then, during the course of investigations in the United States and Great Britain, the gloss was rubbed away from the great disaster, and rather quickly at that. Among other things, investigators discovered that, while aware of ice-warnings, the *Titanic* continued on its prescribed northern course, and that the ship's lookouts—warned, to be sure, to watch out for ice—had no binoculars. Also, while the *Titanic* was not travelling at very top speed when she entered the ice field which would doom her, she was quite close to it. Once the disaster struck, there was considerable delay in loading the life-boats and, once loading began, no small degree of confusion—something which was quite understandable in view of the fact that there had been no formal life-boat drill. At first, boats departed half-loaded and, after the last of them had left, passengers and crew who had worked hard to be sure that all women and children found places in the boats were horrified by the appearance of a wave of humanity which suddenly surged up from below decks. Almost all of these folk were, of course, doomed. After the ship went down, over a thousand human beings, supported by life-vests, were left upon the surface of freezing waters. As they slowly froze to death, their shrieks for help could be heard by those in the boats; but, fearful of being swamped by this struggling mass, they, for the most part, chose to do nothing. Some, in order to drown out the terrible cries, sang as loudly as possible. Finally, when statisticians applied their talents to the disaster, it was discovered that, while 94% of first class women and children were saved, only 47% of those in steerage made it ashore. Almost a third of first class men, 31%, were saved; only 14% of those from steerage. [1] Indeed, as matters turned out, the percentage of first class men saved was higher than that of steerage children.

During the course of the hearings, particularly those in the United States, it became obvious that, while it was untrue that White Star Line personnel had put barriers in the way of people in steerage, even after the extent of the disaster became known they were, in many cases, pretty much left to shift for themselves. Perhaps of greater importance was the fact that "years of conditioning as third-class citizens led a great many of them to give up hope as soon as the crisis became evident." A Swedish immigrant described a scene which particularly appalled him: "Hundreds were in a circle with a preacher in the middle, praying, asking God and Mary to help them. They lay there still crying till the water was over their heads. They just prayed and yelled, never lifting a hand to help themselves. They had lost their own will power and expected God to do all the work for them." [2] Tragically, many of the *Titanic*'s third-class passengers had come to view themselves as "undeserving poor," who, not deserving, it would seem, of life itself, were dependent upon divine intervention on their behalf.

Even as these horrible stories unfolded, well-honed prejudices against the lower classes, particularly if they were from Southern or Eastern Europe, were vented. If groups of men rushed life-boats as the end approached, they were always "Italians" or, in any case, certainly not Anglo-Saxons. Prejudice found expression in a New York newspaper which, in describing the loss of a group of Finns, headed the story with the byline, "Desirable Immigrants Lost." [3] They were from Nordic climes, not from Southern European ones, so they might have been of some value to their destined new home.

By the time the *Titanic* investigations were over, even as ships traversing the North Atlantic were still reporting encountering numbers of bodies upon its surface, the Western world had been provided with a somber view of some of its darker aspects. Exposed for all to see was the rottenness that subsisted at the very heart of an increasingly materialistic civilization which, while self-confident enough to deem an admittedly magnificent ship "unsinkable" and thus expect it to almost willfully defy nature, treated those whose labor sustained it with obscene contempt. In increasing numbers, clergyman, politicians, and other public figures spoke out in condemnation of that worship of material increase and blind faith in technology which had doomed the *Titanic* and two thirds of those who had sailed on its first, and last, voyage. Some went so far as to suggest that, as horrible as the disaster itself had been, it could be interpreted as a Providential omen of far worse things to come. In any event, the sinking of the, up to that point, world's largest ship by one of nature's less complex products caused many to question contemporary social attitudes of a civilization which seemed to be guided by the view that applied human reason could lead to continuous progress.

Indeed, there were those who called into question the role of reason altogether. Friedrich Nietzsche (1844–1900), declaring that, so far as His being of any value in modern times, God was dead, stated that the truly authentic man (literally "man" in this case; Nietzsche was a confirmed misogynist) had to create values of his own and live by them. This would contravene those pitiful remnants of Christian beliefs held to by most humans, being to whom he referred to as "the herd." Condemning all aspects of the mass age, including nationalism, he declared that one who lived according to his own values, the "superman," recognized that he was animated by the "will to power." All humans had this basic drive within them somewhere. The "superman," however, recognized this fact and, further, acted upon it, self-consciously separating himself from spiritually docile beings who adhered to those values espoused by "shopkeepers, Englishmen, females, cows, and other democrats."[4] Nietzsche's "superman" was a kind of warrior of the spirit, who revelled in spiritual combat. Proudly at war with what he perceived to be a degenerate humanity, Nietzsche, in his obviously anti-democratic elitism, spoke in language which, in due course, would make his self-consciously unsystematic philosophy useful for the radical right in general, and the German radical nationalistic right in particular. Nietzsche, who detested nationalism and viewed his fellow Germans with contempt, would have been horrified. In any case, even before he went mad in 1889—he spent the last eleven years of his life ensconced in a kind of "mattress-grave"—his teachings had attained a wide degree of notoriety and, after his death in 1900, they became even more influential.

For those alienated by the modern, mass age, one informed by the grossest forms of materialism even as herd-type folk hypocritically clung to superannuated Christian values, Friedrich Nietzsche became the prophet of a new spiritual order. Especially admired was his assault on reason, or, more precisely, that instrumental form of reason as applied to the material world. While not denying its existence—or even at times its usefulness—Nietzsche, as we have seen, saw the "will to power" as the basic force behind day-to-day appearances. The truly authentic being was one who, joyfully recognizing the reality of this force, drew upon it in setting himself apart (and above) those who applied their, often quite limited, reason to the nauseatingly mundane concerns of mass society.

In challenging those "herd" values which placed emphasis, among other things, upon that sort of "reason" useful to shopkeepers, Nietzsche was calling into question that faith in reason which was crucial to the Western notion of material progress. Those who recognized the "will to power" and were guided by it—the "supermen"—recognized the power of sexuality and revelled in either giving vent to it or self-consciously mastering this drive. Nietzsche, however, did not devote a great deal of attention to sex proper. In the thirty or so years before the outbreak of the Great War, however, there were a number of individuals who did and, in so doing, called into question just how deeply rooted middle class proprieties in fact were.

In the 1880s, the German neurologist Richard Freiherr von Krafft-Ebing (1840–1902) came out with his *Psychopathia Sexualis.* Obviously a labor of love, in several senses of the term, the primary concerns of this widely-read book are plain. Krafft-Ebing, in great detail, devoted himself to examining sexual perversions, sadism and masochism in particular. He seemed to be especially concerned with male masochism and gave myriad examples of such, many of them culled from prostitutes' descriptions of various things which their clients wished to have done to them. Particularly since Krafft-Ebing—here, reflecting a commonly-held perception—thought that, in matters sexual, a woman's role was, by nature, passive, the thought of men receiving gratification from women whipping them, tying them up, or otherwise bashing them about, distressed him greatly. Men who enjoyed this sort of thing were, he thought, either constitutionally weak or had been emasculated by those strident, and hence unnatural, women who were pressing for female emancipation, a phenomenon with which we will concern ourselves in due course. While many professed to be shocked over it, *Psychopathia Sexualis* was extremely popular, and went through several revisions. While it was (and is) hard to tell whether the work was being read as a critique of psychological problems or as a kind of instruction manual, it both reflected and catered to a widely-held, if usually *sub-rosa,* interest in sex.

Sigmund Freud, in his *Interpretation of Dreams,* published in 1900, showed the way to a much more profound, and longer-lasting (if admittedly less exciting) exploration of sexual issues than that proffered by Krafft-Ebing. While his hypotheses on such matters would be fully developed only after World War I, *Interpretation of Dreams* and other pre-war works gave a pretty good idea as to the general motive of them. For Freud, the human psyche was a kind of battleground upon which there clashed repressed sexual wishes and fantasies and those societal norms which, to no small degree, had been constructed to contain them. The realm of the unconscious was the domain of desires and longings which, due to current social usages, usually embodied in parents or parent figures, could not be expressed in the "real" world. It was, however, precisely with regard to what in fact constituted reality, that Freud raised the most distressing questions. For, it was plain to him and to his followers that the ultimate reality was indeed that of our unconscious lives. The world "out there," the realm of politics, art, religion, and social life in general, was an at times quite fragile construct necessary in order that what Europeans had come to know as civilization could be maintained.

Freud, himself the ultimate bourgeois in his personal habits, never questioned the necessity of social controls and the repression of instinctual drives. He pointed out, however, that if, particularly during early childhood, repression were too severe or if trauma in any form were associated with it, healthy sexual development could not take place. Instead, sexual development would become "fixated" at that stage in which untoward occurrences had taken place. An individual thus affected would develop dysfunctional patterns of behavior which then would adversely influence sexual life in particular and social interactions in general. Through examination of dreams, fantasies, and slips of the tongue, the unconscious world of a person thus afflicted could be explored and the source(s) of neurotic difficulties uncovered. While Freud, at least during the early days of psychoanalysis, was very optimistic about the curative potentials of his approach, what he had to say about the human condition was far from comforting. Virtually all elements of our conscious lives had to be seen as being correlated to, if not controlled by, irrational drives at times opaque to rational understanding, even his. That good, middle class life, with all those social usages attaching to it, was, in the end, merely a shield—and, at times, a very frail one—against powerful unconscious forces. Most of the time, our conscious motives for doing things, e.g., creating a work of art, establishing certain relationships, even bending knees in prayer, are not the ultimate reasons for such actions. Indeed, in a very real sense we never really know what we're doing, or, more precisely, why we're doing it. Perhaps if Freud had declared that the most crucial of those unconscious forces lurking below the surface was the manifestation of some sort of divine entity the average person might have found comfort in the thought that our conscious lives were at the mercy of unseen power. As we have seen, however, the most important of these was sex; and, even though Freud used the term in a very broad fashion, most inhabitants of an outwardly self-confident and vital civilization found his hypotheses to be disquieting, if not offensive. At least this was the general public reaction to them.

In truth, Freud's writings, like Darwin's *Origin of Species* which appeared forty-one years before the former's *Interpretation of Dreams,* were published in an environment which was more than ready for them. This had been demonstrated by the popularity of Krafft-Ebing's work, and by the increasing interest in that of Freud's contemporary, Havelock Ellis (1859–1939) who, in 1897 published the first volume of his seven volume work, *Studies in the Psychology of Sex* (the last volume of this monumental work would appear in 1928). Unlike Krafft-Ebing, however, who decried perversions even as he relished describing them, and Ellis, who saw sex as a positive, indeed, often creative force in sustaining civilization, Freud, who enjoyed this selfsame civilization very much, described the relationship between the two in rather cheerless ways. At the same time, he refused to see anything mystical about the unconscious in general and sex in particular. Indeed, with a self-confident certainty which many found infuriating, he rejected religious beliefs of any kind as forms of infantilism. As far as sex was concerned, pre-war Europeans gave every indication of being obsessed with it and the legions of prostitutes which swarmed in all major European cities testified to the seemingly insatiable demands of at least European males.

For many thinkers, the cities of an increasingly urbanized Europe became of great interest. This was particularly the case with regard to the psychic condition of the masses of people who inhabited them. Freud would not address this issue until 1921, when his work, *Group Psychology and the Analysis of the Ego* was published. A strong influence upon him, even though Freud would end up rejecting some of his arguments, was Gustav Le Bon (1841–1931), a French psychologist, whose 1894 work, *The Crowd,* attracted great attention in the pre-war years.

Le Bon saw the urban masses, particularly as portions of them gathered in groups, as the most important factor in current and future social and political life. The "crowd," by nature irrational, could be moved to actions unthinkable for the single individual. By appealing to its most base instincts, a political leader, through appropriate use of speech and symbol, could draw upon its dynamism (however cruel the ways in which this might articulate itself) and use this awesome force for his own purposes, however ruthless or perverse. Politically, Le Bon was himself extremely conservative, and was well-known for his anti-Semitic views. Perhaps it was these which added a certain spice to the, for some, enticing sauce which bubbled richly in his most famous work. In any event, *The Crowd,* while read and appreciated by many of all political persuasions, exercised the greatest influence upon individuals who, after the Great War seemed to demonstrate the validity of Le Bon's hypotheses, would emerge as representatives of European Fascism. In any event, the French psychologist evidenced a somewhat curious, but altogether understandable, split attitude towards "the crowd" (or, perhaps better put, "the mob"). On the one hand, he despised it, seeing those who comprised such an entity as individually cowardly and, in many ways, dim-witted. On the other hand, he seemed to revel in the potentially useful, if often destructive, power which could be generated by mass irrationality—something which, while anticipated to a degree by certain individuals and events in the period of the French Revolution, had been made possible on a wide scale only by the emergence of industrialization and the attendant urbanization of Europe.

As we have thus far considered it, the creation of a modern, industrialized, urban society, something which by its very nature ought to have engendered a ubiquitous rationalism, had had, at least in some very crucial areas, the reverse effect. For Nietzsche, Krafft-Ebing, Freud, Le Bon, and large numbers of people who may or may not have been familiar with all or some of their writing, the world, stripped of mythologies attaching to traditional forms of religiosity, was an alienating place, informed by irrationalities, sometimes of a most perverse and cruel nature. Nietzsche, despising "the crowd" (his "herd"), and Le Bon, also despising the crowd, but seeing in it much potential, however destructive this might be, seemed to find spiritual homes of sorts in this new world. Others, such as Freud, were concerned about dealing with problems generated by the clash between societal forms and those irrational forces perceived of as being well-nigh tectonic. All saw humanity as being in a new place in which traditional social, political, and even psychological usages either would be overthrown or have the truisms in which they were rooted subject to the most searching of examinations.

Impressionism

As is almost always the case, artistic endeavors reflected broader social concerns and issues. In the years immediately preceding the outbreak of the Great War, this resulted in a veritable explosion of creativity which, in the eyes of many critics and historians, Europe had never before (or since) witnessed. From the 1870s until just about the end of the century, the dominant school in art was that of Impressionism, almost all of whose best-known adherents were French. Its emphasis upon capturing the relationship between light and material objects and the almost immediate representation of this upon canvas was responsible for works which had a kind of "blurred effect;" works in which individual features, such as those of the human face, were sacrificed to the artist's impression of what resulted from the momentary confluence of light and phenomena illuminated by it. Initially, some critics and many lay-persons interested in art found paintings rendered in this style to be annoying. In due course, however, Impressionist works became generally accepted, even admired. They tended to have, after all, a soothing effect, and this is probably the reason why, even today, reproductions of them are often found in waiting rooms attached to dentists' offices, or in ante-chambers of lawyers specializing in divorce cases.

For the Impressionists, modernity and problems attaching to it seemed not to occasion any sort of strong emotional reaction. Vincent Van Gogh (1853–1890), unlike the Impressionists, was concerned, at times, almost morbidly so, with rendering the world in terms of his own often violent reactions to it. Yet, one cannot help but feel that so unhappy a being would have been alienated regardless of whatever time in which he lived, though, to be sure, the ways in which he might have expressed this would certainly have been different. The same could not be said of Van Gogh's friend, Paul Gauguin (1848–1903), although it is unlikely that differences in attitudes towards society were responsible for Van Gogh's threatening to kill him during a brief get-together in 1888. Gauguin, increasingly put off by the complexities of modern life, at first retreated to the French countryside, where he produced some impressive landscape paintings. In the 1890s, however, he abandoned European civilization altogether and went to live in the South Sea Islands. There, he produced his best-known works, ones which embodied his deep appreciation for what he saw as the honest sensuality and simple beauty of "natives" living in straight-forward harmony with nature.

Most European artists, though sensitive and, at times, almost overwhelmed by the alienating aspects of modernization, did not flee from it altogether. More complex than Gauguin in their responses to it, they produced works in which this at times astonishing complexity was reflected. What the artists, representing a variety of "schools," revealed in their works was revulsion against an alienating mass society, but, at the same time a fascination with the vitality of urban life; raw sensuality, but also a tender sensitivity for children; and concern, albeit somewhat limited, for religious values. Artists who stood four-square for creative freedom revealed a cruel misogyny, thus reflecting, albeit in exaggerated form, some of the less lovable values of the age. Artists of *all* of the new "schools" which emerged before World War I were united on one point, however—whatever the problems of modernity, in its seeming assault upon traditional values it had opened the way for the artist to undertake some extraordinary explorations into the deepest realms of the imagination; explorations which would lead some of them to reject the phenomenal world altogether. Individual motives crucial to such enterprises were extremely varied. It became plain retrospectively, but also at the time, however, that those who represented such "schools" as German Expressionism, Cubism, and Italian Futurism saw themselves as responding to the new—and often disquieting—challenges of a new age by necessarily journeying deeply inward; there, to discover approaches and styles which both responded to these challenges and offered ones of their own.

One of the most influential of these "explorers" was the Norwegian artist Edvard Munch (1863–1944). While, in later years, his works revealed what can be called a sense of psychic balance, his earlier ones, done mostly during his stay in Germany (with occasional visits home) between 1892 and 1908 revealed concerns, often extremely morbid ones, with inner fears, urban alienation, and sexual lusts. In this regard, what was also revealed was a fascination with women, who, in Munch's works, come across as either corpse-like or possessed of great strength. In either case they were threatening, overpowering figures. Munch, whose works captured a veritable panoply of contemporary concerns and fears, was probably the single most important influence on what became known as German Expressionism, whose adherents picked up upon some of these themes.

The "Expressionists" received that sobriquet because they saw art as a means of articulating a sense of inwardness. As in the cases of van Gogh and Munch, such found articulation in a self-conscious reworking of landscapes, street scenes, still lifes and often somewhat stunned nude models so that such objects became reshaped in terms of the artist's inwardly felt sense of them. In a word, forms—natural or man-made—were made to intersect with emotion. Naturally, this had to lead to distortion and unlike "soft" Impressionist works, those produced by adherents to the Expressionist approach often left the viewer with a sense of disquietude. To be sure, one of the very earliest Expressionist painters, Paula Modersohn-Becker (1876–1907), reacted to encroaching modernity by painting scenes of the North German countryside, and attempting to capture the gentle strengths shown by the people who inhabited it, often children and mothers (ironically, Modersohn-Becker died from complications resulting from childbirth at the age of thirty-one). Most Expressionists, however, appeared to revel in grappling with those immense tensions generated by modernity, particularly with those emanating from harshly alienating urban settings.

Ernst Ludwig Kirchner (1880–1938), became famous for capturing what he saw as the ugliness of city streets which yet coursed with an enticing vitality, and the raw sensuality of urban females. Emil Nolde, alone among Expressionists in this regard, dealt with religious themes, although his depictions of such things as the Last Supper were greatly criticized by clerics as being sacrilegious distortions. (Interestingly enough, Emil Nolde, of all Expressionists, the most concerned with religious themes, was the only one of the movement to be drawn to Nazism). Yet, religiosity was counterbalanced with a fascination with the vitality, often quite sensual, which he sensed in the city. As in the case of Kirchner, Nolde's women were often overpowering, or at least threatening.

Franz Marc (1880–1916), and Wassily Kandinsky (1866–1944), in their respective explorations of inner realms, pushed Expressionism in the direction of non-representational art. Marc, who strove to capture the universal in nature, at first became known for his blue cows and yellow horses (or vice versa)—after all, in efforts to capture the strengths informing animal life, strengths threatened by an increasingly urban civilization, the actual, or "real," external colors meant little. Later, however, Marc's attempts to forge links between his feelings and universal forces in nature led him to depict shapes and images which, rather than representing things "out there" in the "real" world, came from his own rich imagination. In point of fact, Franz Marc was on his way towards total abstraction before he died at Verdun in 1916. By the time his colleague, Wassily Kandinsky, a Russian *émigré* living in Munich, was forced, by the outbreak of war in 1914, to return home, he *had* broken completely with representational art, defending this approach in several influential theoretical essays.

Marc and Kandinsky's breaking with that tradition which saw art, however distorted individual forms of it might be, as attempting in some way to capture an "external" reality, was really a logical consequence of their pushing the Expressionist sense of inwardness to, or perhaps beyond, its outer limits. German Expressionism was a crucial source for that non-representational approach which has predominated in aesthetic circles for much of the Twentieth Century. Expressionism, to no small degree a reaction against the harshness of modernity, was able to draw upon much in modern life (even in terms of rebelling against it) to give it a vitality which challenged traditional artistic forms associated with a past for which not a few artists wistfully longed. With an often feared or hated modernity had come an artistic freedom utterly unprecedented in the history of European art.

"Cubism," some of whose major adherents were Pablo Picasso (1881–1973), Georges Braque (1882–1963), and Marcel Duchamp (1887–1968), reacted to modernity and to the challenges posed by, among other things, photography, by quite literally, offering new perspectives on the human form, landscapes, still lifes, and so on. Such were "broken up" into various constitutive planes, so that the observer was able—or at least was supposed to be able—to perceive objects in day-to-day reality, or day-to-day reality itself, in totally different ways. Bemused patrons, however, often failed to see anything at all and, when Duchamp's "Nude Descending the Staircase" was exhibited at the Armory Show in New York in 1913, it provoked a near riot. Cubists, unlike the more Romantic Expressionists, were seemingly untroubled by modernity, seeing in it right away what the German artists came to see over time—possibilities of liberation from old, in some cases, sacrosanct, forms and shibboleths.

Italian Futurists, greatly influenced both by Expressionism and Cubism (they, in turn, clearly influenced some of Franz Marc's later paintings), not only accepted modernity, but rejoiced in it. In spirit, they were greatly influenced by the poet, Filippo Marinetti (1876–1944), who, in several "manifestos," gloried in a new age of speed, mass agitation, and violence. "'We want to glorify war,'" he declared, "'The world's only hygiene—militarism, deed, destructor of anarchisms, the beautiful ideas that are death-bringing, and the contempt of woman.'"[5] Futurist painters such as Gino Severini (1883–1966), Giacomo Balla (1871–1958), and Umberto Boccioni (1882–1916) sprang to respond to Marinetti's macho challenge, and produced works extolling speeding trains, automobiles, and mass violence. While not attacking women or values seen as "womanish" outright, their paintings—and, in Boccioni's case, sculptures—strove to embody self-proclaimed masculine qualities and truths which, the artists thought, could find the fullest possible articulation in virile, death-defying (and at times, producing) modernity. When war would come to Italy, they, far more than most Italians, would be ready for it.

If the appearance of altogether unconventional paintings produced uneasiness, anger, and near riot, the debut of unconventional, often dissonant, music had even more extraordinary effects. In 1905 the German composer, Richard Strauss (1864–1949), presented an outraged world with his opera, *Salome*, based on the biblical tale as rendered by the English writer Oscar Wilde (1856–1900). The dissonance of the piece was bad enough for many. What made matters far worse was the unbridled sensuality displayed by the scantily-clad main character and, when all was culminated by the beheading of John the Baptists, it suggested a fusion of passion and sado-masochistic frenzy which, if Krafft-Ebing had still been alive, would have qualified the piece for inclusion in his well-known book. The uproar occasioning the performance of *Salome* was dwarfed by that which occurred when the already well-established Russian composer, Igor Stravinsky (1882–1971) introduced Paris to his ballet, *Rite of Spring*. For a 1913 audience, even a Parisian one, the combination of a dissonance which, at times, seemed to border on auditory assault, with raw sensuality—the composer's tribute to passions grounded in nature—was too much. To be sure, Stravinsky had a small clique of supporters in the packed orchestral hall; but, their cries of "Genius!, Genius!" were drowned out by shrieks of protest and the sort of mayhem which one associates today with heavy metal concerts.

In music and in art, one could not only sense, but quite plainly see and hear, values and concerns which, to put it mildly, flew in the face of widely-accepted practices of *bourgeois* decorum. Something was clearly afoot. Obviously, there were moods and tensions which were straining for release. Moreover, while the appearance of one or the other "modernistic" piece of art might have been greeted initially with outrage, even disorder, it was plain that, as in the cases of Krafft-Ebing and Freud, people were ready for such things. Some discouraged European cultural critics noticed that the Old World, or at least a portion of it, was evidencing interest in that ghastly American import, ragtime.

There was one very obvious source of tension in the prewar Western world, and one did not have to plumb psychological depths to discover it. This was the women's issue and, particularly in Great Britain, it was one which, like assaults on artistic sensibilities, produced riots, but on a much more disturbing scale. By the first decade of the Twentieth Century, if rural labor is taken into account, women comprised close to half the work force in some European countries. Yet, by 1910, of the European countries, only Finland (at that time, an autonomous regime in Russia) had given women the vote. By the time of the war, women would receive the vote in Norway. Outside of these two countries, women could vote only in Australia, New Zealand, and several Western states in the U.S.A. Thus it was that, between 1900 and the outbreak of the Great War, the suffrage issue became one of great importance for many thousands of women throughout the Western world. It was of great importance in the United States; but, it was in Great Britain that the issue seemed to be developing an explosive force which many, males in particular, saw as virtually threatening to unravel the very fabric of national life.

Millicent Fawcett (1847–1929) had founded the National Union of Women's Suffrage Societies, an organization dedicated to obtaining the vote for women through the arts of political persuasion and compromise. Most women concerned with the cause of suffrage tended to identify with and support her organization and its methods. In 1903, however, a new organization appeared on the scene. Called the Women's Social and Political Union, it was headed by Emmeline Pankhurst (1848–1928) who, along with her two daughters, Christobel and Sylvia, saw strident action as the way to galvanize women into action on behalf of the suffrage cause while hopefully frightening the government into yielding to ever greater pressures exerted upon it. Within a very brief period of time, the WSPU engaged in a variety of actions which flew in the face of Victorian/Edwardian notions of women's place and role in society. Members of the organization and sympathizers smashed store-front windows, burned mail in letter-boxes, chained themselves to rails of the ladies' gallery of parliament, disrupted parliamentary proceedings and, on one occasion, attempted to storm parliament *en masse.* Male response to such actions, either on the part of the police or bystanders, was sometimes extremely violent, and women were slammed to the sidewalk by their hair, kicked and, perhaps symbolically, punched in the breast. In a society in which respect for women was held up as an important tenet, in fact, one whose supposed existence served to elevate it over all others, women who acted outside of socially-prescribed roles were seen as being women no longer. Thus, what one clergymen denounced as "'These termagants, these unsexed viragoes, these *bipeds*!'," [6] could be treated as noxious demi-beings of some sort. For many, the shallowness of accepted proprieties was visible for all to see. When tossed in jail, WSPU activists engaged in hunger strikes and were force-fed through tubes shoved through nostrils and down throats. In a way, the WSPU protest campaign attained an apogee of sorts in 1913, when a young woman named Emily Davison flung herself to her death beneath horses' hooves at the 1913 Derby. Among those in horrified attendance to this action was the king himself, George V.

As the British suffrage campaign raged on, with the WSPU gaining the greatest publicity, suffrage movements on the European continent, at least in part inspired by it, took hold. While not undertaking actions as strident as those of Pankhurst's organization, their efforts both angered and frightened many, particularly, of course, elements of the male population. In 1912, in Germany, a group of particularly disaffected men, along with a few women supporters, formed The League to Combat Female Emancipation. While this organization was somewhat singular in ideologically-informed purpose, it represented in many ways the anger and, to some extent, the fears, of those threatened by what appeared to be extremely disquieting challenges to accepted social norms and values.

The years before World War I thus saw the emergence of a very disturbing form of activism which many found hard to fully understand, much less assimilate. While relatively few men at the time lent active support to efforts undertaken on behalf of women's suffrage, there can be no question but that many were strongly affected by them. Whether or not the appearance of artistic works in which women appeared as threatening figures of one sort or another was due to an increasing, if probably mostly unconscious, sense of guilt about their suppression is difficult, if not impossible to determine. While, however, Krafft-Ebing's assertion that all would go well if only women would assume those passive roles assigned them by an all-wise nature no doubt represented the public views of many males (and probably not a few women as well), it was plain that actions such as that undertaken by Emily Davison pointed to some extremely crucial issues which would not go away. This was so, even if one attempted to ignore them, or to defame, harass, or humiliate those who voiced such issues into silence.

European society, on the eve of war, presents us with a seemingly schizophrenic picture. On the one hand, there was its "official" aspect—a society immersed in material gain and technological advances and sustained by a sense of cultural (and racial) supremacy which found articulation in world dominance. On the other hand, the actions of Anarchists called attention to the existence of aspects of European social life upon which one, understandably, might not wish to reflect. The *Titanic* disaster, horrible enough in itself, served to heighten awareness of these. Moreover, the new industrial civilization, however much one might benefit from it, seemed to many to have stultifying, indeed alienating, aspects. Also troubling were the hypothesizings of a variety of psychologists who seemed to delight in revealing, at least to their satisfaction, that societal norms, and even the reason which supposedly informed them, were thin—and at times inconsequential—screens behind which, or under, there lurked darkly irrational unconscious forces. Whether we chose to recognize it or not, these were the primary sources, or motives, for our actions.

Spiritual uncertainties spawned by an outwardly self-satisfied and stifling industrial society had found reflection in new varieties of artistic expression which, to many, seemed to embody degeneracy. Women were challenging societal norms which, up to that point, had been widely viewed as Providentially ordained. The times were "out of joint," it seemed, and there had to be a sense of relief.

In 1907, Lord Baden-Powell (1857–1941), convinced by his experiences in the Boer War that increasingly citified British young men needed greater exposure to the healthy outdoor life, founded the Boy Scouts. "'*Be prepared,*' he exhorted his young charges, 'to die for your country . . . so that when the time comes you may charge home with confidence, not caring whether you are to be killed or not.'"[7] By 1913, over 150,000 British young men belonged to an organization which, in the eyes of its founder, had paramilitary purposes. In 1911, a German general founded the *Jungdeutschlandbund* ("Young Germany League"). Through activities directed by officers in the regular army, it undertook maneuvers on a regular basis, preparing to take on enemies foreign and domestic (in the latter case, an anticipated revolt from the left) while emphasizing the grandeur of war. In January, 1913, an editorial in its official journal concluded with the following lines: ". . . it will be more beautiful and wonderful to live forever among the

Sordid

heroes on a war memorial in a church than to die an empty death in bed, nameless . . . let that be heaven for young Germany. Thus we wish to knock at our God's door."[8] In the years immediately prior to the outbreak of the Great War, much of the literature read by young men was concerned with the problems posed by intrusive females who did not respect male values and—the ultimate shock—sought to infiltrate into male realms. War, of course, was the male realm, *par excellence* and, in the final analysis, was the one area, sanctified by nature, where masculine strengths could be exhibited, undisturbed by increasingly prying females.

Coming at a time perceived by many as being alternately boring or degenerate, the war would ". . . liberate . . . many a bourgeois youth from shelves lined with carved cocanuts, arcadian porcelains, gilded lilies of plaster, rooms stuffed with upholstery and damask draperies and sprinkled with handicrafts enjoying the patina of time."[9] At that time when, as Leon Trotsky (1879–1940) would later put it, "History's soldier's boot was poised above the ant-heap," a young British officer admonished his brother to recognize how " 'sordid' " the self-absorbed peace-time life could be. " 'Have you ever reflected on the fact that, despite the horrors of war, it is at least a big thing?' "[10] The fabled "August Days" of 1914 would find many Europeans, including some of the most eloquent representatives of what was generally perceived to be the grandest civilization in human history, more than ready to embark upon a "big thing;" indeed, the biggest "thing" it had ever known.

4

The Most Important Assassination of Modern Times and the Illusive Magic of the August Days

EMPEROR of Austria-Hungary, Francis Joseph (1830–1916), had endured an inordinate amount of tragedy in his long lifetime. In 1889, his son, Crown Prince Rudolf, after (apparently, by previous arrangement) shooting his teen-aged mistress to death, committed suicide. In 1898, his wife, the Empress Elizabeth, became numbered amongst the six heads of state slain by Anarchists during the twenty-four years before World War I. While on vacation in Switzerland, she was stabbed to death by an Italian workingman of Anarchist persuasion because, as he remarked, he wanted to kill somebody important enough so that the story would get into the papers.

In late June, 1914, the by now extremely remote Emperor bade his nephew, Francis Ferdinand (1863–1914), and his wife goodbye as they set off on probably the worst-timed "good will" visits in modern history. The royal pair was to tour Sarajevo, capital of Bosnia which, along with Herzegovina, had been annexed by Austria-Hungary in 1908, an action which had served to precipitate a diplomatic crisis of the first magnitude. Much of the population of Bosnia was (and is) Muslim and, for many of these people, such an event was a matter of little concern. Many Bosnians, however, were South Slavs, and rule under an Empire which, as they saw it, already held several million of their kinsmen under subjugation, was unwelcome, indeed infuriating. Such negative attitudes were encouraged by the government of next-door Serbia, since 1903 ruled by a pro-Russian (and hence anti-Austrian) dynasty, which saw no reason why the only independent Slav

Bosnia hated A-H

state other than Bulgaria and inconsequential Montenegro ought not to extend its control over that area. While the degree to which the Serbian government lent support to the terroristic "Black Hand Society" remains a matter of debate, there can be no question but that this group—active, among other places, in Bosnia—did receive some degree of support from at least a portion of it. In any event, it was no secret, least of all to the Austro-Hungarians, that high-ranking Serbian Army officers either belonged, or lent assistance, to the "Black Hand" people.

Very recently, in fact less than a year before Francis Ferdinand and wife Sophie set off for Sarajevo, Serbia had sustained diplomatic frustration due to Austro-Hungarian involvement in the negotiations ending the Balkan Wars. Desperately concerned that Serbia not obtain access to the sea, the Vienna government had been largely responsible for the creation of the independent state of Albania which had served this purpose admirably. Serbian troops were forced to vacate the area in question. In September, 1913, they returned but, under immense international pressure, withdrew after a brief period; Thus, very recent events had served to put Austro-Serbian relations under something of a shade. While it was widely recognized that Francis Ferdinand favored greater autonomy for Slavs within the Austro-Hungarian Empire, this did very little to mollify frustrated and angry South Slav nationalists. In fact, there were some who viewed him as a threat precisely *because* he was seen as a source of possible compromise. For certain varieties of idealists, compromise was, and is, as hated as those seen as being directly responsible for prevailing injustices.

Bearing in mind the general mood which prevailed in both Serbia and Bosnia, and the well-known presence of the "Black Hand Society" in the region, a royal visit to the capitol of the so-recently annexed territory was extremely risky. In view of this, the date chosen for the couple's arrival in Sarajevo, June 28, suggested that the Austro-Hungarian government was determined to rub salt into wounds already festering. As everybody in Belgrade, Sarajevo, and Vienna knew, June 28 was the anniversary of the Battle of Kossovo when, in 1386, the Serbs suffered a disastrous defeat at the hands of the Turks, an event which led to the country's subjugation for almost five hundred years. Thus, the day was one of national mourning. The point at which arrogance faded into folly was uncertain; but both played a role in bringing about the most significant single terroristic act of modern times.

There were seven young assassins along the route taken by the royal motorcade. All, it was later discovered, were ill with tuberculosis and most of them seemed to have been frail in resolve as well. Of the first six potential assassins, only one took significant action. He threw a bomb which, while striking Francis Ferdinand's car, was deflected away from it, exploding in the street. While several in the royal party were slightly injured, and some spectators more seriously so, no one of importance was hit. Some time later, after deciding to pay a visit to the hospital where those wounded in the attack were being treated, the Archduke and Sophie set off on their mission of mercy. On the way, their car took a wrong a turn and the chauffeur, realizing his mistake, stopped the vehicle before turning it around. Within a few feet of the briefly stationary automobile was eighteen-year-old Gavrilo Princip. He pulled out a small caliber Belgian pistol, effective at only the closest of ranges, and fired twice, hitting the Archduke in the neck, and Sophie in the stomach. As a crowd closed in on him, Princip swallowed a capsule of cyanide. It made him ill for a while; but, he was soon well enough to be interrogated. Sophie, however, died within minutes of the shooting and her husband joined her in death soon afterwards. The very last of seven assassins, and the most determined of them, standing within a few feet of where the royal auto was not supposed to have been, had determined that Europeans would be engaged in the first general war in almost one hundred years. It was almost as if the God of history, sensitive to intertwined prevailing feelings of boredom and anxiety, was concerned to offer some sort of response.

"Terrible! The Almighty cannot be provoked!" Such was the response of Emperor Francis Joseph upon his being told of the death of Francis Ferdinand and Sophie. What he meant by this is unclear. Perhaps in view of the tragic recent history of the Habsburg family, the old man had come to see its very existence as some sort of provocation to the divine order of things; or at least providing a kind of negative instrument by which Providence indicated disapproval of human affairs in general. In any event, there is little evidence that this spiritually-burdened human being had any real influence upon, much less control over, the events set in motion by the terrible deed committed on June 28, 1914.

There can be no question that initial general European response to Princip's action was revulsion. Even leading representatives of South Slav nationalism expressed shock, particularly over the murder of Sophie. Yet, within a week or so it became plain that the atrocity of Sarajevo, horrible as it was, had come to serve as a political lightning rod for the articulation of rage generated by years of accumulated fears and suspicions. Chief of the Austro-Hungarian Army, Conrad von Hötzendorf, had been looking for an opportunity, or pretext, to settle scores with Serbia for some time. So long as Alois Aerenthal (1854–1912) was foreign minister, a cautioning influence had served to keep him in check. In 1912, however, Leopold von Berchtold (1863–1942) succeeded Aerenthal at that post and, while occasionally giving the impression of lacking in resolve, generally lent support to the general's bellicose views regarding Serbia. After the events of June 28, both Hötzendorf and Berchtold agreed that the time to undertake drastic action against Serbia, which virtually everyone suspected as having played some role in at least creating the conditions leading to the murders of the Archduke and his wife, had certainly arrived. During the crisis engendered by the annexation of Bosnia-Herzegovina in 1908, Germany's declaration that she stood foursquare behind her Austro-Hungarian ally had been sufficient to cause Russia to back down and France to suddenly discover that this particular untoward move by the Dual Monarchy was a local matter of no real interest to her. Would Germany back Austria-Hungary if the country undertook a campaign to crush Serbia? Through the Austrian ambassador in Berlin, Berchtold put the question to the German Emperor, William II who, on July 5, expressed his firm approval of the notion that Serbia had to be eliminated as a Balkan power. He then left Berlin to go on one of his customary yacht cruises. The following day, the German chancellor, Theobald von Bethmann-Hollweg (1865–1921) told the Austrian ambassador that his country had to decide what course of action to take regarding Serbia. Whatever decision she might make, however, would meet with German approval. The responses of the Emperor and his chancellor are seen as constituting that so-called "Blank Check" issued the Austrian government during the crucial days following the incident at Sarajevo.

Yet, it was not entirely true that the German government would approve of *any* action undertaken by its ally. In point of fact, with the Emperor—who, as everyone knew, could be bellicose one moment and uncertain the next—out of the country, the chancellor, as well as the foreign minister, Gottlieb von Jagow (1863–1935), urged Austria-Hungary to act immediately and attack Serbia. Only in this way, they said, could this country demonstrate that it was still a serious power in the Balkans in particular and Eastern Europe in general. Both the chancellor and the foreign minister were aware that an attack on Serbia would not play well in Russia, and the Franco-Russian alliance was certainly on their minds. Yet, as they saw it, neither Russia nor France was ready for war at the time, while Great Britain, which had no formal military alliance with either of these powers, was probably out of the picture so far as direct action was concerned. Thus, the reasoning went, an Austro-Serbian conflict—surely a very brief one, in any case—could be a localized one.

With regard to the outbreak of a general war, however, Bethmann-Hollweg at least seems to have been aware of the possibility. In fact, like many Germans, he saw war with Russia as inevitable and, this being the case, the sooner one took place, the better. The chancellor believed this because Helmuth Count von Moltke (1848–1916), chief of the general staff, warned him that, within a few years, improvements in the Russian military would make her a much more formidable foe than she would be in 1914, and this, combined with improvements in the French military, would, in the very near future, render Germany's strategic situation hopeless. So it was that, as Bethmann-Hollweg pressed Berchtold to urge his government to act decisively against Serbia, the German military did the same with its Austro-Hungarian counterpart; and, as we have seen, the commander of this army needed little persuasion in this direction.

Yet, for the moment at least, the German government expressed public concern that, when what it saw as the inevitable Austrian attack upon Serbia took place, the conflict would be a limited one. On July 21, it denounced Serbia, while expressing sympathy for Austria-Hungary. At the same time it expressed the view that, whatever might next occur was a matter between those two countries and must not concern any other powers. Three days later, the Dual Monarchy presented Serbia with a list of demands so severe that both the Austro-Hungarian and German governments thought them to be unacceptable. This being the case, war would have to occur. At first, however, the Serbian government, fearful that Russia would not intervene on its behalf, was inclined to yield to the strident ultimatum which, among other things, demanded that Serbia allow Austrian representatives entrance into the country in order to undertake a thoroughgoing investigation of its possible complicity in the murders of June 28. At the last moment, however, the Serbians, emboldened by assurances of Russian support, decided against acceptance of the Austrian demands *in toto*. They now declared their willingness to accede to all of them except those which would constitute an infringement of Serbian sovereignty. Thus, Austrian investigators would not be allowed to undertake activities on Serbian soil.

Before considering the reaction of Austria-Hungary to the Serbian response, we must deal with the question of why Russia now seemed willing to offer support to Serbia. This was in large part due to a visit to St. Petersburg by the French President, Raymond Poincaré (1860–1934) and the premier, who was also foreign minister, René Viviani (1863–1925), which took place between July 20 and July 22, 1914. This official state affair had been planned long before the assassinations of June 28 and, after the event had taken place, there had been talk of cancelling it. Finally, though, the decision was made to go ahead with the visit as planned. While in St. Petersburg, the two Frenchmen assured the Russian government of strong French support with regard to any actions it might take in defense of Russian interests. At the same time, however, the absence of Poincaré and Viviani from Paris resulted in a temporary hobbling of French diplomacy in general, and the Austrians took advantage of this by making public their demands on Serbia while the two travellers were on their way home. Thus, both the Austro-Hungarian ultimatum and Serbia's reply to it, the latter greatly influenced by Russian assurances which were, in turn, largely due to French guarantees of support, appeared during a period in which French diplomatic responses had to have been limited.

In the meantime, Vienna declared the Serbian response to be unsatisfactory and this thoroughly alarmed the British government which, for the first time seeking to play a role in the mounting crisis, called for the ambassadors of Germany, France, Italy, and Great Britain to meet and discuss the Serbian reply to the ultimatum. The meeting was to take place, of course, on the condition that Serbia, Austria-Hungary and Russia refrain from military operations of any kind. Germany spurned the British request, declaring that it would not participate in any conference which might result in putting pressure upon her ally. At this point, Germany was in fact playing a dual role in the crisis. On the one hand, its foreign office passed on British proposals to Austria-Hungary; on the other, it offered private assurances to Vienna that it did not expect its ally to take any of them seriously.

In the midst of all of this, William II, tanned, fit, and feeling just fine, returned from his cruise and, on July 28, to the horror of the German foreign office and Bethmann-Hollweg, issued a statement in which he declared the Serbian reply to have been sufficiently conciliatory to eliminate all reasons for war. At the very most, the Austrians should occupy a portion of Serbia—although, to be sure, this would include the capitol, Belgrade—and only temporarily at that, to ensure the country's cooperation in investigations into possible Serbian complicity in the assassinations of the Archduke and his wife. Bethmann-Hollweg and Jagow made certain that their Emperor's message was not sent off to Vienna soon enough to influence events. To make doubly certain that matters went their way, i.e., that the expected attack on

Serbia took place, they removed William's statement that, so far as he was concerned, war was unnecessary. In any event, on the very day that William II made his remarks, July 28, 1914—one month after the Sarajevo tragedy—Austria-Hungary declared war on Serbia. The following day, Austrian monitors, cruising the river Danube, began lobbing shells on Belgrade. Russia responded to this action by ordering a partial mobilization, thus indicating that it was ready to go to war with the Dual Monarchy, if not, at this point anyway, with Germany.

Suddenly, Bethmann-Hollweg became alarmed. As mentioned earlier, he had thought that war with Russia was probably inevitable, but, as the possibility of a general European war loomed ever larger, he got "cold feet." In a last minute act of desperation, he attempted to persuade the Austrians to accept British proposals somewhat along the lines of those suggested by the German Emperor. Also, he urged them to enter into negotiations with the Russians over Serbia. By this time, however, Bethmann-Hollweg and the German foreign office were working at odds with the German military which, acting more or less on its own, was putting enormous pressure upon the Austro-Hungarian government to not only press its attack on Serbia but to order general mobilization. This it did on July 31, 1914.

By now, the German high command was virtually running the country's foreign policy, and this was to no small degree due to its inflexible commitment to the Schlieffen Plan. After all, there simply had to be a two-front war and Russian mobilization, even, at this point, a partial one, was the first step in that direction. If, as necessitated by the Schlieffen Plan, Germany was to launch a strong attack in the west against France, whose entrance into the a conflict now seen as inevitable was just a matter of days if not hours, while holding Russia at bay in the east, then general mobilization had to be ordered. Even as the German general staff was pressing the chancellor to order general mobilization, it was, more or less behind his back, pressuring the Austrians to do the same. Bethmann-Hollweg, not wanting his country to bear the onus of responsibility for taking the first step towards a general European war by being the first to order general mobilization, refused Moltke's request—at this point, more of a demand—that the order be given. At the same time, he did warn the Russian government that, unless its partial mobilization was ended, Germany would have to order a general mobilization. In the meantime, however, Austria-Hungary—as we have seen, under strong pressure from the German military to do so—had ordered general mobilization. This was one of several reasons why Russia not only could not accede to

Bethmann-Hollweg's request, but had to order a general mobilization of its own. There were two other reasons of importance. First of all, if Russia rescinded the partial mobilization order, loss of prestige would have been enormous. Yet, as Bethmann-Hollweg had warned, if the order were not rescinded, Germany would be fully mobilized. This being the case, Russia would have to do the same. Finally, and this was perhaps of ultimate importance, the condition of partial mobilization was an awkward one and had brought considerable confusion in its wake. The generals of Tsar Nicholas II (1894-1917) were now declaring that Russia had no choice but to embark on the course of general mobilization.

Even at his best, Nicholas II, though a basically kind person, did not amount to very much. Twisting this way and that, depending on with whom he had last spoken, he yielded to the entreaties of his generals and, on July 31, the day Austria-Hungary declared general mobilization, the Russian government did the same. Immediately upon hearing of it, the German government demanded that the order be rescinded. The following day, it ordered general mobilization of the German armed forces. French general mobilization soon followed. On that day, August 1, 1914, the British ambassador in Berlin, Sir Edward Goschen, sent a telegram to the British foreign secretary, Sir Edward Grey (1862-1933). After describing German reaction to British proposals and concerned with heading off the approaching general conflict, he concluded his report with the following: "Germany's demand to Russia has been published tonight in the extra sheets and large crowds are parading the streets singing patriotic songs."[1] Added onto the telegram was a "Minute" in which Goschen recorded the observations of the Russian ambassador to Great Britain as he travelled by train from St. Petersburg on the way to London. As his train sped through Germany, he noticed that "'The German railways were filled in all directions with moving troops—'"[2] —and this, obviously *before* the formal generalization order had been issued. One wonders if, in some ways, the German military, already known for forcing, or at least anticipating, events was engaged in independent mobilization actions of its own. Or, perhaps the Russian ambassador was being disingenuous or evidencing confusion. It really didn't matter much at this point.

On the evening of August 1, the German ambassador in St. Petersburg, Friedrich von Pourtalés, stood before the Russian foreign minister, Sergei Sazonov (1886–1927). He expressed his government's demand that Russia cease its mobilization. Sazonov refused to comply, and the German ambassador then pulled a paper from his pocket, on which was written a declaration of war. Weeping, the men embraced one another, after which Pourtalés requested that he be provided with his passport.

For the moment, the German government put off declaring war on Russia's alliance partner, France. Wedded though it was to the Schlieffen Plan, it held to the increasingly remote hope that France might not honor its treaty obligations and go to war. Just to make certain that all was in readiness, however, the German ambassador to Belgium was told, on August 2, that, on the following day, he was to inform the Belgian government that it would be necessary to allow German troops to pass through the country. If this move—necessitated, of course, by the Schlieffen Plan—was not resisted, then the German government would indemnify Belgium for any damages which might occur due to the massive German incursion. If Belgium chose to resist, it of course would have to bear full responsibility for what would then take place. On August 3, the Belgian government was presented with the German request. After brief consideration of it, the king of Belgium, Albert (1909–1934) rejected what had amounted to an ultimatum. "Belgium," he said, "was not a thoroughfare," and any infringement of its neutrality, guaranteed by the Treaty of London of 1839, would be resisted. A German declaration of war upon France soon followed, as did the entrance of an enormous German Army into Belgium.

The British government which, as late as August 1 had attempted to play a role in mediating the crisis, declared that it could not allow violation of Belgian neutrality and demanded that Germany pull back its troops. While it was no doubt true that the invasion of Belgium itself sufficed for Great Britain to go to war, possible German possession of the channel coast, especially that of France, was an even more compelling reason for British intervention. In the British statement to the German government, however, the invasion of Belgium was given as being of singular importance. Bethmann-Hollweg's somewhat intemperate response was one which would haunt both him and his country. In a situation in which, he said, Germany was fighting a defensive war for its very existence, "necessity knows no law," and he was astounded that Great Britain was willing to go to war over obligations written down on "a scrap of paper," i.e., the Treaty of London. By the time the sun set on the day of August 4, 1914, Great Britain had declared war on Germany.

All governments took note of the fact that Italy, still formally, if not really seriously, a member of the Triple Alliance, had declared that, since neither Austria-Hungary or Germany was fighting a truly defensive war, she was not compelled to enter the conflict on their side. Behind these noble sentiments, of course, lurked darker motives, and these would become apparent in the not-too-distant future. For the moment, as massive armies were on the move in all directions, accompanied and sustained by an enthusiasm indicative of immense spiritual relief, what a second-rate military power might do or not do was of little concern. In Berlin, William II who, due to the remarkable fertility of his now deceased grandparents, Victoria and Albert of Great Britain, was cousin to George V, the British monarch, and (by marriage) to Nicholas II of Russia, is said to have put his own gloss on the situation. "'To think that George and Nicky should have played me false! If my grandmother had been alive, she never would have allowed it.'"[3]

armies on the move

From the time when Austria-Hungary presented Serbia with its severe demands, all who wished for the preservation of peace were alarmed. Socialists were particularly concerned, and Socialist newspapers throughout Europe called for all measures necessary to prevent war. Acting with dispatch, the leaders of the Socialist Second International called for a meeting to take place in Brussels on July 29. Even before it took place, there were workers' mass meetings and demonstrations. There was even an occasional call for a general strike, although this particular approach had been ignored for so long that no one really knew what it might involve. By the time the Brussels meeting took place, Austria-Hungary was already at war with Serbia. It was hoped however, that, if concerted working class action took place, a widening of the war might be prevented. Yet, while delegates from virtually all European countries met and denunciations of militarism and war flew thick and fast, little of a concrete nature came out of the emergency conference. All that was agreed upon was that there would be a future meeting in Paris on August 9. Of perhaps greater significance was a mass meeting of Belgian working class people held on the evening of July 29. At it, the French Socialist, Jean Jaurès (1859–1914), probably the most eloquent spokesperson for peace and humanitarian ideals in Europe, spoke with dramatic fervor about the necessity of preventing war. At one point, in a moving gesture of Socialist brotherhood, he put his arm around the shoulders of Hugo Haase (1863–1919), representative of the German Social Democratic Party. After the meeting ended, an enormous workers' demonstration took place, and thousands shouted the slogan, "War against war!" Two days later, Jaurès, back in Paris trying to organize parliamentary opposition against the war, was shot dead by a young man representing the nationalist right.

The French government, terrified by the thought of a working class revolt on the very eve of an expected war, appealed for calm. Yet, while there were cries of sorrow and outrage, there was no sign of revolt, not even of any substantial strike action. When, on August 1, general mobilization was announced, young men all over the country report for service. By the time Jaurès was buried, on August 4, 1914, virtually every major city of all the countries involved in the new, great war had seen extraordinary outpourings of enthusiasm which, taken together, have been described as constituting the essence of the magical, indeed mythical, "August Days."

Until the very moment when war had become a certainty, there had been protests against it, particularly, of course, on the left. Once war had been declared, however, its coming was greeted with enthusiasm, even joy. This was particularly the case where one might most expect it, i.e., in the major cities of the warring powers, through which soldiers marched to trains which would bear them off to suddenly materialized fronts, and reactions in smaller towns and rural areas were more muted. Nonetheless, the outburst of a variety of passion, at times bordering on the sensual, has been a subject of amazement. Those who have commented upon the phenomenon, in general, have come to the sad conclusion that, as indicated earlier, large segments of the European population were, for a variety of reasons, ready for war. A time of peace, viewed alternately (or, at times, all at once) as stultifying and degenerate, had been too much to endure. Modernity, either too constraining or too challenging, had brought forth a response which, if antediluvian, was perceived of as being at least authentic.

Thus it was, that not only Le Bon's fabled "mob" cried out for war and the most painful of sacrifices. The French poet, Charles Péguy (1873–1914) who, at the age of forty-one, rushed to enlist (and, as his dates indicate, would very soon be dead), enthused about the joyful atmosphere in Paris as soldiers marched off towards an exploding unknown. "'Who hasn't seen Paris today and yesterday," he declared, "hasn't seen anything.'" A short time before these glorious few days in August, he had written a poem in anticipation of them.

> Happy are they who die for they return
> Into the primeval clay and the primeval
> earth.
> Happy are they who die in a just war,
> Happy as the ripe corn and the harvested
> grain.[4]

Thomas Mann (1875–1955), the great German liberal writer, posed the rhetorical question, "'is not war a purification, a liberation, an enormous hope?'" "'My Russian destiny is fulfilled,'" declared the Russian composer Alexander Scriabin (1872–1915).[5]

It seemed that mediocrities and geniuses alike had been swept up in a mood best captured by Caroline Playne in her book, *Neuroses of Nations:* "At last! At last! We get what we want! We *can* do and *die!* And they felt, in their hearts, intense relief that there was to be no more negotiating, no more thinking, no more heeding, only rushing on, on, gloriously, splendidly on, all traces kicked over, all bridles thrown away!"[6] Looking back on it all, and recalling the lines of happy young men in front of British Army recruiting stations, the poet Philip Larkin, as poets often do, had another "take" on the situation:

> Those long uneven lines
> Standing so patiently,
> As if they were stretched outside
> The Oval or Villa Park,
> The crowns of hats, the sun
> on moustached archaic faces
> Grinning as if it were all
> An August Bank holiday lark;
> . . . .
> Never such innocence,
> Never before or since,
> . . . .
> Never such innocence again.[7]

Probably, though, the final words on the topic were provided by the ordinarily unpoetic Lord Grey, who, watching lamp-lighters working at their tasks on the night of August 4, 1914, turned to a companion and, as if staring into the eyes of some future ghost, remarked, "The lamps are going out all over Europe. They will not be lit again in our lifetime."

5

Two Months of Movement

THE CAMPAIGN IN THE WEST AND THE SHATTERING OF FRENCH ILLUSIONS

CHIEF of the General Staff, Helmuth von Moltke, before the outbreak of fighting, had failed to strengthen the right wing, so crucial, as its author saw it, to the success of the Schlieffen Plan. Instead, he sent several corps to the German left to face the anticipated French onslaught in Alsace-Lorraine. Nonetheless, the German Army in the West initially conducted operations in accordance with its guidelines. War's outbreak saw 1,500,000 German troops massed against the Belgian and French frontiers. They were organized into seven armies. The left wing, facing the French in Alsace-Lorraine, consisted of the Sixth and Seventh Armies, comprising 16 divisions. The Fourth and Fifth Army, consisting of 20 divisions, comprised the "center" of the German line and, after occupying Luxemburg, faced the French from Metz north to just above the Ardennes region in southeastern Belgium and northern France. The right wing, though not as strong as Schlieffen would have liked it to have been, still constituted the "point of concentration" (or, in the somewhat unlovely German phrase, *"Schwerpunkt")* of German operations in the west. It consisted of the First, Second, and Third Armies, which were composed of 34 divisions. It was the right wing, of course, which had immediately to contend with the Belgians should they be so idiotic as to offer any resistance.

Facing well over 600,000 German troops, as mentioned above, organized into 34 divisions, was a Belgian field army consisting of 6 infantry and one cavalry division, and comprising, in total, 117,000 men. There were perhaps 10,000 or so more Belgian troops manning the fortresses of Liège and Namur, but, there were no reserves and, except for the guns of the fortresses, no heavy artillery. What relatively few machine guns the Belgian Army possessed were often borne to the front in wagons which, pulled by dogs, were used in happier times to deliver milk. This army had seen no formal action since the brief war for Belgian independence (1830–1831) and, in the second stage of the conflict, when the previously expelled Dutch began to take it seriously, had not done very well on its own. Only the appearance of French troops saved the country from being reannexed by the Netherlands. Later, Belgian troop were effective in breaking up the slave trade in the Congo, but this hardly amounted to a major campaign. In peacetime, the parliament, placing reliance on the newly-constructed fortresses to defend Belgian neutrality, provided little in the way of funding for the field army. Its infantrymen were allowed to fire one round per man twice a week and this was supposed to have constituted target practice. The Belgian Army was noted for a lack of discipline which bordered on the scandalous. Its men saluted when it suited them to do so and seemed to harbor a particular resentment at having to march in step. It was no wonder that German soldiers viewed their seemingly vaudevillian opponents as *"Schokolade Soldaten"*, or *"chocolate soldiers."*

Yet, when King Albert declared that Belgium would resist a German invasion, the country was swept by a wave of patriotic enthusiasm and the army braced itself to resist it as best it could. The first serious fighting took place at Liège, the fortress city, which was also an important railway nexus. It was in the path of the German Second Army, and 60,000 of its troops were deployed to attack Liège, which was defended by approximately 25,000 troops, with perhaps between 3,000 to 4,000 more occupying the fortresses. On August 5, 1914, German troops attempted to take the fortresses by direct assault. While, as indicated above, peace-time training had not allowed the average Belgian soldier to develop marksman skills, massed troops advancing straight-up provided targets which were hard to miss and field army and fortress troops exacted a carnage which foreshadowed later and greater slaughters. After initial shock, and attendant demoralization, the German Army steeled itself for further attacks, and it soon became plain that the Belgian field army would be overwhelmed. It was withdrawn. Several days later, Liège fell to the invaders, but not before a German Zeppelin, in the first such attack in history, dropped bombs on the city. The fortresses, however, continued to hold out and conventional German artillery had little effect on them. On the way, however, were truly awesome weapons which would put an end to German military embarrassment.

On August 12, 1914, there appeared in Liège the first real "secret weapons" of the war. These were 420 mm howitzers manufactured by Krupp, and 305 mm mortars produced by the Skoda works in Austro-Hungarian ruled Bohemia. By August 16, all of the Belgian fortresses, garrisons blown to pieces, asphyxiated, or stunned into insensibility, had fallen. Now, the German Second and Third Armies, whose advance had been stalled by the resistance at Liège, were once again in motion, and this pleased General Alexander von Kluck (1846–1934), whose First Army, on the far right of the German right wing, had not been able to complete its anticipated rapid sweep along the Belgian coast until the Second and Third Armies were free to keep pace with it.

As the German Armies moved across Belgium, reports of terrible atrocities inflicted upon the civilian population began to emerge. Some of these were gross exaggerations produced by Allied propaganda machines. It was said that German soldiers raped nuns on a regular basis and even, on occasion, were known to eat Belgian babies. While there were no doubt instances of rape, considerations of time, aside from morality, would have made made a systematic campaign of it unlikely. The same held true with regards to consuming Belgian infants, even if the sight of fat, and presumably juicy, Flemish babies might have proved mouth-watering to dust-coated soldiers, exhausted by rapid marching under a pitiless August sun. Nonetheless, many in the Allied camp believed such stories, and the behavior of the German Army was bad enough in any case. " 'Our advance in Belgium is certainly brutal,' " remarked Chief of the General Staff von Moltke, " 'but we are fighting for our lives and all who get in the way must take the consequences.' "[1]

Harsh "consequences" might well have been made inevitable by this army's encountering unexpected, and sometimes effective, resistance from the Belgians. Such produced an initial shock, and then a rage sustained by the near paranoid belief that much of this was being offered by a treacherous civilian population which sniped at German troops from houses and behind fences. Soon, hostages were being taken by the score and executed by firing squads. Priests, who, for some reason, were suspected of having played roles in organizing civilian resistance, were particularly singled out in these actions, but, on occasion, women and children—even infants—were slaughtered.

Villages were burned to the ground and, on August 25, the university city of Louvain (now, Leuven) was largely destroyed, after a German soldier had been wounded by sniper fire. Among the buildings set aflame was a magnificent 14th Century structure in which the world famous university library was located. Totally destroyed, it became a symbol, in this case a very real one, of German ruthlessness. In many ways, it helped to steel the resolve of Allied governments and civilian populations to see the war through to an end, however bitter. It is highly doubtful, however, if Allied soldiers, except perhaps Belgian ones, reflected much on the matter. In the desperate August days, there were other things on their minds.

On August 11, 1914, in accordance with Plan XVII, the French Army began a massive offensive on the center and right flanks of the Allied line. Eventually involving four French armies, totalling around one million men, it was presided over by General Joseph Joffre (1852–1931) a taciturn, hulking *gourmand* for whom, as many historians have seen it, the word "phlegmatic" is most appropriate. At times, it was hard to tell whether Joffre, in dealing with grave issues, was heroically calm or astonishingly obtuse. At any rate, it became almost immediately clear that heavy casualties did not daunt him and, for those under his overall command, this was unfortunate. After initial successes against a German screening force, the French attackers ran into the reinforced German defensive line. As had the Germans at Liège, but with the most minimal artillery support imaginable under the circumstances, the blue coated and red-trousered soldiers advanced straight up, led by sword-wielding, white-gloved officers. Snugly ensconsed in positions which had been prepared with an eye to local conditions ideally suited to the defense, German machine gun batteries mowed down their French opponents with sickening ease. When the stunned survivors finally "took to earth," they could not seek security by digging themselves in. Confident in the power of Bergsonian élan, whose most obvious expression was the bayonet, French planners had not thought it necessary that those captive to their schemes be equipped with anything which might serve to nurture a defeatist defensive attitude. Thus, entrenching tools of any kind were almost totally absent.

Within a very brief period of time, it became obvious that what would become known as the "Battle of the Frontiers" was a French disaster. The "cult of the offensive," confronted with mundane military realities engendered by modern technology, had turned out to be obscenely heretical. Plan XVII was in shambles, and, with tens of thousands of French casualties testifying to its bankruptcy, thousands more were in retreat. As discouragement increasingly yielded to demoralization, a rout seemed inevitable, and the troops on the German left-wing were fully prepared to take advantage of it. Now, however, those same stolid, unimaginative qualities that had allowed Joffre to preside unflinchingly over the, up to that point, most ingenuously suicidal mass offensive in modern military history, proved invaluable in rallying exhausted, disspirited men. The retreat had to stop, he declared, and a firm defensive line established. One was and, to the astonishment of Frenchman and German alike, it held. Gone, however, were the illusions spawned by that military romanticism that had arisen in apparent protest against the unheroic realities of a new, materialistic age. Now, French troops, whose blue and red uniforms had become as faded as many a lost hope, were digging in, some with newly-supplied spades, others, still lacking them, with mess-kit plates and bayonets. With the support of increasing numbers of artillery pieces, the most famous of them, the 75 mm quick-firing gun, they managed, although at great cost, to repulse heavy German attacks. By month's end, however, the battles in Alsace and eastern France had cost the French somewhere between 300,000 and 350,000 casualties. August, 1914, the first month of the war, would be the worst one for France.

Further to the west, matters, at least from the Allied perspective, were not encouraging. Brussels fell on August 20, and its stunned and somewhat fearful inhabitants were treated to a massive German victory parade. All of Alexander von Kluck's First Army, some 320,000 men, in impeccable formations, marched through the city—a "grim, gray, undulating horde," as one horrified but fascinated American correspondent described it. Seemingly as much of an act of God as a collection of soldiers, there appeared to be little that could stop its apparently inexorable advance. On the right of the First Army, the German Second invested the fortress city of Namur, and, fresh from their successes at Liège, the monstrous siege howitzers and mortars were once again in action. Close to the doomed city, the French Fifth Army, commanded by General Charles Lanrezac (1852–1925), while contemplating an attack, was surprised by one mounted by the German Second. This resulted in a retreat which, for awhile, threatened to turn into a rout. In due course, order was restored and Lanrezac's battered and exhausted soldiers were able to slow the German advance in fierce fighting. Slowing, much less stopping General von Kluck's First Army, however, seemed, to all but that redoubtable mountain of impassive flesh, Joffre, a remote possibility. To be sure, there were now British troops available to attempt it, but, for most French generals, this was of small comfort.

Before the war, the British general, Henry Wilson (1864–1922), asked a French counterpart, Ferdinand Foch (1851–1929) what was the minimal number of British troops which he thought would be of use to France in case of war. " 'A single British soldier,' " came the reply, " 'and we will see to it that he is killed.' "[2] The initial British contribution to the fighting during, for the Allies, dark August days of 1914 came out to be somewhat more than that. Yet, the five and one-half divisions, totalling around 80,000 men, which constituted the extreme left of the Allied line, were but a fraction of the French troops engaged in action, indeed, as matters would turn out, a fraction of French losses sustained in three weeks of fighting. Furthermore, the commander of what was called the "British Expeditionary Force" (BEF) was viewed with both distrust and contempt by French colleagues. Sir John French (1852–1925), a cavalryman who, during the Boer War, had established a blandly undistinguished record for himself, was best known for a coleric temper and massive libidinal appetites. Of the commanders of the two corps which comprised the BEF, that of the First, Lieutenant General Douglas Haig (1861–1928) thought him unfit for command, while, in turn, Sir John seemed to harbor a strong grudge against the commander of the Second, General Sir Horace Smith-Dorrien (1858–1930).

From the French perspective, however, what made Sir *John* French (who, despite his name, spoke the language of his Ally rather badly) so unsatisfactory a guardian of the left flank was his seeming reluctance to commit his admittedly undersized force to combat. Indeed, his well-known outbursts of temper, which often served to give the pudgy, under-sized, ferociously-moustached man the appearance of an enraged fox terrier, seemed to be more than counterbalanced by a timidity when it came to wartime variety combat. Within a very brief period of time, relations between the commander of the BEF and virtually all French commanders were quite poor and those between him and the commander on his right, the sorely-tried Lanrezac, disastrous. It was only with difficulty that the French could persuade Sir John to move the BEF into assuming a combative stance and coordination between it and the soon to be smashed French Fifth Army was haphazard at best. Yet, whether or not its commander desired it, British soldiers would, in due course, have to engage in combat and, one day after Lanrezac's defeat, they took part in their first battle.

Near the Belgian industrial town of Mons, on August 23, 1914, the heavily-outnumbered BEF clashed with forward elements of Kluck's First Army. While the British Army would prove to be ill-prepared for that trench warfare which would soon await them, it was well-trained in marksmanship (of course associated with "open field" varieties of fighting) and, man for man, its soldiers were probably the best "shots" in the world. Compensating somewhat for the spiritual confusion of their commander, they beat back German assaults with a rifle fire of such deadly intensity that many German commanders thought that they were using exclusively machine-guns. As attack after attack wilted in the face of the determined British defense, the German brought their immensely superior artillery into action and soon British casualties began to climb. By day's end, the men of the BEF withdrew some in order to minimize their losses. Yet, because they had succeeded in repelling all German infantry attacks, the battle at Mons came to be viewed as a British victory, even though the German First Army had received the most temporary of checks.

BEF losses at Mons totalled around 4,200, a mere drop in the blood bucket compared to those being sustained by their French Ally. While its soldiers had reason to congratulate themselves on their marksmanship and a stout defense, it was soon compelled to retreat before the overwhelming numbers of Kluck's legions. Yet, at least in the eyes of many Britons the Battle of Mons became elevated to legendary proportions. In due course, members of the BEF became known as "Mons Men," and a special "Mons Medal" was struck for all who had participated in the August fighting. Later, it was claimed that, during the fighting, legions of angels illuminated the sky as they shielded British soldiers from harm and, during the inevitable retreat, they had constituted a kind of divine rear guard, hindering German pursuit. In their glorification of the events of August 23, Britons revealed the sort of nationalistic lunacy that had been responsible for the war in the first place, and would help to sustain it long past that point by which the losses suffered at Mons would be viewed as being almost ridiculously minuscule.

After a rapid retreat, the BEF soon found itself in France where, at Le Cateau, it turned to confront the pursuing Germans. Once again, its sharp-shooting riflemen inflicted heavy losses. Once again, in the end, German superiority in artillery proved decisive. After sustaining over 8,000 casualties, the British were again in retreat, while their commander, Sir John French, teetered on the edge of spiritual collapse. On their immediate and far right, French armies, while fighting heroic defensive battles, were also in retreat. The Belgian Army, having withdrawn to positions in and around Antwerp, far to the northwest, was out of the picture for the moment, although it served the purpose of compelling the Germans to detach several corps to keep an eye on it. From the Allied perspective, matters were grave and, indeed, by the end of the month, numbers of Parisians were fleeing the French capital. Yet, if Allied commanders had been able to read the minds of their German counterparts, they might have discovered reasons for hope.

By the end of the month, not only were German soldiers exhausted by days of enforced marching, not to mention occasional fighting; but, the advancing armies were rapidly losing cohesion and Commander in Chief von Moltke, his mind. What that revered prophet of total war, Carl von Clausewitz had called its "frictions" had put in an appearance and such matters as the energy-draining August heat, breakdowns in communication, and the awesome difficulties posed by adequately controlling the movements of the most massive armies the world had ever seen—issues barely considered by Schlieffen—were beginning to cause his bold scheme to unravel. This was particularly true for the soldiers of the First Army, whose advance was to pace those of the others. By the beginning of September, its soldiers at least as exhausted in advance as were the Allies in retreat, and still confronted by an enemy which, though frequently beaten would not acknowledge defeat, were showing signs of demoralization. Their commander, General von Kluck, on the other hand, was showing both strain and impatience, and this would cause him to make a decision the consequences of which would prove to be beyond measure. Before we consider this, however, we must devote attention to events in areas which, taken together, would come to constitute the Great War's "Eastern Front."

THE CAMPAIGNS IN THE EAST: GERMAN SUCCESS AND AUSTRIAN DISASTER

In formulating his famous plan, General von Schlieffen had assumed that the Russians, never known for efficiency in matters military, would mobilize slowly. Once the war began, however, and in part due to the pleading of their French Ally, the Russian Army mobilized with startling speed and almost immediately was in motion towards the west. In point of fact, it was in motion long before it was really ready to undertake a sustained offensive campaign. Even before it clashed with the enemy, it was clear that supplies were lacking and that many soldiers were lacking in that training necessary to see a modern campaign through to a successful conclusion.

Under the circumstances, it might have made sense to assume a threatening bit defensive posture towards the Germans, while, if there had to be an offense, undertaking such against the weaker Austrian forces. The Russian high command knew, however, that East Prussia was held by the German Eighth Army, numbering 135,000 effectives, and that it could bring to bear a far larger army against it. It was also, as mentioned above, being bombarded by French requests to do something to help to relieve seemingly irresistible pressures in the west. Thus it was that a massive Russian army, numbering 650,000 men, embarked upon an invasion of East Prussia.

Besides problems of lack of training and supplies, there was that of leadership. The Russian mass was comprised of the First Army, commanded by General Pavel Rennenkampf (1854–1918), and the Second Army, commanded by General Alexander Samsanov (1859–1914). Neither was known for possessing either strategic vision or tactical prowess and, worse than that, they hated each other. During the Russo-Japanese War they were supposed to have engaged in a fist-fight on a platform of the Mukden, Manchuria railway station. In any case, relations had been decidely sour ever since. Even in a campaign as crucial as the one in which they were now prematurely engaged, neither could be counted upon to render assistance to the other. To be sure, the commander of the German Eighth Army which confronted them, Colonel General Max von Prittwitz (1848–1917), also was no luminary. As the Russian threat to East Prussia became plain, however, the high command added to his staff Lieutenant Colonel Max Hoffmann (1869–1927). Well over six feet tall, and weighing more than 250 pounds, he blended dedication to established military procedures with a healthy contempt of those, above or below him, who did not interpret them the same way as he did. Before the war, he had been mainly known for gargantuan eating and drinking capacities, and his "wake-up call" sometimes consisted of two litres of wine before breakfast. Of greater interest to the German high command, however, was his profound knowledge of things Russian. Knowing the language well, he had spent six months in Russia as an interpreter for German military representatives stationed there, and later was attached to the Russian section of the German General Staff. He had crucial insights into Russian military thinking and, of course, was quite familiar with the animosity between generals Samsonov and Rennenkampf.

In 1902, an avaricious Russian officer had sold Hoffmann a copy of the proposed Russian plan in case of war. Since that time, there had been alterations; but, he had been able to determine what he thought a Russian offensive against Germany would be like and, in the final analysis, Hoffmann's appraisal would turn out to be correct. Naturally, geographical concerns are important to any military operation and, if the Russians attacked each Prussia, it was plain that the interconnected

Masurian Lakes would play an important role. If there was to be a large-scale Russian offensive (and common sense dictated that there couldn't be a small one) then, in a relatively rare portion of Germany in which there were few roads, the lakes would serve the purpose of splitting any army attacking from the east into two wings. Such being the case, a defender, even if heavily outnumbered, might have a good chance of defeating one or the other "wing" of an advancing Russian Army and then defeating the other one—in a word, of beating the enemy "in detail."

At first, however, it appeared as if circumstances would not allow for Hoffmann's hypotheses to be translated into reality. After some initial successes, a German army contesting the advance of Rennenkampf's Second—which constituted the northern (right) flank of the Russian invasion force—was decisively beaten at Gumbinnen on August 20, 1914. Some German units had shown signs of panic, and over 7,000 of them wound up in Russian prisoner of war cages. The defeat had been bad enough, but Prittwitz was sent into near hysteria by it and succeeded in persuading Chief of Staff von Moltke that he ought to become hysterical as well. Responding to the Eighth Army's commander's report of massive disaster in East Prussia, Moltke ordered three corps and a cavalry division to be detached from the right wing of the German army in the west and sent east as rapidly as possible. This move not only obviously weakened the right wing, but, at a time when confusion was starting to prevail between the armies comprising it, made it increasingly difficult for the German First and Second Armies to maintain cohesion. As we will see, this would have extremely important, if not, from the German perspective, grave consequences.

Moltke did more than to reinforce the Eighth Army. He replaced its commander and appointed, in his place Paul von Hindenburg (1847–1934), summoned from retirement. Before retiring from the service in 1911, he had established a reputation for good judgement and for being calm in the most trying of circumstances. What he lacked in imagination would be more than compensated for by that of his new chief of staff, Erich Ludendorff (1865–1937), who already had established a considerable reputation for himself during the Belgian campaign. By the time the two arrived at Eighth Army headquarters, Prittwitz's panic had subsided somewhat and he had pretty well fallen in with Hoffmann's idea of defeating the Russian Army in detail, it having lost cohesion, as anticipated, by being divided into two rather distant wings by the Masurian Lakes. It was Ludendorff, however, who received the message from Berlin that, in response to Prittwitz's earlier entreaties, three corps and a cavalry division had been removed from the German army in the west and now were on their way to restore the situation in East Prussia. By now, however, this didn't matter any more, for what became known as the "Battle of Tannenberg" was underway.

While the thinnest cavalry screens kept watch over Rennenkampf's First Army, almost all of the Eighth Army focused its attention on Samsonov's Second. The men of both of the Russian armies were not only exhausted, but hungry. They had long since outrun their supply lines, and soldiers were short, not only of food, but ammunition and good boots. The rough nature of the terrain over which they had advanced had been responsible for terrible wear and tear and, with no fresh boots available, many soldiers had been forced to bind their feet with rags. This nasty situation possibly could have been at least ameliorated, if not avoided, if the invading Russians had marched in the daytime and thus had seen where they were going. But, in an almost childlike effort at concealment, they had marched at night, sleeping in the daylight hours. Furthermore, whatever chance they had of fooling the Germans by this move was rendered *totally* null and void by an oversight so monumental that even the word "blunder" is inadequate to describe it—the commanders of the two Russian armies often sent messages to each other and to the overall commander of both armies, General Jilinsky, and responded to one another "in clear." In other words, messages asking for instructions, providing crucial information as to tactical dispositions, lines of march and so on, often were not sent in code. Thus, understandably curious Germans could eavesdrop whenever they wished to do so and have an almost total understanding of their enemy's dispositions and intentions.

It was thus that, in due course, the German generals knew that Rennenkampf probably was going to stay put—long enough, at least for the Eighth Army to crush Samsonov's force. The process commenced on August 26th and, as in western battles, the German artillery played a crucial role. The famished and exhausted soldiers of the Second Army were short of ammunition; but, it didn't really matter. The big guns and field pieces of the Eighth Army shredded most of them before they could get within small arms range. Within a few days, Samsonov's force was shattered. By August 30th, around 30,000 men were killed or missing, while the victorious Germans counted over 92,000 prisoners. General Samsonov, whose pleas for instructions and assistance from anyone who might have been listening had gone largely ignored (except, of course, by the Germans) was heart-broken. To his chief of staff, he muttered, over and over again, " 'The Tsar trusted me. How can I face him after such a disaster?' "[3] At about 1:00 A.M., on the morning of August 30th, he committed suicide. The great German victory had taken place on a wide-ranging battlefront which included a number of small towns (some of which were burned and ransacked by retreating Russian soldiers). For awhile, bemused staff officers scratched their heads over a proper name for the engagement. Finally, someone, probably Ludendorff, remembered that, in 1410, the German Teutonic knights had been defeated by a Polish/Lithuanian Army near one of the towns, an otherwise undistinguished place named Tannenberg. Hence, the victory went into the books as the "Battle of Tannenberg." Historical memory runs deep in some parts of the world. By the time the forces dispatched from the west by a panicky Moltke had arrived, all was just about over, and there was nothing much of importance left for them to do. Perhaps, though, their rail journey had been an interesting one. General Rennenkampf who, for awhile, entertained the notion of capturing the East Prussian capitol of Königsberg, thought better of it and began pulling his First Army back, harried all the way to the Russian frontier by the Germans in a series of battles which, taken together, became known as "The Battle of the Masurian Lakes." Yet, although its commander was soon sacked, this army was able to rally and prevent their foe from carrying the pursuit very far onto Russian soil. The German troops, by now themselves exhausted and running short of supplies, could not force the issue and their commanders soon learned that, in this new, grinding war, one battle, even if a seemingly decisive one, would not serve to win it. Battered, shaken but, for the time being, unbroken, the Russians held on close to—and, at one point, still slightly over—the German frontier in East Prussia. As the opposing armies dug in for the winter season, German commanders pondered as to how they could, once and for all, finish off a stubborn foe which seemed not to realize that it has sustained monumental disasters. On their parts, Russian commanders perhaps were cheered somewhat by the better fortunes enjoyed by their countrymen in the south.

Commander in Chief of the Austro-Hungarian Army, Conrad von Hötzendorf (1852–1925), was a highly educated man who spoke seven foreign languages fluently. He also had a well-schooled military mind, and, aware of this, had a tendency to "think big." This might have been a virtue if he had had a truly first rate army at his disposal. Such, alas, was not the case. While the Austro-Hungarian Army contained a number of excellent units and was equipped with some excellent artillery pieces by the Skoda works (as we have seen, the 305 mm mortars which reduced the Belgian fortresses were produced by this firm), it was not the sort of fighting force which could be counted on to undertake bold offensive operations, especially the ones envisioned by its commander in chief. On the whole, standards of training were not what they ought to have been, and leadership abilities of many of its junior officers were not high. Probably of greatest importance, however, was that, in an age in which massive free-willed (to be sure, often mindless) sacrifices had to be sustained by nationalistic enthusiasm, the Austro-Hungarian Army was not a truly "national" one. As seen earlier, as was the Empire it was sworn to defend, the army was a polyglot. Numbered in its ranks were some tens of thousands of Slavs. When war first broke out, they showed a loyalty which some found surprising. It was not, however, the sort of devotion which could be counted on to survive sustained, costly campaigning to say nothing of serious setbacks. The latter were perhaps assured by Conrad von Hötzendorf's grandiose strategic vision.

When the war began, the Austrian commander immediately began assembling his armies for a bold, two-pronged offensive enterprise. While a relatively small portion of his army would invade and conquer Serbia, most of it would assume the offensive against the Russians. Striking north out of that portion of Austrian-occupied Poland known as Galicia, it would slash through Russia Poland. In the meantime, after repelling anticipated Russian attacks, the German Army would move east and south, thus linking up with its Austro-Hungarian ally. Those Russians who had not already been chewed up by Conrad von Hötzendorf's advancing legions, would be either captured or annihilated.

It all looked very good, even kind of inspiring, on paper. In reality, however, it began to unravel almost as soon as it was set down. First of all, Commander in Chief of the German Army, Helmuth von Moltke, informed his Austrian counterpart that the German armies in the east were not going to take part in such an operation. At the time he communicated this unhappy news, East Prussia was being invaded, and there was considerable doubt as to whether the vastly outnumbered Eighth Army could hold its own. Obviously, future *offensive* operations on its part were under something of a cloud, at least at that point. Then, there was phase one of the Austro-Hungarian commander's scheme—the invasion of Serbia, an operation as much informed by national hatred as it was by sober tactical considerations.

The relatively small Serbian Army, with toughening provided by the recently-concluded Balkan Wars under its belt, was well-suited to fight in the mountainous terrain of its homeland. The Austro-Hungarian Fifth Army, whose task it was to conquer Serbia, was not. Moreover, it was commanded by a military nitwit, General Oskar Potiorek, whose task it had been, while governor general of Bosnia-Herzegovina, to provide security for the Archduke and his wife on June 28th. Thus, within a few days after the invasion began—August 12, 1914—the Fifth Army was in trouble; stopped cold by the Serbians, who then launched a ferocious counter-attack. Even after reinforcements from another Austro-Hungarian army, the Second, were rushed to the Fifth's gradually crumbling front, defeat could not be stayed and, by the end of August, Serbia was swept clean of its unwelcome foreign visitors. At the very least, the ill-conceived operation had cost them 40,000 casualties, a very high percentage of the number of men involved in it. Several months later, Conrad von Hötzendorf would have another go at taking out Serbia, and this effort, too, would fail.

As early as August 18, the Austro-Hungarian high command knew that the Serbian operation was in trouble. Also, it had known for some time that the Germans would not be part of the commander in chief's ambitious schemes regarding the Russians. Nevertheless, on August 22, three Austro-Hungarian field armies, the First, Third, and Fourth, totalling almost 800,000 men, boiled out of Galicia. On August 26th, they made first contact with the Russians and, from that point on, went from disaster to disaster. Unlike the two numbskulls of the north, Samsonov and Rennenkampf, Russian commanders facing the Austro-Hungarians were extremely competent by any standard. Indeed, one of them, Alexei Brusilov (1853–1926), would later be associated with one of the most successful, if one of the most costly, Allied offensives of the war. Four Russian armies struck at the flanks of the already somewhat disorganized Austro-Hungarians and, within a few days, had driven them across the River San, which separated Galicia from Russian Poland. Then, the Russians were deep into Galicia and, on September 1, 1914, they invested the important city of Lemberg (now Lvov), which fell two days later. Soon, the fortress city of Przemyśl was surrounded and, trapped within its walls, were over 150,000 Austrian soldiers. After heroically enduring a six months siege, during which disease, badly-attended wounds, and starvation took a terrible toll, the city surrendered.

By the end of September, an extraordinary Russian advance which, in some places, had taken them to the edge of the Carpathian Mountains, had to come to an end. Men and horses were exhausted, and supplies were running low. To ensure that such could be delivered from the mother country, the gauge of railways in newly-won expanses of Galicia had to be widened in order to accommodate the locomotives and rolling stock of the Russian ones. Large numbers of Russian soldiers had to devote their energies to this task, one in which forced assistance was provided by Austro-Hungarian prisoners of war. In all, 120,000 of them had been taken, while well over 200,000 of their comrades had been killed and wounded in just about one month's fighting. The Austro-Hungarian Army would never fully recover from the disasters visited upon it by its commander in chief's overblown ambitions. Yet, as happened with the victorious Germans up north, the victory-flushed Russians on the southern portion of the Eastern Front soon discovered that even seemingly overwhelming victories did not suffice to win this new kind of war. In the end, realities imposed by mass-mobilized levies and mind-boggling logistical concerns dictated that, for now, the opposing armies dig in and wait upon events. Though heavy fighting flared up from time to time in Galicia, there, as along the East Prussian frontier, 1914 ended on a note of disquieting uncertainty.

6

The War of Movement Ends

FIRST MARNE AND THE RACE FOR THE SEA

AFTER the joys of the "August Days," "official" and civilian Paris waited anxiously for news of victory. By mid-August, the government at least knew that the French attacks in Alsace and Lorraine had been bloodily repulsed. It also knew that French armies in those regions were now in retreat and that the rapid advance of the German left-wing was continuing. By month's end, the threat to Paris itself had become plain to everybody and thousands of Parisians began to flee the city. The military governor of Paris, however, General Joseph Gallieni (1849–1916), was fleeing from no one and, after bidding farewell to a dreary succession of weeping government ministers, prepared to defend the city against a German attack that had to come very shortly. There would be none; this, due to human exhaustion, logistical realities, and military miscalculation.

In attempting to keep pace with that envisioned in Schlieffen's wildly optimistic vision, the German left wing, with Alexander von Kluck's First Army taking the lead, had to cover an average of between 20 to 25 miles a day. By the end of August, the broiling heat, at times choking dust, and annoying skirmishes had taken their toll on the men. Burdened with 65 lbs. of equipment carried on their backs, they were also oppressed by the knowledge that their enemy, while being constantly driven back, showed no signs of giving up the struggle. As exhaustion grew, morale began to sag. Officers tried to keep spirits up by having their sorely-tried men sing lusty soldiers' songs. In the end, however, this was counter-productive. Furthermore, as noted earlier, the very rapidity of the advance began to cause the

German left-wing to lose cohesion even as the German commander in chief, Helmuth von Moltke, began to show signs of losing control altogether. Loss of cohesion was in part due to his yielding to panicky pleas from his generals in the east and detaching two corps to send to East Prussia to help to stem the Russian advance. As we have seen, by the time they got there, the Russians had been defeated at Tannenberg and there was little for them to do.

Suddenly, however, the French Army became very active. As seen earlier, the French, after the terrible defeat in Alsace-Lorraine, had rallied as the German forces now held eastern France. On August 29, its Fifth Army which, up to that time, had been retreating before the German Second, launched a counterattack which stopped its pursuers cold. The German commander, General Karl von Bülow, called for help, and this came from Kluck's First Army, on his right. It was at this point, that Schlieffen's bold scheme began to unravel. After the French counterattack was contained, Kluck became convinced that the best chance for finally defeating the French in a truly decisive battle would be for his and Bülow's army to press the attack in the general area of the now-defeated French assault, i.e., considerably to the east of the earlier line of advance. One of the factors which influenced him in this decision was the exhaustion of his men, which was certainly known to Kluck by this time. A no doubt costly, but massive victory, if won quickly, would be better than recommencing the forced march to the west, something that had taken an enormous toll of his army's strength and morale. Also, First and Second Armies had lost a considerable amount of cohesion, this in large measure due to the detaching of the two corps from the latter's right wing. In fact, by September 2nd, there was only a thin link between the two armies, and both commanders were of course aware of this. So were the Allies.

It was thus that Alexander von Kluck, with, of course, Moltke's approval, decided to swing his army to the east. There was no longer any thought of that southwest march which would bring the right wing, with First Army in the lead, south of Paris. The Schlieffen plan, or what was left of it, was abandoned. A British airman observed Kluck's, as matters turned out, fateful swing towards the east. He was, at this point, only about twenty-five miles from Paris, but far north of where Schlieffen said the crucial turning maneuver should have been made. Yet, Kluck was confident in the wisdom of his decision and, in truth, it is perhaps possible that, in view of the condition of his army and the breakdown in cohesion of the German right-wing in general, he had no choice. In making this move, however, Kluck showed an uncharacteristic carelessness.

For, on his right, he had the BEF which, while it had been driven back in constant retreat, was still intact. He also had the French Sixth Army, which was a fresh unit and hence at full strength. As the German First Army swung east, its right flank was exposed to attack from these Allied units. The ponderous Joffre did not at first grasp the possibilities but, in Paris, Gallieni had. Frantically, he attempt to call his phlegmatic commander's attention to them and, and, in due course, succeeded in doing so. On September 5, 1914, the Sixth Army struck out at Kluck's right wing and, because the fighting which now commenced all along the line took place in the valley of the Marne River, the largely disconnected series of engagements came to be known as the "Battle of the Marne."

Kluck's right wing, hard-pressed, began to fall back. To reinforce it, he sent two corps over from First Army's left-flank, thus weakening even further the tenuous connection between it and Bülow's Second. The two armies were now linked only by the thinnest of cavalry screens. On September 6, the BEF, and, on its right, the hard-tried but now inspired French Fifth Army, began to move in the direction of this gap and Bülow's exhausted force. In attacks on September 8 and 9, the Allies pushed the German Second Army back while all but severing its connections with the First. On the left of the once seemingly unstoppable able German right wing, the Third Army was able to contain French attacks. This was the only good news for an increasingly distraught Moltke. The First and Second Armies had been stopped in their tracks and pushed back. At one point, the First Army seemed about to gain the upper hand over the French Sixth, which put out a frantic call for reinforcements. These were to be had in Paris, but, getting them to the embattled Sixth presented a problem. General Gallieni solved it by assembling 1,200 taxicabs and troops were sped to the front in these. For many Parisian cabbies it was probably the first (and last) time in their professional careers that they were seriously concerned about finding the shortest distance between two points. In any case, Gallieni's measures were successful and the French Sixth Army fought Kluck's First to a standstill. At the same time, Bülow's Second, fought out and defeated, was struggling to maintain links with Kluck. German bravery and fortitude, which were considerable, could do no more. In the valley of the Marne, the recovered Allies, less exhausted in retreat than their opponents had been in the advance, and showing no small degree of bravery and fortitude of their own, had triumphed. On September 10, the German Armies began a general retreat. By September 14, they were able to stabilize their line on the Aisne River, still deep in France, but far enough from Paris as to pose no threat to the city.

In the eastern portion of France, there could be no question of further German advances. After stabilization had been achieved in the west, however, both sides concentrated upon gaining as much of the French and Belgian coasts as possible. There thus commenced what became known as the "race to the sea." The German armies were now commanded by General Erich von Falkenhayn (1861–1922). Helmuth von Moltke, who was forced to assume total blame for the September failures, had been forced out of his position and replaced by the former Minister of War, an apparent cool, indeed cold, soul seemingly less jittery than his predecessor. Almost immediately, he commenced a furious attack on the strategically crucial port of Antwerp, within and around which the Belgian Army had taken up defensive positions. The port was well-fortified, but the German siege artillery, already having established a fearsome reputation for itself at Liège and Namur, was too much. One by one, the fortresses were pounded into rubble. The Belgian Army, isolated and exhausted, seemed ready to collapse. Upon the urging of Lord of the Admiralty, Winston Churchill (1874–1965), the British Imperial General Staff dispatched reinforcements to help it out. Unfortunately, only two Naval Brigades and a scattering of British Army troops were available and they, plus the Belgian Army, were not enough to hold Antwerp. The city fell on October 8, and political opponents furiously condemned Churchill's "Antwerp Expedition" as a ridiculous exercise in futility.

In a familiar scenario, Belgian and British troops retreated south, uncovering as they did much of the crucial Belgian coast. Finally, however, making contact with Allied troops in what was left of Belgium, they were able to establish a thin and shaky line between the Belgian city of Ypres to a position slightly north of the port of Nieuport. The Belgian Army held the extreme northern portion of the line, along the Yser River, while the BEF, switching position in the Allied line, moved west to cover Ypres. On their left, next to the Belgians, was a relatively "fresh" French Army, the Eighth. Falkenhayn ordered that massive assaults be commenced, and the Belgians were hit first. They sustained enormous losses but, supported by the fire of British warships succeeded in holding firm. Then, the Belgians opened up dikes, producing an artificial lake which shielded them from further German assaults. Frustrated on the Yser, Falkenhayn's next blow came at Ypres, an important transportation hub linking the Allied-held hinterlands to the coast. From October 20 to mid-November, German troops, many of them fresh, and including the elite Prussian Guard, launched ferocious attacks around the city, against the exposed salient which constituted the Allied position. They were supported, as usual, by excellent artillery which wholly outranged that of the Allies.

German infantry assaults, however, were directed by officers who either had forgotten or never learned the lessons BEF riflemen had provided in earlier, smaller engagements. As we recall, while the British had invariably been forced to retire after these battles, they had inflicted heavy casualties against an enemy advancing straight up, in the open. Thus, as had happened with their countrymen at Mons and Le Cateau (and, for that matter, the French in Alsace-Lorraine), German infantry, advancing straight up and bunched together, were cut down in windrows by the British and French, firing from behind stone walls and shallowly-dug trenches. Walls and shallow trenches could not shelter the Allied soldiers from the superior German artillery, however. Thus, as they took a heavy toll of German infantrymen, German shellfire, raining down on the salient from several directions, tore them to pieces by the hundreds.

The Allies, at times fighting with the courage of despair, held on, while their equally heroic enemy was able to garner a legend useful for morale and propaganda purposes. On November 11, 1914, regiments which had an unusually high number of young volunteers, many of whom had been in the prewar youth movement, launched several courageous, but completely unsuccessful, assaults against the Allied line. The attack took place near the village of Bixchote and resulted in several thousand German casualties with no ground gained to show for it. Yet, as German dispatches had it, regiments comprised almost entirely of youths had captured the Allied first trench line, and this took place near the village of Langemarck. While it was true that the regiments involved did contain many young people and that, in turn, large numbers of them counted midst the slain, everything else contained in the dispatches was false. The regiments involved were not exclusively youthful in complement, the attacks had not been successful, and, finally, they had taken place near Bixchote, not Langemarck. Why there was a change of venue with regard to the assaults is unclear. One author has suggested, however, that Bixchote, a Flemish name which rang strangely on German ears, was not appropriate for the purposes of national symbolism. Langemarck, which was at least close-by, sounded a bit more Germanic. [1] Hence, arose the myth of the free-willed sacrifice of youthful regiments the so-called *"Kindermord of Langemarck."* The very phrase was supposed to summon forth a sense of national pride while arousing hatred against the enemy. "Children" had indeed been "murdered," albeit closer to Bixchote. But, they were only a portion, though, to be sure, a larger one than usual, of those mowed down in unsuccessful attacks upon enemy trenches.

Of significance, though, was the appearance of the word "trench" in the German dispatch. As the battle raged on, Allied commanders became aware that, in the exposed conditions of what was becoming known as the "Ypres Salient," their men had to dig in on a massive scale if they were to survive. Their German counterparts were gradually learning of the stupidity of hurling massed soldiers against an entrenched enemy. By the time what became known as "First Ypres" ended in mid-November, 1914, both sides were "dug in." Since generals on either side of the line assumed that such arrangements were temporary, these were somewhat haphazard in nature. In their construction, however, one could see a grim foreshadowing of what was to come in an age in which shrapnel and machine-gun fire were king.

Sorely pressed, the British and French soldiers had held on under the most trying of conditions. They lost 108,000 men, slightly more than half of them members of the BEF which, for all practical purposes had been shattered in the engagement. The Germans counted 130,000 killed, wounded, or missing. Back home, in London, war secretary Kitchener cried out, "This isn't war!" Yet, as horrible as First Ypres was, much worse lay ahead. In June, 1916 Kitchener died just a few weeks before a new, mass British Army would lose 60,000 men in one day.

The Ypres Salient would see two more massive battles, in 1915 and 1917, and a seemingly endless stream of minor engagements. By war's end the town would be over 90% destroyed—included in the destruction was its magnificent cathedral and a 13th Century cloth guild hall—considered by many to be the finest of its kind in Europe—while surrounding pulverized villages and shell-torn fields were turned into a virtual mass grave. Even at century's end, place-names such as Steenstrat, Pilckem, Westhoek, Langemarck, Bixchote, Poelcappelle, Passchendaele, and, of course, Ypres itself, evoke pangs of sadness for anyone familiar with what occurred there.

For the new Chief of the German General Staff, Erich von Falkenhayn, however, judgements grounded in humanistic concerns were not of immediate importance. Having wasted 130,000 men in efforts to capture Ypres, and having seen the emergence of, to be sure, still primitive trench warfare in response to tactical realities, he caught a glimpse of the grim future. The days of successful mass attacks and significant breakthroughs were over, at least on the Western Front. The palm had passed to the defense, and the German Field Army would have to make crucial adjustments in view of the new circumstances. In this regard, the British and French generals would be much slower to see matters for what they had become, and would pay for this; a far higher price being exacted from tens of thousands of those unfortunate enough to be at their disposal.

TRENCH WARFARE AND ITS LEADING CHARACTERISTICS

> If you want to find your sweetheart,
> I know where he is, I know where he is
> If you want to find your sweetheart I know where he is
> He's hanging on the frontline wire.
>
> —British World War I Ditty

The exhaustion of all of the armies was an important reason why they dug-in during the last months of 1914. Another reason was that, after unimaginable expenditures of bullets and shells, they were virtually out of ammunition. Thus, if the war were to be continued at a proper pace in future, vital stocks had to be replenished. Nobody, except perhaps, Falkenhayn, expected that trench warfare would become the best known aspect of the Twentieth Century's first great war. All armies on the Western and Eastern Fronts, and a few others as well, fought from trenches and this type of warfare, while hardly unprecedented, had never before been conducted on such a scale. The "Eastern Front," however, stretched over a vast expanse of territory with often widely-varying terrain. Also, and this is of greater importance, the rather large qualitative difference between the German and Russian Armies allowed for a certain "fluidity" lacking in the West, where, in terms of equipment, organization, and leadership, the opposing forces were more equally balanced. Thus, while one can say that trench warfare was a general characteristic of war on the Eastern Front, it never hardened into that seemingly inflexible "given" that it became in the West. Much as Stalingrad came to apotheosize military nightmare in World War II, Western Front trench warfare in general, and several enormous horrors generated by it, provided such in World War I. Because of this, the description of trench warfare which follows is of the variety which, between late 1914 and early 1918, prevailed on the Western Front.

By the spring of 1915, it had become obvious that, despite the romantic musings of some commanders, particularly British ones, over the possible future use of cavalry, the forces which now mattered were massed infantry, machine-guns, and artillery. Further, that the particular way in which these meshed with, and determined, tactical realities, meant that the trench system was here to stay, at least for the foreseeable future. What this produced was a six-hundred mile gash from the Channel coast to the Swiss frontier. A series of roughly connected trenches, manned, west to east, by Belgian, British, and French troops (with occasional variations between the latter two armies) faced a series manned almost entirely by German troops with, occasionally, an Austro-Hungarian unit thrown in as demonstrative of Central Power unity. In several areas of the front, the Allied and German trenches were separated by less than one hundred yards; but, in all cases and for very good reasons, the ground between the two became known as "no-man's land."

Most people at the time believed in national character and thought that the respective trench systems of the major armies reflected this. French trenches, it was observed, reflected the national propensity for sloppiness and slap-dash construction. British trenches, while still a bit make-shift, were somewhat more orderly, while reflecting that stolid practicality associated with Anglo-Saxon peoples. German trenches, in large part because the German High Command had become convinced that its forces would be fighting mainly on the defensive, at least in the West, were constructed with a kind of scientific precision. They were, in fact, masterpieces of defensive planning created by and for an army that intended to stay where it was. In some areas of the front, deep dugouts in the German trenches had wooden floors and walls, always with pictures on them, and were furnished with occasional pieces of furniture and reading lamps.

While there were differences between the several trench systems, they did have certain features in common. The front line, or "fire" trench was fronted with barbed wire and, more often than not, sandbags. It was dug in a zig-zag fashion so as to limit the effects of a shell which might explode inside it and also to prevent enfilade fire from enemy soldiers who might have gained access to the trench. Trenches were dug an average of six to eight feet deep, so that soldiers therein could be invisible to the outside. For purposes of observation, they often used periscopes to view the outside world. There was also a "fire step", generally two to three feet high, upon which a soldier could stand for observation purposes, or from which he could fire upon an advancing enemy or engage in gratuitous sniping. During raids or major attacks, this step was a convenient "jumping off" point. The average trench was four to five feet across and, in sectors which were often the scene of raids or prolonged fighting, barbed wire was sometimes stretched across the top. There was a "support trench," a "fall back" line, dug in about the same style, several hundred yards to the rear. Usually, this was linked to reserve areas by a communications trench. The German and British armies maintained formal reserve trenches in order to shelter rear-area troops from long range artillery fire. Often, however, the French Army did not provide these for its soldiers. As indicated earlier, trenches contained dugouts, the German ones being exceptionally elaborate, and these, angled into trench walls and often quite deep, could shelter up to several dozen men. They were convenient places to sleep and could be extremely useful during bombardments or bouts of inclement weather. Artillery support, in the form of light, medium, and heavy batteries, were deployed to the rear and, yet further back, were the forward (or advance) aid or casualty clearing stations.

Unless major offensives were underway, soldiers usually spent a week to ten days in the front line and support trenches, a week in reserve, and the rest of the month in rear areas. Since the trench systems of the Western Front were in regions known for fairly heavy rainfall, mud was a constant problem. Duck-boards were useful in providing walk-ways of sorts, but they were often unequal to the task, and, after rainstorms or bombardments, men could find themselves ankle deep, sometimes thigh-deep, in mud. During quiet times, lice and rats posed more immediate problems than enemy action and what became known as "trench rats" could be the size of cats. They raided soldiers' packs for food and, with good reason, were suspected of becoming fat on the dead. There were latrines in the forward areas and, after the trench systems had been in place for awhile, these could be quite sophisticated. Often, though, there were problems of drainage and overflow and, during bombardments or sustained fire-fights, it was impossible to get to them. Men then had to relieve themselves in dug-outs, or sometimes in the trenches themselves.

In past wars, soldiers had had to get accustomed to the sight and smell of dead bodies. The nearly static conditions which prevailed in the Great War, however, particularly on the Western Front, were responsible for men having, quite literally, to live amongst the dead. One reason for this, of course, was that it was often impossible to provide a proper burial for them. So, they were interred in the walls and floors of trenches. Exploding shells or hard rains could uncover these corpses in various stages of decomposition. Over time, soldiers grew accustomed to their presence. They stood guard among them, ate among them, took cat naps among them, and often made jokes at their expense. Robert Graves, in his autobiographical work, *Goodbye to All That,* described a situation in which the hand of a not-yet-buried corpse reached into a trench from the fire-step. As British soldiers passed it as they strode about the trench, they jokingly shook it. "'Put it there, Billy Boy!,'" was the gleeful phrase generally used on such occasions.[2] Naturally, there were often large numbers of corpses in no-man's-land and these were interred, disinterred, and reinterred as the result of shell fire. As bodies decomposed in the open under a hot sun they turned yellow, green, and then black. Sometimes, as they vented gases, these bloated forms would go into obscene gyrations.

Conditions in the trenches were responsible for an incredible stench in which were blended odors of cordite, chloride of lime (used in burials to hasten decomposition), excrement, frying bacon, literally tons of decaying flesh and, after the spring of 1915, residual poison gas. A person approaching the front line from rear areas could smell it long before it actually came into view. Soldiers became accustomed to the stench, just as they had to the bodies in large measure responsible for it. They also became accustomed to various illnesses in part arising from unsanitary conditions (to put it mildly) and, it seemed, everyone suffered from colds and intestinal disorders at one time or another. A good part of the time, the soldiers suffered from boredom. There would be "stand to's" at dawn and dusk, with soldiers on the alert for enemy activity. There usually being none, or nothing out of the ordinary, they would attend to a myriad of tasks—widening or draining the trench, an activity that generally turned up bodies or pieces of them, making minor repairs to dugouts and duck-board, delousing themselves, stringing or restringing wire. In between, they might play cards, take the time to write a letter (often on a heavily censored form), or engage in rat-hunting expeditions in which shovels and rifle-butts were wielded with enthusiasm. They functioned as filth-encrusted housewives in a surreal domestic setting.

Projecting out into no-man's land from the fire trench there were listening posts, or "saps," whose job it was to detect enemy activity. Sometimes, usually at night, there might be a raid on the enemy trench, almost always for the purpose of obtaining prisoners to be questioned about enemy plans about which they usually knew very little. Trying to escape detection by listening posts, "freezing" against the landscapes to avoid being illuminated by flares—green, white, sometimes red, always very beautiful—a raiding party would attempt to slip or cut through the enemy wire and, behind a shower of grenades, leap into the trench, making ample use of specially designed clubs, knives, sharpened trench spades, rifle-butts, bayonets, and pistols. The sawed-off shotgun made its first appearance as a trench-raiding tool. Raids could expand into something bigger, perhaps something nobody really wanted. Nevertheless, raiding parties, at least in the early stages of trench warfare, seldom lacked for volunteers—anything to escape the tedium or, worse, being a passive target for artillery fire directed by crews who, working with coordinates, rarely saw the enemy.

In fact, most soldiers rarely saw the enemy—alive—except during raids or general offensives. Corpses apart, no-man's-land appeared to be literally that—a shell-pitted moonscape from which all animate life had been pumped, except for rats. Occasionally, if one looked closely, he might see a blur of head and shoulder above the enemy parapet. And one might hear occasional outbursts of laughter and obscenity from across no-man's-land, smell foreign cooking odors, or gain insights into the enemy's musical tastes from listening to singing or faint, scratchy Gramophone recordings. On the whole, however, the enemy was distinguished by his general invisibility, and this had pronounced psychological effects for many men on both sides. It was as if, between major engagements and raids, the war was being fought by armies of ghosts. Of course, there were some soldiers who, specialized in sniping, took the general invisibility of the foe as a challenge.

If the enemy was not present in person, soldiers were constantly reminded that he was thinking of them. Witness was provided by artillery, the war's single greatest producer of casualties, if not necessarily, fatalities. By 1915, an extremely wide range of pieces had appeared, each one designated for a specific purpose. There were light field pieces, such as the French 75 or German 77 mm cannon, whose purpose it was to slaughter infantry in the open; medium ones, such as 150 or 155 mm pieces used by all of the armies in sustained bombardments of front line areas, and the heavies, ranging from 210 mm on up to 380 mm cannons and 420 mm mortars, the primary targets of which were fortifications and targets far to the rear of the front lines. After gas was introduced in April, 1915, gas shells began to take the place of projectors, which simply released clouds into the air and were thus often wildly inaccurate. Each shell had its own sound and, for experienced soldiers, associations. Their occasional malevolent visitations brought explosions and enormous pieces of shrapnel that mutilated human beings in ways unimaginable up to that time. Quite ordinary days, between major assaults would see ". . . men squashed, cut in twos, or divided from top to bottom, blown into showers by an ordinary shell, bellies turned inside out and scattered anyhow, skulls forced bodily into the chest as if by a blow with a club." [3] The devastating effects of shrapnel could not be ignored and, by the end of 1915, the soldiers of all armies on the Western Front were wearing helmets of steel or alloyed tin. British soldiers were the last to receive them, to some extent because some of their officers thought the wearing of them to be "unmanly." Soldiers who, despite all precautions, were wounded often benefitted by the extraordinary advances in medicine made before the war and surgical techniques during it. By now, anesthetics were in general use and this allowed for less rushed, and hence more sophisticated, surgical techniques. The use of X-ray machines made excruciatingly-painful probing and manipulating mostly things of the past. All armies had access to anti-tetanus serum, and the typing of blood, a discovery of 1917, made transfusions possible, although, due to its appearance relatively late in the war, few benefitted from the new technique at the time. Motorized ambulances allowed for quicker evacuation from aid stations to hospitals, while generally well-run hospital trains provided for transportation to urban centers, where more sophisticated medical techniques could be brought to bear. While there were physicians on both sides of the line who established reputations for using the wounded as guinea pigs upon which to try out new surgical techniques, most doctors and nurses tended to their needs with extraordinary dedication and fortitude.

advances of med

Yet, the terrible wounds inflicted by shrapnel and bursts of machine-gun fire, and, during periods of heavy fighting, tens of thousands of casualties—on occasion, sustained in the course of one day's combat—created pressures and conditions which could overwhelm medical facilities and personnel. In response to this, the French military introduced the technique known as *"triage."* The wounded were divided into three groups. There were the lightly wounded who, after relatively brief treatment, could be sent back into combat. There were those who required more substantial treatment; but, whose recovery was probable. Then, there were soldiers who, having sustained truly hideous wounds, either were clearly beyond help or, if they were to be saved, would require so much medical attention that the needs of other wounded comrades could not be adequately met. Thus, category three of the *triage* would be placed in tents where, heavily sedated and soothed by nurses especially selected for the purpose, they awaited death. Although never institutionalized in the manner of the French, this response to situations which overwhelmed medical facilities and personnel came to be used by all armies. In considering the fate of the wounded, at least passing mention must be made of those who, hit in no-man's land, were trapped between the lines. Occasionally, truces were called to allow for their evacuation. For the most part, however, they died unattended. Sometimes, sheltering or trapped in shell-holes, they lay helpless while, during rainstorms, the craters filled up with water and they drowned. Their cries, and those of other stricken souls trapped in no-man's-land, got on everybody's nerves. But, as there was usually nothing that could be done about it, soldiers became as hardened to them as they did to the presence of those who they would soon join in death.

For soldiers, trench warfare, in which stultifying boredom alternated with, at times quite literally, unimaginable horror, was probably the worst form of warfare conceivable. Living in death and filth, subjected to furious shellings called down upon them by an enemy which, while invisible, was often but one hundred yards away, soldiers learned to endure the unendurable on an almost daily basis, at the same time steeling themselves for suicidal assaults on well-fortified positions. There were, to be sure, "quiet" portions of the front—places set aside by unspoken mutual agreement, where there would little or no fighting. These were places where men could relax a bit without going on formal leave before they were whisked off to more active areas. Still, even with the existence of these sectors and even with the usually fairly extended periods between major engagements the combination of bombardments, raids, sniping, and, after spring, 1915, gas attacks, produced significant losses over a period of time. In the British Army, these losses were called "normal wastage" and they could amount to approximately 8,000 casualties a week, slightly less than losses accrued by General Bernard Montgomery's Eighth Army during the first week of the decisive Battle of El Alamein in World War II.

By the end of 1914, soldiers were beginning to become accustomed to a form of warfare unprecedented in modern history. Things were relatively quiet now; but all knew that matters would only get worse. The battlefields were now frozen over and major operations by either side were thus precluded, at least for the moment. With spring, however the earth's rebirth would be the occasion for massive actions of one sort or another. Perhaps because they knew that such was on the way, some hundreds of British and German soldiers participated in one of the most extraordinary events of the war.

On Christmas Day, December 25, 1914, soldiers on both sides of a now quiet front were opening packages from home, reading cards which, under the circumstances, seemed almost preternaturally cheerful, or engaging in bouts of carol-singing. In some freshly-hewn dugouts, pathetic "trees," with sparse, thinly decorated branches, stood for painful memories of other, happier seasons. No one now knows who started it, but, someone on one or the other side of no-man's-land joined in the carol-singing of the enemy. Probably the song was "Silent Night," which, while originally a German carol, has a well-known English version. Soon, Christmas greetings were being shouted across the lines and then, as if in a dream, soldiers from both sides emerged from the trenches and, at first furtively, almost shyly, approached each other. Then, there were handshakes, some embracing, laughter—at first nervous then joyous—and tears. As time passed, presents of sorts were exchanged and groups of British and German soldiers were photographed standing together. Some of these pictures have survived and, today, even after more recent horrors and the ironies generated by them, it is impossible to look upon these photographs without feeling an almost overwhelming sense of sadness. There are smiles; but these are rather faint. These boys-become-men are no longer naive. They know what will soon come. They seem to know that this will be the last such Christmas. Indeed, at least on the Western Front, this proved to be the case. Officers on both sides of the line were scandalized by the event and were concerned that such an incident not occur again. While exhortations, indeed, in some cases, threats, came down from on high, the dedicated professionals need not have worried. As in all wars, this one had developed a momentum of its own, and, from the military view, untoward events such as those which took place on Christmas Day, 1914, would not occur again.

Even without the more dramatic major offensives, the general effect of trench warfare, in which boredom and horror complemented each other—indeed, occasionally becoming conflated—was a brutalization unique in modern society. As time went on, this brutalization deepened and, as trench warfare moved into other areas, widened as well. And major offensives were planned with regularity from the spring of 1915 on, even as trench life helped to inure increasingly benumbed soldiers to what these offensives would produce:

> A man's brains splattered on
> A stretcher bearer's face;
> His shook shoulders slipped their load
> But when they bent to look again
> The drowning soul was sunk too deep
> For human tenderness.
>
> —"Dead Man's Dump" [4] Isaac Rosenberg

7

Nineteen Fifteen: First Full Year of the Great War

ESTABLISHMENT OF SAD PATTERNS ON THE WESTERN FRONT

AS 1915 dawned, the French and British high commands were beginning to face a challenge to their collective military wisdom. With regard to winning a now seemingly bogged-down war, this wisdom ran as follows: for the British and the French, the war which mattered was that being waged in France and Flanders, and thus it would be won or lost on that front. From this, it of course followed that every soldier, artillery piece, and draft-animal had to be concentrated in that area. There could be no thought of diverting vital human and material resources for purposes, say, of opening up another "front." By the beginning of 1915, however, there were those who had come to believe that, with the emergence of the increasingly complex trench systems, a decisive offensive in the west had been rendered virtually impossible. Thus it was that, in some circles, there was increasing talk of a kind of "end run" by virtue of which a new front would be opened up. By September, 1914, Turkey, which, since the turn of the century had become increasingly a German client state, was in the war on the side of the Central Powers. The strategically-important Dardenelles, linking the Black Sea to the Mediterranean were thus in enemy hands and a wedge had been inserted at a point where the Western Allies might establish vital contacts with the Russians. On top of that, a hostile Turkey might conceivably pose a threat to the Suez Canal. Why not, reasoned some, open up some sort of military action in that Turkish region which appeared to be the most vulnerable, the Dardenelles themselves? Not only could the, it was assumed, less-than-competent Turks possibly be knocked out of the war; but, the German high command might deem it necessary to send troops to this new front, thus weakening their strategic reserve in the west.

Imaginative schemes of this nature were a horror to those who commanded the Allied armies on the Western Front. "Diversionary" schemes were not for them. No, *Germany* was the enemy which mattered and all efforts had to be devoted to defeating this, the strongest of the powers arrayed against them. As the year waxed on, however, it became plain that a rather large operation of some sort would be undertaken against the Turks. The Allied commanders had already contemplated offensives in the west. This new scheme stiffened their determination. Whether or not an offensive against Turkey were undertaken; whether or not it succeeded, the war could only be won in the west and thus a decision had to be obtained there as soon as possible. Between March and October, 1915, the world would come to know what trench warfare was all about.

The British and French General Staffs decided on a joint operation in a region called Artois, not far from Belgium. They hoped to capture a series of low-lying ridges and thus force a general German withdrawal in the area. The French, however, were planning on launching operations in a region far to the east, Champagne, and thus, before the assault in Artois was to take place, their command announced that French soldiers, needed elsewhere, could not participate in it. The British commander, Sir John French, feeling betrayed, decided that the BEF would carry out its portion of the operation anyway. On March 10, 1915, after a short but very intense bombardment by around 500 British guns, British troops attacked near the village of Neuve-Chapelle. In comparison to later battles this was a "small show." The German defenders had thinned out the area around Neuve-Chapelle in anticipation of actions elsewhere. The attack was on a very narrow front—only 3,500 yards. Because of these two factors, the very intense shelling allowed the attacking British to actually achieve a clean break-through and, three days later, the shattered village was in their hands.

A major victory was proclaimed in the British press. The generals, however, had counted on going quite a bit further. In their collective heart-of-hearts, they knew that what became known as "The Battle of Neuve-Chapelle" had been a disappointment. There were reasons for this. In the first place, while attacking on a very narrow front with heavy artillery support did allow for a breakthrough (one of the very few on the Western Front), it eventually exposed the attacking troops to murderous fire from two directions once the Germans on both flanks of the initially broken line recovered. Also, as soon as they regained their balance, the defenders were able to reform in a second trench line very quickly. On their part, the British were unable to move in reserves quickly enough to exploit the initial success. Finally, those on the scene couldn't help but notice that, even during the relatively successful first stage of the battle, heavily outnumbered defenders succeeded in taking a terrible toll of their British assailants. The reason, of course, was skilled use of the machine gun. As a result, the 60,000 man First Army, commanded by Douglas Haig, lost 13,000 of this number in three days. At the same time, 100,000 shells, a fifth of those at the disposal of the entire British Expeditionary Force, had been expended. The primary lesson learned by Haig, and his commander, Sir John French, was that an attack delivered in greater strength and supported by heavier weight of shell could succeed against a well-entrenched enemy. After all, had not the Neuve-Chapelle enterprise come close to success? The machine gun factor had yet to be assimilated by those at high levels of command.

Besides providing a graphic demonstration of just how effective automatic weapons fire could be, the technologically forward-looking German military soon offered another lesson in applied technology. On April 20, 1915, they commenced a murderous bombardment of the forlorn town of Ypres. Lasting two days, it was but a prelude to a new, for many, ultimate horror. Early on the morning of April 22, Allied troops in the ghastly Salient heard a peculiar hissing sound. Slowly over the German lines, there arose two greenish-yellow clouds. As the winds moved them towards the Allied lines, many soldiers were fascinated by their awesome beauty. Within minutes the first soldiers in the way of this interesting phenomenon, French colonials, were transformed from a transfixed spectators into a panic-striken mob of gasping, wretching, men. Those who could, fled to the rear. Over 15,000, however, didn't make it. They were dead, soon to die, or condemned to live with lungs forever scorched by the first use of poisonous gas on a mass scale in warfare. The lovely clouds, it seemed, were of chlorine.

For awhile, as survivors attempted to save themselves by holding or tying urine-soaked pieces of cloth to their faces, there was a large gap in the Allied lines. Canadian troops, many of whom would also be shaken by a soon-to-be experienced encounter with the unknown, were sent in to fill it; but, if the Germans had moved fast to exploit their initial astonishing success they could have had Ypres, now filled with terrorized soldiers and civilians. Many of the latter were fleeing the city. The German command, however, had not anticipated just how effective the use of gas would be. On the other hand, the attacking infantry, like the initially-routed defenders, having no protective masks of their own, were fearful of moving too rapidly into areas where the gas had not yet lifted. So, the attack stalled and the Canadian defenders were able to fend it off until the arrival of British reinforcements. The Allied line held, though at a terrible cost. Whenever the wind direction was right, gas, released from cylinders as it turned out, was used against them. Heavily outgunned, they were subjected to murderous bombardment from more "conventional" artillery pieces. What became known as "Second Ypres" dragged on until almost the end of May. There were 70,000 Allied, 35,000 German casualties. Most of the Allied losses had been sustained during the first few terrible days, the German in their later, increasingly badly coordinated, attacks.

What served most, of course, to attract the historian's often morbid interest to Second Ypres, was the first use of poison gas on a mass scale. In point of fact, the Germans had tried it out, in a limited way, earlier. This had occurred, in January, 1915 on the Eastern Front, however, and, in conditions of extreme cold, gas is relatively inert and hence not very effective. Certainly, though, the Russian troops at the scene knew that something quite different was being tried out on them. Yet, for reasons which still remain obscure, they did not inform their Western allies of it. Furthermore, shortly before the attack on Ypres, a German deserter spilled the beans to Allied interagators, who did not take his tales of soon-to-be used gas cylinders very seriously.

After Second Ypres, everyone appreciated that a new, nightmarish dimension had been added to a conflict which already had rendered the common phrase "horrors of war" pathetically inadequate. By September, the Allies were employing chlorine gas, as in the German case, released from cylinders. Soon cylinders gave way to projectors, and then to shells, whose effectiveness was less dependent on weather conditions. Cumbersome gas-masks, which, at times, could be almost suffocating themselves, put in an appearance, as did new gases. By 1916, phosgene, almost twice as deadly as chlorine, was in wide use; by 1917, "yellow cross," or mustard gas, which had the advantage of both burning and asphyxiating. While most casualties in the Great War were inflicted by conventional weaponry—artillery, machine guns, rifle-fire, hand-grenades, etc.—poison gas, the use of which had been anticipated since the beginning of the century, served to demonstrate what ghastliness could result when scientific minds applied themselves to increasing technical options in an age of total war.

As we have seen, by the end of May, 1915, the Battle of Second Ypres had drawn to a close. Already, however, it was being eclipsed, in terms of numbers involved and casualties sustained, by other battles. First of all, on April 25, 1915, with Second Ypres just underway, Allied troops landed at Gallipoli, in the Dardenelles. The great "diversionary" effort was underway. We will consider this daring enterprise in due course. In any case, the (what turned out to be) disastrous attack on Gallipoli would soon devolve into the sort of battle characteristic of those being waged on the Western Front. While, as mentioned earlier, the British and French High Commands were skeptical of operations such as that currently being undertaken against Turkey, they certainly did not wish the operation ill. They remained firm, however, in their belief that the war would be won, or lost, in the west, and this virtual matter of faith informed operations throughout the year. Thus, it was thought, even as Second Ypres was still raging, offensive pressure had to be maintained.

On May 9, 1915, in Artois—the region in which the Neuve-Chapelle battle had taken place—the British and French struck out in a joint operation. Once again Haig's First Army constituted the British effort, and it struck out in an effort to seize Aubers Ridge. At this point, the BEF was running short of shells, so the preliminary bombardment was less than an hour in duration. Furthermore, the Germans, persuaded by the Neuve-Chapelle engagement that entrenched machine guns were the answer to attacks mounted by an enemy enjoying preponderance in numbers, had reinforced the threatened area with hundreds of them. On the first day of the assault, the British lost almost 12,000 men with almost no gains at all to show for it. "It had been a disastrous fifteen hours of squandered heroism, unredeemed by the faintest glimmer of success."[1] The British pressed on for awhile, enduring punishing losses. Then, the attack petered out. Sir John French, while claiming success, blamed whatever problems there had been on a shortage of shells. While this played a role, to be sure, he failed to give appropriate credit to the role of the machine gun.

At this point, there were vastly more French than British forces on the Western Front, and Joffre was determined that good use be made of them. So, while Haig's soldiers were being cut down in windrows before Aubers Ridge, French infantry, after an impressive bombardment from over 1300 guns, attacked in the direction of the city of Lens. Their spirit was remarkable and this, plus a bombardment that had been far more systematic than the British one at Aubers Ridge, was responsible for a three mile advance on the very first day. Then, however, German resistance began to stiffen, the rains—which many an Allied soldier came to believe were orchestrated by the German High Command—set in, and the advance was slowed to a dismal crawl. Intensive German artillery fire blocked the arrival of reserves needed to sustain the effort, while machine gunners—the emerging elite of the German Army—began to take an increasingly heavy toll. By early June, 1915, the French attack in Artois had ground to a halt. Well over 100,000 men had been lost, while German losses were about half that number.

After the failed Franco-British Artois offensive, there were grumbles of protest in London and Paris. In response, French and subordinates pressed the shells issue. If only the British Army had enough at its disposal to provide for a really sustained bombardment, then success would be assured. The "system" itself was proceeding just fine. Marshal Joffre, whose phlegmatic willingness to accept losses commands the attention of a psychiatrist, insisted that the battle had been a success after all. "Je les grignotte." "I am nibbling them," he declared, even as he admitted that attempts at any sort of rapid breakthrough had been costly failures. As in the case of his British colleagues, he had come to believe that ever more massive employments of artillery were the answer and one gets the uneasy impression that the losses sustained in the Artois attack were almost welcomed by him as proving that point.

Obviously, the answer to failures of massed infantry attacks upon well-prepared defensive positions was simply heavier attacks supported by greater masses of artillery. In a word, more of the same, but much more of it. On September 25, 1915, this elemental hypothesis was put to the test. Once again, there was an attack in the Artois. This time, however, it was a two-pronged affair, with the French attempting to take the vitally important Vimy Ridge, while their British colleagues aimed to take the town of Loos and, pressing beyond it, joining the French in a combined thrust at the important transportation and industrial city of Lille. As massive as this assault was, it was supposed to have been a diversionary one. The Allied attack in the Artois was designed to force the Germans to keep troops in the area and away from a French attack in the Champagne region, scheduled to take place on the same day. If the French could break through in that area, vital German road and railway connections could be severed and this in turn would compel the German Army to retire from almost all of that area of France. The Germans knew that an attack was coming, the Allies knew that they knew, and thus operations in the Artois were meant to keep the former from reinforcing the threatened region.

In the Artois attack, the role of artillery was seen as being of great importance, and indeed the assault was preceded by an enormous bombardment. The British artillery, however, still suffered from a want of high explosive shells, so, in the first British use of this weapon, gas was employed to compensate for this lack. The French came close to taking Vimy Ridge; but, stiffening German resistance was assisted by the weather, which turned bad within a few days of the first attack. The fighting dragged on until mid-October, but there was little to show for it, at least not in terms of ground gained or prisoners taken. The British, according to plan, also attacking on September 25, were able to make some minor gains in front of Loos. Haig, of Aubers Ridge fame, saw that if advantage were to be taken of them, the attack had to be pressed hard on the following day, September 26. Reinforcements were needed and several newly-arrived divisions were at hand. Unfortunately, they had just very *recently* arrived, exhausted from a forced march. Haig had wanted them available on the first day. Unaccountably, however, his boss, Sir John French, had kept them far to the rear. As a consequence, these divisions had to be virtually driven like cattle in order to participate in the early stages of what became known as the "Battle of Loos." They had missed the first day. Certainly, they would be ready for action on the second. They were not. After the forced march, they had experienced much difficulty finding their way into the line, and the morning of the 26th found them still extremely tired and, in many cases, hungry. Haig knew of their condition but hurled them into the day's attack none the same. The Germans had reinforced the area around Loos with scores of fresh machine gun crews. The far-from-battle-ready troops attacked as if they weren't there. "'One of the German battalion commander's spoke later of the revolting and nauseating impressions made on them as they watched the slaughter; so much so that after the retreat began they ceased fire.'"[2] In German military circles, the second day's battle at Loos would be remembered as the "Leichfeld von Loos" ("corpse-field of Loos"). In a matter of a few hours, the British had lost 385 officers and 7,861 men. In the second day's fighting, the Germans lost not one man. To a great extent because of the disaster, Sir John French would lose his job.

British loose Loos

By October 14, 1915, the British had succeeded in taking Loos, but not in going much further. The French, having been held at Vimy Ridge, had repelled inevitable German counterattacks, but there could be no further thought of an advance. So, on that day the Allied High Commands declared operations—costly, to be sure, but successful—to have ended. Between them, the British and the French had lost over

250,000 men. German losses were close to 180,000. As can be seen, while not as high as Allied casualties, they were hardly insignificant, and this was due to the fact that, after being forced to yield ground, no matter how little of it, German commanders, often behaving like their Allied counterparts, hurled their men forward in desperate efforts to regain some scores of metres of land. In the end, however, the German lines had held firm, and it was the machine gun that was primarily responsible for this.

As we have seen, the attack in the Artois had been designed as something of a diversionary effort for the French attack in the Champagne region. It had developed a momentum of its own, however, and once started, seemingly could not be stopped. In this regard, it can be seen as prototypical of many World War I battles. Ironically, what was to have been the primary operation of September 25—the Champagne attack—ended eight days earlier than the assault in the Artois. At first, things seemed to be going well. Marshal Joffre had been determined that this attack would be supported with every artillery piece available to the French Army. Even the great forts around the city of Verdun—in a move which would later have unfortunate consequences—were stripped of much of their artillery to add further weight to the bombardment. After three days intense shelling by over 2,500 guns, the French infantry left its trenches, in some cases being play "played into battle" by bands playing the *Marseillaise.* For many French soldiers, this stirring concert would be the last one they would ever hear. After a successful first day's assault which carried the first two lines of German trenches, the attack began to fold. Advances over the shell-torn landscape had exhausted the men. Furthermore, it seemed that the Germans had gotten into the annoying habit of husbanding men and artillery until their enemy had committed himself and was fully exposed in open country. Under the cover of massive counter-bombardments, German infantry, including many hundreds of the now dreaded machine gun crews, began moving into prescribed positions. Stopped cold, the French attempted another massive attack. By October 6, it had become plain that exhausted men, drained of *élan,* and attacking in open country against an enemy heavily-entrenched upon slightly higher ground could do no more. Thus it was that, on October 6, Marshal Joffre declared the Champagne Offensive to have been a success. Some thousands of metres of territory had been liberated and 25,000 prisoners taken. For some time, however, France would not know that it had lost 145,000 of its sons killed, wounded, or missing in the effort. Joffre, seemingly not inordinately disturbed about this, might well have kept the offensive going if the supporting artillery had not run out of shells. In about ten days of fighting, the French batteries had fired off close to five million rounds, and precious stocks had to be replenished to keep things going.

The combined Artois and Champagne offensives of September–October, 1915 had cost the Allies almost 400,000 men. Total German losses were around 250,000. Gains were next to nothing and it was the German machine gunner who emerged with the best-established reputation. Yet, even as their men inflicted heavier casualties than they sustained, German generals knew that, particularly as more British troops were committed to battle on the Western Front, their situation could only become more perilous in the future. Particularly concerned with this issue was now Chief of the German General Staff, Erich von Falkenhayn. Already, as we shall see, at odds with many of his generals, he would draw conclusions which would result in helping to make 1916 the worst single year of the war.

As 1915 ended, however, General von Falkenhayn still had his job. An Allied counterpart, however, Sir John French did not. He was a victim of his own incompetence, and the holding back of reserves at Loos was representative of this. He also fell victim, however, to the intrigues of one of his army commanders, Sir Douglas Haig, a man much favored by important elements of the British press and by the royal family. He had groused about Sir John's inadequacy almost from the time the BEF had first landed on the continent, and now the Loos disaster added weight to his arguments. Thus it was that, in December, 1915, Sir John French was replaced as commander of the BEF by Douglas Haig. Many in the army and out of it were relieved. Exuding quiet confidence and looking far more to fit the role of commander of the BEF than the roly-poly French, he was seen as a soldier's soldier whose plans had been undone by an incompetent superior. Forgotten, for the moment, was the Aubers Ridge disaster. Also forgotten, or at least overlooked, was the fact that, while it was true that French had held back reserves and thus compelled them to undertake an exhausting forced march to the point where their support was needed, Haig, knowing their condition, had no hesitation whatsoever in sending them into battle. Thus, his share in the disaster of the second day at Loos was not a small one. Before, however, this disquieting effect had been duly assimilated, he would send the BEF into one of the most grinding and soulless battles in the history of warfare.

For his part, Marshal Joffre was continuing to succeed in convincing Frenchmen who mattered that he was indispensible. One of the reasons that this was the case was that this peasant's son acted as an absolute ruler of yore. His generals were forbidden to talk to politicians (even the minister of war was off-limits), and newsmen who visited the front spoke only with officers selected by the commander in chief to disseminate often misleading information, and saw only what Joffre wished them to see. Some Frenchmen knew what had resulted from his offenses but, for the moment, it appeared that little could be done to prevent more of the same in the future. As 1915 ended, Joffre was indeed masterminding such, unaware that his disasters of that year had inspired his German counterpart to preempt him.

Nineteen fifteen, the first full year of the war, saw the realities of trench warfare on the Western Front demonstrated for all to see. How much of it was actually seen is hard to tell. Censorship prevailed on both sides of the line, although that which prevailed in France, perhaps because it was the country of revolution, seems to have been a bit more egregious. What appears to have been more astonishing, however, is the probability that the Allied High Commands either chose not to see what was really going on or, having been made aware of it, chose to ignore or understate its significance. In the face of the trench systems, unprecedented in their complexity, and of tactical realities posed by machine guns and massed artillery, they persisted in their belief that, almost by sheer will plus artillery (albeit, to be sure, in vastly increased amounts) prewar offensive doctrines could be translated into reality. To be sure, there was will aplenty shown by French and British soldiers, and there was more artillery than could possibly have been imagined, even during the early months of the war. When dissolved, however, in the ghastly solvent which was the new variety of technologically-sustained war, prewar tactical usages plus more artillery resulted in gains measured in yards paid for by unimaginable losses. British soldiers, a German general remarked at the time, had the stubborn courage of lions. Alas, he went on, they were led by donkeys. The singular stubbornness of these people—and that, of course, of Joffre—translated into deaths or wounds for tens of thousands of their soldiers.

The German military, perhaps because it had been thrown back on the defensive, had shown somewhat more ingenuity in adjusting to the newer conditions imposed by a trench warfare system to which they had made immense contributions. Yet, it was in many ways as entrapped by the new realilities as anyone else, and this would soon be demonstrated by the commander in chief, desperately eager to find a way out of the nightmarish imbroglio.

EASTERN FRONT(S): QUALITATIVE DISPARITY = A MORE "FLUID" WAR.

After Erich von Falkenhayn became Chief of the German General Staff, headquarters of the Supreme Command was in the northern French city of Charleville-Mezieres. Early in 1915, he had it transferred to the castle of the Prince of Pless, located in Silesia, one of the easternmost regions of Germany. The move was symbolic of the commander in chief's new strategy. Falkenhayn believed that the war eventually would have to be won in the west. For the moment, though, a truly decisive breakthrough was impossible on that front. What could be done, he thought, was to defeat the Russians in a series of large battles in which German and Austrian armies would not allow themselves to be drawn too deeply into trackless eastern regions. If the Russians endured enough heavy defeat, Falkenhayn thought, they might be persuaded to come to terms with Germany or endure a revolution. In the meantime, the Allies could be held off in the west until that point at which German armies released from a now collapsed Eastern Front could be sent to the Western Front. Hopefully, such could be done before Great Britain, which thus far had played a relatively limited role in the war but which the German commander in chief saw as his country's most dangerous enemy, became more fully involved in military operations.

Generals Hindenburg and Ludendorff, encouraged by Colonel Max Hoffmann, viewed Eastern Front operations from a somewhat different perspective than Falkenhayn. As they saw it, the only way in which Russia could be compelled to leave the war was if its armies were totally annihilated. They saw Falkenhayn as far too cautious with regard to the east, far too obsessed with Western Front concerns in general and Great Britain in particular. Not unexpectedly, the commander in chief of the thus far undistinguished Austro-Hungarian Army, Conrad von Hötzendorff, shared their views. Thus, as Falkenhayn planned massive, but controlled, battles, German and Austrian generals in the east began to put together grandiose schemes involving huge pincer movements.

At first, though, it was necessary to deal with the last Russian force remaining on German soil. Between February 8 and February 22, 1915, there occurred the Second Battle of the Masurian Lakes, in which, at a relatively low cost to the victors, virtually the entire Russian Tenth Army was destroyed. By the time it was over, Hindenburg and Ludendorff, bearing in mind earlier engagements, thought that they were able to take the measure of their Slav opponent.

Certainly, the Russian Army contained some excellent units, such as the elite Semonovskii and Preobrezhanskii Regiments. The Cossacks could be ferocious enough, while some of the artillery units could be counted on to fight with distinction. There even were a few Russian generals who were on par or better than those of the Western Allies. Yet, on the whole, it was now plain that Russia had not been ready for war in 1914, at least not one against Germany. Its ferociously-disciplined soldiery could, and often did, fight with immense courage. Modern warfare, however, seemed often to bewilder them and, on their own, they showed little initiative. In this regard, it seemed obvious that soul-paralyzing discipline had been meant to substitute for poor training. While, as mentioned earlier, the German generals had to take note of several Russian counterparts of stature, most of the enemy commanders came across as bungling incompetents. Furthermore, even those Russian generals who had shown tactical abilities had done so against Austro-Hungarian opponents. Furthermore, by early 1915, it was plain for all to see that the Russian Army was suffering from problems of supply. The still-primitive Russian transportation system was not up to the task of supplying a large army engaged in modern warfare. The usually quite good Russian artillery was not receiving enough shells, and a high percentage of those which did reach it were duds. Prisoners were beginning to speak of shortages with regard to machine gun and rifle ammunition—in some cases, even of rifles themselves.

For Hindenburg and Ludendorff, Eastern Front conditions were ideal for a massive battle of annihilation against an enemy whose disordered state seemed almost to invite one. To be sure, such a battle would necessitate the involvement of at least a portion of the discredited Austro-Hungarian Army. If, however, this were placed under German command then perhaps a good deal more could be expected of it. The main portion of the Austro-Hungarian Army, still under the direct command of Conrad von Hötzendorf, should be able to deal with what was left of the Russian Army after a mostly German one had disposed of almost all of it. What Hindenburg and Ludendorff envisaged—the Austro-Hungarian commander in chief had a similar plan—was a giant, two-pronged attack. While one wing would strike out against the Russians on the Carpathian Front, sweeping to the northeast, another would undertake a massive offensive in Courland and Lithuania, heading east and south. Between the two wings, almost all of the Russian Army in Poland—which was, in fact, virtually all of the Russian Army, period—would be annihilated.

Falkenhayn, as we have seen, was certainly committed to offensive operations. In fact, under his direction, a new army, the Eleventh, had been formed with these specifically in mind. Commanded by the aging but still intelligent and ram-rod tough August von Mackensen (1849–1945) it consisted of three excellent German and one Austrian corps, plus two extra German infantry and one Hungarian cavalry division. With this army functioning as a hardened core, German and Austro-Hungarian troops would shatter the entire Russian Carpathian Front. The German commander in chief did not approve of the proposed attack, which was to be directed by Hindenburg and Ludendorff out of Courland and Lithuania. Such a maneuver was a trifle too risky, he thought. Furthermore, as commander in chief of all German armies, he had to bear in mind factors and conditions that perhaps had eluded those of his eastern commanders. By late April, 1915, Allied troops were ashore at Gallipoli, and who could know what new demands this situation could create? For the time being, the Western Front was quiet. But, Falkenhayn anticipated Allied offensive efforts and, while he thought that there were sufficient German troops to deal with them (as we have seen, such proved to have been the case), one could not afford to be overly committeed to grandiose, perhaps reckless, operations designed to utterly destroy an enemy which could be knocked out of the war through more limited engagements. Thus, much to the fury of Ludendorf and Hindenburg, Falkenhayn vetoed their bold pincer-movement plan. To make matters worse, the commander in chief remained at his new Supreme Command headquarters in Silesia to oversee operations.

Such began on May 2, 1915. While a diversionary gas attack—largely unsuccessful—was staged at Skierniewice, near the center of the front, Mackensen's llth Army and the Austrian Fourth, after a ferocious artillery bombardment against which the Russians could offer little in reply, smashed through the enemy positions in the Tarnow-Gorlic area of Galicia, the northernmost point of the Carpathian Front. Other German and Austrian units struck out all along the rest of the Carpathian Front, and soon the outgunned and, in strategically-crucial places, outnumbered Russians were falling back all along the line. Russian trenches, shallowly dug and unsophisticated, offered little protection against the devastating artillery fire directed against them, while the attacking German and Austro-Hungarian troops did not have to contend with Russian artillery fire to any significant degree. By mid-May, Mackensen's army had reached the San River, eighty miles from the starting point of the attack. By this time, having suffered, by Western Front standards, relatively light casualties, the German and Austro-Hungarian armies had killed or wounded over 100,000 Russians, while taking 150,000 of them prisoner.

On June 3, 1915, the Russians abandoned the fortress city of Przemysl, which, after a prolonged siege, they had finally taken in March. Without question, the Tsarist legions were absorbing an enormous beating. Yet, despite this, and despite being driven into rapid, morale-sapping retreat, they were still intact, still offering determined resistance whenever possible. Their overall commander, Grand Duke Nicholas, the Tsar's uncle, while very far from being a military genius, was proving to be surprisingly adept at extricating at least the bulk of his forces from seemingly impossible tactical situations. Furthermore, the very rapidity of the German/Austro-Hungarian advance had taken respective staff by surprise, and movements of supplies had not been able to keep pace with it. Thus, at possibly crucial moments, the pursuing armies had to pause to be reequipped.

It was against this background of enormous, nationalism-honing victories, and nagging worries that an important military conference took place at Falkenhayn's headquarters. The chief of the general staff had become increasingly concerned over the Gallipoli situation. Also, his confidence in Germany's ability to hold the Allies in the west had been shaken somewhat. Allied attacks in the Artois and at Aubers Ridge had been contained; but, the German attempt to take Ypres had been repulsed, despite the use of gas. Falkenhayn suggested that operations in the east be reduced or suspended and troops be made available for employment elsewhere.

To make matters worse, Italy had entered the war against Austria Hungary in May and now, Conrad von Hötzendorf, one of the original supporters of a strong eastern campaign, wanted to detach Austrian units and send them to the now new Italian Front.

All Germans present at the conference were opposed to Hötzendorf's request. Just about everyone at Pless, including the Emperor, who put in a sort of cameo appearance, was opposed to closing down or cutting back on operations in the east. In fact, as before, Hindenburg and Ludendorff talked of expanding them. This did not occur, but Falkenhayn was forced to concede that the eastern front attacks be continued. They were, and further enormous gains were made as tens of thousands of Russian soldiers were killed, wounded, and captured.

During its retreat, the Russian Army took out its frustrations on Poland's Jewish population. Many Polish Jews were accused of spying for the German Army and, in view of the policies of Tsarist Russia, there was no question that most Jews in Poland were pro-German—from the point of view of future history, a cruelly ironical situation. In any case, sometimes with the grim approval of Christian Poles, who hated Jews at least as much as they did Russians, many hundreds of them were slaughtered. Poland as a whole suffered enormously during the offensives of 1915. Both sides looted and burned to an extraordinary degree and masses of refugees, caught between opposing forces, were often fired upon, sometimes deliberately and, always deliberately, run down or sent flying into ditches by columns of cavalry and horse-drawn artillery. Nobody on either side seemed to take Polish suffering very seriously and the future revelation that the 1915 fighting had killed or made homeless some four million of them was received with muffled tongue-clucking and little else.

The campaign ground remorsely on and, on June 22, Lemberg fell. Yet, as had happened a month before, problems emerged. The Russian Army was still perversely intact, although badly shaken, and supplies were not keeping pace with the advance. Another conference was called, this time on July 1. Once again, Hindenburg and Ludendorff pressed for a vast, enveloping attack sweeping through Courland and Lithuania down to the south, to trap the Russians being driven north-east by Mackensen's offensive. Falkenhayn, fearing that, if the German Army extended itself too much further in operations such as those envisaged by the eastern commanders it might suffer the fate of Napoleon, and worried about having enough troops available to send west to meet the anticipated new French attacks in the west, rejected this scheme. This time, he received the Emperor's approval. What would take place instead was the following: the Mackensen-spearheaded armies, up to this point advancing in an east by northeast direction, would turn sharply northward between the Bug and Vistula Rivers, where almost the entire Russian Army was located. German armies, led by Hindenburg and Ludendorff would attack out of East Prussia and head south to trap the Russians. Falkenhayn had ruled out the bold, sweeping maneuver originally proposed by the eastern commanders as too risky and involving the commitment of too much of Germany's hard-pressed armies. The modified pincer approach would have to do.

The combined attack certainly did inflict further heavy damage on the Russian Army. On August 5, 1915, it abandoned Warsaw and, by month's end, had lost over 750,000 men in prisoners alone since the offensive had begun. Almost as many had been killed and wounded, and this put total Russian losses at well over one million, perhaps close to a million and a half. Yet, the Russian Army had not been trapped. As General Ludendorff predicted, the attack out of East Prussia had not been on a broad enough front; and, this being the case, the Grand Duke had been able to pull most of his army out of danger. Later, in September, Hindenburg and Ludendorff finally got their wish and were allowed to try their sweeping maneuver to the east. The key city of Vilna fell, and forward German cavalry units appeared to have cut rail lines to the east. By this time, however, much of the Russian Army was already away, and the German forces on the scene were too few in number to contain what was left behind.

For the Russian Army, 1915 had been the most disastrous year in its history. In a country that, in many ways, had grown jaded to mass suffering and death, the losses endured as a result of the campaign begun at Gorlice-Tarnow were hard to take. Grand Duke Nicholas, assuming blame for the catastrophe, resigned and, in a singularly ill-advised move, his nephew, Nicholas II, whose military acumen was about on par with his acumen in other fields, took personal command. There were rumblings of discontent at home; some riots, some strikes, and widely believed rumors emerged. Probably the most disturbing of them was that there was treason in the highest circles of government. Quite unjustly, suspicion began to center on Nicholas's German-born wife, Alexandra. In high government and social circles, many were focusing their frustrations and rage upon the mysterious figure of Grigori Rasputin (1872?–1916). We will have more to say about these individuals later.

The end of 1915 saw the Russian Army, no matter what its condition or that of the country as a whole, still in the field. This being the case, Germany could not bring to bear all of its military potential in the west. Later, Ludendorff, Hindenburg, and Hoffmann would declare that, if Falkenhayn had allowed them to pursue their bold plans in the east, Russia could have been knocked out of the war and the Western Allies either defeated or forced to come to terms before the entrance of the Americans. A good case can be made for this argument although, as always, those of the "what if" variety can never really be decided with any certainty. Certainly, the campaigns of 1915 had inflicted massive damage on the Russian Army and, by autumn, deficiencies in supply had gotten to the point where soldiers in a second attack wave would wait for comrades in the first wave to be killed or wounded in order to make use of their rifles. Looking back on it all, it strikes one as amazing that this badly-armed, insufficiently-trained, often miserably-led force was able to hold out as long as it did. Yet, at times fighting with the courage of despair, it was still able to fend off the Germans, thus preventing a strategic defeat, while, when catching them alone, managing to defeat the Austrians. In September, 1915, for example, as the Grand Duke was extricating most of his thoroughly thrashed army from northern Poland, a large Austro-Hungarian force attacked on the southern end of the front. The attack miscarried, there was a successful Russian counter-attack, and Conrad von Hötzendorf's sorely tried army lost another 250,000 men even as its more powerful ally was celebrating a massive, if inconclusive, victory. It was obvious that Germany could not move large numbers of troops to other fronts if an Austro-Hungarian collapse were to be prevented. Thus, the heroic Russian effort which, in the end, would bring about the end of the Romanov dynasty was of incalculable value to her Allies.

THE SOUTH SLAV EMBARRASSMENT PUT TO REST

One of the positive results of German successes in the spring and summer of 1915 was to bring Bulgaria into the war on the side of the Central Powers. Since the Balkan Wars of 1912–1913, the country had nurtured a variety of grievances against her neighbors, Serbia in particular. It was Serbia, after all, viewed by most in the Balkans as a client state of Russia, which had gained the most from the wars, much of this at Bulgaria's expense. Now, with Germany seemingly victorious everywhere on the Eastern front, the Bulgarian government saw its chance, as an ally of this powerful country, to settle scores once and for all with the hated Serbs. Naturally, Austria-Hungary, which had suffered great military embarrassment at the hands of Serbia, was eager to have revenge and, with the campaign in Poland drawing to a close, Falkenhayn promised that German troops would be of assistance in helping its ally to obtain it.

With Bulgaria about to enter the war in early October, 1915, with new Austro-Hungarian moves to open up yet another Serbian front, and with the realization that the ruthlessly decisive General von Mackensen was heading towards the country with a substantial German force, the Western Allies, having endured stalemate on the Western Front and, as we shall see, disaster in Gallipoli, thought it imperative to come to the aid of Serbia. To this end, around half a million troops were landed at Salonika in benevolently-neutral Greece. The Greek government had been kind of divided over whether this should have been allowed to take place. The king of Greece, Constantine, had a wife who was not merely German but indeed Wilhelm III's sister. Most Greeks, however, nurtured a profound hatred of Bulgaria and their feelings found embodiment in the person and policies of the prime minister, Eleutherios Venizelos. Royal objections were overruled and, while Greece chose not to enter the war at this time (it would eventually do so in June, 1917) on the side of the Allies, its government allowed the British and French to land troops at Salonika, early in October, 1915. Before they could move north to aid Serbia, however, Bulgaria declared war and sent a large army west into Serbia, blocking any Allied efforts. At the same time, Serbia was attacked by German and Austro-Hungarian forces. As always, the Serbian Army fought back bravely but this time, massive disparities in numbers and equipment were too much. Between October 7 and November 20, 1915, as Allied troops remained hopelessly penned-in in Salonika, Serbia was overrun.

There thus commenced a truly horrific retreat of the Serbian Army. In bitter cold, still led by the 71-year-old king Peter—who every few hundred feet had to stop to pause for breath—the 130,000 man army conducted a fighting retreat through the mountains which constituted the border between Serbia and Albania. Some thousands died of cold, hunger, and disease. Most, however, made it to the Albanian coast where, in January, 1916, Allied ships evacuated them to the island of Corfu. There, they were rested and refitted and, later that year, were sent to join their Allies, idling in Salonika. Blocked off by the Bulgarian Army to the north—the Allies greatly outnumbered it, but the Bulgarians, with some German and Austro-Hungarian backing held the high ground and all approaches—the forces in the Salonika expedition did little fighting. Men loafed, drank wine by the gallon, fought among themselves, and yielded to the beguiling invitations of prostitutes, which constituted a rather large army of their own, one which proved to be far more active in pursuing its avocation than were the more formal armies in pursuing theirs. The venereal disease rate soared. Until the fall of 1918, this was just about the only significant development of any kind in Salonika, an area which German generals referred to—and not without a measure of truth—as "our largest internment camp." In the meantime, however, Serbia, if not most of its army, had been knocked out of the war, and Germany and Austria-Hungary had gained a new ally in the form of Bulgaria. While matters on the Eastern Front had not turned out to be as decisive as Central Power military establishments had hoped, 1915 had been a good year, and things appeared to augur well for an even brighter future. Few imagined that patterns set in that year would find hideous amplification in the very near future.

8

"Other" Fronts

ITALY AND THE ISONZO TRAGEDIES

ITALY had been formally allied with Austria-Hungary and Germany since 1882; but, the reasons which drove her into what became known as the Triple Alliance revolved mainly around grievances against France which proved to be transient. After 1890, with Bismarck gone and Germany now far more consistently committed to Austria-Hungary, the Italian government evidenced diminished enthusiasm for an alliance in which the country was tied to an ally which, in the not too distant past, had occupied much of northern Italy and which, in the Tyrol, still ruled over many thousands of Italians. By the turn of the century, Italian-French relations had improved to a remarkable degree, and many German and Austrian diplomats and military people were beginning to doubt that, if and when war came, Italy would be on the "right" side. During the negotiations which ended the Balkan Wars Italy, for reasons of her own, did come down on the side of her presumed allies. This was the last comfort, diplomatic or otherwise, which she would provide them.

When war broke out in 1914, the Italian government was quick to point out that the Triple Alliance was supposed to have been a defensive one. Thus, the Austro-Hungarian attack on Serbia obviated the need for Italy's entering the war on the side of her supposed allies. Of course, the real reason that Italy did not enter the war was that, by this time, the government—indeed, probably most Italians—had long ago decided that the alliance with Germany and Austria-Hungary no longer served the country's interests. Indeed, perhaps the British, French, and Russian governments were in a better position offer more. As matters turned out, they were, and sordid arrangements were brought together in the Treaty of London, signed on April 26, 1915. In exchange for entering the war on the side of the Allies, Italy was promised the Cisalpine Tyrol, Dalmatia, Trentino, Istria, including the key and coveted city of Trieste, the Dodecanese Islands, taken from Turkey as a result of the war of 1911, and claims on whatever German colonies and Turkish-held territory that would be gained as the result of an Allied victory.

While Italian support for the country's entering the war was rather mixed—it was especially weak in the impoverished south—most were probably in favor of fighting on the Allied side, and against a traditional enemy. In any event, Italy declared war on Austria-Hungary on May 23, 1915. The declaration of war against Germany would not be made until August 27, 1916. A Socialist turned nationalist, the newspaper editor, Benito Mussolini (1883–1945) had been pressing for some time for Italy's entering the war on the side of the Allies. Many believed that French bribes were behind this. In any case, he was joined in his bellicose bellowings by violence-starved Italian Futurists, and by the decidedly eccentric Romantic poet, Gabriele D'Annunzio (1863–1938).

An alternately impressive and amusing collection of nationalistic ideologues and aesthetes was ready for war. How about Italy as a whole? On paper, matters looked good. The country was able to field an army of almost 900,000 men. It was headed by General Luigi Cadorna (1850–1928), by background, an artilleryman who had some administrative abilities and appeared to promise more of the same in the areas of strategy and tactics. From the beginning, however, there were problems, and just about everybody, Cadorna included, seemed to be aware of them. Despite rapid industrialization in the north, Italy was a poor country on the whole, one that was hardly in the position to sustain a major war effort. Poor in resources and capital, its armaments industry was antiquated. Worse than this, when Cadorna took over the army in 1914, its officer corps was of miserable quality, and morale, overall, was extremely low. Here, it was noted that troops from southern Italy seemed to be particularly disaffected. In a country which was still sharply divided along regional lines, their devotion to a war which, in many ways, seemed to be waged in defense of north Italian interests, was less than acute.

From a strategic point of view, things did not augur well for latecomer Italy. By the time Italy entered the war, Russian armies were being rolled back by the great German and Austro-Hungarian offensives in Poland. To be sure, for the moment at least, Austro-Hungarian forces were still almost exclusively absorbed in these operations. Thus, initially, Austria-Hungary could commit only eight divisions, totalling a little more than 100,000 men, against an Italian force which, from the first, could bring to bear 300,000, with the promise of much more to come. Yet, if Russia sustained severe defeats in 1915, then it was plain that, in due course, Austria-Hungary could well afford to make a far greater commitment to what would become known as the "Italian Front." Added to this worry, was the problem posed by geographical realities.

All along the emerging front, Austro-Hungarian troops held the high ground, i.e., the region now generally known as the "Italian Alps." If Italy were to assume the offensive, her soldiers, except in one limited area, would have to attack "up-hill" in circumstances which naturally (in a literal sense) favored the defense. At the same time, for Austria-Hungary, the mountains proved to be an imposing barrier behind which, when available, masses of troops could be assembled for a push down into and upon the northern plains of Italy. As General Cadorna saw it, there were, from the beginning, two crucial areas of the new Italian Front. First of all, there was the Trentino region to the north. This was that portion of Austria which bulged into northern Italy, a mountain fastness which defied Italian attack. At the same time, though, as we have seen, it was a place which could serve as a convenient staging area for an offensive into Italy once Austria-Hungary had the forces necessary to mount one. To the east, there was the relatively flat region drained by the Isonzo River, beyond which lay the important Austrian fortress city of Gorz (called Gorizia by the Italians). Cadorna decided to hold the Austro-Hungarians in the Trentino region and attack in the east, in the direction of the Isonzo River, and with the eventual objective of taking Gorz, possibly even pressing onto Trieste. What resulted were the studies in military horror known as the "Battles of the Isonzo."

Austro-Hungarian soldiers had not established a particularly distinguished record for themselves in combat against the Russians. Some of this can be attributed to the fact that Russian soldiers, as badly trained and outfitted as they were, were nonetheless extremely tough fighters. Also, a not inconsiderable number of the Emperor's soldiers were Slavs and many of these were not overly enthused about fighting people perceived of as brothers. Probably, though, the most important reasons why Austro-Hungarian soldiery proved to be extremely tenacious on the Italian front were two: (1) geographical circumstances were very much in their favor, and (2) troops on this front, many of whom came from the Tyrol, a region threatened by Italian domination, were animated by a genuine hatred of their enemy. Certainly, Austro-Hungarian successes on the Italian front in 1915 and 1916 were not due to a lack of Italian courage.

Soon after the declaration of war, Italian armies began a limited offensive in the Trentino. It didn't get very far; but, in some ways, this did not matter. One of its purposes was to forestall a possible Austro-Hungarian thrust from that direction, the other to be a sort of covering operation for the main Italian attack along the Isonzo, far to the east. On June 23, 1915, the assault began, and against an enemy which was fully expecting it, there really being no other place where one of this nature could have been launched. By July 7, after negligible gains, the first of the Isonzo Battles came to an end. Cadorna commenced the Second Battle of the Isonzo ten days later. While pressed with resolution by his soldiers, this more prolonged version of the first effort (it was called off on August 30) gained next to nothing. By this time, it was apparent that the gallantry of his men could not compensate for mediocre training and certain substantive lacks. Particularly ironical in this regard—considering the background of the commander in chief—was that of artillery. As indicated earlier, Italy had hardly been ready for war in 1915, and the terrible results attendant upon a variety of deficiencies were now plain for all to see. Nonetheless, Cadorna was determined to make a go of it on the Isonzo; so, a third massive attack began on October 21. Lasting until November 4, it registered some minor gains. Since the previous two assaults had gained hardly anything at all, Cadorna took these gains, however meagre, as a good sign—good enough, in any case, to warrant a Fourth Battle of the Isonzo. Such began on November 10 and, by the time it was brought to an end on December 2, almost nothing whatsoever had been gained by it.

As Italy entered the holiday season, it was determined that the four Isonzo offensives had cost 280,000 casualties. Austro-Hungarian losses totalled about 150,000. As on the Western Front, the superiority of the entrenched defense over attackers, no matter how gallant in their efforts, had been established. As in France and Flanders, trench warfare had become the prevailing idiom of war on the Italian Front. As if part of some cosmic joke, trench warfare with, all those dreary aspects attaching thereto, put in an unwelcome appearance in colorful Alpine settings. The Austro-Hungarians discovered how costly assaults on the Italian Front could be during the course of their own offensive in the Trentino between May 15 to June 26, 1916. Around 100,000 men were lost for gains best measured in metres. For the Austro-Hungarian commanders, it was a crucial learning experience and, not until far more promising circumstances—in October, 1917—would they again attempt a large scale offensive.

Cadorna, however, was a somewhat slower learner although, to be sure, 1916 saw one of his five more Isonzo crowned with a success of sorts. Fifth Isonzo (February 15–March 17, 1916) accomplished nothing. Sixth Isonzo, however, begun on August 6, resulted in the capture of Gorz, which now, quite suddenly, was officially Gorizia. After taking the city, Cadorna probably should have rested on laurels, however thin. As was the case after the third of the Isonzo battles in 1915, his appetite was whetted by success, in this case, a fairly palpable one. Thus it was that, in autumn, 1916, there occurred three more "Battles of the Isonzo," none of which accomplished a great deal. By year's end, Italy's armed forces had lost close to 490,000 casualties, almost all of them on the Isonzo Front. Italy already had sustained more battle deaths than it would during the whole of World War II. In the midst of the 1916 campaigns, the government took a moment to declare war on Germany.

Italy, more than any other of the large powers except, perhaps, Russia, was almost totally unready for war and no small number of people, civilian and military, knew this. Yet, territorial lures functioned to bring a country poor in resources and military traditions into the most destructive war in European history. Italy's soldiers, by and large, had fought with immense gallantry, giving far more than anybody had a right to expect of them. Some of its units, particularly the *Arditi* shock troops, were as good or better than any of those in other armies. After more than a year and a half of fighting, however, it was plain that the Italian Army as a whole was undersupplied and often miserably led. As indicated earlier, a large number of Italian enlisted men were peasants from the south of the country. While many of their officers were southerners as well, most of the leadership, including, of course, Cadorna himself, were from the north. As in the case of other armies, there were immense class gaps between officers and men. In the Italian case, however, regional ones were also of importance. By the end of 1916, General Cadorna was presiding over an army whose morale was, for the most part, quite low. Maybe, he seemed to think, it could be elevated by a few more Isonzo offensives plus, for a change, one in the Trentino as well. At least as much as the enemy, General Cadorna was priming those legions unfortunate enough to be at his disposal for a disaster the effects of which would be felt long after the war was over. Some would later maintain that the bitterness engendered by the Italian military experience in World War I—no small part of which was influenced by the commander in chief—contributed to a mood that, in turn, was responsible for the rise of Fascism.

THE WAR AGAINST TURKEY AND A FLING AT GENOCIDE

Ever since the last two decades of the 17th Century, the Ottoman Empire, more commonly referred to as Turkey, had been in decline. The neighboring Russian and Austrian states bit off territories with disturbing frequency, sometimes in fact quarreling with each other over the spoils. Throughout the 19th Century, previously conquered peoples, such as the Greeks and the Serbs, staged successful revolts against Turkish rule; revolts which, for power-political reasons of their own, one or the other of the great powers often supported. Indeed, as the century waxed on, it became plain that probably the most important reason that Turkey did not collapse altogether was that powers such as Great Britain and France—but Great Britain in particular—did not wish for this to happen, particularly if that great unknown, Russia, might benefit from it. In the last decades of the 19th Century, however, for a variety of reasons, the western European powers began to lose interest in shoring up a decrepit Empire in decline. Germany, engaged in diplomatic, military, and economic muscle-flexing, was happy to leap into the breach and, from the late 1880s on, its influence within and upon Turkey became very great.

In 1909, probably one of the most reactionary rulers of all time, Sultan Abdul Hamid (1876–1909), was overthrown by a body of reformers which came to be known as the "Young Turks." They were determined to return Turkey back to the glory-days of yore. Yet, this was not to be the *old* Ottoman Empire, a rather loosely, if at times very cruelly, ruled conglomeration of conquered peoples presided over by an *imperium* exercised in the name of Allah. No, unlike preposterously outfitted mossbacks like Abdul Hamid, the Young Turks were inflamed with modern nationalism. They viewed Turks in national, indeed, at times, almost racial terms and, if there was to be a new empire, it would be created in the name of Turkish national pride rather than in the name of vague, now seemingly quite irrelevant, other-worldly considerations. German penetration of Turkey would ensure the opening up of another front in the Great War and the emergence of problems which have bedeviled the world ever since. The emergence of modern nationalism, at least in the circles which mattered in the end, assured Germany of a firm ally. It also was responsible for actions which many see as constituting the first attempt at genocide in the Twentieth Century.

German attempts to improve the Turkish military did not, at first, appear to bear fruit. After some early embarrassments, Italy was able to defeat Turkey in the war of 1911–1912, receiving Libya as the prize. In the Balkan Wars of 1912–1913, Turkey endured military humiliation in a conflict which saw her lose virtually all of her holdings in Europe. Yet, when war came in 1914, Turkey's future role in relation to it was a source of great concern for the Allies.

While Turkey was not formally tied to the Triple Alliance, there were various diplomatic and military arrangements with Germany. On August 2, 1914, these coalesced into a formal alliance. Yet, with Germany already at war with Russia, and soon to be with France and Great Britain, there was no formal Turkish declaration of war. Perhaps, some on the Allied side thought, Turkey would remain on the sidelines, perhaps "benevolently neutral" towards Germany and her allies, but not an active participant in the impending conflict. This, the British, French, and Russian governments wanted desperately. To be sure, in recent years Turkey had not demonstrated much in the way of military prowess. It was widely-known, however, that German officers were continuing to work long and hard at training and helping to re-equip the country's up to then moribund armed forces and no one could say for certain how the Turks might perform in another war. At the same time, Turkish armies in the Near East greatly outnumbered British forces shielding the Suez Canal, and thus this vital water artery could be put at risk at any time. Furthermore, Turkish fortresses guarded the Dardenelles and thus this other vital water route, the one real possibility for establishing links between western and eastern allies, could be eliminated if the Turks, with German support, decided to close it off. Thus, however weak Turkey had been in the past, the Allies viewed the possibility of its entrance into the war with great alarm.

As far as formal entrance into the war was concerned, the Turkish government was divided. The formal ruler of Turkey, Grand Vizier Säid Halim, was rather cautious about involving his country in a war for which he suspected it was not prepared. On the other hand, Minister of War Enver Pasha and Minister of the Interior Talaat Pasha, while cognizant of various Turkish military deficiencies, were eager to enter the conflict on the side of a powerful Germany which they saw as having an excellent chance of winning it. Imbued with the Young Turk nationalist philosophy, they thought that if a new Turkey—with greatly expanded borders—was to be created, now was the time for it.

In the end, the two ministers had their way. Two German ships, the *Goeben,* and the *Breslau,* after skillfully evading Allied naval units in the Mediterranean, arrived in Constantinople. There, they were formally sold to the Turkish Navy. In fact, the crews of the two vessels remained almost entirely German and German sailors took over a variety of other Turkish ships. On September 27, 1914, under immense pressure from the German government to do so, the Dardenelles were closed to Russian shipping. Certainly, by this time, the Western Allies and Russia must have known that the war-hungry duo of Enver and Talaat Pasha had the upper hand with regard to Turkish foreign policy and that, this being the case, the country already was in a virtual state of war with them, even if one had not been formally declared. Throughout October, 1914, the German admiral who had brought *Goeben* and *Breslau* to Constantinople, and who, at this point, was in fact in charge of all naval operations, German or Turkish, in the area, Wilhelm Souchon, sent his ships around the Black Sea, hoping to provoke the Russians into attacking him. Nothing along these lines happened. So, to press the point a bit, Souchon had several of his putatively Turkish ships attack the port of Odessa, sinking several ships at anchor and shelling the shoreline. This happened on October 29. Three days later, Russia declared war on Turkey, France and Great Britain following suit almost immediately. Minister of War Enver Pasha tended to think in rather large terms. Within a matter of weeks after Turkey's entrance into the war, Turkish armies were engaged in two offensives. One of these was coming out of then Turkish-ruled Palestine, and was aimed at the Suez Canal. The other was taking place in eastern Turkey. Here, an enormous army was plunging into the Caucasus mountain range which constituted the frontier between Turkey and Imperial Russia. The goal of this offensive was the oil-rich region around the Caspian Sea, the crucial city of Baku in particular. Each of the offensives failed, one after a particularly hideous fashion.

According to the Bible, Moses took forty years to cross the Sinai Desert. Now, a relatively small Turkish army, moving a bit faster and, of course, in the opposite direction, was heading across this terribly inhospitable region. By the end of February, 1915, most of this force—somewhere between two and three divisions—had crossed the Sinai and was in fact threatening to take the Suez Canal. As small as the Turkish force was, there were far fewer British defenders in the area. Yet, within a week or so, the Turkish army was being withdrawn and the threat to the Suez Canal had disappeared. There had been a few clashes between the Turks and British forces. These, however, had not been decisive. In the end, what had mattered was an overextended supply line and shortages resulting from this. Fairly close to their goal, the Turks had to abandon their attack because hungry soldiers were short of supplies, ammunition in particular. Whatever the reason for the failure of the Turkish attack out of Sinai, a certain level of military incompetence had been revealed.

However embarrassing the failure of the Suez Canal campaign might have been, it was not terribly costly in lives. Such was not the case with regard to the Turkish invasion of the Caucasus, which commenced in December, 1914. At first, the Russian government, shaken by defeats inflicted by the Germans, panicked and almost begged the Allies to intervene somewhere in the region in order to distract the Turks. In due course, however, it became very plain that, at least with regard to this portion of the war, Russia needed no assistance. Enver Pasha's grand Caucasian design seems not to have taken either the geography or the weather into consideration. The 150,000 man Turkish force was attacking in the dead of winter, and not just any winter, but a very bitter Caucasian one. The Russian defenders, outfitted for winter and well-equipped for the sort of war to be fought in the unforgiving Caucasus, repelled Turkish attacks with heavy losses. In less than a month, all Turkish troops had been driven out of Russian territory. Out of 150,000 men who, in one of the most crack-brained military adventures of modern times, had been sent into the Caucasus in the dead of winter to accomplish the impossible, over 100,000 were lost, with 50,000 of these having frozen to death.

By the end of March, 1915, Turkish threats in all areas had eased. Indeed, Allies who, not so long ago were terrified at the prospect of Turkey's entrance into the war, now saw her as an easy mark; in any case, certainly an easier one than that with which they were being confronted on the Western Front. Russian requests for aid against Turkey, plus the miserable performance of the Turks themselves in the Suez Canal enterprise and the more tragically botched Caucasus campaign, served to focus the attention of many in the Allied camp upon possibilities in the Near East. As we have seen, by early 1915 there were those who had pretty much given up on being able to accomplish much on the Western Front, with its sophisticated trench systems. Certainly the Turkish disasters of late 1914 and early 1915 showed that Allied success against a seemingly incompetent opponent was virtually assured. All that was needed was a bold plan, and one was soon on the way.

Towards the end of November, 1914, First Lord of the Admiralty, Winston Churchill (1874–1965), raised the question of a combined land and sea attack in the area of the Dardanelles. As he saw it, the

Western Front was hopelessly bogged. At the same time, there were specific concerns generic to the Near East, the defense of the Suez Canal being of greatest importance. Also, of course, there was the question of protecting British access to Middle Eastern oil and, in order to provide for this, a British brigade (later augmented by other units) had been dispatched to the Persian Gulf state of Kuwait within days after war with Turkey had officially broken out. By early 1915, as we have noted, there were added reasons for a sustained attack upon Turkey. Besides the miserable failures of the country's first military efforts—which seemed to suggest "easy pickings" for the Allies—there was the Russian request for assistance.

As mentioned earlier, those in command of British forces on the Western Front were most unenthusiastic about any enterprise which might result in dilution of the military effort in that area. Consequently, the thought of a major ground offensive in the Dardanelles was anathema to them. In part due to this, in part due to his growing belief that, with the military incompetence of the Turks having seemingly be established, naval operations alone could break the stranglehold on the straits, Churchill came around to the belief that sustained bombardment from British and French battleships was all that was needed. No ground assault would be necessary. The person who was ultimately in direct charge of all naval operations, First Sea Lord Fisher, had his doubts. In due course, however, Churchill's increasingly monomaniacal insistence on the exclusively naval approach won him over. Yet, even after yielding to Churchill's arguments, the crusty old admiral remained in many ways unconvinced as to the wisdom of it. "'You are simply eaten up with the Dardanelles and cannot think of anything else,'" he wrote in an angry note to his boss. "'Damn the Dardanelles! They will be our grave!'"[1] It is doubtful that Fisher could have suspected just how terribly true this strident admonition would prove to be.

On February 19, 1915, Allied warships bombarded the Dardanelles fortresses. The results appeared to be impressive; but, due to bad weather further naval action had to be put off until February 25th. At this time, under heavy covering fire, parties of Royal Marines were landed to blow up those guns that had not been destroyed by the bombardments. At first, these landings were barely contested. In due course, however, resistance stiffened and, by the middle of March, many in British governmental and military circles, including Churchill himself, were beginning to believe that a strong land assault would be necessary if Turkish positions commanding the Dardanelles were to be permanently neutralized. Nonetheless, on March 18, 1915, British and

French warships attempted to force their way through the straits on their own. Three battleships were sunk and a fourth badly damaged by mines. Obviously, a purely naval approach to the Dardanelles problem would not work. Yet, some have argued, if properly pressed, it might have. After the March 18 engagement, the Turks were woefully short of heavy ammunition and there were signs of demoralization amongst the gun crews. "What if" questions, especially, it seems, in military matters, are pointless, however. The British reaction to the disaster of March 18th was to plan major landing operations on the Gallipoli Peninsula and take the fortifications from behind. The French, with muted enthusiasm, offered to provide what support they could, though, with offensives planned for the near future, it couldn't be all that much.

Selecting a commander for the Gallipoli operation proved to be relatively easy. Sir Ian Hamilton (1853–1947), besides having established a good reputation for himself in the Boer War, had been commander of Great Britain's Mediterranean forces since 1910. Presumably, then, he knew that part of the world very well. He had a brisk quality about him, appeared to be almost preternaturally youthful, and was noted for writing orders which were of an almost literary quality. Alas, some of his subordinates complained that, while these made fine reading, they were, at times, almost impossible to understand. Reflected in them was a kind of abstract quality which augured ill for the campaign soon to be undertaken.

Hamilton's opposite number was General Otto Liman von Sanders (1855–1929). One does not have to be well-versed in the Turkish language to notice that the name has a distinctly non-Turkish ring to it. In fact, before the war, the man had headed the German military mission to Turkey. In this capacity, he had labored long and hard to improve the Turkish Army. Early Turkish operations, described above, seemed to indicate that his efforts had been in vain. After the March naval bombardment, Liman von Sanders was placed in command of the Turkish Fifth Army. Consisting of six divisions, its task was to defend Gallipoli against that ground assault that everybody now knew had to take place.

Liman von Sanders was concerned that the Allies might land soon after the bombardment of March 18th. This worried him because he was uncertain if he would have the time necessary to prepare his army to meet a sustained assault. Delays in assembling troops to take part in the landings and in gathering together enough ships to carry them and provide support were responsible for the Gallipoli attack being put off until April 25th. By this time, the Turkish defenders, while still not up to their commander's exacting standards, had regained some of the confidence that had been shaken somewhat by the bombardment of mid-March. Also, by the time the Allies attacked, the Fifth Army was, in some respects, superior to their opponents in terms of equipment. This was certainly true with regards to artillery. The Turks on the Gallipoli Peninsula were well supplied with howitzers and these guns, which "lobbed" their shells, were far better suited for use in the rugged, hilly terrain of the peninsula than were Allied pieces, most of which had nearly flat trajectories. Turkish grenades were more reliable and, while somewhat underequipped in terms of machine guns, at least by Western Front standards, the Fifth Army disposed of more of them than any other Turkish unit. Also, those who manned them were directly trained by German instructors, and, at this point in the war, German machine gunners were the best in the world. Finally, if the battle-to-be were to turn attritional, then the Allies would be faced with severe problems with regard to supplies. Theirs had to be brought in by ship over long distances, while the Turkish defenders could be supplied "overland" with relative ease.

On April 25, 1915, after two feints which fooled nobody, Allied troops came ashore at several points on the Gallipoli Peninsula, Cape Helles, and Ari Burnu. According to Hamilton's scheme, multiple landings would serve the purpose of throwing the Turks into confusion. While some of this did take place, it was the Allies who, from the beginning, were the most confused. At Cape Helles, troops came ashore at five separate beaches so, at least at first, there could be no effective concentration of forces and no mutual support. In places, there was no resistance at all because there was no enemy there to offer any. But, British commanders on the scene were indecisive and would not move their men forward. In other places, there was slaughter on the very first day.

For many, the *River Clyde* incident came to symbolize the horrors of Gallipoli. While some specially-designed landing craft (Admiral Fisher was responsible for them) would put in an appearance later in the campaign, troops were initially landed from conventional ships, which would be beached, or from what really amounted to glorified row-boats. In running down gangways attached to the sides of larger vessels, or leaping over the gunnels of boats, disembarking soldiers were, of course, dangerously exposed. The *River Clyde* was beached at a portion of Cape Helles called "V Beach." As infantrymen swarmed down the gangways or leapt from small boats they were mowed down in waves by Turkish machine gunners. Within a few hours, an enormous crimson stain had spread over the waters of

"V Beach." Within this stain, at the shoreline, in aimlessly drifting boats, and before strands of uncut barbed wire a few metres inland there were hundreds of fallen soldiers. Many were dead; but many still lived and " 'the wounded cried out all day—in every boat, lighter, hopper, and all along the shore. It was horrible.' "[2] Some hundreds of yards away, at "S Beach," a British battalion had landed with no opposition at all. Its men could hear the sounds of slaughter coming from "V Beach," but, they didn't move.

At Ari Burnu, the northernmost of the beach-heads, troops of the newly-formed "Anzac" units—consisting of Australians and New Zealanders—went ashore and within a few hours were engaged with newly-arrived Turkish reinforcements. By day's end, the lads from "down-under" had not been able to advance beyond some very low-lying ridges near the beach; and, from higher ones, howitzer shells rained down upon them. Their overall commander, one General Birdwood, sent a message to Hamilton in which he warned him that, unless the troops were reembarked at once, disaster would occur. In return, General Hamilton sent the following: " 'You have got through the difficult business. Now you have only to dig, dig, dig until you are safe.' "[3] By the end of the first day, it would appear, the commander in charge of the Gallipoli operation knew that any quick victory was out of the question and that, in due course, tactical circumstances would come to approximate those on the Western Front. In any event, while containing a large element of truth in it, Hamilton's advice reflected the mentality of one who, in many respects, never really took charge of the Gallipoli Campaign.

By the end of the first day of fighting on the peninsula, a pattern had emerged, one which would remain until the last days of the botched Gallipoli Campaign. Virtually all tactical decisions were made by local commanders, i.e., those on the scene. In a sense, there was a certain wisdom which informed this approach. After all, those closest to the fighting ought to have maximum flexibility. With regard to Gallipoli, however, this just didn't work. General Hamilton, without question one of the least intrusive generals in modern history, was vague with regard to overall plans, often unclear in his instructions, and, at times, gave the impression of being kind of bored with what was going on. He certainly knew of trials, tribulations, and occasional lost opportunities, but often seemed to assume an almost neutral stance with regard to the operation's success. As hell exploded around him, he took it all in as if he were observing some sort of natural disaster about which he could do very little. Everyone knew, of course, that, eventually, the troops put ashore at various beaches were to link up and, as a unified line, move eastward across the Gallipoli Peninsula, taking the Turkish fortifications from the rear, while routing any Turkish forces which got in their way. But, beyond these extremely general goals, General Hamilton offered little advice. Commanders, some maddeningly cautious, others maddeningly daring, seemed to be operating on their own, at times, almost independently of each other. So accustomed did some of them become to this state of affairs that when, on rare occasions, the commander of chief actually made some sort of decision, he was likely to be overruled.

An interesting, and fateful, example of this was provided on the first day. British forces who landed at "Y Beach" soon found themselves hotly engaged in fighting, much of it of the bayonet variety, with the Turks. Losses were heavy on both sides; but, in the end, the Turks withdrew. Somehow, this didn't register with the British commander and, after deciding that it was, after all, *they* who had been beaten, he had his force reembarked on boats and taken away. So, for awhile, there existed a most curious, very limited, battlefield. Not only was there no battle taking place on it, but nobody around to engage in one. The commander of the "Y Beach" force, who frequently complained about Hamilton's lack of direction, resented his commander-in-chief whenever he tried provide it. He knew that, as Hamilton saw it, the landing at "Y Beach" was crucial to the success of the campaign. He, however, chose to disagree and not only refused to accept reinforcements which might have ensured his position, but, when informed that battalion commanders were deciding to withdraw, agreed with alacrity with the decision, not at all concerned with whether tactical realities called for it.

By the end of April, soldiers on both sides, to paraphrase the commander in chief, had "dug, dug, dug," and trench warfare had become a fact of life (and death) just as had happened on the Western Front, to some degree on the Eastern Front, and as soon would happen on the Italian Front. Now, the once despised Turks were demonstrating that they could be just as good at it as anybody else. As for the Allies, General Hamilton was demonstrating that, at times, a cautious approach eschewing concentration of forces could be, in the end, just as costly as the opposite approach currently being undertaken on battlefields in France and Flanders. On occasion, the "Turkish" commander, Liman von Sanders, demonstrated that he could be just as profligate with the lives of his men as anybody else. On May 1st, with the Allies seemingly hopelessly pinned down not very far from the beaches upon which they landed, he sent his men into furious counterattacks. Everywhere, they were hurled back with enormous losses. No sooner than the Turkish attacks had been repulsed, then the Allied forces had a try at it, with approximately the same results.

Up to this point, General Hamilton's dispatches to the government had been almost cheery in nature. Gains measured in yards were counted as major victories and all was going according to plan. Now, however, things began to unravel. Previously muzzled pressmen began to represent the operation as hopelessly botched, and the commander-in-chief began calling for reinforcements. To make matters worse, German and Turkish naval units sank several Allied battleships. In a fury, Admiral Fisher resigned his post. Within a few days, Churchill also was forced to step down. Under furious attack in the press and condemned not only by traditional political foes but by many in his own party, he requested that he be posted to a front-line battalion in the west. In due course, he was and, seeing conditions on the Western Front first hand, came to the conclusion that, even if the Gallipoli Campaign had not gone as it ought to have been, there had to be a better way of waging war then that utilized by Haig, Joffre, and colleagues.

Trench warfare Gallipoli style was, however, bad enough, and it had its own singular miseries. Even with Allied reinforcements, the lines moved very little and, for a large part of the campaign, Allied units were not very far from the beaches. In a way, this was somewhat inviting. Water was scarce on the parched peninsula. There was barely enough to drink, much less to bathe in, and men were encrusted in filth. Thus, on occasion, whole companies of them would bathe in the ocean. Often, however, this was under Turkish artillery fire, the distances between Turkish positions and the beach being very little. In the ferocious heat, bodies of the slain bloated up and rotted very quickly, and the wounded between the lines endured the agonies of hell. Among the Anzac troops the rumor spread that the British military leadership, less sensitive to the fate of "colonials," was throwing them into the most hopeless of situations. Yet, they fought with a dogged bravery which won the respect of the world. In due course, the slim sliver of beach held by them became known, at least in Allied circles, as "Anzac Cove," and, from this point, the tenacity of the Australians in holding on to their trench positions at all costs would be responsible for the word "Diggers" to be used to represent them and, eventually, their country.

Battles raged throughout June and July, 1915. As in the case of Western and Italian Front engagements, there was little to show for them except in terms of steadily mounting casualties. On August 6th, General Hamilton attempted to open up a new front. Some 5,000 troops, many of them conveyed in the special landing craft designed by Admiral Fisher, landed at Suvla Bay, about five miles to the north of Anzac Cove. To achieve total surprise, they were landed at night. It proved to be a disastrous move. Amphibious operations were still rather a novelty, and one conducted in darkness taxed human resources beyond endurance. Men became separated from their units, units themselves lost all cohesion, and officers seemed to lose their minds. By the time the confusion was sorted out, and men, many of whom were already suffering from thirst and exhaustion, were moved off of the beaches, Turkish reinforcements were on their way to the threatened area. Now fighting with desperate courage, the Suvla forces managed to link up with those at Anzac Cove, but, even this combined force was unable to register meaningful gains. In the meantime, Allied attacks around Cape Helles had proved to be equally fruitless.

The Turkish Fifth Army was suffering terribly as well. Just as in the case of German soldiers on the Western Front, their officers often sent them on ludicrous missions to recapture whatever hundreds of metres they might have lost during a particular engagement. They, however, were fighting on their own soil and doing a good job of it. Allied soldiers, fighting on enemy soil—and also, particularly considering their abominable leadership, doing very well—were aware that they were involved in a losing cause. More important for the career of General Ian Hamilton, so were those in high places.

On October 16, 1915, General Hamilton was relieved of his post. He would never again hold one of any consequence. Less than two weeks later, his replacement, General Charles Monro, a man who had opposed the Gallipoli operation from the beginning, arrived from the Western Front to take over operations. Almost at once, he determined that nothing at all could be accomplished by continuing the campaign, and that the Allied forces had to be evacuated as soon as possible.

Yet, as in the case of most World War I battles—perhaps most battles in general—the Gallipoli contest had developed a ghastly momentum of its own and could not be broken off at will. Thus, despite General Monro's belief that the campaign should be brought to a close, fighting continued through November. Casualties continued to mount up in engagements in which the lines changed little, if at all; and, there was another, altogether unexpected, disaster. A sudden change in the weather brought in a violent storm, which lasted for three days. Rain, sleet, and snow tormented soldiers who, just a short time ago, had suffered from blistering heat and thirst. Over 250 of them were drowned in flooded trenches, others froze to death, and there were thousands of cases of frostbite. If God was on the side of this particular Allied effort, He had the most curious ways of showing it. By the end of November, Monro had decided that evacuation had to take place and plans were made for it.

As matters turned out, the evacuations, which began early in December and were completed by January 9, 1916, were the most successful operations of the Gallipoli Campaign. Planning was precise, staff work excellent, and the rigors of winter had negative effects on Turkish vigilance. Over 50,000 British and French troops were evacuated without the loss of a man.

Yet, between April and November, 1915, the Gallipoli Campaign had involved 480,000 Allied soldiers, of whom 410,000 were British; 70,000 French. Casualties—killed, wounded, died of disease or exposure, or evacuated sick—totalled around 250,000, i.e., over half of those who took part in the operation. In the end, the Turkish defenders suffered in almost equal numbers. Their casualties were officially counted as 249,000. Yet, as jubilant Turkish soldiers, who had subsisted largely on rations of olives and bread, struggled to open abandoned tins of potted meat and other delicacies, they were aware that they had won an extraordinary victory. In due course, April 25, the day of the invasion, would be celebrated in Turkey as a jubilant national holiday. In Australia, it came to be commemorated as a day of national pride in the role played by countrymen in a heroic but doomed enterprise. The Gallipoli Campaign would be the last major "diversionary" effort undertaken by the Allies during the course of the Great War. From then on, Allied generals, in most matters, strategic and tactical, would have things their own way. On various notable occasions, this would result in casualties even greater than those sustained at Gallipoli, and in shorter periods of time, too.

As the last Allied troops were being withdrawn from Gallipoli, others were coming to grief at the hands of the Turks. The reader will recall that, in November, 1914, a small British force had been dispatched to Kuwait in order to secure access to oil in the region. Over time, this force was gradually built up until, in February, 1915, a 12,000-man Anglo-Indian army under the command of General Charles Townshend, was ordered to advance up the Tigris River valley towards Baghdad. At first, this relatively small force accomplished wonders. Advancing over inhospitable terrain, and harassed as much by disease as by the enemy, it triumphed in several sharp fights with the Turks. By the end of November, however, it was plain that Townshend's army had overextended itself and, after further fighting against an enemy steadily increasing in strength, it fell back to the city of

Kut-al-Imara in Mesopotamia (modern-day Iraq). By December 7, 1915, the now heavily-outnumbered force was under siege.

In January, 1915, the Russian Army undertook an initially extremely successful offensive in the Caucasus. Turkish armies were thrown back and, for awhile, it appeared that this might serve to relieve pressure on Townshend's force. Eventually, though, the Russian advance, for largely logistical reasons, came to an end. Thus, between December 7, 1915, and April 29, 1916—143 days in all—this small army, weakened by hunger and malaria, endured a heroic, but, of course, ultimately hopeless, siege. When Townshend finally did surrender his force, it had been reduced to around 10,000 men, over 2,000 of them sick. The newly-taken prisoners were then forced to march across the Mesopotamian and Syrian deserts to the Syrian city of Aleppo, where they were to be interned. During the course of this 500-mile trek, over half of Townshend's men died of exposure, hunger, disease, or brutal treatment. Only later on was it revealed that General Townshend, at first hailed as a hero for holding out so long against overwhelming odds, had been treated extremely well by his captors even as so many of his men died miserable deaths. It would also come out that this did not seem to bother the general all that very much. Quite probably, this was in large part due to the fact that 8,000 of those surrendered at Kut-al-Imara were Indian. In any case, as Britons were attempting to assimilate the Gallipoli disaster, they were confronted with having to deal with yet another Near Eastern calamity although, to be sure, it was on a somewhat smaller scale and, involving as it did mostly non-white troops, did not touch white hearts to the same degree as did the results of the earlier botched campaign.

Thus, so far as the war against the Turks was concerned, 1915 and the first months of 1916 was a disastrous period for the Allies. It was also a period which bore witness to what many consider to be the century's first fling at genocide. Involved were what became known as the "Armenian Massacres," and it is to this doleful topic that we must now turn.

At the beginning of 1915, there were approximately 1.8 million Armenians within the greatly reduced Turkish-controlled lands. Almost all of them were concentrated in that area which had once constituted an independent Armenian state, the first Christian state in history. This was in eastern Turkey, near the Caucasian Mountains. During the days of the old Ottoman Empire, the Christian Armenians, like most conquered minorities, were generally left to their own devices within the framework of the relatively loosely-controlled Muslim *imperium*. At times, though, there were outbursts against them, in times of trouble, sometimes fomented by the government, and there were anti-Armenian outrages in the early 1880s and between 1894–1896. After the Young Turk revolt, there were further attacks on the Armenians, this time in 1909. As terrible as the earlier depredations had been (particularly those of 1894–1896, in which between 100,000 and 200,000 Armenians were slaughtered), the most recent one was also the most ominous. The motive behind it was the new Turkish nationalism, mentioned earlier. As indicated earlier, this could turn out to be far more intolerant of differences in nationality than religious doctrines with an otherworldly focus.

In 1909, the Young Turks, still a bit uncertain of themselves and concerned about gaining and holding onto international credibility, tried to shift the blame for atrocities against the Armenians to surviving and vindictive remnants of the old regime of Abdul Hamid. Many observers, however, saw these as resulting from efforts at some sort of national purification—the sort of thing which would be associated with the new Turkish nationalism.

When Turkey formally entered the war in November, 1914, the Armenian community was placed at risk almost immediately. There was no question but that Armenian Christians felt some sort of tie to Russians, also Christian. The fact that, from time to time, the Armenians had been subjected to persecution certainly served to strengthen pro-Russian sympathies. Also, as mentioned earlier, most Armenians lived in eastern Turkey—the site of the old Armenian state, but also the region closest to Russia. Of course, during earlier conflicts, the same geo-political circumstances prevailed. The regime which brought Turkey into the Great War, however, was imbued with the new, at times, massively intolerant, nationalism. Apart from religious considerations, the nation of Turkey had been rendered virtually sacrosanct by a history and national genius that was its alone. Thus, foreigners living within the Turkish lands could come to be viewed as dangerous, and this was particularly the case with a people which, not only had a strong sense of national consciousness, but also in fact had played a crucial role in the nation's economy; something which, of course, had done nothing to endear the Armenians to their Turkish neighbors. The Young Turks and those associated with them were, for the most part, hardly bastions of Muslim orthodoxy. But, the Christianity of the Armenians came to represent crucial national differences which served to set them apart from the majority Turks. In any case, in times of trouble, the religion of the Armenians—which, in the eyes of the average Turk, caused them to stand out as infidels—could be used to rally support against them. This could be done even if the motives informing a new anti-Armenian campaign had more to do with the secular religion of nationalism rather than previously hallowed Islamic causes.

As seen earlier, at least at first, the war seemed not to be going all that very well for Turkey. The grab for the Suez Canal had failed, and the attacks in the Caucasus had resulted in an enormous debacle. Now, in April, 1915, everyone expected the Allies to mount an invasion in the Dardanelles. With military disaster in the background, and a massive threat looming in the immediate future (nobody could have possibly foreseen the extent of Allied military incompetence), the regime found it necessary to seek out a group upon which one could place the blame for military catastrophes otherwise very hard to assimilate. Many Armenians were pro-Russian, most Armenians lived in lands adjacent to Russian territory, and these people had been for the most part, stubborn and unassimible. Obviously, they were somehow responsible for everything that had gone wrong in the war up to that point. Maybe they were mostly, if not all, Russian spies. In any event, with the exigencies of war prevailing in all areas of life, now was the time to settle the "Armenian Question" once and for all.

Late in April, 1915, shortly before the anticipated Allied landings, Turkish police and soldiers arrested many Armenian intellectual and political leaders in Constantinople. All were removed from the city to the Turkish interior, where almost all of them were executed. The following month, Minister of the Interior Talaat Pasha, declared that the Armenian population as a whole was disloyal and, in fact, in a state of rebellion against the Turkish government. He issued orders calling for an "evacuation" (a word which would turn out to have euphemistic value in a variety of contexts) of Armenians from areas in which they currently resided to new living spaces in Mesopotamia and Syria. This was being done, it was said, because these people, now officially deemed to be in rebellion, represented a danger to the Turkish fatherland, now fighting for its existence. Also, it was maintained, it was necessary to remove the Armenian population from its homes to protect it against the well-deserved wrath of the Turkish people, furious at its perfidious conduct. Armenians living in Constantinople, apart from the intellectuals eliminated in April, were not affected by the order, nor were those living in the city of Smyrna. There were too many foreigners living in these communities to bear witness to actions of this sort. Beginning in May, 1915, Armenians throughout Turkey—with exceptions mentioned above—were removed from their homes and, escorted by Turkish soldiers, force-marched towards Mesopotamia and Syria. There was some scattered resistance from Armenian self-defense groups, enough, as the government saw it, to lend credence to its claim that this largest of Christian minorities was engaged in rebellion. Generally, though, operations preceded along smoothly. As hundreds of thousands of helpless men, women, and children were on the move, soldiers began to slaughter men and older boys without mercy. Women and girls were gang-raped and then hacked to pieces. Sometimes, in order to spare themselves from shame, women killed themselves, after killing their daughters. Those boys and girls not massacred were enslaved as prostitutes. As would Nazis in times to come, the Turkish government was able to make much use of intercommunal national and religious hatreds. Armenian families by the thousands were abandoned in the region occupied by Muslim Kurds, traditional enemies of the Armenians, who had a hatred for these infidels which was even more visceral than that of the government. They set about their ordained tasks with a ferocious enthusiasm. Those Armenians not slaughtered by Turkish soldiers or Kurdish irregulars died of thirst and hunger in the stark wastelands of the Anatolian interior.

By early 1916, anywhere from 600,000 to 1,200,000 Armenians had perished in what some have called the first major genocidal action of the Twentieth Century. Some have maintained that, because Armenians in Constantinople and Smyrna were spared, this was not a *true* genocidal action. After all, the Turkish government, even if only because it did not wish to accrue bad publicity, wasn't out to kill every single Armenian. Such an argument, however, strikes one as a trifle pedantic. In any even, all aware of what was occurring in Turkey at the time knew that something quite unprecedented—certainly in scope, if not design—had taken place.

One of those who was well aware of what had happened was the American ambassador to Turkey, Henry Morgenthau. He recorded an episode which, in terms of sheer cynicism, still stands out even in a century replete with acts of bureaucratic barbarity. The author of the latest, and most thorough-going of Armenian massacres, Talaat Pasha, approached him with a most unusual request. It was known to the interior minister that two American insurance companies, The New York Insurance Company, and the Equitable Life of New York, had had many Armenian clients. Talaat Pasha asked Morgenthau to request that these companies send the Turkish government " 'a complete list of their Armenian policy holders.' " Since the Armenians were " 'practically all dead now and have left no heirs to collect the money,' " vast sums would now " 'escheat . . . to the state.' " Thus, " 'the [Turkish] government is the beneficiary now.' "[4] The astonished and horrified ambassador refused to comply with the request.

As word of the slaughter got out, many Allied propagandists tried to blame the episode on the Germans. But, while the German government of course had to refuse to acknowledge what its loyal ally had done, it is plain that the Turkish government acted on its own. In so doing, it had provided a graphic illustration of what can occur when, in wartime conditions, extreme nationalism, making abundant use of social, communal, and religious prejudices, was pushed to a logical conclusion. To its shame, the Turkish government, even up to now, never has owned up to the very existence of the Armenian massacres of 1915–1916. And, for a variety of reasons grounded in considerations of power-politics, very little pressure has been put upon it to do so. Sometime after it was all over, a former German common soldier drew appropriate conclusions. In pondering policies towards another group stigmatized as inimical to national life, Adolf Hitler posed the rhetorical question, "Who now remembers the Armenians?"

WAR IN AFRICA AND ASIA

While, as we shall see, there would be challenges to British command of the sea, one of them quite grave, the Royal Navy pretty much "ruled the waves" (though it would have problems with what moved around under them) throughout the war. This allowed the British to pretty much determine what went where during this time. An important result of this was Great Britain's ability to prevent Germany from sending reinforcements to colonial holdings throughout the world while making certain that British and friendly forces in these regions could be reinforced and supplied. This was of immense significance, because, unlike in Europe, German military power in Africa and Asia was quite weak. On the other hand, not only did Great Britain, at least in Africa, have fairly large military forces to bring to bear (for the most part, "native," commanded by white officers), but, it could count on assistance from white-officered "native" armies from the French, Belgian, and Portuguese colonies.

Thus, from the beginning, the disparity in numbers and material made itself felt. Almost immediately upon the outbreak of war, a relatively small British army—it was commanded by a captain, an officer usually in charge of an army company—headed out from the British-held Gold Coast and into the neighboring German colony of Togoland. On August 26, 1914, in what turned out to be the most quickly attained British victory of the war, Captain Barker was accepting the surrender of the German garrison at Kamina. More success was to come to the

British in west Africa, although it would take a little bit longer to achieve it.

Most of the white population of the Union of South Africa was Boer, and many of these Dutch-speaking people still harbored resentments towards the British. During the Boer War, 1899–1902, the latter had suffered military humiliation before finally overwhelming their often better-armed opponents by sheer numbers. Boers remembered this with some pride. With bitterness, they also remembered that, when attempting to deal with Boer guerrillas once victory against the regular armies had been obtained, the British had imprisoned thousands of men, women, and children in what turned out to be some of history's first concentration camps. While few died of deliberate mistreatment, many perished from hunger and disease.

Thus, it was perhaps understandable that many in German governmental and military circles assumed that the Boers—who, after all, spoke a Germanic language—would be sympathetic to the German cause. If war came, so this line of reasoning went, the Boer inhabitants of the Union of South Africa would be less than enthusiastic about lending the Allied cause any support. The Boer head of the Union, however, Premier Louis Botha (1862–1919), was suspicious of Germany. Also, he was friendly with Winston Churchill. The friendship, to be sure, had a rather odd beginning. Botha had participated in Churchill's capture when the latter was a news correspondent covering the Boer War. When he engineered a well-publicized escape from a Boer prisoner of war camp, he gained Botha's grudging admiration, and the friendship took off from there. Thus, for reasons personal and political, Botha was committed to supporting the British war effort.

Support came in the form of around 50,000 troops including some excellent cavalry. Useless on the Western Front and of limited value in the eastern theatre, good cavalry could be crucial in regions characterized by plains and deserts, especially in view of the fact that there were neither the men nor material available for the introduction of trench warfare. German Southwest Africa was just such a region and, after some delays due to problems of logistics and training, South African forces invaded the territory in October, 1915. The German defenders were vastly outnumbered; but, unlike in Togoland, put up considerable resistance. The outcome, however, was never really in doubt and, on July 9, 1915, all surviving defenders of German Southwest Africa were forced to surrender.

The other German colony in western Africa, the Cameroons, was adjacent to French Equatorial Africa, British-held Nigeria, and the

Belgian Congo. Hence, immediately after the outbreak of war, it was invaded by armies coming from several directions. Again, as in the cases of Togoland and the Cameroons, the German forces were heavily outnumbered. They fought back as best they could, however, and, in this case, the defenders were assisted by climate and by a variety of diseases which positively thrived in a region dominated by jungle and dense bush. Harassed as much by sleeping sickness, malaria, and dysentery as by the German enemy, the Allied armies were forced to suspend the dismal campaign until adequate medical supplies were brought to the scene. When this occurred, and the Allied forces were able to resume their advance, the outcome could not be in doubt. By January, 1916, almost all German resistance in the Cameroons had been broken. A very small detachment of "native" troops, commanded by a handful of white officers, continued to hold out at the small town of Mora. When, on February 18th, they finally did surrender, their British captors, in recognition of a gallant stand against hopeless odds, allowed the officers to keep their swords. It was a romantic survival from a bygone age that witnessed the imperialistic land-grabbing responsible for Africa's being embroiled in the first of two world wars.

The Allied military effort in German East Africa was not nearly as successful as that in the west. The German commander in the area Colonel (later General) Paul von Lettow-Vorbeck (1870–1964) was something of a minor military genius. Bold and resourceful, he thought it futile for his heavily outnumbered forces to simply sit on their hands waiting to be attacked. No sooner had war been declared, then he astonished just about everybody by launching a three-pronged German attack, striking against surrounding British colonial territories. With some difficulty, the assaults were contained and then beaten back by November, 1914. Lettow-Vorbeck, however, continued the struggle and, until the end of the war—in fact, not finding out about the German defeat until quite late, his force did not surrender until around two weeks after the armistice—he succeeded in thoroughly baffling, and often defeating, armies far larger than his own. Thus, German East Africa was not securely in British hands until the war was over, indeed, as we have seen, not until some time after that. It would seem that the thrill of combat was very much in Lettow-Vorbeck's blood for, after the collapse, he joined a vicious, right-wing German paramilitary organization called the "Free Corps," a group which, at one point, attempted to overthrow the Weimar Republic. For the hero of German East Africa, as would prove to be true for some thousands of other lesser known souls, the war would rage on in their hearts long after the battle fields had fallen silent.

Probably the oddest, in fact, almost unbelievable, episode in the war in Africa concerned how the British obtained naval superiority on Lake Tanganyika, a strategically-important body of water separating German East Africa from the Belgian Congo. Under the direction of a British naval officer, one Commander Simson, two large armed river launches were dispatched from Cape Town, South Africa. Heading northeast, they made use of waterways, of course. At times, however, there *were* none. In those cases, the launches were simply dragged through jungles until the next available river. Then, the two boats were taken off of crude rollers and were able to travel in a more conventional manner. Moreover, the goal, Lake Tanganyika, is more than 6,000 feet above sea level, so that a large part of this most interesting cruise took place going uphill. The two vessels did eventually arrive at their destination, and German naval supremacy on Lake Tanganyika came to an end. Later, the novelist, C. S. Forester would write a work based on this episode entitled *The African Queen.* In the 1950s, there would be a movie bearing this name, and it would turn out to be one of the last starring Humphrey Bogart.

Compared to the battles raging in Europe, those in Africa were small potatoes. Yet, both sides took them extremely seriously, realizing that, in future, possession of the colonies might be useful as bargaining chips in peace negotiations. Naturally, of course, if there was a decisive victory, the conquest of new colonial territories could be of immense political, economic, and strategic value—to say nothing of matters of prestige. Having conquered all of Germany's African colonies—with the important exception of German East Africa—by mid-February, 1916, the Allies certainly planned on holding on to them, rationalizing their conquest through doubtful assertions that they could run the new possessions better than the previous owners had done.

The casualties sustained in the African fighting in no way approached those endured in Europe. Yet, proportionally, losses were sometimes quite high, and, as we have seen, losses due to disease could cripple armies. In any event, some thousands of folk indigenous to the region died fighting for European masters. And, it is entirely possible—if one adds to the toll of those Africans killed in combat there those slain in combat in Europe—that more Africans died in the white man's Great War than in all the tribal wars that had taken place during the preceding three centuries.

Germany had several colonial holdings in the Far East, and here, even more than in Africa, British, and, to some extent, Japanese, command of the sea proved to be decisive. In the Pacific, British sea and land power was in fact largely represented by Commonwealth forces. Thus it was that units from New Zealand captured New Guinea and Samoa, while the Australians seized the island of Neu-Pommern, which had served as an important German wireless station. In due course, the island was renamed New Britain. Japan, which had been somewhat loosely tied to Great Britain by the naval agreement of 1902, was hardly obligated to enter the war. Seeing the opportunity of gaining some strategically-important territory on the cheap, however, the Japanese government joined the war on the side of the Allies on August 23, 1914. Especially coveted was the German-held base of Kiaochow, on the Shantung Peninsula, extorted in 1897 from a then supine Chinese government during the more aggressive phase of German imperialism. To get to it, however, the Japanese had to take port city of Tsingtao, held by an undersized garrison of German troops. The assault by Japanese naval and army units began on October 31 and, after seven days of heavy bombardment, the city fell and Japanese presence on the Shantung Peninsula was assured. The German garrison had not offered determined resistance, and this caused Japanese military men to form a somewhat low opinion of the fighting qualities of an army to which, in the future, they would be linked by alliance. Other German holdings, the Marshall, Mariana, and Caroline Islands, located in the Central Pacific, were almost devoid of defenders, and fell to the Japanese like so many ripe plums. For around 300 dead, a skirmish-sized toll by standards of the war in Europe, Japan had greatly strengthened her strategic position in Asia.

The course of the war in Africa and Asia had demonstrated the crucial role played by sea power. As mentioned before, it was soon obvious that Britannia ruled the waves, and this seemed to have been demonstrated by several relatively small, but costly, naval engagements. At the same time, however, another dimension—and a very crucial one—was being added to naval warfare. And, as matters turned out, the most critical role played by navies in World War I was one that, in its extent, had not been anticipated by most naval establishments before the outbreak of the conflict. These issues are the subject of the chapter which now follows.

9

Naval Engagements and the Emergence of Submarine Warfare

"SMALL SCALE" TRADITIONAL ENGAGEMENTS

THE pre-war "naval race" between Great Britain and Germany had done much to exacerbate tensions between the two powers. When war came, Great Britain found itself still well in the lead in terms of numbers of ships. It was assumed, however, that the smaller German High Seas Fleet, known for high standards of training and for disposing of some excellent new ships, would present the Royal Navy with a formidable challenge quite soon after the commencement of hostilities. At first, though, the High Seas Fleet pursued a policy of caution. Naval Minister, Alfred von Tirpitz and his admirals knew that, confronted with a still quite large disparity with regard to numbers of ships, a general fleet action could result in disaster for the young German navy. Thus, while Germany went about the task of preparing less orthodox approaches to naval warfare, units of the High Seas Fleet were to avoid engaging opponents, especially British ones, unless the odds seemed to favor a good outcome. The Royal Navy, however, justifiably proud of having succeeded in bringing the BEF to the continent without losing a man, displayed a somewhat more aggressive approach, its chief, Winston Churchill, knowing full well that it could afford to do so. There was, perhaps, another reason for a quick display of naval vigor—the successful transport of the BEF was counterbalanced by the navy's inability to prevent the *Goeben* and *Breslau* from reaching Turkey. This embarrassment needed to be redeemed, and a quick, decisive naval victory would be the best way to do it. On August 29, 1914, in a most daring move, a British battle cruiser squadron steamed into an area of the North Sea known as the "Helgoland Bight," in a manner of speaking, Germany's maritime back-yard. The much lighter German ships in the area, some light cruisers and destroyers, were caught completely off-guard and three light cruisers and a destroyer were sunk with heavy loss of life. No British ships were sunk, and loss of personnel was slight. It was an extraordinary achievement. Yet, almost immediately, the ever capricious fortunes of war took a turn which served to cast a shadow over it. On September 22, three British cruisers steaming in the North Sea off the Dutch coast were sunk within a very brief period of time. The relatively few survivors could say little about their attackers. This inability did not result from battle trauma of any kind, but because almost nobody had been able to see them. In point of fact, the three cruisers had been sunk by a single German submarine. It became immediately obvious to the Admiralty that a new, if in the eyes of some, untoward, dimension was being added to naval warfare. As if to drive home the point, on October 27, the battleship *Audacious* struck a mine off of the Irish coast, sinking within minutes. The mine most probably had been "laid" by a German submarine. As if matters weren't bad enough, a British surface unit met disaster in a more conventional battle. On the night of November 1, 1914, steaming off the island of Coronel near the Chilean coast, three British cruisers under the command of Admiral Sir Christopher Craddock encountered a much larger German force, in fact the German Far East Squadron, commanded by Admiral Maximilian von Spee, which had been in the vicinity for purposes of refueling. Outnumbered and heavily outgunned, Craddock nonetheless thought himself duty-bound to obey the Admiralty's order to engage the enemy wherever he might be encountered. In a rash "do or die" move, the British cruisers sallied forth and, in what followed, there was little British doing, but much dying. Two cruisers were sunk, and nobody on board lived to tell about it. Admiral Craddock was among those who died, no doubt convinced to the end that, in dooming himself and a thousand of his men, he had made the right decision. Revenge was not late in coming, and, in large measure, it was made possible by a blunder on Spee's part which more than counterbalanced that of his late British adversary. He knew that, after the Coronel Island battle, the British had dispatched a large force to the South Atlantic in order to confront him as he headed around Cape Horn on the way home. Under these circumstances, Spee decided not to head home anyway. Rather, he thought, he might amuse himself by bombarding British installations at Port Stanley, in the Falkland Islands. Close to his goal, he was informed by horrified lookouts, that the large British force he was supposed to avoid was *at* Port Stanley, where it was fuelling up. The German Far East Squadron, outnumbered, outarmored, and outgunned—and, unfortunately, by speedier ships—had about as much of a chance as that enjoyed by Craddock when he confronted it five weeks earlier. Flight was impossible and, on December 8, 1915, the battle cruisers *Scharnhorst* and *Gneisenau* were sunk almost immediately and with heavy loss of life, with two light cruisers being sunk soon afterwards. Only one German ship, the light cruiser *Dresden,* escaped the massacre, one in which close to 2,000 German sailors died, and it would be sunk a few months later. As in the case of Craddock, Admiral von Spee did not survive the carnage resulting from a blunder of the highest order. In the meantime, closer to home waters, the German Navy was becoming somewhat daring. In November and December, 1914 some of its units bombarded several cities on Britain's northeast coast, inflicting considerable damage and some loss of life. On both occasions, the attackers got away unmolested. In January, 1915, a German cruiser squadron took a third try at it and, at this point, the law of averages put in an appearance. It was intercepted by a fleet of British battle cruisers and, fighting against hopeless odds, one German cruiser, the *Blücher,* was sunk, while two others were heavily damaged in what went down in the history books as the "Dogger Banks Action." In one of the most famous—and heart-wrenching—photographs to come out of the Great War, the *Blücher* is seen lying on her starboard side. Parts of the ship are dark with sailors, hundreds of them, a large proportion of which are doomed. We are told that many of them were singing hymns. Shortly after the photograph was taken, the cruiser foundered. Over 900 German sailors perished in the Dogger Banks Action, while British losses were astonishingly light.

By early 1915, then, the Royal Navy had engaged the German High Seas Fleet in four "limited" actions, winning three of them. The Admiralty had reason to be pleased and most Britons felt confirmed in their opinion that anyone foolish enough to challenge their navy would suffer disaster. Of course, the German naval establishment was not at all pleased with the overall results of these encounters, although it could perhaps take some comfort from the fact that its officers and men had fought with great bravery against immense odds. "Moral victories" in warfare do not count for much, however, and what was perhaps of greatest positive significance for the German naval leadership was that one, astonishing victory gained through somewhat unconventional means—the sinking of three British cruisers in one day by a German submarine in September, 1914. This was a good augury, and German naval strategists were quick to seize upon it. Perhaps, until some more favorable balance could be attained with regard to the surface fleet situation, it would be best if most, if not all of it, were to remain in port while the burden of Germany's war effort at sea would be borne by submarines. In order for it to be successful, a submarine offensive would have to be conducted in the most aggressive manner imaginable. Very quickly, Germany's naval leaders realized that the submarine could serve a double purpose. On the one hand, it could attack British warships, i.e., engage "traditional" naval targets. On the other, it could do what the outnumbered German surface vessels could not accomplish—attack on a more or less regular basis those merchant ships upon which Great Britain was dependent for food and materials. This marvelous discovery was of that variety which has consequences unimagined by those who make them.

SUBMARINE WARFARE AND TWO BLOCKADES

Shortly after the outbreak of war, the world became aware of the daring exploits of the German light cruiser, *Emden,* commanded by Captain Karl von Müller. A "commerce raider," this relatively light ship—she displaced only 3,500 tons—wreaked havoc on Allied shipping in the Indian Ocean. At one point, acting completely on his own, Captain von Müller had succeeded in virtually eliminating merchant shipping in that region. Finally, though, the Australian cruiser, *Sydney,* a much heavier vessel armed with heavier guns, caught up with the *Emden,* and, on November 22, 1914, her career came to a flaming end. Captain von Müller, however, and the officers and men who served him, had established an extraordinary reputation, not only for excellent seamanship and daring, but, for fighting "according to the rules." The *Emden* fired only upon legitimate targets, took pains to rescue survivors, and treated all prisoners with courtesy, indeed, kindness. Even in an atmosphere which very rapidly was being filled with hate, his captors had to admit that the officers and men of the *Emden* were rather extraordinary sorts and, when they entered into captivity, officers were allowed to keep their swords, while all who served on the valiant ship were treated very well. In the whole, sorry history of the Great War, the *Emden* story is one of the very few which, in any way, shape, or form, could be described as "heart-warming." Very rapidly, as on the land, naval warfare began exhibiting some very "dirty" aspects. As the Allies came to see it, just about the "dirtiest" of these was provided by Germany in the form of submarine warfare.

In 1902, a British admiral described the submarine as " 'underhanded, unfair, and unEnglish.' " He must have been musing upon future uses of it, for, up to that point, its employment in warfare had been slight. As is well known, Leonardo da Vinci (1452–1519)—a man who seemed to enjoy counter-balancing his splendid, often religious, works of art with diagrammatic excursions into realms of mass destruction—designed a submarine. During the Revolutionary War in America, a New England college student by the name of David Bushnell designed, and in fact, built, a submarine. Dubbed the *Turtle,* this curious, barrel-shaped device was operated by one man—the inventor himself. It was armed with a long drill. The hope was that the *Turtle* would be able to position itself under a British warship. Then, the intrepid one-man crew would assault the unsuspecting vessel by drilling a hole in its wooden bottom—or, if required, a number of them—thus sinking it. Alas, the very first (and, as matters turned out, last) effort ended in failure. The *Turtle's* innovative inventor and captain had not counted on running into, or, more accurately, under, a ship possessing a copper bottom. Poor *Turtle* was almost immediately "defanged."

Throughout the first half of the nineteenth century, there was some planning and Robert Fulton, the inventor of the first steam boat, even made a prototype. It was not until the American Civil War, however, that submarines were taken seriously. The Confederacy, even more heavily outmanned and outgunned on the sea than it was on land, was being subjected to a Union blockade, and there seemed to be little that could be done about it. An unconventional approach was thought to be necessary, and what resulted was the *Hunley,* the world's first operational (sort of) combat submarine. It was armed with a mine placed on the end of a spar extending from the bow of the vessel, certainly, from a technological point of view, an improvement over Bushnell's approach, but something which would prove fatal to the submarine itself. Even before it went into combat, the *Hunley* proved to be something of a problem child. During her initial trials, she sank to the bottom three times, drowning her entire crew on each occasion. Finally, in February, 1864, the *Hunley* was able to sneak up on the Union blockader, *Housatonic,* cruising off of Charleston, South Carolina. The spar-mounted mine (in the parlance of the times, a mine was a "torpedo"), made contact with the Union ship. There was an explosion, and the *Housatonic* sank, the first victim of a submarine in history. The force of the explosion, however, also sufficed to sink the *Hunley* which, as on three previous occasions, took her entire crew to the bottom, this time, permanently. For awhile, hypotheses regarding the use of the submarine were under something of a cloud.

In 1898, however, the American inventor, John P. Holland (1840–1914), succeeded in building the first truly practical submarine. As in the case of Hiram Maxim, the inventor of the first truly practical machine-gun, an American invention attracted considerable interest abroad. By the time of the First World War, Great Britain had 74 of the "unBritish" vessels. They were designed, however, mainly for coastal patrol duties, and only 18 of them were capable of long-range action. Of Germany's 33 submarines, 28 were long-range. As we have seen, their effectiveness was demonstrated very quickly. Within six months, they would be fulfilling a novel function, one largely unanticipated by pre-war strategists. Shortly after the Dogger Banks Action, the German government announced that it would consider certain foodstuffs destined for Great Britain to be contraband. The British government responded by impounding the *Wilhelmina,* an American—and hence neutral—ship docked at the British port of Falmouth. It was carrying a cargo of food to Germany. Shortly thereafter, the German government responded by declaring that, after February 18, 1915, the waters around the British Isles were a war zone, and that any enemy ship entering it was liable to be sunk without warning. On March 1, 1915, the British government declared a *total* naval blockade of Germany. *No* ship, no matter *what* its nationality, would be allowed to enter German waters, and any ship leaving a German port would be liable for immediate destruction. Thus, by the beginning of March, 1915, there were two officially-declared blockades underway. In the end, each would prove to be quite effective—but, one of them especially so; in fact, as some have seen it, perhaps decisive.

Germany's advantage in long-range submarines allowed her to undertake an, up to then, quite unconventional blockade of Great Britain. Since the Royal Navy pretty much "ruled the waves," the Germans would have to utilize this approach. Pretty soon it became plain to all that, while German submarines (or "U-boats") would attack naval targets of opportunity, their usual victims were merchant ships. And, more often than not, these would be sunk without warning. The reason for this was obvious. If a German submarine commander took the time—and, at first, some did—to warn the crew of a merchant ship that he was about to torpedo it, he would be taking a terrible chance. What was to prevent the captain of the threatened vessel from wiring the submarine's position to interested naval authorities? Since World War One submarines had to travel on the surface most of the time—this due to their limited cruising range underwater—they were vulnerable to attack for relatively long intervals. Thin-skinned, and equipped with cannon effective only for shelling unarmed ships, they could be easily sunk if caught on the surface (later, of course, when underwater listening devices were developed and "depth bombs" brought into play, they were liable for destruction under it as well). Thus, it was soon obvious, that effective submarine attacks would have to be made without warning. Allied propagandists, for obvious reasons insensitive to German tactical problems, made a great deal of German submarines torpedoing merchant ships without warning. In May, 1915, they were provided with an impressive reason for indignation, real or feigned.

Towards the end of April, the Imperial German Embassy placed a notice in New York papers in which it declared that, " 'in accordance with formal notice given by the Imperial German Government,' " any ship flying the colors of Great Britain or any of its Allies was a legitimate target for destruction and " 'that travellers . . . sailing on ships of Great Britain or her allies do so at their own risk.' "[1] On May 1, 1915, the Cunard liner, *Lusitania,* weighed anchor and set sail for Liverpool. Several hundred American citizens planned to travel on the *Lusitania,* but only one of these, a clergyman, cancelled his reservation. Perhaps his more intimate appreciation of the often "strange ways" of a Providence which, at times, seemed less than benign, caused him to take the German warning more seriously. In the early afternoon of May 7, 1915, the German submarine, U-20, under the command of Commander Walter Schwieger, was patrolling at periscope depth off the coast of Ireland. Suddenly, there hove into view the plumpest, most enticing target imaginable. It was the *Lusitania,* of course, astonishingly enough, unescorted, and even more astonishing, unaccountably not adhering to the zig-zag pattern prescribed for ships steaming in submarine-infested waters. Commander Schwieger later stated that he would have preferred to have surfaced and warned the *Lusitania* of her impending fate. His ship, however, was short of fuel, he had but three torpedoes left, and he knew that British merchant ships, even passenger ships, had been instructed to attempt to ram U-boats should they be caught on the surface. He was also aware that, shortly before the war, the *Lusitania* had been extensively overhauled in order to provide for the carrying of troops and munitions, and that there were gun emplacements on board. He was uncertain whether or not they were in fact armed. What was certain was that this putatively innocent ship was in fact of a semi-naval nature, and that it was described by the British Admiralty as an "auxillary cruiser." It was shortly after lunch had been served to her passengers, few of any of whom knew of "Lucy's" (as the great liner was affectionately dubbed) secret identity, that Commander Schwieger, quashing whatever personal doubts he might have had, ordered the launching of a single torpedo.

The day before the *Lusitania* was due to sight the Irish coast, the Admiralty had warned its captain, William Turner, that there were U-boats in the area, and that precautions had to be taken. These precautions were of particular importance since a cruiser which was supposed to provide escort for him would not be available for that purpose. Extra lookouts were put in place, and life-boats swung out on davits, just in case. Yet, for reasons which are still unclear, Captain Turner had not taken measures which would had made an actual attack more difficult in the first place. First of all, as we have seen, he was not following a zig-zag course. Secondly, the *Lusitania,* which was capable of steaming at 25 knots, was steaming at 18 knots. If steaming at full speed, she would have been much more difficult to hit. Commander Schwieger's aim was true, and the *Lusitania* was hit on the starboard bow. There was an explosion, then, a second, more muffled roar. Almost immediately, the ship listed sharply to starboard and began to sink. The angle of the list, and the rapidity with which she took on water, made it impossible to properly fill and launch but a fraction of the life-boats. In fact, of 48 boats aboard, only 6 reached the water's surface filled and intact. There was enormous confusion, rapidly yielding to panic, aboard the *Lusitania,* so much so that, according to Commander Schwieger, he could not bring himself to launch a second torpedo into the mass of terrified humanity. He didn't need to, anyway. The explosion from the initial hit might have caused cases of ammunition carried aboard to explode in turn, and it was this second blast that was responsible for the great ship's rapid demise. Unlike, in the case of the *Titanic,* her former short-lived competitor, there was no time for gallantry or moving farewells. Eighteen minutes after U-20's torpedo had struck, the *Lusitania* was gone. Of slightly under 2,000 passengers and crew aboard, 1,198 died, among them 128 Americans, as in the case of the *Titanic,* some of them socially prominent.

In general, American reaction to the sinking of the *Lusitania* was that of outrage and such was not assuaged by the German government's claim that the *Lusitania* had not been, after all, an innocent passenger vessel and thus, according to the rules of war, her sinking was thoroughly justifiable. Nor was public opinion in the United States much influenced by this government's seeking to absolve itself from blame for the loss of American lives because, after all, those foolish enough to have booked passage on the ship had been warned of what might lie ahead. As an editorial in the *New York Nation* put it: " 'To speak of technicalities and the rules of war in the face of such wholesale murder on the high seas is a waste of time.' " The editorial went on to declare that " 'The torpedo that sank the *Lusitania* also sank Germany in the opinion of mankind . . .' "[2] From the point of view of what would occur in the years ahead, this last statement would prove to be of immense importance. When all is said and done, one can still declare that the Germans were justified in sinking the *Lusitania.* After all, it was carrying a rather large cargo of munitions, was probably armed, and, in any case, had instructions to ram any German submarine it might be fortunate enough to catch on the surface. Moreover, America's claims—voiced, among others, by President Woodrow Wilson—that its citizens had the right to go wandering about all over the world in a time of general warfare and not expect to be in anyway harmed, struck many Germans (and now, many years after the fact, many non-Germans as well) as being informed by an odd blend of arrogance and naiveté. Ultimately, however, whatever one's opinion on British underhandedness with regard to the role of the *Lusitania,* her sinking was, moral issues to the side, a monumental blunder. Naturally, Allied public opinion, particularly, of course, British, was reinforced in its belief that the war against Germany was a veritable crusade against cold, remorselessly cruel "Huns" who were capable of anything. In neutral America, already, for the most part, inclined to favor the Allied cause (for reasons we will examine later), the liner's sinking was an atrocity of the first order, and the fact that a large number of Americans died made most of their countrymen even less willing to consider legal, much less strategic, justifications for the deed. Most Americans who followed public affairs knew that the United States, from the beginning, had been willing to sell ammunition and materials useful in its manufacture to anyone who could come across the Atlantic and purchase such. German merchant vessels had been driven to port by the Royal Navy almost from the start of the war. Thus, Great Britain and her allies had the seas pretty much to themselves so far as trade was concerned. Most assuredly, they were taking advantage of this. Certainly, then, it was only fair that Germany "be allowed" to use whatever means at its disposal to interdict shipments of materials which would be used to kill or maim its soldiers. Yet, somehow, the sinking of the *Lusitania,* however justifiable it might have been from a legal or technical point of view, was not worth the cost Germany had to pay with regard to public opinion, particularly, and ominously, that of the United States. All of the explanations, justifications, and disclaimers provided by the German government could not efface from mind's eye the sight of terrified people struggling, mostly in vain, to get into life-boats; of separated and desperate family members, using their last minutes of life trying to find one another; of children, last cries for fathers and mothers stifled in their throats by sea-water. Maybe it was unfair, but, for most familiar with the *Lusitania* horror, these images outweighed by far the rationalizations, however justifiable, proffered by the German government and those who sympathized with it. However much cant and hypocrisy might have prevailed in British government and Admiralty circles, it was in fact Great Britain which gained the most from the sinking of the *Lusitania.* And, by Western Front standards, a major "gain" which cost under 1,500 lives was, after all, something of a bargain. Germany's sinking of the *Lusitania* pointed to a problem that country had throughout the war. While certainly not insensitive to world opinion—indeed, its pained efforts to justify its action shows that it was—the German government often was astonishingly insensitive in areas of public relations. Shortly after the terrible event of May 7, 1915, it was revealed that it had celebrated this "victory" by striking a medal. On one side, there was death in the act of selling tickets to passengers. The scene is crowned with the saying "Business above everything." On the reverse side, there is depicted the great ship descending to its grave. Beneath the scene, there is reference to its being sunk by a German submarine, above it, the slogan, "No Contraband." There were some who declared that the medal was a fake, planted by British intelligence to discredit Germany. Most familiar with the topic, however, accept it as authentic—the only argument being over if it was struck before or after the sinking. That it revealed an insensitivity so gross as to be almost beyond belief cannot be argued. In the vital areas of propaganda and public opinion, the German government often displayed the same stolid stupidity and unwillingness to learn as did their often befuddled opponents on the Western Front.

Whatever its obvious lack of skills in the crucial area of public relations, the German government was very much concerned to keep the United States neutral. Thus it was that, after a *westbound* British vessel, the *Arabic,* was torpedoed on August 19, 1915, and three Americans were numbered amidst those lost, it responded to American protests by declaring that, in future, passenger ships would not be sunk without warning. On September 18, in order to further reduce the possibility of running afoul of American shipping or sinking ships with Americans on them, the German Navy pulled its submarines out of the western approaches to Great Britain, and out of the Channel. Such caving in to American pressure had to have created problems for the German war effort and, under pressure from the naval high command, the government, on March 13, 1916, declared that German submarines would be allowed to sink British ships in the waters around the British

Isles without warning if such did not appear to be passenger vessels. Naturally, this left a great deal to the individual submarine commander's discretion and, eleven days later, the channel steamer, *Sussex,* was torpedoed. Though it did not sink, there were many casualties, several Americans among them. Rejecting all German protestations, the United States government threatened to break off diplomatic relations. The eventual German response, presented on April 24, 1916, was the so-called "*Sussex* Pledge," in which the German government stated that it was instructing its submarine commanders not to sink passenger vessels without warning. Essentially, it was merely a new version of the promise made after the sinking of the *Arabic.*

German concessions with regard to submarine warfare were made under American pressure. They were done in the hope of keeping the United States out of the war. Many in both German naval and army circles were opposed to them. As they saw it, America was really neutral only in name. After all, American industry was making substantial contributions, in munitions and raw materials, to the Allied war effort. Nobody wanted the New World power to enter the war, but, as many military people came to see it, German strategic necessities could not be held captive to pious hopes. Anyway, if, somehow, the Allies could be knocked out of the war before America entered it, victory would be assured. It was only a matter of time before perceived military realities would cause the German government to order the commencement of completely unrestricted submarine warfare. In truth, it is entirely probable that strategic realities regarding not only military conditions on land and sea, but the country as a whole gave Germany little choice. For, as Germany's U-boat fleet, after gaining impressive but isolated successes, was forced to hobble itself in response to American protestations, another, far more thorough-going blockade was beginning to have truly devastating effects on the German nation as a whole.

Shortly after the outbreak of hostilities, British and French ships began intercepting merchant vessels bearing goods to Germany. At that point, they let foodstuffs through. As we have seen, however, after the seizure of the *Wilhelmina,* and the German response to it, a total blockade of Germany was announced on March 1, 1915. With no German surface fleet around to contest it, and Germany's relatively small submarine fleet (it remained such throughout the war, despite a crash U-boat building program) stretched too thin to both harass merchant shipping while taking on the Royal Navy, the British blockade—with, of course, French support—proved to be almost immediately effective. By May, 1915, the month which saw the sinking of the *Lusitania,* food rationing had been introduced in Germany. Within a little more than a year, there were massive shortages in certain crucial foodstuffs and, by the winter of 1916, genuine hunger in almost all urban areas. It was a ruthlessly effective blockade in which British ships committed outrages which brought strong protests from neutral countries, including the United States.

Yet, with regard to the general public mood, at least the American one, it was plain that a general pro-Allied position prevailed. In a word, so far as American public support was concerned, it was there for the British to lose. In the German case, except for some German and Irish-Americans, and some Jews, who, while not anti-British, loathed Tsarist Russia and thus were ambivalent about the Allied cause, it was there for them to win. Naturally, the latter is by far the more difficult of tasks. Also, the British blockade—something which, in due course, became known as the "starvation blockade"—did not involve spectacular, one-shot atrocities such as the sinking of the *Lusitania.* Indeed, such were not needed. To be sure, shots were fired across bows, and occasionally a neutral merchantman was blown up (usually after the crew had been evacuated). Royal Navy ships involved in intercepting merchant vessels bound for Germany did not face most of the problems confronting German submarine commanders. Hence, they could go about their appointed tasks with an efficiency which, if at times grim, could also be almost cheerful. Thus it was, that the British blockade, which was never marked by spectacular, and thus, attention-getting atrocities, was *itself* an atrocity. While it is doubtful that few, if any, land-bound Britons died as a result of the German submarine blockade, as increasingly fierce as it became (particularly in 1917) hundreds of thousands of Germans, a horrifying percentage of them children, died from the results of a blockade which might have claimed more German civilian casualties than the air attacks of World War II. Some historians have declared that the "starvation blockade" imposed upon Germany by Great Britain was the single most significant factor contributing to the Allied victory in the Great War. We will be taking a closer look at its terrible effects on the German home front in a later chapter.

Most certainly, the role played by naval warfare in World War I was one that was not anticipated by prewar planners. To be sure, many had thought that fleets would be involved in blockades. Almost everybody, however, had expected major fleet actions. There would be one, in due course, but *only* one. That naval units, underwater and of the more conventional surface variety, would be primarily involved in blockading activities was something that nobody of consequence seemed to have anticipated, even though historical memory offered the example provided by the blockade of the Confederacy. The short-lived Confederate States of America, however, was a largely pre-industrial society which, with regards to food, was largely self-sufficient. The terrible shortages experienced by its army were due to the new country's poor distribution and miserable transportation systems. Germany was a modern, industrialized nation and, like most European industrial powers, was greatly dependent upon imported foodstuffs to feed its largely urban population. At a time when the seas were ruled by an enemy willing—as, of course, was Germany—to use all means possible to win the most bitter or wars, this had to result in an extraordinary degree of suffering on the "home front." Naturally this unanticipated anguish would have unanticipated consequences, none of them pleasant.

10

The Emergence of Aerial Warfare

FROM RECONNAISSANCE TO AIR COMBAT

ITALY'S armed forces, in their eventual victory over the Turks in the war of 1911–12, had not emerged with much luster. It had been a slipshod performance against an, at the time, third-rate opponent. In one area, however, the Italians had shown much imagination, and that was in the use of aircraft. Given important tasks with regard to scouting and reconnaissance, Italian airmen (or, as they were usually referred to back then, "aviators") had done extremely well, and it was obvious to many that airplanes would have roles to play in future wars.

During the Balkan Wars of 1912–13, the airplane served in a variety of capacities, the Bulgarians in particular being distinguished in this regard. Besides being used for scouting and reconnaissance, they assisted in directing artillery fire and, on several occasions, even undertook bombing attacks against ground troops. Yet, it was plain that, as valuable as airplanes could be on various occasions, their role in this war was that of being an adjunct to ground operations and, so far as the general staffs of the major military powers were concerned, that was to be their function in the next major war.

By the time the Great War had ended, aircraft still had to be seen as having served in a largely adjunct capacity. Overall, the Allied blockade probably had been the single most important strategic factor in the final victory and, so far as actual fighting was concerned, the enemy had been defeated on the ground. Yet, as the war dragged on, aircraft had played increasingly large roles in it and, by 1918, those it would play in World War II and beyond had been largely defined, albeit in embryonic form.

At the very beginning of the war, the warring powers disposed of less than one thousand aircraft altogether, and none of them were armed. The maximum speed of these machines was, on average, around 65 miles per hour. By the time the war ended, the warring powers had at their disposal over 10,000 aircraft, and Great Britain now had an independent air-force. All the warring powers had fighter aircraft, and these were usually armed with two machine-guns, while the average maximum speed—125 miles per hour—was almost double that of 1914 variants. Even more astonishing, there were now multi-engined planes capable of flying considerable distances and, after reaching respective destinations, disgorging loads of bombs upon enemy cities far behind the lines. Ancillary though its role still might have been, the airplane was a factor which, at the very least, had to be taken into account by military establishments.

Quite early in the war, airplanes demonstrated their usefulness in the more-or-less established realms of reconnaissance and scouting. The reader will recall that it was a British airman who, in September, 1914, observed General von Kluck's fateful turn in the direction of the Marne. At this time, every plane in European skies was serving in an observing capacity and pilots were united in a kind of brotherhood of the air. Fairly often, aircraft of the opposing sides would pass each other on the way to peeking in on respective troop dispositions and, when this happened, enemy airmen would wave at one another or, at worst, make obscene gestures. In due course, however, it dawned on just about everyone, that it would be advantageous to be able to gather valuable data while, at the same time, denying an enemy the opportunity to do the same. Thus it was that, within a matter of a few months, pilots and observers (often one and the same person) were taking aloft pistols and rifles. It was only a matter of time before some tactical genius thought of arming an airplane with machine-guns. This latest prospective "advance" in aerial technology presented aircraft designers with a conundrum of considerable proportions. Where would these weapons be placed? Machine-guns would be most effective in a "fire-forward" position and, with older "pusher" type aircraft—i.e., planes where the propeller was located behind the cockpit—this was not a problem. Newer aircraft, however, had the propeller in front of the cockpit, and it was obvious that, since this arrangement allowed for much improved performance, it represented the wave of the future. If machine-guns were to be mounted on the newer aircraft—and, at the time, they had to be attached to the fuselage; wing-mounted guns were a thing of the future—there was the very strong possibility that, when fired, they would shoot off the plane's propeller, an uninviting prospect in the best of times.

Early in 1915, a pro-German Dutchman, Anthony Fokker, came up with a timing device which caused the propeller-blade to be out of harm's way when a machine gun was fired. Thus, aircraft, at least German aircraft, could now be armed with one or two forward placed machine-guns and these could be fired through the propeller-arc. By May, 1915, the Germans were using the Fokker EI aircraft. Travelling at somewhat over 100 miles per hour, it was armed with a machine-gun synchronized to fire "through" the aircraft's propeller. Known by Allied airmen as the "Fokker scourge," it was responsible for Germany's rapidly gaining aerial supremacy. Of considerable interest with regard to the future of air warfare, the Fokker, although it could serve in traditional reconnaissance and scouting capacities, was really not designed with these in mind. It was, in truth, a "fighter"—a machine designed for the sole purpose of shooting down other planes, whether they were of the observation variety or badly-equipped Allied craft attempting to protect observers from attack.

In due course, the Allies produced aircraft equipped with synchronizing devices. Also, by mid-1916, they were putting *their* new fighters together in squadrons, allowing for a greater concentration of fighting power. The new Allied aircraft and the new tactical approach regarding their use led to Germany's loss of aerial supremacy.

In 1916, the primary tasks of airplanes were still those that had been established during the Italian-Turkish conflict and the Balkan Wars—scouting, reconnaissance, and (along with observers in stationary balloons) helping to direct artillery fire. Furthermore, their reconnaissance role was indeed strengthened by the emergence of aerial photography. Yet, by this time the airplane was beginning to capture the attention and imagination of ground-bogged soldiers and civilians alike, not because of its success in going about its important but somewhat prosaic tasks, but because of the exploits of the new "fighter" pilots.

As we have seen, the "fighter" aircraft originally was supposed to keep skies free for observation planes to carry out their missions, unhindered by aerial opposition. After the Allies countered the "Fokker Scourge" with new planes and tactics of their own, however, plane-to-plane battles took on a dimension of their own. Far above the trenches and shell-pitted seas of mud in which traditional military glories seemed to have been forever entombed, daring, at times almost maddeningly individualistic, young men engaged in a new century's version of single combat. In frail machines of fabric, wood, and wire—in the first year or so of air combat, a pilot would be as much concerned about having a wing drop off as he would about being downed by enemy action—they seemed to embody a kind of updated knightly ethic. Soon, by a kind of unspoken universal agreement, it was decided that anyone who downed five or more enemy aircraft would be known as an "ace," and folks on respective home fronts and, at times, even soldiers (who, to be sure, more often than not had other things on their minds) would follow their exploits with enthusiasm. Naturally, as in the case of all war-related activities, knightly duelling in the skies had its dark side. Machines caught fire easily and, under certain circumstances, could burn up in a matter of seconds. At the war's beginning, nobody carried parachutes—these would not be widely distributed until fairly late in the war and, even then, many pilots would not have access to them—and, if a plane were on fire, one had the choice of either jumping to a quick, but horrible death, or burning up in an often much slower one. Most who followed the aerial exploits of their favorite aces, however, chose not to reflect on such issues and, to be sure, the extraordinarily daring exploits of World War I aces would suggest that they rarely did either. For civilians in particular who, even though they were rarely, if ever, told the truth about the nature and progress of the Great War, certainly knew that things were not proceeding according to earlier expectations, the airman provided a kind of link to a better, more heroic past. German aces such as Manfred von Richthofen (known as the "Red Baron," he apparently has been reincarnated as the nemesis of "Snoopy," the canine member of the "Peanuts" family), and Oswald Boelcke, French air heroes such as Rene Fonck, and Charles Nungesser, the leading British aces, Edward Mannock and Billy Bishop (the latter, a Canadian, was driven by an intense hatred for the enemy which was rather unusual) and Belgium's Willey Coppens became legendary figures at a time when old mythologies were being either heavily shaken or mortally wounded. Even as daring young men, in ways reminiscent of knights of old, fought their individual duels for the sky, aerial warfare became more sophisticated, more modern. By the spring of 1915, airplanes were attacking ground troops, strafing them with machine-gun fire and dropping primitive bombs—at first, very ineffective—upon them. By the following year, air-raids on enemy supply and transportation systems were taking place and, while the "air forces" involved were not extensive enough—nor was their equipment sophisticated enough—for these to do extensive damage, patterns for future developments were being set.

While home-front folk were fascinated by one-on-one air combat, there was an increasing tendency for planes to travel in larger groups, and in formation. Thus it was that, by the end of 1917, air combat often involved fifty or more planes on each side. By this time, it should be noted, the Allies, due to a steadily increasing advantage in numbers, generally ruled Western Front skies, although, to be sure, there were occasional, sometimes crucial, exceptions. Also, it should be noted that Germany produced probably the most effective fighter of the war, the Fokker DVII, a biplane machine which was fast for the time (130 miles per hour), and had an unusually rapid rate of climb. Yet, as matters would work out in the next world war, there were simply too many, and steadily improving, Allied aircraft and, in the end, Germany's fine aircraft and often excellent pilots were overwhelmed by French Nieuports and S.P.A.Ds and British Sopwith Camels. As in the case of the one on the ground, the air war turned out to be attritional. As early as 1915, Germany did produce an all-metal monoplane, far in advance of its time. For a variety of reasons, however, it was never mass-produced, and none of this type found their way into combat. Even if they had, it is highly doubtful that there would have been enough of them to turn the tide and, in any event, one of the advantages most quickly lost in military affairs is that of technical superiority.

ATTEMPTS AT STRATEGIC USE OF AIR POWER

During the German attack on the Belgian fortress city of Liege, in August, 1914, a monster airship, called after its inventor, a "Zeppelin," dropped bombs on the town in an effort to demoralize the population. While crude, they sufficed to kill nine people. Towards the end of the month, as German aircraft dropped propaganda leaflets on Paris urging the inhabitants to surrender, a Zeppelin dropped bombs on it, killing one woman. In 1915, Germany introduced the new year by launching Zeppelin attacks against British coastal cities and, within a very short period of time, London was being bombed. Damage was usually slight, as were casualties, but, there could be grim exceptions and the raids were disruptive and disconcerting. At first, there was precious little that could be done about them. The Zeppelins flew at an altitude which rendered them inaccessible to the British fighter aircraft of the time, and anti-aircraft artillery was in its infancy. Eventually, though, the British produced planes which could intercept the almost obscenely grotesque balloons. Furthermore, since it was known that they were filled with highly inflammable hydrogen, the machine-guns with which the new fighters were equipped fired incendiary bullets. At the same time, anti-aircraft artillery was improving rapidly. Over time, conditions in British skies became increasingly uncomfortable for Zeppelin crews (they were supplied by the navy), and, although some raids continued into 1918, the airships were gradually phased out, to be replaced by airplanes which, if not necessarily more efficient in going about their tasks, were at least less vulnerable. Paris, however, remained much more lightly defended than London, so Zeppelins began to devote attention to the city on a fairly regular basis. Raids on Great Britain killed almost 600 civilians.

Early in 1917, Germany began sending twin-engined "Gotha" bombers against British targets, London in particular. Raids by aircraft were more frequent and thus deadlier than those mounted by the Zeppelins, and they killed close to a thousand British civilians. By the summer of 1918, British air defenses, especially around London, had become efficient to the point where steadily mounting German losses forced a reduction in the number of raids on Britain. As in the case of Zeppelin attacks, Paris was now seen as the target of opportunity.

The German air attacks on London and Paris marked the introduction of what is known as "strategic bombing." Such is concerned with striking at the heart of an enemy—disrupting or, to the greatest extent possible, destroying his economic and transportation systems, while damaging morale. Since, even at the time, it was known that aerial technology had not gotten to the point where aircraft could seriously damage what we now call the "infrastructure" of a country, the ultimate, perhaps sole, purpose of these raids was to lower morale. At first, urban populations *were,* at the very least, discomfited by this new form of warfare. Over time, however, Londoners and Parisians got used to being under air attack, some apparently even revelling in the excitement of it all. As military brass hats would discover in World War II, while "terror raids" might very well produce fear, this is not the same as destroying morale; that, indeed, such raids usually have the effect of stiffening resolve to combat an enemy now perceived even more as criminal if not subhuman. Nonetheless, German attacks on British cities soon brought forth retaliatory raids on the Ruhr, the British employing twin-engined Handley-Page bombers for that purpose. By the end of the war, these raids—which took place mostly at night—had killed around 700 German civilians, while wounding 1,800 more. Interestingly enough, while the British and Germans were alone in engaging in consistent strategic bombing, Russia and Italy produced the largest bombers, ones capable of carrying over two tons of bombs. Neither power found much use for them.

In 1918, due to the pressures posed by German raids on Great Britain (now, due to better defensive measures, somewhat diminished in number), and to perceived future tactical and strategic uses of her own aircraft, Great Britain established an independent air force, and the Royal Flying Corps, previously attached to the army, became the Royal Air Force, headed by Sir Hugh Trenchard (1873–1956). The new air chief was immensely enthusiastic over the role his newly established service could play in the war and, by its end, had husbanded around 1,000 bombers in order to be able to raid the Ruhr on a consistent basis, while possibly hitting other urban and/or industrial targets as well. It was widely-suspected that at least some of the bombs used would be filled with poison gas. It would be difficult to maintain that the role of air power in the Great War had been decisive. Throughout the course of the conflict, however, its role had grown both in terms of aircraft used and, more crucially, sophistication. By war's end, those tactical and strategic uses which would be brought to ghastly maturity in World War II had been demonstrated for all to see and, by the early 1920s, some forward-looking sorts in armed forces throughout the world were convinced that, in future wars, air power would supplant ground and naval forces as playing decisive roles in the fates of nations. Over 50,000 airmen on all sides died in World War I. The goal of at least some of them was to make some sort of precedent-setting point. For these at least, their sacrifices had not been in vain, even if more recent wars have shown that air power by itself usually has not sufficed to assure those total victories predicted by visionaries who probably would have resented being labelled dystopian.

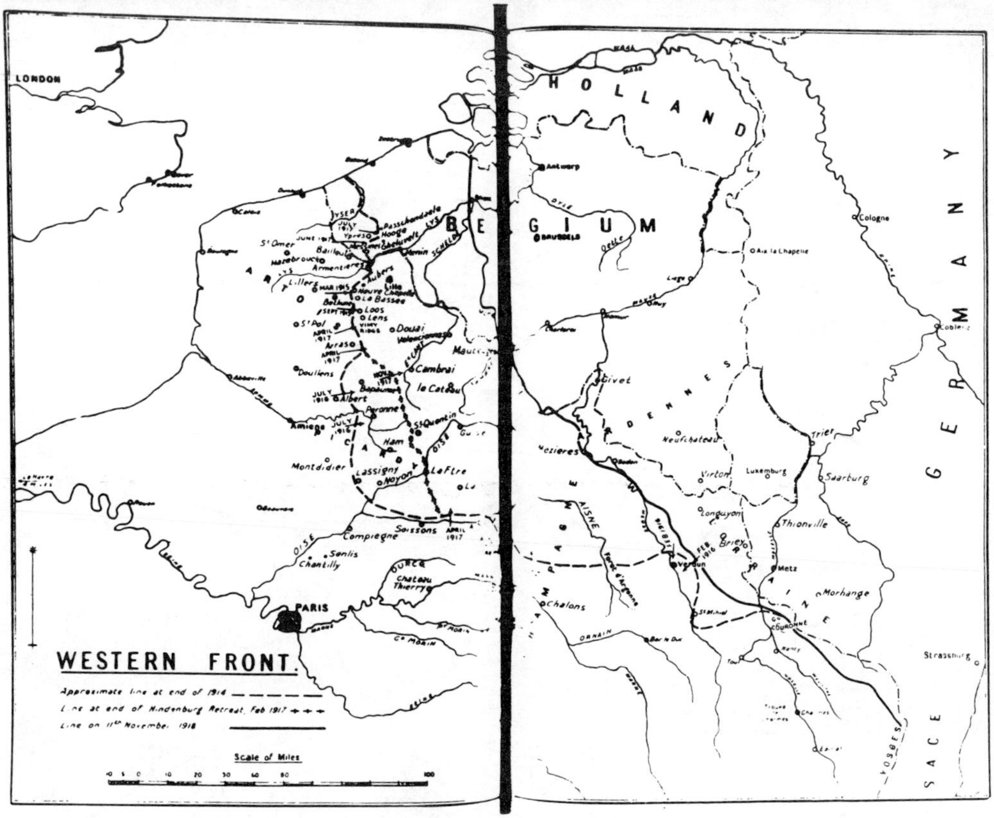
WESTERN FRONT.
Approximate line at end of 1914
Line at end of Hindenburg Retreat, Feb 1917
Line on 11th November, 1918
Scale of Miles
LONDON
HOLLAND
BELGIUM
GERMANY
ARDENNES
CHAMPAGNE
LORRAINE
ALSACE
ARTOIS
PICARDY
Antwerp
BRUSSELS
Cologne
Aix la Chapelle
Coblenz
Liege
Namur
Trier
Luxemburg
Saarburg
Thionville
Metz
Morhange
Strassburg
Verdun
Mezieres
Sedan
Givet
Neufchateau
Virton
Longuyon
Briey
Chalons
Ypres
Passchendaele
Hooge
St Omer
Hazebrouck
Bailleul
Armentieres
Lille
Menin
Aubers
Neuve Chapelle
La Bassee
Bethune
Loos
Lens
Vimy Ridge
Douai
Valenciennes
Maubeuge
St Pol
Arras
Doullens
Cambrai
le Cateau
Albert
Bapaume
Peronne
St Quentin
Amiens
Ham
Montdidier
Lassigny
Noyon
La Fère
Compiegne
Soissons
Senlis
Chantilly
Chateau Thierry
PARIS
OISE
OURCQ
AISNE
MARNE
MEUSE
MOSELLE
VOSGES
YSER
LYS
SCHELDT
SOMME
SEINE
ORNAIN
St Mihiel
COURONNE
Bar le Duc
Toul
Nancy
Epinal

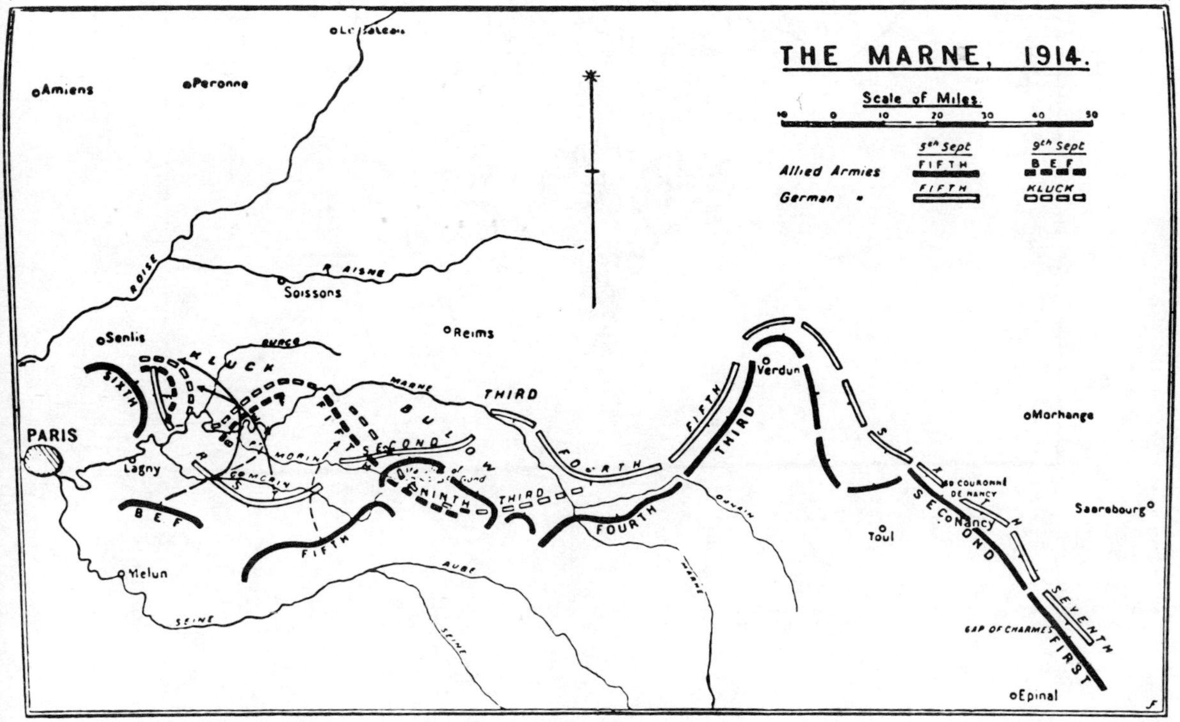
THE MARNE, 1914.
Scale of Miles
10 0 10 20 30 40 50
5th Sept
9th Sept
Allied Armies
FIFTH
BEF
German
FIFTH
KLUCK
Le Cateau
Amiens
Peronne
OISE
AISNE
Soissons
Senlis
OURCQ
Reims
MARNE
PARIS
Lagny
Melun
SEINE
AUBE
ORNAIN
Verdun
Morhange
Saarebourg
Toul
Nancy
COURONNÉ DE NANCY
GAP OF CHARMES
Epinal
SIXTH
KLUCK
BULOW
SECOND
THIRD
FOURTH
FIFTH
NINTH
BEF
SIXTH
SEVENTH
FIRST
SECOND
Gd MORIN
St MORIN

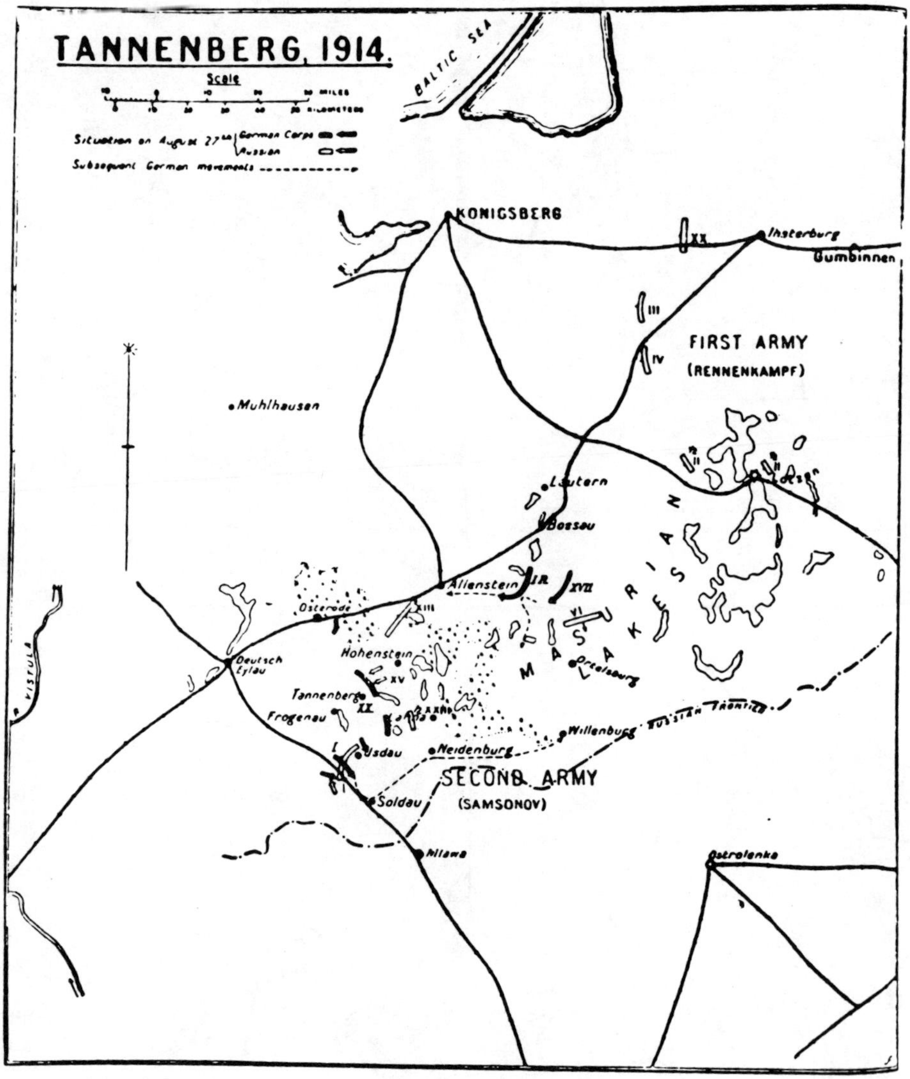
TANNENBERG, 1914.
Scale
Situation on August 27th
German Corps
Russian
Subsequent German movements
BALTIC SEA
KONIGSBERG
Insterburg
Gumbinnen
XX
III
IV
FIRST ARMY
(RENNENKAMPF)
Muhlhausen
Lautern
Bossau
Allenstein
XVII
XIII
VI
Osterode
Hohenstein
Deutsch Eylau
VISTULA
MASURIAN LAKES
Ortelsburg
Tannenberg
XV
XX
Frogenau
Willenburg
RUSSIAN FRONTIER
Usdau
Neidenburg
I
SECOND ARMY
(SAMSONOV)
Soldau
Mlawa
Ostrolenka

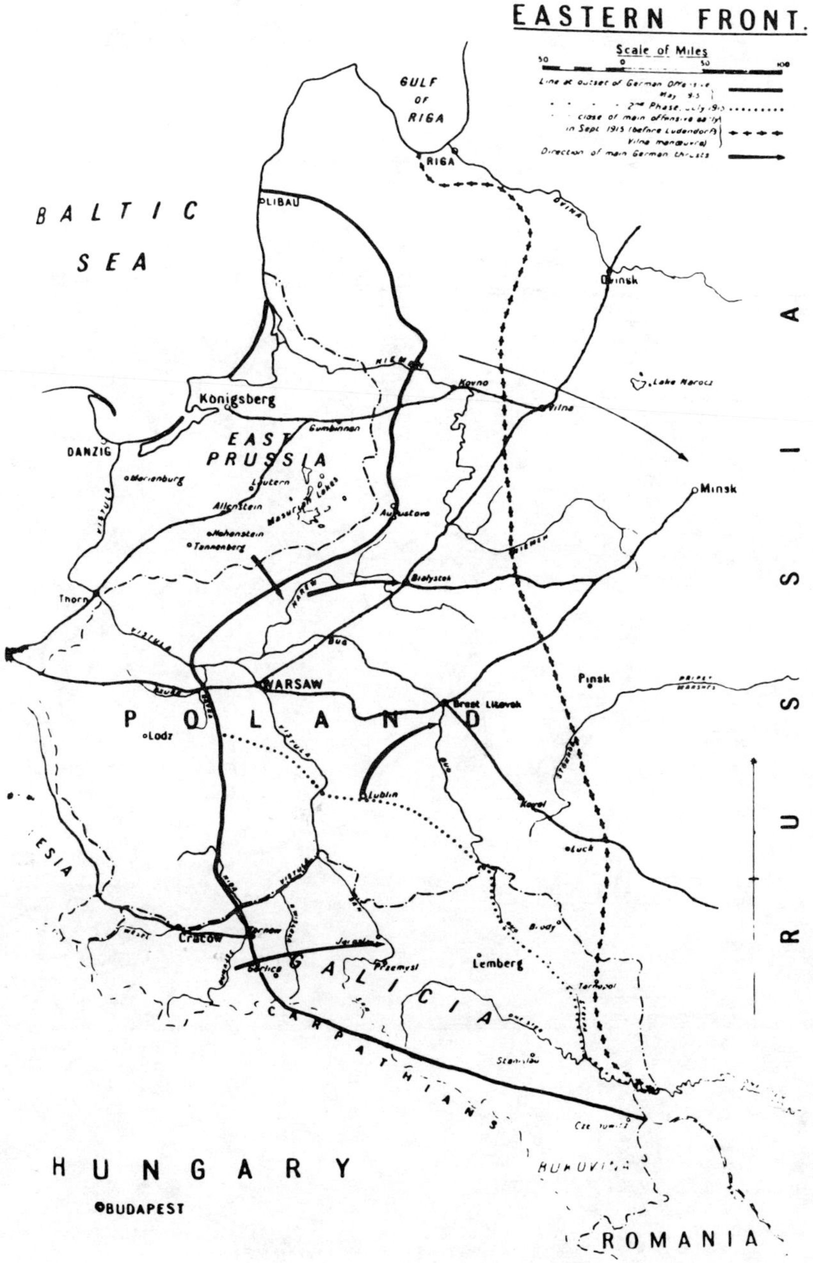
EASTERN FRONT.
Scale of Miles
GULF OF RIGA
RIGA
BALTIC SEA
LIBAU
Dvinsk
Lake Narocz
Königsberg
Kovno
Vilna
DANZIG
EAST PRUSSIA
Gumbinnen
Minsk
Allenstein
Masurian Lakes
Augustovo
Tannenberg
Bialystok
Thorn
VISTULA
WARSAW
Pinsk
Brest Litovsk
POLAND
Lodz
Lublin
Kovel
Luck
Brody
Cracow
Tarnow
Jaroslav
Przemysl
Lemberg
Gorlice
GALICIA
Tarnopol
CARPATHIANS
Stanislau
RUSSIA
HUNGARY
BUDAPEST
ROMANIA

Istabulat
R. Diyala
BAGHDAD
Diyala
Ctesiphon
R. EUPHRATES
Aziziya
R. TIGRIS
PERSIA
PERSO-MESOPOTAMIAN FRONTIER
Sanniyat
Sheikh Sa'ad
Kut al Imara
SHATT AL HAI
Amara
R. TIGRIS
KARUN R.
R. EUPHRATES
MESOPOTAMIA.
BASRA
SHATT AL ARAB
Mohammerah
PERSIAN GULF
Scale of Miles
10 0 50 100

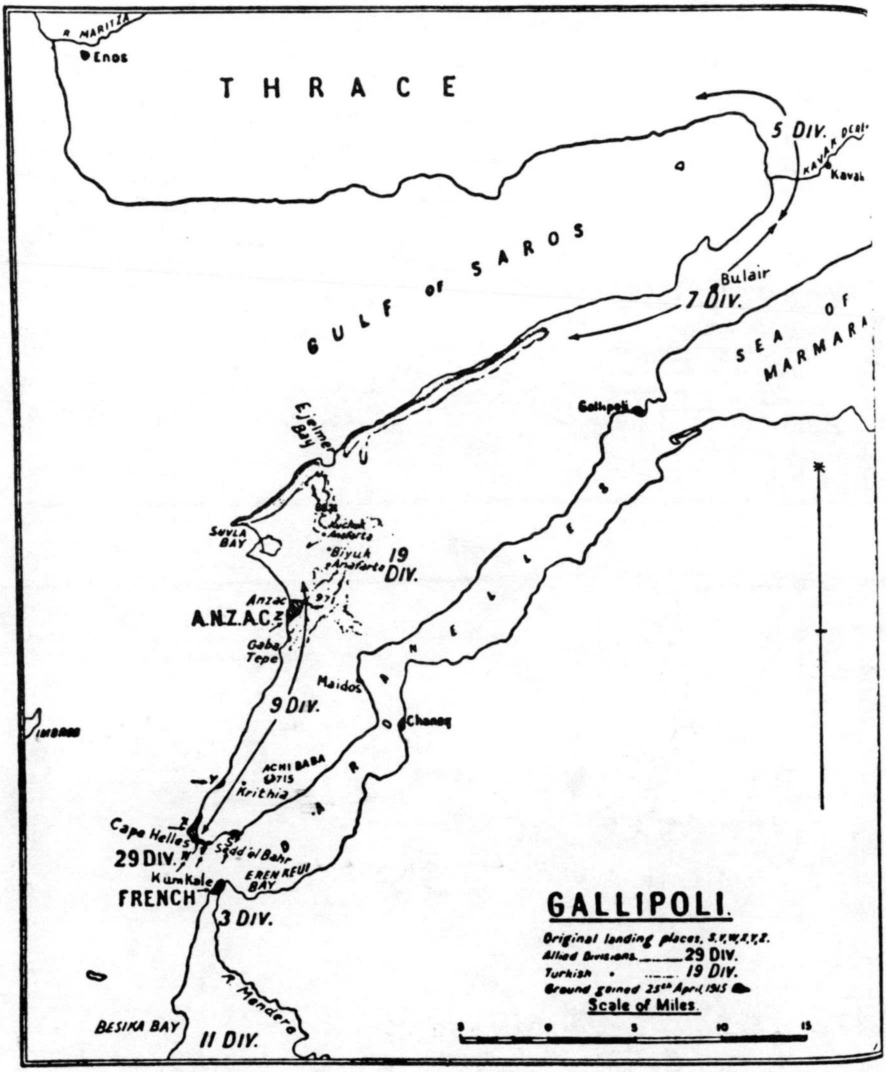

R. MARITZA
Enos
THRACE
5 DIV.
KAVAK DERE
Kavak
GULF OF SAROS
Bulair
7 DIV.
SEA OF MARMARA
Gallipoli
Ejelmer Bay
SUVLA BAY
Kuchuk Anafarta
Biyuk Anafarta
19 DIV.
Anzac
971
A.N.Z.A.C.
Z
Gaba Tepe
Maidos
9 DIV.
Chanaq
IMBROS
ACHI BABA
715
Krithia
DARDANELLES
Y
X
Cape Helles
29 DIV.
W
V
S
Sedd'el Bahr
Kumkale
EREN KEUI BAY
FRENCH
3 DIV.
R. Mendere
BESIKA BAY
11 DIV.
GALLIPOLI.
Original landing places, S, V, W, X, Y, Z.
Allied Divisions 29 DIV.
Turkish " 19 DIV.
Ground gained 25th April 1915
Scale of Miles.
5 0 5 10 15

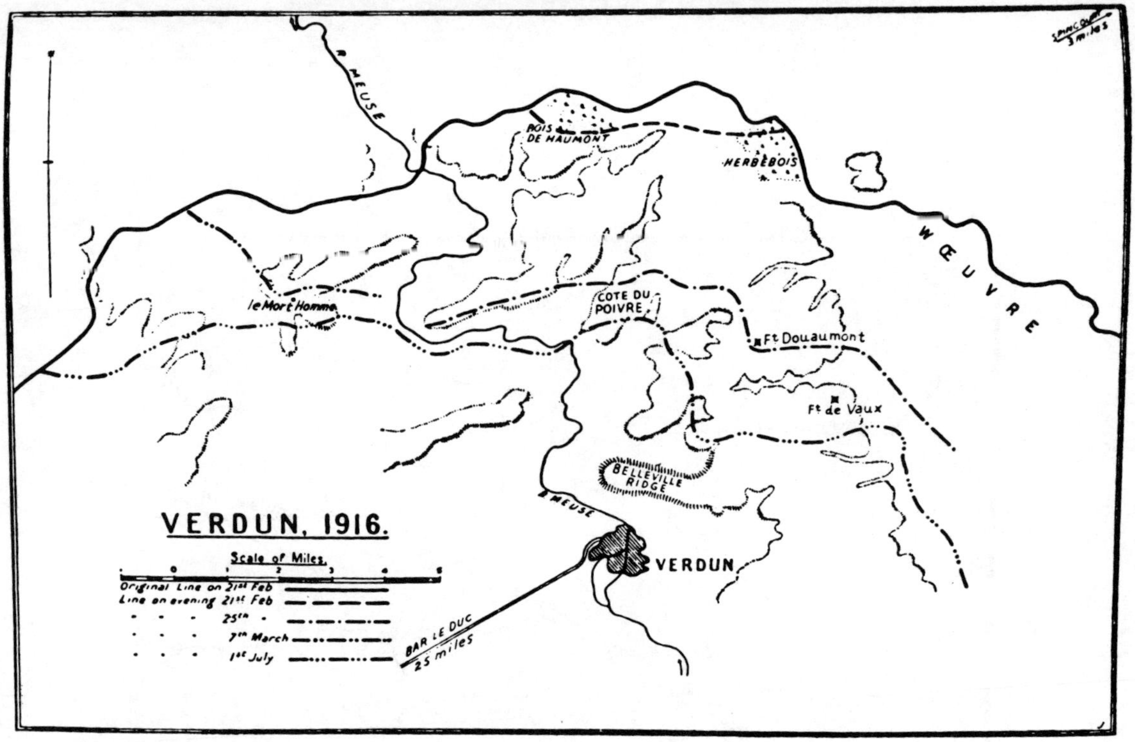

VERDUN, 1916.
Scale of Miles
Original Line on 21st Feb
Line on evening 21st Feb
25th
7th March
1st July
R. MEUSE
BOIS DE HAUMONT
HERBEBOIS
WŒUVRE
le Mort Homme
COTE DU POIVRE
Ft Douaumont
Ft de Vaux
BELLEVILLE RIDGE
R. MEUSE
VERDUN
BAR LE DUC
25 miles

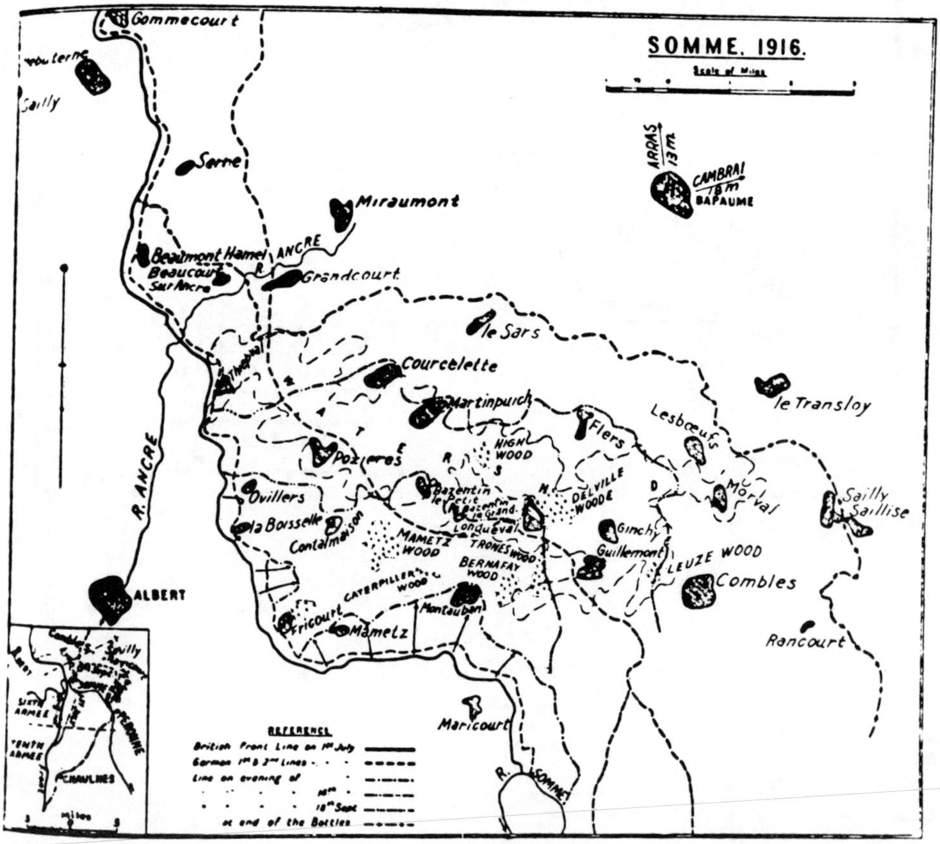

SOMME, 1916.
Scale of Miles
Gommecourt
Sailly
Serre
Miraumont
ARRAS 13m
CAMBRAI 18m
BAPAUME
Beaumont Hamel
ANCRE
Beaucourt Sur Ancre
Grandcourt
le Sars
Courcelette
Thiepval
Martinpuich
le Transloy
Lesbœufs
Flers
HIGH WOOD
Pozieres
DELVILLE WOOD
Morval
Sailly Saillise
Ovillers
Bazentin le Petit
Bazentin le Grand
Longueval
La Boisselle
Contalmaison
MAMETZ WOOD
TRONES WOOD
Ginchy
Guillemont
LEUZE WOOD
BERNAFAY WOOD
Combles
R. ANCRE
ALBERT
CATERPILLER WOOD
Fricourt
Mametz
Montauban
Rancourt
Maricourt
R. SOMME
REFERENCE
British Front Line on 1st July
German 1st & 2nd Lines
Line on evening of
18th Sept
at end of the Battles
SIXTH ARMEE
TENTH ARMEE
PERONNE
CHAULNES
Miles

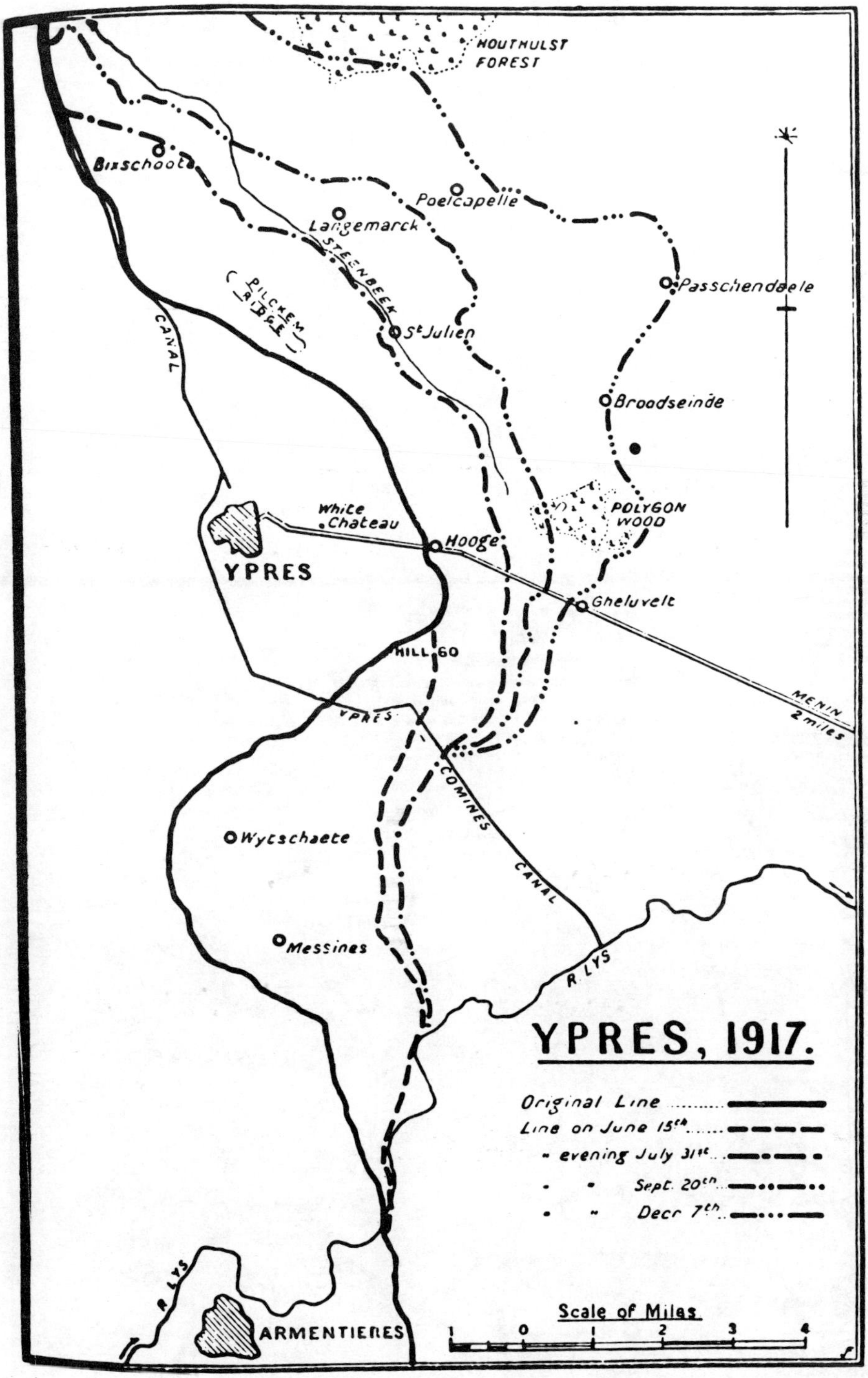
HOUTHULST FOREST
Bixschoote
Poelcapelle
Langemarck
STEENBEEK
PILCKEM RIDGE
Passchendaele
St Julien
CANAL
Broadseinde
POLYGON WOOD
White Chateau
Hooge
YPRES
Gheluvelt
HILL 60
MENIN 2 miles
YPRES
COMINES
CANAL
Wytschaete
Messines
R. LYS
YPRES, 1917.
Original Line
Line on June 15th
" evening July 31st
" " Sept. 20th
" " Decr 7th
R. LYS
ARMENTIERES
Scale of Miles
1 0 1 2 3 4

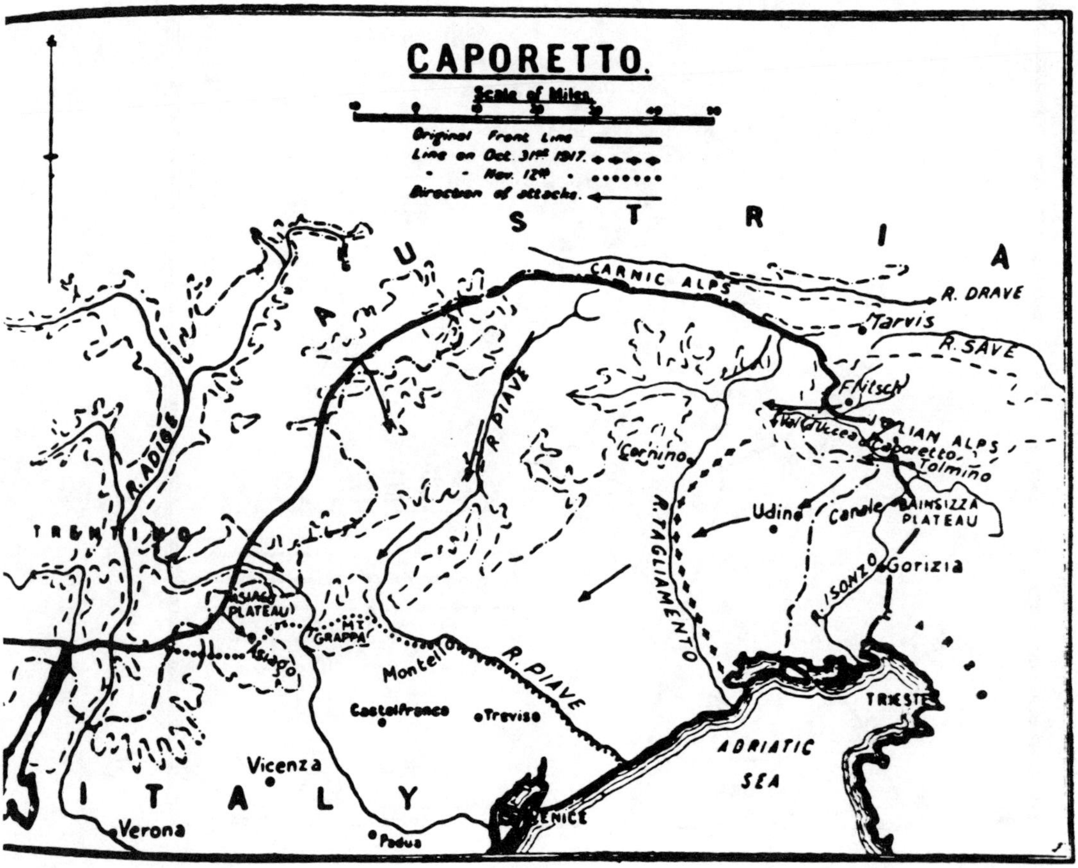

CAPORETTO.
Scale of Miles.
Original Front Line
Line on Oct. 31st 1917.
" " Nov. 12th "
Direction of attacks.
A U S T R I A
CARNIC ALPS
R. DRAVE
Tarvis
R. SAVE
Flitsch
Caporetto
Tolmino
BAINSIZZA PLATEAU
Canale
Udine
Cornino
R. TAGLIAMENTO
R. PIAVE
ISONZO
Gorizia
TRIESTE
ADRIATIC SEA
VENICE
Padua
Verona
Vicenza
I T A L Y
Castelfranco
Treviso
Montello
MT GRAPPA
ASIAGO PLATEAU
Asiago
TRENTINO
R. ADIGE

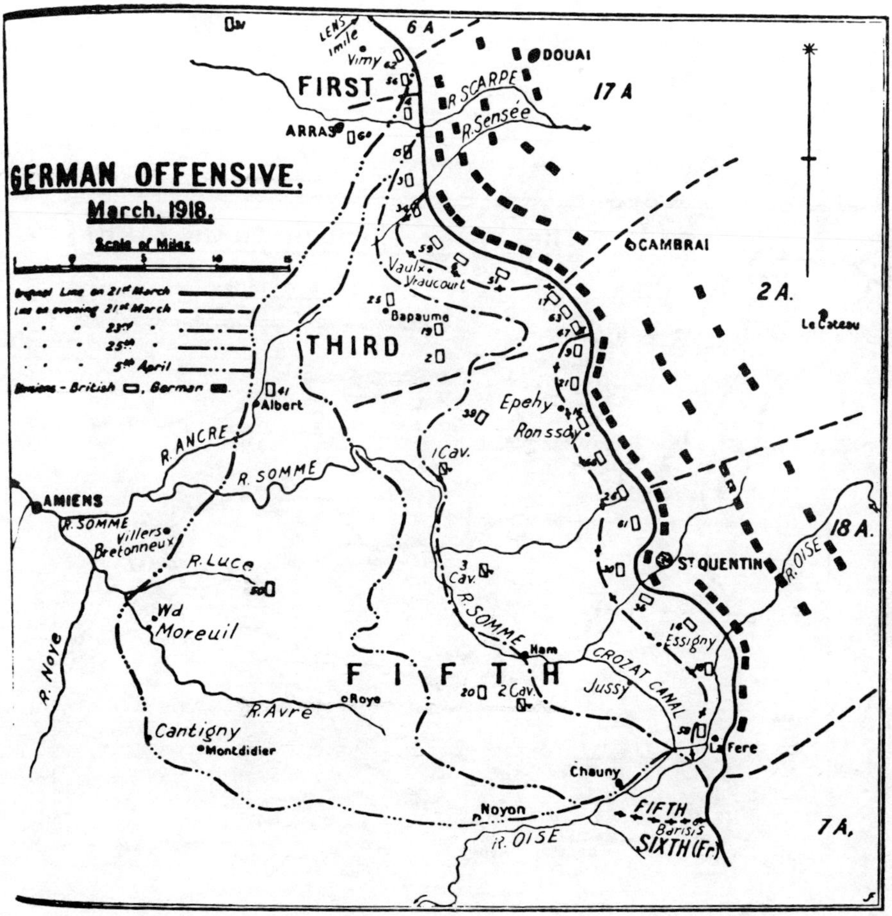
GERMAN OFFENSIVE.
March, 1918.
Scale of Miles.
Original Line on 21st March
Line on evening 21st March
23rd
25th
5th April
Divisions - British, German
FIRST
THIRD
FIFTH
6 A
17 A
2 A.
18 A.
7 A.
SIXTH (Fr)
DOUAI
CAMBRAI
Le Cateau
ST QUENTIN
ARRAS
Vimy
LENS
Bapaume
Vaulx
Vraucourt
Albert
Epehy
Ronssoy
AMIENS
Villers Bretonneux
Wd
Moreuil
Cantigny
Montdidier
Roye
Ham
Essigny
Jussy
CROZAT CANAL
Chauny
La Fere
Noyon
Barisis
R. SCARPE
R. Sensée
R. ANCRE
R. SOMME
R. Luce
R. Avre
R. Noye
R. OISE
1 Cav.
3 Cav.
2 Cav.

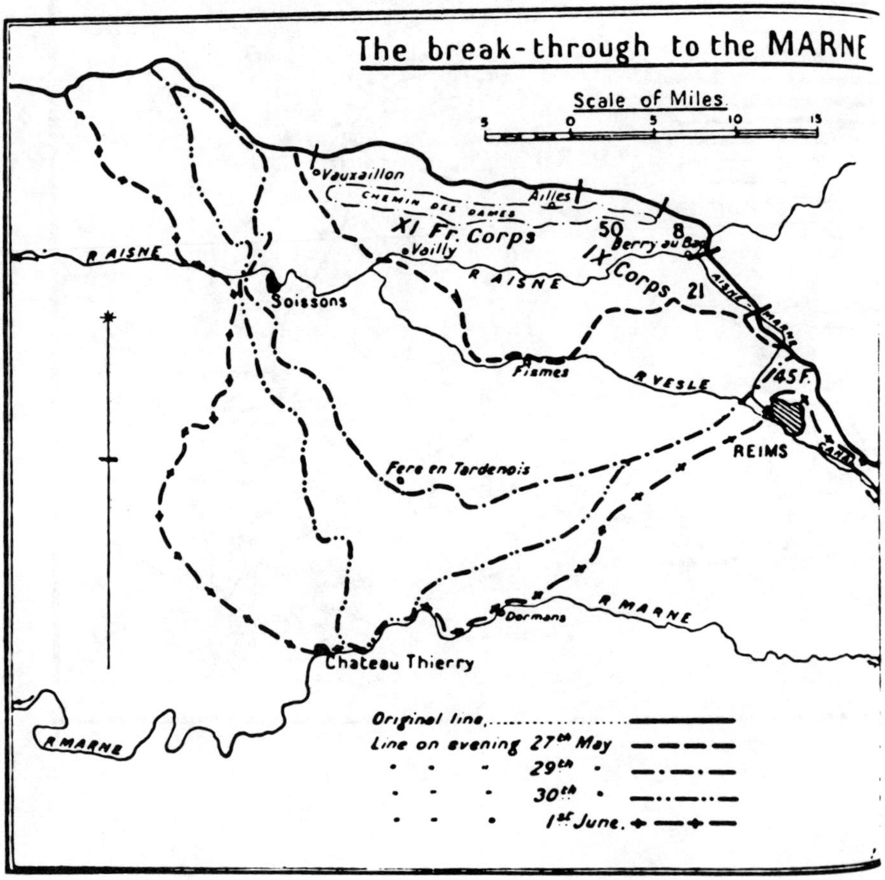
The break-through to the MARNE
Scale of Miles
5 0 5 10 15
Vauxaillon
CHEMIN DES DAMES
Ailles
XI Fr. Corps
50
8
Berry au Bac
Vailly
R. AISNE
R. AISNE
IX Corps
21
Soissons
Fismes
R. VESLE
REIMS
Fere en Tardenois
Dormans
R. MARNE
Chateau Thierry
R. MARNE
Original line
Line on evening 27th May
29th
30th
1st June.

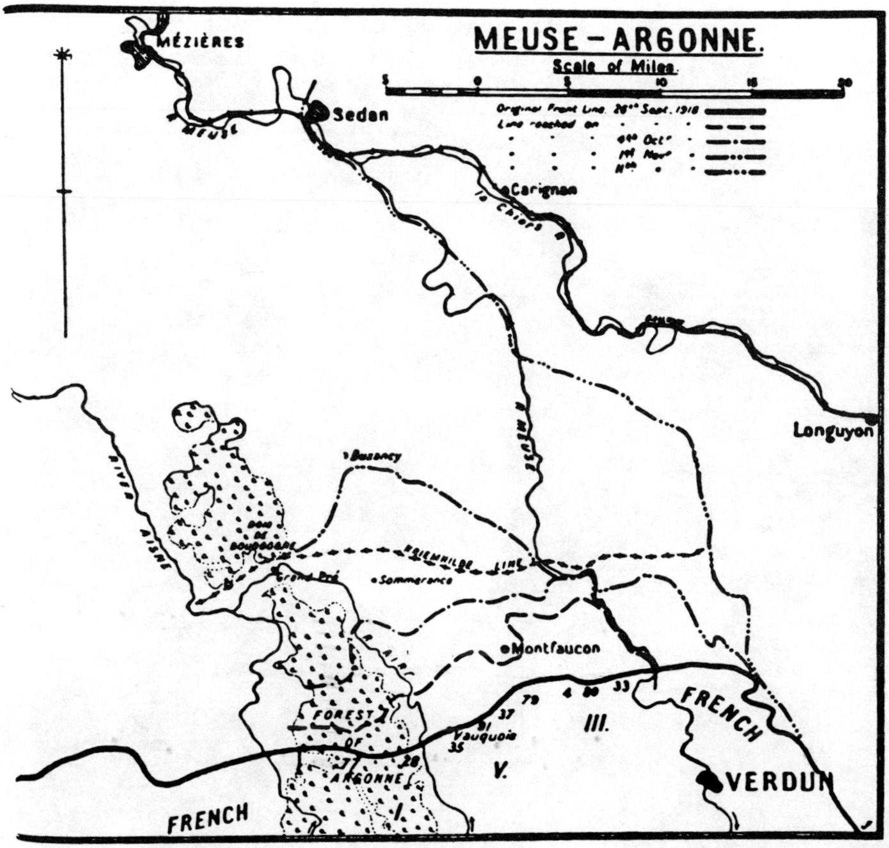

MEUSE – ARGONNE.
Scale of Miles.
5 0 5 10 15 20
Original Front Line. 26th Sept. 1918
Line reached on
4th Oct.
1st Nov.
11th
MÉZIÈRES
Sedan
MEUSE
Carignan
Chiers R.
Longuyon
Buzancy
RIVER AISNE
KRIEMHILDE LINE
Grand Pré
Sommerance
Montfaucon
R. AIRE
FOREST OF ARGONNE
79 4 80 33
37
91
Vauquois
35
77
28
III.
V.
I.
FRENCH
VERDUN
FRENCH

Fig. 1 One big happy family–much of European royalty was related, either directly or by marriage, to Queen Victoria, who appears to be not particularly happy about it. Wilhelm II of Germany is seated at far left. At his left, in a bowler hat, is Nicholas II of Russia.

Fig. 2 Francis Joseph, between 1848 and 1916, the increasingly remote Emperor of the Austro-Hungarian Empire.

Fig. 3 The doomed Franz Ferdinand and wife Sophie with their children, arguably the first orphans of the Great War.

Fig. 4 Wilhelm II, Germany's last emperor (1888-1918), strikes a characteristically bombastic pose.

Fig. 5 Gavrilo Princip, dying of tuberculosis, has just assured, wittingly or not, that he will take no small number of souls with him—Sarajevo, June 28, 1914.

Fig. 6 What a great send-off ! (Paris, August 1914)

Fig. 7 In the trenches, 1917. A British soldier stands guard while comrades sleep.

Fig. 8 French troops advancing into a barrage, near Verdun, 1916.

Fig. 9 *Inferno,* a painting by Georges Leroux.

Fig. 10 The terrible Serbian retreat, winter, 1915.

Fig. 11 A Russian soldier wearing a quite primitive gas mask. Despite improving war production, his country's miserable transportation system would always make certain that he and his comrades were badly equipped.

Fig. 12 War in an Alpine setting—Italian light artillery piece being winched into position, winter of 1915-1916.

Fig. 13 Christmas festivities—British and German troops fraternize in no-man's land, Christmas Day, 1914. Carols were sung, and gifts exchanged.

Fig. 14 Boiler room, British warship. If the vessel were fatally struck, these sailors would have little chance.

Fig. 15 Dogger Banks action, January 24, 1915—German sailors swarm over the capsized hull of the battle cruiser *Blücher*. Over nine hundred will go down with her.

Fig. 16 Early efforts at strategic aerial bombardment: German Gotha bomber being loaded up.

Fig. 17 Damage from German air raid, London—knowledge that damage and casualties were inflicted by relatively primitive machines would have been of small comfort.

Fig. 18 Italian women employed to service an ammunition dump—several hold the shells as proud mothers would their children.

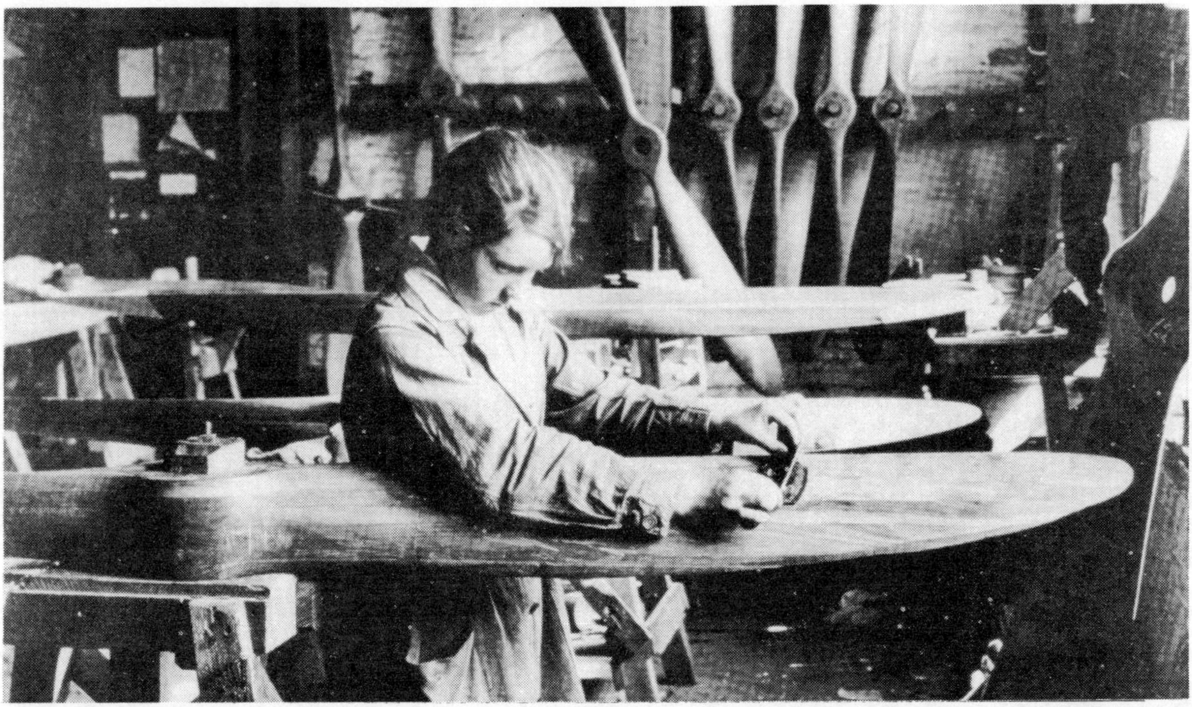

Fig. 19 An obviously determined young Englishwoman puts the finishing touches on an airplane propeller.

Fig. 20 A French woman serving her country by providing a soldier on leave with "sweet moments" which he "will always remember."

Fig. 21 The ultimate realists? Representatives of what will soon be known as the "Women's International League for Peace and Freedom" (WILPF) meet in the Hague, April 28–May 1, 1915, to address problems caused by modern history's most pointless war.

Fig. 22 Field Marshal Sir Douglas Haig, whose implacable determination and insensitivity to casualties made him ideally-suited for the Great War.

Fig. 23 Canadian troops dug in near Passchendaele, autumn, 1917—"Third Ypres," July–November, 1917.

Fig. 24 British stretcher-bearers struggling in the mud, "Third Ypres."

Fig. 25 Harry Tonks' painting, *Advanced Dressing Station at the Front,* captures the desperation, agony, and valiant efforts to deal with the conditions characteristic of such a place.

Fig. 26 A common sight—a French position after intense German shelling, probably during the spring of 1916.

11

Nineteen Sixteen: Slaughter Apotheosized

WESTERN FRONT AND THE SANCTIFICATION OF ATTRITION: VERDUN AND THE SOMME

GENERAL Erich von Falkenhayn prided himself on approaching wartime problems in a cool, logical manner. As he saw it, the war would be won or lost in the west. The Eastern Front was certainly important enough, but, the Russians, while demonstrating astonishing powers of endurance, were, by themselves, too weak militarily to constitute Germany's most dangerous foe. Moreover, it was entirely possible that even with a fairly limited commitment in the east, Germany, with whatever assistance their moribund Austro-Hungarian ally could offer, would inflict defeats upon the Russians which might drive them into revolution. On the other hand, if Germany committed herself too strongly in the east, her armies, superior though they obviously were, might find themselves drawn into the sort of morass that, slightly over one hundred years earlier, had doomed another superior army—that of Napoleon. No, a decisive victory had to be won in the west as, Falkenhayn reasoned, war-weary Russians would either rebel against their incompetent, corrupt leaders or be driven to conclude a separate peace.

In pursuing his Western Front oriented policy, Falkenhayn created some powerful enemies. Generals Ludendorff and Hindenburg, arguments bolstered by those of the wily Max von Hoffmann, declared to the Emperor, fellow generals, politicians—indeed, to anyone willling or compelled to listen to them—that the best course of action was to win a decisive victory in the east, where disparities between the opposing forces were far greater than they were in the west. If Russia were to be knocked out of the war, then Germany would be able to concentrate enough forces in the west to achieve victory there. Now, as they saw it, Falkenhayn, in pursuit of his own perverted strategic vision, seemed willing to endure costly stalemate in the west, while squandering enormous opportunities in the east.

In the face of what he perceived to be self-serving attacks mounted by subordinates lacking an overall strategic perspective, Falkenhayn remained firm in his commitment to achieving some sort of decisive decision in the west. Like Ludendorff and Hindenburg, however, he was appreciative of the terrible toll being taken by the stalemate on that front. The war had become an attritional one, to be sure, and Falkenhayn knew that, in the long run, Germany did not have the resources to win such a contest. Especially vexing for him was the fact that, in 1915, Great Britain had still not fully committed itself on the Western Front. Despite the BEF's costly failed offensives of that year, the French had still borne the burden of doing most of the fighting. This would not, could not last forever, though. The German Commander in Chief was convinced that 1916 would see Great Britain fully committed to increasingly intensive and long-term operations on the Western Front. Germany already was feeling strains posed by attritional warfare. Once the British came in, these would become far worse, and Germany could be bled to death.

Around Christmas time, 1915, Falkenhayn began to plan an operation which, he thought, offered the best chance of assuring German victory in the west and, as he saw it, the war in general. He put down his thoughts in a famous letter which he sent to his Emperor, incidentally, a letter the contents of which he chose not to share with those who would be immediately involved in what he had in mind.

First of all, he pointed out that, while Russia's offensive power had been blunted, there was no hope of annihilating its armies. In all events, there might be some collapse from within. The terrible stalemate in the west was taking an immense toll. The German troops were suffering terribly and, although their courage was unwavering, such a situation could not go on forever. A mass attack on the Allied lines would not improve matters. The failed Allied offensives had demonstrated the impossibility of a breakthrough of any consequence. As Falkenhayn saw it, Great Britain was Germany's primary enemy. Yet, for the British, "the campaign on the continent of Europe with her own troops is at bottom a side-show. Her real weapons here are the French, Russian, and Italian armies."[1] What had to be done was to weaken the most important of these armies, the French, to the point where it would be compelled to give in before England was ready to make a full-fledged commitment involving her own troops. Bearing in mind Germany's "limited resources," the best that could be done was to undertake a limited offensive in the direction of an objective "for the retention of which the French General Staff would be compelled to thrown in every man they have. If they do so the forces of France will bleed to death—as there can be no question of a voluntary withdrawal—whether we reach our goal or not."[2] Verdun was such an "objective;" i.e., one which the French would be forced to defend with all their might, exhausting themselves in futile mass counter-attacks, while Germany would be "perfectly free to accelerate or draw out her offensive, to intensify it or break it off from time to time, as suits her purpose."[3]

Obviously, at least as stated in this letter, a breakthrough as such was not important, nor was it even envisaged. In fact, if the French Army was to be bled to death, it was best that such not occur. The purpose, after all, was not to gain ground but to kill as many enemy soldiers as possible. Yet, when the commander of the 5th Army, the one which would undertake the offensive, Crown Prince Wilhelm, and his Chief of Staff, General Schmidt von Knobelsdorf, were told of the operation, mention was made only of an attack "in the Meuse area in the direction of Verdun."[4] This led the Crown Prince and Knobelsdorf to assume that capture of the fortress town was indeed the objective. Falkenhayn, aware of this assumption, never informed the commander of the 5th Army of his real intentions.

With regard to the misleading directive to the 5th Army and to Falkenhayn's allowing its commander to believe that capture of Verdun was his intention all along, we should bear in mind a statement of his made at a late stage of the Verdun battle: "Nevertheless, this fighting without visible or—for the man at the front—tangible result afforded the sternest test imaginable of the capabilities of the troops."[5] In a word, as Falkenhayn planned his offensive, he was aware that he could not tell the leadership of the army to be involved that they were engaged in a bleeding operation. The soldiers involved had to believe that they were supposed to take Verdun by storm. Otherwise, their commander in chief could not count on a sustained effort over what could become a prolonged period of time. In fact, while Falkenhayn knew the battle could not be allowed to degenerate into one of attrition—one which Germany could not win—it had to last long enough to be sure that France would bleed to death. Thus, it had to be a controlled battle, with Falkenhayn doing the controlling. In order to be certain that the assault "in the direction of Verdun" proceeded at a proper pace, neither too slowly or too rapidly, the initial area of the assault was limited. The attack was to be mounted only on the left bank of the Meuse River, which bisected the front and Verdun as well. Not only would this rule out the possibility of an immediate breakthrough, but it would serve to bring the assaulting German troops under murderous artillery cross fire from French batteries behind the west bank of the river. Yet, while an attack on only the left (or east) bank of the Meuse, involved some risks, it was perfectly consonant with the notion of a limited offensive, the object of which was to draw in as many French troops as possible while allowing the German Army, at least hypothetically, to limit its overall commitment, even if those troops immediately involved in it were put at considerable risk.

There was another way in which Falkenhayn could control what he had come to see as "his" battle. If the possibility of a breakthrough emerged, he would be certain not to send in enough reinforcements to bring it about; just enough to keep things going at the prescribed pace. Yet, the French, in order to hold the line and launch counterattacks, would have to make maximum commitments. In a word, what Falkenhayn saw as a limited effort for Germany would turn into an attritional massacre for France.

If the German commander in chief had wanted to stage a breakthrough, the French had made things easier for him to do do. Earlier, to support his failed offensives of 1915, General Joffre had stripped the French fortresses around Verdun of much of their artillery. Also, French higher ups, when told by commanders in the area that the Germans seemed to be planning some sort of major operation, simply couldn't believe it. The area which appeared to be involved was far too small for a genuine offensive. The idea of one designed not to gain ground of any consequence, but simply to kill people never occurred to them. Falkenhayn's cool logic, from which his own subordinates had to be shielded, eluded representatives of a culture known for philosophical rationalism.

While Falkenhayn did not want an initial rupturing of the French line, the attention of his enemies had to be drawn to the area of assault, as limited as this assault was supposed to have been. Thus it was that the initial German attack was to be preceded by an artillery bombardment of unprecedented intensity. At 7:15 on the morning of February 21, 1916, the bombardment commenced. It was of an intensity which the world never before had seen, or probably even thought possible. With the exception of the Eastern Front in World War II, there has been nothing like it since. The shells came down at the rate of 100,000 rounds an hour. As gunners collapsed from exhaustion, fresh comrades took their place. French troops in front-line positions were blown to pieces or churned into bloody gruel. Surprisingly enough, the relatively few survivors of the carnage still had enough of their wits about them to offer strong resistance. But, it was not enough and, by day's end, all of the front-line trenches were in German hands. Four days later, Fort Douaumont, stripped of most of its artillery, and with an undersized garrison, fell to the enemy after only brief resistance.

Many at the time, and later, thought that, at this point, the Germans could have captured Verdun. This was not, however, Falkenhayn's intention. Rather, as we have seen, he was concerned about killing as many Frenchmen as possible. Thus, while he did allow for some reinforcements to be fed into the line, there were just enough of them to keep the battle going. Nonetheless, as the French saw it, the Germans were in the process of mounting a successful attack which, even if it were taking place on a surprisingly narrow front, was threatening to capture not only the fortresses around Verdun, but the city itself. On February 26, the stunned defenders learned that they were being led by a new commander, one who, in many ways, cut across the grain of French military thinking of the time.

Henri Philippe Pétain (1856–1951) had established the reputation of being a dour, pessimistic spokesman for defensive warfare at a time when, even after the ghastly experiences of 1914–1915, there were many who held to prewar offensive doctrines. Now, however, with the Germans apparently in the position to take Verdun (Falkenhayn's true purpose had not yet been divined), what was needed was an expert in defensive warfare. At the time Pétain assumed his post, the battle had died down somewhat. Having fired off over one million shells on the first day of the battle alone, German gunners had just about run out of ammunition. On the other hand, French supplies had been exhausted. Pétain, anticipating a prolonged fight, saw that the most crucial issues would be those of communication and supply. Thus it was that Pétain, taking advantage of what, by Verdun standards, was a lull in the fighting, saw to the repair and widening of a crucial road linking the town to the rear. At the same time, he created an ingenious transport and supply system by virtue of which over 3,000 trucks were kept in constant motion, bringing men and supplies forward, dropping them off, and heading back along the road for more. Later, the road became known as the *Voie Sacrée* (or "sacred way") which, in view of the fact that many on both sides of line had come to view the war as a kind of modern crusade, is not surprising. Over time, Pétain's ingenious method was responsible for bringing 65 divisions and 27,000 tons of military material into the line. Soon, the battle was raging with full intensity and, by March 6, 1916, the German 5th Army was attacking *west* of the Meuse River. This represented a considerable departure from Falkenhayn's original approach, for now, the Germans were no longer engaged in the tightly-controlled, limited attack he had once favored. Yet, he had no choice but to do this. French artillery on the hitherto undisturbed west (right) bank of the Meuse had been wreaking havoc on his soldiers attacking on the narrow front of the east bank alone. After having to endure days of continuous protest from subordinates, Falkenhayn gave in. Now, the 5th Army was attacking on both sides of the Meuse and it was by then plain that the battle "in the direction of Verdun" was becoming an attritional one for Germans as well as for Frenchmen. Falkenhayn's harsh logic had been overtaken by the yet harsher one imposed by contemporary logistical and tactical realities. Once again, a graphic example of the Great War's running according to its own rules had been provided.

By the end of March, Falkenhayn's masterpiece had degenerated into a series of ferocious engagements over extremely discrete pieces of earth, and places such as Hill 304 and another infamous protuberance, *"Le Morte Homme"* ("Dead Man"), came to symbolize not only the horrors of Verdun, but the tactical pointlessness of the war as a whole. To be sure, the Germans had introduced a new technological innovation (it had been tested on a very limited scale earlier), the flame-thrower, and it proved to be a marvelous device for spreading terror and agonizing death. By itself, however, it could not be decisive and, as in earlier engagements, that of Verdun became a monument to ghastly persistence and squandered heroism. In May, 1916, shortly before he was killed, a young French lieutenant named Albert Joubaire recorded in his diary, "Humanity is mad! It must be mad to do what it is doing. What a massacre! What scenes of horror and carnage! I cannot find words to translate my impressions. Hell cannot be so terrible. Men are mad!"[6] The reader will note Lt. Joubaire's use of the word "translate." It was as if he were trying to render another world, articulating itself in its own tongue, accessible not only to anyone who might on some future occasion peruse his diary, but to himself.

By the time the twenty-one-year-old lieutenant was recording what turned out to be some of his last written words, it would seem that Falkenhayn, the ultimate author of his distress, had pretty much lost sight of what he had intended to do in the first place. Now, in a battle which, at this point, had become even more attritional in nature than earlier engagements, the taking of the two forlorn hills, *304* and *Le Morte Homme,* was viewed as constituting an enormous success. On

June 2, Fort Vaux, an east-bank strong-point that had been under siege for some time, finally fell to the Germans. On June 23, a massive German assault nearly succeeded in breaking the French line. In the end, though, it failed, and from that point on, it was the French who were on the attack. On October 24, a ferocious French counter-offensive was launched east of the Meuse. Fort Douaumont was retaken on the very first day, Fort Vaux, on November 2. The attack was directed by Robert Nivelle (1856–1924) who, having garnered considerable luster for its success, would soon come to replace Joffre as commander of the French Army. The results would not be pleasant.

All this lay in the future, however, one as shrouded in uncertainty as was the smoke and gas-choked Verdun landscape. By the time Nivelle launched his offensive in late October, 1916, the man who once, seemingly ages ago, had tried his hand at directing a "controlled" one was gone. On August 27, Erich von Falkenhayn was removed from his post of commander in chief and replaced with two of his most persistent critics, Hindenburg and Ludendorff. By that time, it had become obvious that his Verdun scheme had failed. To be sure, it had succeeded in one sense—the French had been compelled to commit far more of their own forces to the fray than had Falkenhayn. In fact, by the time it was all over, in December, 1916, the French Army had sent over two times the number of divisions to Verdun than did the Germans. Yet, it was plain to all that, in terms of casualties, French losses were not significantly higher than those sustained by the constantly embattled 5th Army. Falkenhayn had been proved correct in his belief that 1916 would see a major British commitment on the Western Front. On July 1, 1916, far to the west of Verdun, they launched a major offensive on the Somme. Obviously, however, he had been incorrect in assuming that his Verdun assault would knock France out of the war before Great Britain launched a major offensive of its own. In fact, despite Verdun's attritional horrors, the French High Command had been able to send several hundred thousand men to the Somme to support the British.

Things were not going all that well on the Eastern Front. On June 4, 1916, the Russians launched a major offensive against Austro-Hungarian forces, shattering several of their armies. If, Hindenburg and Ludendorff argued, Falkenhayn had allowed them to pursue their 1915 Eastern Front offensives with greater vigor, the Russian Army, even if it hadn't been completely destroyed, would have been in no position to conduct operations so massive. On August 27, there was the final straw. Romania, whose foreign policy was characterized by rapacious opportunism, decided, now that Russian armies seemed on the verge of winning decisively, to enter the war on the side of the Allies. Falkenhayn, who had assured one and all that this could not happen, at least not at that time, was fired on the same day.

Yet, as we can see, even when its progenitor had departed the scene (his next stop was Romania), the Battle of Verdun dragged on, having acquired, as in the case of all World War I battles, a momentum of its own. By the time it ground down to the point where day-to-day violence occurred in the form of raids and random shellings, over 40 million rounds of artillery had been expended in an area but several times larger than New York's Central Park. If casualties sustained in ancillary actions related to the giant battle area taken into account, French losses were close to 500,000, German, upwards of 400,000. Never before, perhaps never since—even if Stalingrad is taken into consideration—has so much suffering and horror been crowded into so small a space.

After the battle, it was noted that Falkenhayn's hair had turned virtually white. About a year before his death, in a letter to a former subordinate, he wrote, "My complaint is an inflammation of the kidneys with horrible consequences, which I have been suffering from since the New Year . . . the real cause of it is doubtless psychological, not physical . . ."[7]

As I write, 76 years after this most extraordinary event, unexploded shells still pose dangers to those who wander off of well-marked paths. It is said that, on *Le Morte Homme,* no birds sing. It is estimated that there are, as yet, possibly up to 100,000 skeletons which remain to be discovered. It is as if, in some odd way, perhaps in a dimension mercifully inaccessible to our senses, the battle is raging on even as a cruel but shaken God of history holds His breath.

Douglas Haig, John French's replacement as commander of the BEF, would later claim that his own, ill-starred 1916 military adventure had been undertaken to save the French from disaster at Verdun. In truth, however, he had a rather large-scale enterprise in mind almost from the time he assumed command. First of all, like Falkenhayn, he saw his country playing a greatly increased role in the war. Furthermore—also, very much like his German counterpart—he saw the Western Front as the area of decision. The disastrous Dardenelles operation, something which, even if it had succeeded would not, as Haig saw it, have been decisive, served simply to confirm him in his opinion that operations on in the west were the ones which really mattered.

Initially, he had mused about undertaking a massive offensive in Flanders. The Admiralty much favored such an operation. British naval chiefs assumed, incorrectly, as matters turned out, that a large proportion of Germany's submarines operated from bases on the Belgian coast. Thus, an offensive which resulted in its capture would greatly hamper the ever-growing U-boat offensive. Joffre, however, at the time, still commander of French forces, insisted that an offensive further to the southeast, in the valley of the Somme River, would be more beneficial, especially with regard to supporting his own operational plans. After some hesitation, Haig agreed, and, by the second week in February, 1916, he had planned a major offensive in the area designated by Joffre. He assumed that there would be a major breakthrough, with his beloved cavalry serving to turn the expected German retreat into a rout. Once the massacre of Verdun commenced, Joffre certainly did push Haig to undertake his offensive (in fact, before he wanted to do so); but, it was something he had planned on doing some time before Falkenhayn launched his "limited" attack on the French fortress city.

While the French 6th Army, under the command of General Marie Emile Fayolle, would participate in the attack, it would be a largely British operation. A newly-formed 4th Army, under the command of General Henry Rawlinson, plus one corps from the British 3rd Army, would constitute the major force in the Somme Offensive. Unlike the Verdun bloodbath, it would take place over, by Western Front Standards, a rather wide front. The British would be striking out over an eighteen-mile front, while the French, on their right flank, would be attacking on one of eight miles. General Fayolle's troops were mostly veteran. The same could not be said for the British soldiers.

The old professional British Army had been pretty well killed-off in the battles of 1914–1915. To take its place, conscription had been introduced early in 1916. Most of those, however, who entered the army in droves were volunteers, eagerly responding to Lord Kitchener's 1915 call for a million of them. Some young men were probably influenced to some extent by evocative recruiting posters such as one depicting a little girl confronting an obviously ashamed father with the question, "What did you do in the great war, daddy?" There were also cases, isolated, but well-publicized, of women thrusting white feathers at young men not in uniform. There could be no denying the fact, however, that those who constituted what became known as "Kitchener's army" (or, less charitably, "Kitchener's mob") were, on average, chock-full of youthful enthusiasm. All who commanded them were impressed with their optimism and their seeming immunity to cynical gibes from those who had survived earlier actions.

It soon became plain that British generals would have to place a great deal of stock in enthusiasm to carry the day for the new levies were being rushed into the lines with a minimum of training. Furthermore, what training they did receive was largely along pre-war lines, with few concessions to the harsh realities of the utterly unprecedented conflict under way. Some British commanders, to be sure, having witnessed the carnage inflicted upon troops attacking straight-up, were suggesting that other, more sophisticated, approaches to the assault be used. In the end, however, it was decided that emphases on approaches in which individual initiative might play a leading role would be too much for the still semi-civilian brains of Kitchener's lads to assimilate. Thus, when the assault on the Somme would take place, at least the major, i.e., British, portion of it would be spear-headed by soldiers advancing straight-up, in line, towards the enemy positions.

By the spring of 1916, however, the British artillery arm had been greatly strengthened, and the shell shortages of the previous year were seen as having been largely surmounted. Thus, it was assumed that even soldiers advancing straight-up would be well-supported. As we will see, this assumption would prove to be tragically erroneous. In any event, beginning on June 24, the British and French artillery commenced a ferocious bombardment. The shelling continued day and night and, within a fairly short period of time, some portions of the German front-line trenches had been reduced to cratered ruins. On June 26, the British began releasing clouds of chlorine gas from projectors as the bombardment continued unabated. Surely, when the Allied infantry went over the top they would find nothing much left to oppose them. As British soldiers watched fountains of earth intermixed with pieces of timber and wire soar heavenward and whole trees, blasted from their roots, sailing into the air, they laughed and cheered.

Only later would it be discovered that the massive bombardment of June 24–July 1, 1916 was woefully ineffectual. It was known to Haig that German positions in the Somme sector of the Western Front were the strongest to be found anywhere. The enemy had been able to fortify the area at their leisure, undisturbed by major British or French actions. What resulted was not merely an unusually labyrinthian trench system, but dugouts located deep underground. Protected from all but a direct hit from the heaviest of shells, they offered shelter to German soldiers who, unlike their British opponents were, for the most part, seasoned veterans. Some of the dugouts, particularly those inhabited by officers, had wood-paneled walls to which pictures, some rather obscene, had been affixed. In some portions of the line, dugouts were equipped with electricity, and more literary sorts could peruse the writings of Nietzsche and, one of the latest poetic hits, Stefan George, by soft lamp-light. Certainly, during the week-long intense shelling the thoughts of most German soldiers did not wander in esoteric directions and, from time to time, there *were* direct hits, tearing men to pieces and leaving survivors badly shaken. Trapped like rats in dugouts which, for all of their relative sophistication, were becoming almost unbearably fetid, hearing the world exploding all around them, almost all suffered a diminution of morale, while some indeed went mad. Yet, considering all the sound and fury, German casualties from the bombardment were relatively light. This was due not only to the strength and staying power of the German positions, but to the character of the bombardment itself.

As mentioned earlier, the British artillery arm had been greatly strengthened since 1915. Almost three million rounds of artillery had been made available for use in the Somme attack, and there were 50,000 artillerymen to see to their employment. During the week's bombardment, 1500 British guns had fired off over 1,500,000 rounds, in other words, about 15 rounds for every foot of the eighteen-mile long front. As mentioned earlier, in some areas, the German front-line trenches were all but obliterated. The vast majority of German soldiers would emerge from their dugouts shaken but quite alive, however, because the British artillery was, on the whole, not heavy enough to do what it was supposed to, i.e., cave in the dugouts, crushing, blasting to pieces, or burying alive those within. Most British artillery was of the light to medium variety and,in fact, before the British commenced their bombardment on June 24, they borrowed over 100 heavy artillery pieces from the French. They seemed to recognize that their own artillery, however much more guns and shells had been made available, possibly was not adequate for the job at hand. Even with the borrowed pieces, the number of "heavies" at the disposal of British artillerymen was not enough. There was yet another problem.

All knew that the German trenches to be attacked were shielded by unusually thick rows of barbed wire. It was assumed that the shrapnel in shells fired by light and medium artillery pieces would serve to cut the wire and thus carve paths through it for the attacking infantry. On the day of the attack, well-trained observers noted with some alarm that, in most places, the wire was still intact. The shrapnel scheme quite simply hadn't worked. The attack took place as scheduled and, at 7:28 A.M., on July 1, 1916, as German soldiers were emerging from their bunkers and setting up machine guns in what was left of their trenches, 110,000 British soldiers climbed over parapets to begin their walk across no-man's-land. They were led by a star football player who, from the edge of a trench, kicked off a ball and commenced to dribble it down to the German lines.

The British soldiers had been ordered to walk, not run, since they were to have energy enough to make liberal use of bayonets once they had reached the enemy trenches. They couldn't have advanced on the run in any case since the ground separating British and German trenches had been heavily pitted with craters created by the week-long bombardment. Within seconds after the assault began, hundreds of young men who, once in a time which might as well have been years ago (for all it now mattered) had been brimming with confidence and hope, were being mowed down by scores of intact machine guns manned by the best gunners in the world. Some of those hit were observed to simply bow their heads and fall, as if into a sudden sleep. Others cried out wildly and, as they fell, grabbed at the legs of still advancing comrades who sometimes had to use quite brutal means of fighting them off. Some soldiers reached the German wire and, finding it largely intact, tried to use wire-cutting shears to cut their way through the deadly maze. In most cases, such intrepid souls, as well as scores attempting to follow them, were cut down by machine gun and rifle fire. Many of those hit fell into the wire and, thrashing about in agony as bullets tore into them, were horribly shredded by it. The air was filled with a terrible din as sounds of machine gun and rifle fire blended with the deep-throated roar of artillery, much of which was now German, firing in support of the defenders. Occasionally, screams from wounded or dying men could be heard amidst the general uproar and, for some who would later remember the terrible day of July 1, it was as if they were hearing a hideous symphony which could have been composed only in hell.

In some cases, British infantrymen did succeed in getting through to the German forward positions. In view of the staggering losses sustained, however, there were often not enough of them to accomplish a great deal. In one case, a private, sergeant, and a lieutenant found themselves on the German side of the wire, close to the enemy trench. The rest of the company, however, was nowhere to be seen. Some time after the event, the private remembered his lieutenant's despairing query, " 'God, God, where's the rest of the boys?' "[8] By day's end, there had been shallow penetrations, of some hundreds of yards, of the German forward positions. On the British right, the French troops under General Fayolle, attacking on a narrower front and enjoying better artillery support, did somewhat better. Here, too, though, there was no breakthrough. British losses on the first day of what would become known as the "Battle of the Somme" totalled 60,000 of which 21,000 were dead. It was the worst day in history for the British Army. Many of those who died had been wounded who, trapped in no-man's land, could not be evacuated. Later, during a truce, it was discovered that a large number of these people had crawled into shell holes, wrapped themselves up in their "waterproofs," and died with field-issue Bibles in their hands. In at least some cases, there were prayers for speedier deaths and, so far as mortals looking back on events so stomach-wrenching can tell, these were the only ones answered in this tiny portion of God's earth on July 1, 1916.

Douglas Haig had thought that the first day's battle would see a massive rupture of the German lines, with his beloved cavalry pouring through to complete a rout. Indeed, it would seem that he had convinced himself that the paltry gains of July 1 constituted an enormous success. Among other lines set down for the day in his diary there were the following: " 'Reports . . . [are] most satisfactory. Our troops had everywhere crossed the enemy's front trenches.' "[9] Even the wounded encountered by Haig seemed to be "quite cheery." Rather soon, however, it penetrated his mind that there would be no one day shattering of the German lines. Quietly adjusting himself to the circumstances, he now declared that the Somme Campaign had been designed, from the beginning, to be a "wearing-out battle," the object of which was to severely, if not fatally, damage the German Army through attrition. This being the case, there was no choice but to keep it going as long as possible.

By the end of July, British casualties totalled 165,000. Haig, however, was not much bothered by them. Taking into account what the British Army called "normal wastage," he came to the conclusion that losses in July "were only about one hundred and twenty thousand more than they would have been had we not attacked." In his view, these were not "sufficient to justify any anxiety as to our ability to continue the offensive."[10] Thus, the British commander-in-chief—who, throughout the war, convinced that he was inspired by divine guidance—thought it only logical that the offensive be pressed on, even though he certainly knew by this time that gains would probably continue to be measured in yards.

In mid-November, 1916, the British captured the forlorn town of Beaumont-Hamel (about a half-mile or so from the jumping-off point of July 1), and, with that, the Somme offensive came to an end. The maximum advance had been about seven miles, average advance, four. Over 600,000 Allied troops, well over two-thirds of them British, had been lost. German losses, however, were also extremely high, and this was due to Falkenhayn's, and his successors', insistence that every metre of ground be contested, and that territory lost, no matter how small the amount, be gained back. Thus, while the first day of the Somme saw a one-sided slaughter of British troops (German losses had been around 6,000 men, one tenth of those sustained by their attackers), losses of both sides tended to become more equal as time went on. By the time the Somme fighting ended, the Germans counted over 500,000 casualties. It helps to put matters in perspective if one bears in mind that the 21,000 dead lost by the BEF on the first day of this massive, heart-breaking battle represented considerably more than one-third America's total loss of dead for the entire Vietnamese War.

In his dispatch of December 23, 1916, General Haig was enthusiastic about the results of the Somme battle. As he saw it, all the "main objects had been achieved." As matters turned out, there had been three of them. "Verdun had been relieved, the main German force had been held on the Western Front, and the enemy's strength had been considerably worn down."[11] With regard to the first point, it was certainly true that, particularly with the enormous pressures created for France by the purgatory of Verdun, Joffre had pressed Haig to commence the Somme operation. Yet, by July 1, major German attacks had been contained and, within a short period of time, the French would be counter-attacking. As for the second point, it was certainly true that the Somme offensive necessitated that Falkenhayn and successors maintain an enormous commitment of men and materiale in the west. At the same time, though, it must be pointed out that this did not prevent them from being able to detach several corps and send them east to bolster their Austrian ally, sagging in the face of an astonishing soon-to-be-described Russian offensive.

With regard to Haig's third point, however, one would have to say that he was completely correct. German strength had indeed "been considerably worn down" and, in a situation in which Germany had fewer men to lose, this was of decisive importance. By 1916, it was plain to military and civilian chiefs on both sides of the line that an attritional war was one that Germany simply could not win. Thus, all that need be done was to keep matters going to the point at which, as one British general put it, there would be two British soldiers confronting a single German one. Douglas Haig, obstinate, inflexibly-committed to fixed schemes, unwilling to hear or to see anything that might divert him from providentially-ordained tasks, was probably the ideal leader for such a conflict. As the Battle of the Somme began, the soldier-poet Siegfried Sassoon declared that "Armageddon is too immense for my solitary understanding . . . my thoughts are powerless against unhappiness so huge."[12] But, he was merely a poet, by definition alienated from "real" concerns. The British government, despite some dissenting voices, was aware of what was needed to see the war through to a proper conclusion. On December 22, 1916, one day before issuing his self-justifying dispatch concerning the Somme operation, Haig, described by some as being the "dunce" of his whiskey-making family, was promoted from general to field marshal. Later, we will provide an overall evaluation of his approach to war.

EASTERN FRONT: A RUSSIAN SURPRISE

The year 1915 had seen the Russian Army go from defeat to defeat. Yet, by year's end, it was still intact. Probably no other army could have held together under the dismal circumstances created by perpetual shortages of ammunition and supplies, bad training, at times, even worse leadership, and continuous disaster. In due course, it would be demonstrated that this seeing conglomeration of badly armed ragamuffins could be an extremely formidable force.

By the spring of 1916, the material condition of the Russian Army had improved somewhat although, to be sure, by Western Front standards, there were vast shortages and deficiencies in a number of areas. A portion of this army which, in some ways, was materially better off, was the Southwest Army, commanded by General Alexei Brusilov (1853–1926). General Brusilov was himself a first-rate commander. In the 1914 fighting against the Austro-Hungarians he had shown excellent offensive abilities. Much to the embarrassment of the Central Powers, he was about to do the same again although, as in the 1914 case, cruel logistical realities would, in the end, supervene, once again depriving Mother Russia of a decisive victory.

At the beginning of June, 1916, matters were not going well for the Allies. The Germans were still pressing hard at Verdun, and it was plain that besieged Fort Vaux could not hold out much longer. On the Italian Front, Austro-Hungarian forces were mounting an offensive in the Trentino, and the Italian Army, weakened by earlier marginally successful offensives of its own along the Isonzo, was very hard-pressed to hold its own. In desperation, the Italians pleaded with the Russians to do something to compel the Austro-Hungarians to ease up in the Trentino or, at the very least, to prevent them from sending more troops into the area. Some Russian assaults south of the Pripet

Marshes, in south-central Poland, had been planned for awhile. Now, much as Russian armies in 1914 had undertaken offensive operations before they were ready due to pleas from their Allies to ease their situation in the west, General Brusilov's Southwest Army did the same. On June 4, 1916, after the most minimal of preparations, and supported by an artillery bombardment which, on the Western Front would have been deemed to have been lamentably insufficient, four Russian armies struck out against their Austro-Hungarian opponents along a two hundred mile front, from just below the Pripet Marshes to the Romanian frontier.

Precisely because the Austro-Hungarian high command had perceived no special concentration of Russian troops at any particular point along this front, and because there had been so brief a preliminary bombardment, total surprise was achieved. While Austro-Hungarian armies at the center of the line held for awhile, those on both flanks collapsed, the Fourth and Seventh being almost completely destroyed. In three days, Brusilov's Southwest Army took over 200,000 prisoners. Threatened with the possibility of a Tannenberg-variety battle of annihilation—only on far larger a scale—the Austro-Hungarians thought it necessary to cut back operations in the Trentino, truly a God-send for Italy at that time. Hindenburg and Ludendorff, screeching that Falkenhayn's unwillingness to press issues on the Eastern Front in 1915 had made the current debacle possible, sent eighteen German divisions from their portion of the front further north to bolster the Austro-Hungarians. It was something of a familiar situation, only this time, there was a far more ominous dimension.

Up to this point, Slav units in the Austro-Hungarian Army, while often not exactly distinguished in combat, had remained loyal, albeit after a somewhat glum fashion. Now, as this most extraordinary of all Russian offensives enjoyed astonishing success, Slav soldiers, particularly those from Bohemia and Ruthenia (now, within the broken-up state of Czechoslovakia), deserted in droves. The entire Austro-Hungarian Army seemed to be teetering on the verge of imminent collapse and, as mentioned earlier, Chief of the General Staff Falkenhayn, normally opposed to extensive commitment of German forces on the Eastern Front (especially since the Verdun attacks were still being pressed at this stage, and a major British assault on the Somme was expected), was compelled to send several corps from the Western Front to help to stem the Russian tide. In heavy fighting, German troops, plus whatever Austro-Hungarian soldiers as remained in the vicinity, managed to halt the Russian advance in the north. Towards the south, however, the Russians were able to advance to the edge of the

Carpathian Mountains. At that point, drained by losses sustained in increasingly severe fighting, exhausted and short on supplies of all kinds, they could go no further.

By the end of June, the front seemed to have stabilized somewhat. A month later, though, Brusilov's forces struck again, along its central and northern portions. All through August, and well into September, the Russians were on the attack. By now, though, those grim logistical realities that had handicapped the Russian war effort from the beginning of the war began to assert themselves. Some units had all but run out of food and this had led to a ruthless pillaging of the countryside. Ammunition was becoming increasingly scarce, and, on some portions of the sprawling front, Russian artillerymen were rationed to five shells per gun per day. Now, as before, Russian infantrymen in the second wave of an attack would have to wait for comrades in the first to be shot down in order that they be able to use their rifles. In an increasing number of cases, however, there was no ammunition available for them. Therefore, Russian infantrymen would sometimes have to undertake assaults with unloaded rifles, placing exclusive reliance upon bayonet and rifle-butt.

By September 20, 1916, what became known as the "Brusilov Offensive" had ground to a halt. In terms of length of front attacked, there had been nothing like it in the west. Neither of Russia's better-armed and better-fed partners in the west had been able to mount an offensive that had gained anything approaching the amount of territory taken in this amazing campaign. In some places, Russian armies had advanced almost fifty miles. In so doing, they had inflicted staggering losses on their Austro-Hungarian and German opponents. The armies of the Central Powers lost over 600,000 men, more than 400,000 of them as prisoners. It had been an extraordinary, heroic effort on the part of an army which, in virtually every area that mattered—except courage—had never really been ready for anything approaching this new "Great War" in the first place. Yet, however amazing its achievements might have been, however much it may have provided needed services for Russia's allies, the overall results of the Brusilov Offensive were disastrous.

The unprecedented and unexpected successes of June-September, 1916 had cost the Russian Army over one million casualties. Those who survived had been offered numerous examples of how deficiencies in transportation and supply had led to massive—and, for any other army, unthinkable—suffering. Many of the finest units in the Russian Army were all but gone now. What was left had much about which to ponder, and the results of such musings (always unhealthy for states under stress) would become plain just about a half year later. General Bruslilov's offensive did not by itself lead to the Russian Revolution. Perhaps it was not even the factor most important in its taking place. Nonetheless, it is rather hard to imagine its taking place when it did without the extraordinary and terrible events that unfolded along the south-central portion of the Eastern Front between June and September, 1916.

Not surprisingly, Romania, which was "next door" to the cataclysmic events exploding on the Eastern Front, followed the goings on with considerable interest. There were reasons for this other than the obvious one provided by simple geographical proximity. Officially, the country had been linked to the Dual Alliance since the 1880s. Thus, when war broke out in 1914, one might have expected Romania to enter it on the side of Germany and Austria-Hungary. Instead, Romania chose to follow the Italian example and sit it out, waiting upon the course of events to determine what side to join if, indeed, it entered the war at all. In so doing, it was following an extraordinarily duplicitous course, one thoroughly representative of a country whose government(s) had established a reputation for corruption so mind-boggling that, in frustration, a British diplomat once defined Romania as "not a country, but a profession." At one point, the German government, in a fury over Romania's perfidy, compelled the fence-sitter to enter into trading agreements with both Germany and Austria-Hungary in order that their blockaded peoples could have access to the country's grain. Otherwise, Romania succeeded in remaining neutral.

Brusilov's initially very successful offensive, however, caused the Romanian government to decide that its interests—if not necessarily those of the Romanian people—necessitated that the country enter the war on the side of the Allies. Thus it was that, on August 27, 1916, Romania, whose Latin-based language always had allowed for a sense of cultural affinity with France, entered the war on the side of the *Entente.*

From a geographical standpoint, Romania's coming into the conflict against Austria-Hungary and Germany posed some considerable risks. Shaped like a reversed L, much of it was wedged in between the Hungarian region of Transylvania and Bulgaria, which was allied with the Central Powers. The German General Staff had anticipated that Romania might enter the war on the wrong side and had provided for large concentrations of German and Austro-Hungarian troops in Transylvania, while bringing together Bulgarian, Turkish, and a limited number of German troops to form a second powerful force along the Danube, separating Romania from Bulgaria. Thus, the newcomer could be confronted with invasions from the west and south. There was another, more crucial reason why the Romanian declaration of war was a very dangerous, perhaps even reckless, act, and that concerned the state of the Romanian Army.

In terms of sheer numbers, this army was not insignificant. On the day war was declared, over 500,000 men were ready to move. Hypothetically, at least, they could have moved very fast; but, this was due to the unhappy fact that it was pathetically ill-equipped. It can be assumed that the Romanian General Staff had had ample opportunity to observe how the conflict was being fought. Nonetheless, the roles played by machine guns, mortars, and heavy artillery seemed not to have registered with it. In any event, the army was short in all three areas. The Romanian Army was not prepared for gas warfare. Indeed, throughout the entire country, there were hardly any gas-masks to be found. By 1916, the growing importance of the airplane had been demonstrated. The very few aircraft possessed by the military did not add up to anything approaching an air force. Then, there was the question of military leadership.

While there were a few extremely lonely souls at the top who seemed to have a modicum of brain-power, the Romanian officer corps presented a picture of incompetence and corruption consonant with the general state of the country. Symptomatic of this was an official injunction declaring that, on the outbreak of hostilities, officers had to remove whatever facial rouge they might be wearing at the time. By the end of August, these merry men were leading their troops on very cautious advances into Transylvania to the west and Bulgaria to the south. By the end of the third week in September, disaster beckoned on both fronts.

The German and Austro-Hungarian forces in Transylvania were commanded by Erich von Falkenhayn who, besides having a few things to prove after the Verdun massacre, was especially embittered at Romania's entrance into the war. After all, such had been the proximate cause for his being replaced as commander of the German Army. The Bulgarian-Turkish-German force in Bulgaria was commanded by the iron-willed and extremely competent August von Mackensen, who, in the Polish campaign of 1915, had established a very good reputation. Thus it was that, on both western and southern fronts, Romanian offenses were turned back and, within a very brief period of time, the Romanian Army was in rapid retreat. At times, this army showed more courage than anyone had a right to expect from it. Whenever it chose to stand and fight, however, such a decision usually resulted in a one-sided slaughter. On December 6, 1916, German and Austro-

Hungarian troops entered Bucharest, while what was left of the Romanian Army retreated to the northeast portion of the country where, on a line running along the Siret River, it managed to link-up with Russian forces and stand firm. Almost all of Romania, however, with its considerable resources of grain and oil, was now in enemy hands.

For perhaps very understandable reasons, the very brief—and extremely one-sided—Romanian campaign has rarely been the subject of much historical scrutiny. Some commentators have suggested that, if the Romanian advance in Transylvania had been more rapid, such could have resulted in some initial military embarrassment for the Central Powers. In view of the vast disparities between the opposing forces in terms of equipment, training, and leadership, however, it is difficult to see how the final result could have been much different. Nonetheless, it is certainly true that historians representing the great powers often tend to underestimate the efforts made by not-so-great ones while, at the same time, paying little attention to the human cost often engendered by these efforts. Driven into battle by a government which can be described as being criminally irresponsible, miserably-equipped Romanian soldiers often fought hard against hopeless odds. The end of the war would see over 300,000 of them dead, a large proportion of the toll having been accrued between August and December, 1916. America's participation in World War I would cost the country about a third of this number. Often treated by historians as a "sideshow" to more crucial events, Romanian involvement in the Great War represented an enormous national tragedy. And, as is often the case in such matters, what reckoning there was would open the door to more of the same in the not-too-distant future.

JUTLAND: THE COSTLIEST ANTICLIMAX IN THE HISTORY OF NAVAL WARFARE

After a brief flurry of small unit, but nonetheless costly, naval encounters during the first six months or so of the war, German submarines and attempts to counter their activities constituted the bulk of what could be called "naval warfare." A great *fleet* action had yet to take place. In due course, one would occur, and this, largely because of accident.

In the last days of May, 1916, Admiral Sir John Jellicoe, who commanded the Grand Fleet, received a warning that a large number of

German submarines was moving towards the English coast. On May 30, this fleet steamed out from its base at Scapa Flow, rendezvoused with a force of battle cruisers under the command of Admiral Sir David Beatty, and headed towards where the submarines were suspected to be. As matters turned out, problems posed by weather conditions and logistics had forced the U-boat force to turn back. As the British would discover later, their activities had been part of a broader German plan to lure the Grand Fleet out in order that the High Seas Fleet, commanded by Admiral Reinhard Scheer, catching the British ships at a tactical disadvantage, could destroy them. The German fleet had never before ventured from home ports and Admiral Jellicoe had no idea that he was about to encounter it now.

In the afternoon of May 31, 1916, about 70 miles west of the Jutland Peninsula, the Grand and High Seas Fleets blundered into each other, and, at a range of 18,500 yards, began exchanging fire. Within an hour, British complacency with regard to naval superiority was badly shaken. The flagship of the battle cruiser fleet, HMS *Lion,* was severely hit. Then, the battle cruiser *Indefatigable* was mortally damaged, sinking in less than thirty minutes and taking with her more than 1,000 of her crew. The *Queen Mary* blew up and sank within minutes. There were no survivors among her crew of 1,266. Evidencing distress, the commander of the battle cruiser fleet, Admiral Beatty, remarked to his flag captain, "Chatfield, there seems to be something wrong with our damned ships today." [13]

There was indeed "something wrong." British naval construction had been lax in a number of crucial areas, British gunnery, at least insofar as a general fleet action was concerned, was inferior to that of the High Seas Fleet, and shells fired from its big guns had a tendency to break apart upon impact without exploding. Thus, even when British sailors did score "hits," damage was often negligible. Despite the terrible losses that resulted from these deficiencies, Admiral Beatty pressed on in engaging the obviously superior German battle cruisers. These were in retreat, but one designed to draw their British counterparts towards the main body of the High Seas Fleet which would annihilate them. With the shielding battle cruisers gone, the Grand Fleet would be at a considerable disadvantage and perhaps, at that point, the German fleet could risk engaging it. Fortunately for the British, towards nightfall, Beatty decided to turn away and head back towards the Grand Fleet. The German battle cruisers turned about in pursuit and, in the running battle which followed, it was their turn to sustain heavy damage although, due to superior ship construction, none of the stricken German vessels sank immediately.

Throughout the early evening of May 31, opposing battle cruisers, later joined by cruisers and destroyers, slugged it out, with battleships putting in occasional cameo appearances. Ships on both sides were sunk and the British finally obtained a significant success when one of their destroyers succeeding in sinking the German battleship *Pommern.* By this time, Admiral Scheer, although fully aware that his ships had "given" far more than they had "gotten" in return, had decided that a full-scale engagement with the Grand Fleet would be very dangerous, if not suicidal, and had ordered the High Seas Fleet to break off the engagement and head home. By 8:00 P.M., the British heavy units were also headed back to base, but, there were continued clashes between rival cruisers and destroyers. These lasted long enough to extend what would become known as the "Battle of Jutland" into the early hours of June 1, 1916.

Losses on both sides had been heavy, but, it was obvious to all that the British Grand Fleet had absorbed far greater punishment. It had lost three battle cruisers, three heavy armored cruisers, and eight destroyers. British tonnage sunk totalled over 117,000. Worse, over 6,000 British sailors had died in the action. The German High Seas Fleet lost one battleship, one battle cruiser, four light cruisers, and five destroyers. Tonnage lost totalled 61,180, while somewhat over 2,500 of its sailors had been killed. By all standards, Germany's officers and seamen had won a striking tactical victory. Yet, in the end, it amounted to a strategic defeat. Admiral Scheer, observing the vast number of British ships that, not yet committed to the action, were on the verge of entering it, made the no doubt wise decision that a full scale engagement could only have ended in disaster for the High Seas Fleet. Thus, he had been the first to break off the action, and this fleet headed back to home ports, never to venture forth again. In war, enforced idleness can be very dangerous for morale and, over time, German sailors, with nothing but time on their hands, would find a host of grievances to nurture. As Germany faced defeat in November, 1918, this would have grave consequences indeed. For German military men, the Jutland battle must have seemed like a microcosm of the war as a whole. German fire control, ship construction, and, as some saw it, seamanship as well, had proved superior. Yet, in the end, there had been simply too many British ships and the watery "field" had had to be abandoned to the somewhat battered but still very much intact Grand Fleet. If the battle had turned into an attritional one, German defeat would have been certain. Those who studied the battle must have been struck by a singular irony: the great *battleships* of both sides, construction of which before the war had played an important role in increasing those tensions which led to it, had not exchanged one shot between them.

German naval men knew that its qualitatively excellent High Seas Fleet could never prevail in a war of attrition against the Grand Fleet. As we have seen, General Erich von Falkenhayn had come to the realization that a war of attrition on land was one that Germany could not win. His, as he no doubt saw it, skillfully crafted Verdun scheme was supposed to have resulted in an engagement in which one side, the French, would be worn down by attrition, while the other managed to fight it in a limited manner. As we have seen, this approach failed in the end, and the result was a more-or-less conventional attritional battle in which the two sides lost around 900,000 casualties.

General Haig, at first entertained (in every sense of the word) the hope that he could achieve an immediate rupture of probably the strongest portion of the German line on the Western Front. When this failed, he seemed to accept the fact that his Somme offensive would devolve into a battle of attrition—a "wearing-out battle," as he liked to call it—and this resulted in his army gaining a maximum of seven miles of shell-churned earth. Allied (mostly British) and German losses totalled close to 1,200,000 men.

On the Eastern Front, General Brusilov's offensive, which, in terms of enemy prisoners taken and territory overrun, would be the most successful Allied offensive until the one of 1918 which ended the war, cost his armies over one million casualties, his Austro-Hungarian and German opponents, over 600,000. Thus, if the butchers' bills for major campaigns on Western and Eastern fronts are added together, we come up with the dismal total of 3,700,000 casualties, the Western Front contributions in offensives which went more-or-less nowhere. Between major engagements there were, of course, those thousands lost every week to "normal wastage." Only if one bears in mind the losses endured in the terrible land campaigns of 1916, the costliest year of the war, can the Battle of Jutland be described as "a casual item in the long butcher's bill." [14]

12

Spiritual Traumatization, Home Front Concerns, and Doomed Efforts at Peacemaking

WITNESSES TO SPIRITUAL DECAY: THE REAL "LOST GENERATION"

The term "Lost Generation" was first applied by Gertrude Stein to a group of expatriate American writers in Paris in the 1920s. Talented, sensitive, certainly alienated from a Prohibitionist America, they were also self-indulgent enough to see themselves as heroic souls doomed to suffer at the hands of intellectually vapid philistines. In the context of the American culture of the time, perhaps people such as Ernest Hemingway and F. Scott Fitzgerald did qualify as lost. But the real lost souls of the 1920s were those who either were crushed by the war or, in some terrible way, had so internalized it that the war raged on in their psyches, providing a spiritual bridge to another era of horror.

In 1916, Henri Barbusse (1874–1935) published *Le Feu,* later translated as *Under Fire.* At one point in this shockingly realistic view of life in the trenches, Barbusse reaches out to embrace his doomed comrades: " 'Poor unknowns, it is your turn to give battle. Another time it will be ours. Perhaps tomorrow we will feel the heavens burst over our heads or the earth open under our feet . . . and we will be swept away.' "[1] For him as for the German Erich Maria Remarque (1897–1970), who in 1929 published *Im Westen nichts neues,* later translated as *All Quiet on the Western Front,* World War I was what French scholar Antoine Prost called " 'a transgression of the limits of the human condition.' "[2] The old, respected values of bourgeois civilization—patriotism, honor, adherence to form—had been rendered meaningless. The war had certainly provided ample opportunity for displays of courage, but it was courage of the desperate kind, the frenetic struggles of doomed souls not so much against a palpable enemy as against the war itself. For men who watched comrades drown in mud, or saw them reduced to shredded fragments by artillery or carbonized by the new flame-throwers, the "shadow of death" had spread out of its biblical valley and had come to enclose life itself, shrouding it in a perpetual twilight illumined by flares instead of stars. In this new shadow world only the cries of men in agony and fear testified to human presence, and the passage of time was measured in putrefaction.

Of course, those combatants who survived World War I had varying reactions to it, and it would be foolish to see those of unusually sensitive and articulate literary people as typical. The average ex-soldier, come home in victory or defeat, generally went back into the workaday world and tried to pick up where he had left off, now seemingly an eternity ago. Over time, some veterans would attempt to glean meaning of sorts from their wartime experiences and, joining veterans' organizations (Barbusse himself would found one), would emphasize positive experiences such as devotion to duty or comradeship.

But if it is true that literature reflects basic social concerns and issues, even if in attenuated form, then one must conclude that the terribly singular aspects of World War I had immensely important effects. One of these effects can be described as a mixture of sensitization and psychic numbing. "I believe we are lost," said Paul Bäumer, chief protagonist of *All Quiet on the Western Front.*[3] These were the men who, as Remarque wrote in the dedication to his book, "while they may have escaped its shells, were destroyed by the war." They were destroyed because they had no values left, or at least none of the values that had sustained them, often really as children, before the war began. For these men, the younger of whom had matured in a stinking world of shadows, the war itself had become a sort of life-alien, self-sustaining universe. It aroused sensitivities that one had to numb to preserve one's sanity in this environment where, as young Lieutenant Joubaire put it, men were mad.

When Europeans, once all was over, attempted to put the madness behind them, they discovered that this could not really be done. All too soon they found that men ravaged and brutalized by the war were the bearers of new values for postwar society. For Second Lieutenant Edwin Campion Vaughn (1898–1931), the war had entered his soul, absorbed all that had been in it, and remained. At the end of an eight-month term that concluded in the terrible fighting in Flanders in 1917, he was about to go home. His last diary entry read, "So this was the end of "D" Company. Feeling sick and lonely I returned to my tent to write out my casualty report; but instead I sat on the floor and drank whiskey after whiskey as I gazed into a black and empty future."[4] The war itself had triumphed over one who had nothing left in him but memories associated with it. Even a possibly peaceful future held out no hope, nothing of value.

Naturally, not all soldiers reacted as had Vaughn, and certainly not every civilian was left bereft of meaning. There can be no question, however, that if old values survived the war, they now shared the stage either with newer ones engendered by it or with a sense of purposelessness equivalent to nihilism.

For some soldiers, but particularly those who would come home in defeat, the war raged on. There could be no end to it. In place of peace-time values now deemed pallid or artificial, there were more "authentic" ones, the new values of a "new man" forged in remorseless conflict. Ernst Jünger, who entered the war as an enthusiastic nineteen-year-old volunteer, recognized its horrors. Yet it had given him a sense of purpose. Perhaps largely because Germany had lost the war, he rejoiced in memories of combat and looked forward to a future filled with more of the same. With approval, he wrote of bayonet-fighting in the confines of a trench. "There is no mercy and no retreat then. Blood sounds in the shrill cry that is wrung like a nightmare from the breast."[5] In the lives of Vaughn and many like him, the war had left a gap that could be filled only with more of the same, even though they never went so far as to glorify war. Restless with civilian life, Vaughn himself went back into combat within the year, and joined the RAF once the war was over. His death in 1931 was due to the eventual consequences of wounds sustained in combat. A few, like Remarque, turned to pacifism. Most of those who had been affected by the experience were simply never fully at home in postwar life. People like Jünger, particularly those who, while finding purpose in war, had had to experience defeat, felt that it must rage on until revenge could be achieved. They would build a bridge to a terrible future, one of the chief bridge-builders being, of course, Adolf Hitler. The troubled musings of the literary were unhappy harbingers of times to come. At the war's end, one side would triumph; but if there had been a victory of the human spirit, it was obscure.

THE HOME FRONT

ECONOMIC CENTRALIZATION FOR TOTAL WAR

In references to World War I, the expression "centralization" must be used cautiously. In none of the warring powers did socialism come to prevail (at least without revolution). Indeed, captains of industry on all sides had to endure few sacrifices. Yet, governments certainly played unprecedented roles in directing economic life. In each of the major powers, governments were compelled to maximize production of military goods, but they also needed to maintain civil harmony in order to ensure a united effort. They were generally astonishingly successful in the first effort, but experienced difficulties in the other.

Prewar Germany had seen the government often working hand-in-hand with heavy industry. The government played an even greater role in economic planning and resource allocation. To assure maximum cooperation on the part of industrialists, the German government, by 1916 really run by the military, allowed industrialists to reap whatever profits they could as they strove to meet the demands of total war. While Germany's workers were guaranteed, at least on paper, their right to bargain for higher wages, and while wage controls were hypothetically balanced by controls on prices of basic commodities, German economic centralization basically favored management. This fact, along with the government's unwillingness to raise taxes (it sold war-bonds instead) resulted in a wartime inflation, whose consequences would be especially disastrous after the conflict had ended. Price controls broke down, and with the country under Allied blockade, there was terrible suffering on the home front. From 1916 on, patriotic enthusiasm was counterbalanced by growing working-class resentment. Traditionally autocratic Germany experienced a growing number of strikes, accompanied by an increased radicalization of elements of the Social Democratic Party, a phenomenon that resulted in its internal breakup. Of all the warring powers with the exception of Russia, which would endure revolution, Germany experienced the worst labor unrest. While it was true that German wartime production achieved remarkable levels, the economy as a whole failed; and this failure, accompanied by the effects of the "Starvation Blockade," not only sapped civilian morale in general but also created enormous tensions among different groups on the home front.

Germany did not succeed in substantively coordinating its economic war effort with that of Austria-Hungary, and probably had no intention of doing so. Great Britain and France did largely achieve coordination.

In a way, France had no choice. German armies had occupied some of its most crucial industrial and agricultural areas in the north, and thus France became in many ways dependent on British assistance almost from the beginning of the war. What resulted was a coordination of those aspects of the economy involving vital elements such as coal, shipping, and wheat. And coordination between the two major Allied powers generated tighter controls within the French economy proper. Through a "consortium system," the government established tight controls over industrial prices and supplies. While reasonable profit margins were assured, no single firm was allowed to gain untoward advantages. Thus unlike Germany, where the military had virtually protected the conflation of patriotic endeavor with economic rapacity, France did not experience a disastrous inflation. Working-class suffering in France never approached that which obtained in Germany. As the war dragged on, however, substantial price increases did occur, particularly with regard to basic food items and coal. These resulted in a wave of strikes in 1917, in which women workers played an especially crucial role. While wage increases alleviated some of the distress, French workers and some middle-class people, were feeling the strains of war by 1917, and a decline in civilian morale had become noticeable.

Great Britain, the home of "private enterprise," had to face the unprecedented problem of all-out involvement in a major continental war. France required massive economic assistance, and for the first time in British history, a true mass army had to be equipped, even as enlistments and then conscription placed immense strains on the British work force. While, like France, Britain had increasingly to rely on material and later fiscal assistance from the United States, her own effort was prodigious. A Ministry of Munitions was established to assure adequate supplies for the army, industries deemed unnecessary had resources denied to them, railroads were nationalized "for the duration," and eventually wage and price controls were imposed. While the British government relied mainly on bonds to raise money for the war effort, it obtained 30 percent of its revenues through taxation, a higher amount than in France, and far higher than in Germany. This policy helped to prevent inflation, but did not prevent labor unrest stemming from price rises and poorer working conditions. By 1917, the government, while still laying down general guidelines, had decided that specific labor issues should be worked out between the managements of industries concerned and their workers. As a result, within the framework of a more centralized economy, the power of the unions actually grew in many areas of the economy. Strangely enough, economic chaos did not supervene, Britain was able to continue to provide substantial assistance to France, and the British "muddled through" in their time-honored way even though, as in all countries, increasing war-weariness took a spiritual toll in the population at large.

Even in countries with relatively backward economies, such as Russia and Italy, impressive achievements in wartime production were recorded, although the pressures on civilian economies were immense. In Russia, such pressures would contribute to the eventual collapse of the Tsarist regime; in Italy in 1917, bread riots had to be ruthlessly suppressed. In all European countries involved in the war, however, marked increases in the production of military goods occurred, even as enthusiasm for the war effort was increasingly offset by weariness and depression. Ivan Bloch had underestimated the staying power of governments and economies in the face of total war. There would indeed be revolution in Russia, but that revolution would be due to the special problems of this most autocratic of nations, which had somehow found itself fighting on the side of "democracy."

MASS WARFARE AND "WOMEN'S LIBERATION"

One of the cherished legends about World War I is that women "came into their own" as a result of it: that almost overnight they appeared in overwhelming numbers in industry, releasing hundreds of thousands of their countrymen for service at the front. This simply was not the case. Women had worked at a variety of industrial and agricultural jobs before the war. What was different about the war years was not that they worked, but *where* they worked. Women had always worked in white collar and service industries, and it was in these areas that the greatest *permanent* increases occurred during World War I. Now, briefly, women appeared in areas from which prewar social niceties had largely excluded them: the munitions industry, the railroads (as signal personnel), and heavy farm labor. Once the war was over, they would generally be excluded from these areas once again as jobs were taken by returning soldiers.

What the women of all the warring powers had demonstrated was that they could do jobs traditionally assigned only to men—while continuing to function in traditional household capacities. At the time, nobody seemed to take much notice of this.

Few women played an active role in combat. Particularly in Great Britain, however, women increasingly served in semi-military capacities, sometimes taking over police roles and, when the first air raids began, becoming air-raid wardens. Indeed, it was generally in Great Britain that women's service was most noticeable.

As we have seen, the issue of votes for women had been central to British political life before World War I. With the outbreak of war, many active in the campaign for women's rights threw themselves headlong into the war effort, in order to prove that they deserved the vote. Millicent Fawcett took a predictably moderate position: "'Let us prove ourselves worthy of citizenship, whether our claim be recognized or not.'"[6] Less predictably, even more aggressive—and thus more persecuted—suffragists such as the Pankhursts now supported the very government that had been jailing them. While some active in the suffrage campaign refused to recognize the legitimacy of the war effort and worked with the No-Conscription Fellowship, founded in December 1914, Emmeline Pankhurst and daughter Christabel plunged into the war effort with enthusiasm. While daughter Sylvia distanced herself from them, her mother and sister abandoned the suffrage cause, adopting in place of the slogan "Votes for Women" a new one, "For King, for Country, for Freedom." Fawcett at least continued to stand for women's issues during the war. For the two Pankhursts, however, and for many of their supporters, the war was a golden opportunity to show that women could do just about anything as well as men, and they were not about to squander the opportunity of demonstrating this.

Middle and upper class women who might formerly have been involved in the suffrage campaign now joined Voluntary Aid Detachments, serving in various capacities not only in Great Britain, but close to the lines in France and Belgium as well. They were cooks, nurses, and, most dramatic of all, ambulance drivers. Helen Zenna Smith's 1930 novel *Not So Quiet . . .* , a sort of response to Remarque's *All Quiet on the Western Front,* which had appeared in the preceding year, was based on the diary of a VAD ambulance driver. At one point, the narrator, whose super-patriotic mother is intensely, almost morbidly, proud of her, describes cleaning out an ambulance after a day's service:

> The stench that comes out as we open the doors each morning nearly knocks us down. Pools of stale vomit from the poor wretches we have carried the night before, corners the sitters have turned into temporary lavatories for all purposes, blood and mud and vermin and the stale stench of stinking trench feet and gangrenous wounds. Poor souls, they cannot help it. No one blames them.[7]

Unlike the lower-class women who were formally attached to the army, the members of the VAD were unpaid, being wholly sustained by patriotic devotion and a desire to prove themselves. Even as their enthusiasm wilted in the face of accumulated horrors, they certainly succeeded in doing just that.

As a reward for their services, most British women received the vote in 1918, all obtaining it by 1928. Whether as a reward or not, German women received the vote in 1919, while French women would not get it until after World War II. Meanwhile, basic social attitudes and vocational patterns did not significantly change, and, to some extent, a sort of collective amnesia concerning the role of women in the war set in. *Not So Quiet . . .*, first published in 1930, would not be republished until 1989, when feminist issues were taken more seriously. Now it must serve as a belated memorial to those women who labored, suffered, and occasionally died in the worst-yet example of a largely male activity.

Mass Propaganda for a Mass War

For as long as human beings have engaged in warfare, it has been necessary for the participants to stereotype "the enemy" often as something considerably less than human. "He" was brutal, stupid, cowardly, dirty, or immoral, or maybe all of these at once. Warriors or soldiers departing for battle steeled themselves to dangerous or unpleasant tasks by depersonalizing the foe.

From the time when war began to involve whole societies, a phenomenon often dated from the French Revolution, it has been necessary to sustain the fighting spirit not only of the soldiers themselves, but also of those who support them on the home front. Farmers, workers, the families of the departed millions, have had to believe in the "justice" of the cause at hand. Moreover, such a belief has had to be sustained in the face of possible heavy casualties and increasing privation.

World War I took place when mass communication was, by present-day standards, in its infancy. The wireless had been around for a while, but there was no functioning radio system anywhere in the world. Mass journalism had been a fact of life for some time, however, and literate populations—in some ways more literate than present ones—read an enormous variety of newspapers and magazines. These periodicals presented obvious opportunities to nurture hatreds. The term "propaganda" also had been around for a long time, but it was in

World War I, the first mass, technological war, that its extraordinary potential was realized for the first time.

Prewar tensions and crises had paved the way for wartime propaganda by raising suspicions against potential enemies. In Germany, where fears of "encirclement" had turned out to be a self-fulfilling prophecy, the public mood was reflected in slogans such as "Jeder Schuss, ein Russ," "Jeder Tritt, ein Britt," "Jeder Stoss, ein Franzos" ("Each shot, a Russian," "Each kick, a Brit," "Each thrust, a Frenchie").[8] The government provided official amplification for Ernst Lissauer's "Song of Hate against England," a poem that reflected the attitude of many Germans who felt betrayed by Britain's entrance into the war. Problems with traditional foes, France and Russia—these were understandable. Great Britain, however, in recent years so perfidious in her efforts to deny Germany her rightful "place in the sun," was now a subject of special hatred. "'We have but one foe, England,'" shrieked the poet, up to then justifiably unknown:

> Hate by water and hate by land
> Hate of the head and hate of the hand
> Hate of the hammer and hate of the crown
> Hate of seventy million choking down
> They love as one, they hate as one
> They all have but one foe: England.[9]

Throughout the war, German propaganda would emphasize the perfidy and materialism of England, and the primitivism of the Slavs. As for the French—well, what could one expect of a sissified, degenerate people who were willing to use black colonial troops in Europe and thus expose the continent to the possible ravages of racial decay? German wartime propaganda, when focused upon the enemy, was characterized by a mixture of grim moral earnestness, cynicism, and a sense of racial superiority. When focused upon the nature and events of the war itself and the role of the German soldier in it, German propaganda was rather similar, as we shall see, to that of the Allies. The horrors of war were trivialized and reverses were ignored, denied, or played down. On war-loan posters and postcards and in newspaper sketches, German soldiers appeared resolute, unafraid, or revelling in the comradeship of frontline life. In a sense, the post-1918 Germany that would not recognize defeat was foreshadowed in wartime propaganda.

Retrospectively, commentators have come to see the German propaganda effort as hampered by the unwillingness of the German government, to say nothing of the military, to work effectively with the newspapers—especially the liberal ones, some of which were owned by Jews. German leaders really distrusted public opinion, and their propaganda tended to be pedantic or patronizing in tone, as if talking down to the population. As wartime stresses accentuated class differences, the impact of such propaganda upon working people became increasingly ineffectual, perhaps even counterproductive. Ex-soldier Adolf Hitler, recording his thoughts on the subject in *Mein Kampf,* was highly critical of its lack of emotional appeal. Whether any kind of propaganda could have sustained the will of a half-starved population facing eventual defeat must of course remain a moot point.

Allied propagandists were faced with a somewhat easier task than their German counterparts. After all, whatever the underlying causes of the war might have been, Germany had struck first. And the words of her leaders, as well as actions of some of her soldiers, provided welcome grist for propaganda mills. In 1900, in offering a model for soldierly behavior to German troops departing for China to assist in putting down the Boxer rebellion, Wilhelm himself had furnished the epithet "Huns"; and German Chancellor Theobald Bethmann-Hollweg had called the 1839 treaty proclaiming Belgium's neutrality "a scrap of paper." Above all, there was the conduct of German armies in Belgium.

For British propaganda, the German invasion of Belgium was crucial. Britons may still have harbored a residue of suspicion regarding the French, but German behavior in the face of unexpected Belgian resistance aroused genuine indignation. As we have seen, there were certainly atrocities enough to warrant it, and British propaganda experts elaborated on them. The German foe soon became a monster who not only committed hideous crimes against Belgian civilians but crucified a captured Canadian soldier, torpedoed civilian vessels without warning, and processed the dead bodies of soldiers for soap. Fabricated, as were the crucifixion and soap factory stories, or one-sided, as was the omission to mention that certain "civilian" vessels were carrying military supplies, these stories were used effectively by the British government, which, unlike the German, worked hand-in-glove with the press. The Church of England, too, was brought into the propaganda effort. The Bishop of London, Dr. Winnington Ingram, pulled out all the stops in broadsides that were hardly compatible with the biblical warning that vengeance was the Lord's alone. To save "'everything that is noble in Europe, everything that loves freedom and honour,'" Britain had "'in a great crusade—we cannot deny it—to kill Germans: to kill them not for the sake of killing, but to save the world; to kill the good as well as the bad, to kill the young men as well as the old . . . and to kill them lest the civilization of the world be killed.' "[10] Once the war was over and the falsity of many of the atrocity stories was revealed, cynicism and distrust would set in, dulling reactions against later, very real atrocities. For the duration, however, such stories served their purpose. One of the immediate results was anti-German rioting, often directed against the persons and businesses of anybody unfortunate enough to have a foreign-sounding name.

French wartime propaganda was often far more artistic than that of other countries, and of a far more varied quality. Postcards, posters, and newspaper pieces covered themes ranging from sentimental representations of Allied unity to more practical suggestions concerning ways for French women to offer soldiers on leave "sweet moments" that would sustain morale and be long remembered. More than in any other country, the French propagandistic effort blended together patriotic idealism with frankly sexual appeals. At the same time, of course, it depicted the bestiality of the enemy—in this case, an enemy ensconced on native soil and ravaging much of northern France. Traditional Franco-German hatreds, from the French side nurtured by bitter memories of defeat in 1870 and the loss of Alsace and Lorraine, provided French propagandists with an especially receptive audience. Of course, once the war was over, particularly in the late 1920s and early 1930s, cynicism would set in as experience increasingly called into question not merely the truth of the propaganda but the results of the four years of sacrifice.

In all three countries, as well as others not discussed here, propaganda efforts had certain features in common. All of them, perhaps necessarily, trivialized the horrors of war while emphasizing the inhuman or bestial qualities of the enemy. All glorified the comradeship of the trenches, virtually sanctified national life, and suggested that, in nurturing national hatreds, increasingly deprived civilians were, in fact, being idealistic. World War I was a true "people's war," and whether being exhorted to buy bonds, work until they dropped in the factories, or attend to the carnal needs of soldiers, peoples of the warring nations were always to bear in mind that they were engaging in a virtual holy war—to quote the Bishop of London, a "crusade."

Whether propaganda sustained morale on the home front is debatable. That it sustained national hatreds is not. In the new "mass" age, mass passion was crucial to any country's war effort, whatever the form of its government. While propaganda had been used before, its role was infinitely greater now that increased literacy and greater means for providing information were facts of life. In an age of mass nationalism, seen by some as virtually a secular religion, the originally religious meaning of the term (something that "propagates the faith") had been fully realized in a secular context for the first time.

In presenting its case to neutral parties—particularly, of course, the United States—Germany was at a great disadvantage. The Allies controlled the world press services, and thus stories, true or false, of German atrocities were more generally known. Russian atrocities in East Prussia in 1914 were not widely known, nor were Russian actions against Polish Jews, who were (correctly) assumed to be unsympathetic to the Tsarist cause. Moreover, the Allies had at their disposal the services of one of the most effective cartoonists of the time, the Dutch artist Louis Raemaekers. The Netherlands were neutral in 1914, but, since they shared a border with Belgium and Flemish Belgians, at least, had a linguistic link with Raemaekers' country, refugees' tales of German atrocities there had become well known. His cartoons, while often depicting the horrors of war in general, just as often focused upon German atrocities, and his savagely anti-German caricatures led the German government to place a 12,000 mark price on his head. There is no question that the picture that reached the public in neutral countries such as the United States was very unbalanced; but the German government had never shown much aptitude for public relations. In an age in which the power of advertising was increasingly becoming a crucial factor in public life, this was perhaps suicidal.

EFFORTS AT PEACE AND THE PERVERSE LOGIC OF WAR

Many frontline soldiers knew that large numbers of the missing and presumed dead were alive after all, hiding out in underground caverns between the lines. At night, hordes of deathly pale ghouls, wearing the tattered uniforms of all armies, would emerge to loot and sometimes feed off of the dead and dying. Their animal-like cries occasionally could be heard amid the ordinary sounds of war. Once it was all over, the opposing armies would have to get together and gas these monsters who had come to the valley of the shadow to live in war forever. As brutalized as the men of the trenches had become, many of them recognized that the war was a degrading experience. To exemplify its hideousness, they conjured up a legion of demonic beings even more dehumanized than themselves.

Many soldiers, on both sides of the line, also knew that at one time a slight, bespectacled man, clad in the vestments of the Roman Catholic Church, had suddenly appeared in the French trenches, accompanied by a tall, young priest. In wonderment, combat troops stared at the pale intruder. Suddenly, there was a cry of recognition—" 'C'est le pape!' " " 'It's the pope!' " Benedict XV, whose strong position against the war was well known, was among them. Boldly, as weeping men dropped to their knees around him, he rose above the parapets and walked into no-man's-land. " 'La guerre est finie!' " " 'Der Krieg ist beendet!' " " 'The war is over,' " he cried. Magically, the shooting ceased, and, in all languages, soldiers joined in the "Lord's Prayer." Suddenly, the pope collapsed and was assisted back into the trench by the young priest. In a few seconds he had disappeared, and after a brief interval the fighting resumed.[11]

These two stories were opposite sides of the same coin. However fantastic, they were less absurd than the war itself, and they pointed to the deeply felt wish for peace even on the part of those most brutalized by it.

Beginning in 1915, there were a number of efforts to bring the war to an end. Socialists of many countries met at Zimmerwald, Switzerland, in September 1915 and drafted a widely ignored resolution calling for the soldiers of all nations to give up the struggle and to devote their energies towards establishing a more equitable world community. There would be two more such meetings: at Kienthal, also in Switzerland, in 1916, and in Stockholm, Sweden the following year. The resolutions became ever more strident, but they accomplished nothing.

In the spring of 1915, a group of women who had been involved in social reform all over the world, including the well-known American reformer Jane Addams (1860–1935), met at the Hague, where so many forlorn hopes had once found articulation. This group, the foundation of what would become the Women's International League for Peace and Freedom (WILPF), consisted in part of women representing the warring countries. Declaring their opposition, as women, to the war, they embarked on missions all over Europe and to the United States as well, visiting heads of governments and urging them to use their good offices to end the slaughter. Only the King of Sweden, neutral in the conflict, lent them encouragement. While the organization that they established at the Hague would survive and grow, their immediate efforts proved vain. Some of these women joined male colleagues on the famous "Peace Ship" sponsored by Henry Ford, which sailed for Europe in December 1915. Ford, who travelled with them, dismayed some of the delegates by blaming the war in part on the Jews, whose supposed perfidy was becoming a fetish with him, but delegates, some of them Jewish, swallowed their outrage and held to the desperate hope of persuading heads of state to end the war by Christmas. The only result of note was Ford's coming down with a severe head cold.

After the Verdun and Somme massacres of 1916, the German government sent out feelers, through several neutral embassies, indicating that it was ready to talk peace—but only on Germany's terms, i.e., with its armies still on foreign soil. This "effort" understandably fell on deaf ears. So did the Landsdowne Memorandum, a document circulated by Lord Landsdowne, British minister without portfolio. The memorandum, which stated that the war was turning out to be a catastrophe for England, and that the only way out was a negotiated settlement, was rejected by the rest of the British cabinet, and British generals declared it the work of a coward.

Woodrow Wilson, who had just been narrowly reelected as president of the then still neutral United States, in part thanks to the slogan, "He kept us out of war," undertook a peace-making campaign of his own. In December 1916, he asked the governments of the warring powers to state their aims, at the same time declaring that he could see little difference between the concerns of the two sides. The Allies, infuriated even though they had received much in the way of war materials from the United States, wondered if Wilson had been in collusion with the German government, since his message came so soon after the feeler from Germany. For its part, the German government was about equally contemptuous of Wilson.

In March, 1917 there was a revolution in Russia, and in April America entered the war. Fearing growing unrest in Germany, the *Reichstag* passed a "Peace Resolution" in July. While somewhat more conciliatory than the government feeler of late 1916, it was deemed too advantageous to Germany and thus not taken seriously. Peace feelers by the harassed government of Austria-Hungary late in the year also achieved nothing, in part because of German intransigence with regard to territorial concessions.

The war really had developed an attritional logic of its own, it seemed, and it would have to be fought through to the bitter end. Government rearrangements on both sides seemed designed to assure this would continue. David Lloyd George (1863–1945), who had served as chancellor of the exchequer, minister of munitions, and minister of war (after Kitchener died when a ship he was on struck a mine) replaced Sir Herbert Asquith (1852–1928) as British prime minister late in 1916 because it was thought that he would be a more effective wartime leader. Georges Clemenceau (1841–1929), dubbed the "Tiger," became premier of France in November 1917 for the same reason. In Germany in July 1917, Theobald Bethmann-Hollweg (1856–1921), whom the military had come to distrust, was replaced by a political nobody, Georg Michaelis, and military rule tightened even further. Revolution had put Russia's role in doubt, but America was on the way.

Despite increasing disillusionment on battle and home fronts, the war, like Dr. Frankenstein's monster, plodded on, seemingly sustained by inertial forces initially spawned by industrialization and mass nationalism. Russia, which had stayed in the war far longer than a variety of deficiencies should have permitted it to, was about to drop out altogether. It would do so, however, in circumstances that would be responsible for yet more historical trauma, trauma that would scarcely have been possible without the impact of World War I.

13

A Revolt and a Revolution

THE IRISH EASTER MONDAY UPRISING

DURING the Great War, thousands of Irish young men served in the British Army. Perhaps, especially if they were Catholic, they thought that they had a point to prove, and their performance in combat was generally excellent. Yet, the "Irish Question" remained and just how critical it was for the Irish people and the British government was demonstrated in April, 1916.

Before the war, Home Rule had been proposed for Ireland; but, this appeared to have raised more problems than it had solved. Most in the Catholic south of the country supported it. More militant sorts, however, thought that it did not go far enough, and pressed for total independence. Protestants were in the majority in the six northern counties and most of them, not wishing to reside in a country in which a Catholic majority would be in charge of domestic affairs, were bitterly opposed to Home Rule, and, on the eve of war's outbreak, there existed the very real possibility of civil war in Ireland.

With the coming of the war, the Irish issue, for Irish and English alike, appeared to have been relegated to the political back-burner. Certainly, this *was* the case for most people. For members of the nationalistic *Sinn Fein* ("We Ourselves") party, however, the question of Irish independence remained primary. This was much more the case for an organization called the Irish Republican Brotherhood, a kind of underground army, widely rumored to be receiving secret arms shipments from Germany. In 1916, as Haig planned his offensive on the Somme, radical Irish nationalists were planning to embark on one of their own.

The leading 19th Century crusader for the Irish cause, Charles Stewart Parnell, had been a Protestant. The same was true for Sir Roger Casement who, after the outbreak of war in 1914, snuck into Germany and, while there, attempted to win over Irish prisoners of war to the cause of rebellion against Great Britain. At the same time, of course, he was working with the German government to garner support for the cause. The vast majority of captured Irish soldiers remained loyal, if not necessarily enthusiastically so, to the British cause. Some, however, lent Casement support and a rebellion was planned for April, 1916.

British intelligence was very much aware that untoward schemes were afoot and, on April 20, 1916, a German vessel, heavily-laden with arms, was intercepted off the Irish coast. That evening, as planned, a German U-boat landed Casement himself, something that also had been anticipated by British intelligence. He was almost instantly captured, and Good Friday of 1916 would turn out to be his last. With expected arms having been seized by the British, and their most important leader in captivity, the Irish Republican Brotherhood was in a quandary. Very soon, however, the leadership decided to go ahead with the anticipated revolt anyway and, on Easter Monday, April 23, 1916, several thousand armed men seized several public buildings in Dublin, most prominent of them, the post office. An Irish Republic was then declared, with Padraic Pearse its president.

During this time, the British military was husbanding its forces for anticipated future operations. Enough were available, however, to deal with the Easter Monday revolt and, after a week of bitter fighting, all was over. Initially, the rising had not had wide-ranging public sympathy. Due to a harsh action of the British government, this changed very quickly. Fifteen leaders of the ill-fated revolt, Roger Casement and Padraic Pearse among them, were executed. To be sure, what they had done had amounted to high treason in wartime, and this point was underscored by the British government. Nonetheless, the vast majority of Irish people, particularly, of course, in the Catholic south, were shocked and infuriated by the executions. Also, they did not play very well in the United States where they were widely condemned in the press. Of course, Irish Americans were just about uniformly outraged and this was a group whose political importance had been established for some time. Summer, 1916, saw Anglo-American relations at their lowest point since the outbreak of the war. At the same time, the Irish cause had been provided with new martyrs and, after the war, there would be no small number of Irishmen willing to die and to kill in their name. As had been (and still is) so often the case, ruthless suppression of a cause "gilded o'r" with the patina of idealism, had served only to strengthen it.

THE RUSSIAN REVOLUTION

THE LAST OF THE ROMANOVS: WRONG PEOPLE AT THE WRONG PLACE AT THE WRONG TIME

The Romanov Dynasty came to rule over Russia in 1613. Nicholas II (1894–1917), would be its last representative. While certainly a good family man and kindly disposed towards his people, he was, overall, a somewhat vapid, weak-willed person who added several dimensions to the term "mediocrity." At the same time, however, he took his role as autocratic "Tsar of All the Russias" very seriously indeed. After the 1905 Revolution, Russia had a parliament of sorts, the *Duma.* It had few real powers, and in fact, functioned more as an advisory body than as one concerned with the creation of policy. Nonetheless, Nicholas resented it, and seemed to view its existence as an almost personal affront. Weak-willed though he was—and he appeared to be aware of this condition—he remained convinced that his presumably God-given imperial prerogatives allowed for, in fact, demanded, that absolute authority remain in his hands. Weak-willed, not terribly bright autocrats can often provide students of history with much mirth. History itself, however, is rarely kind to them.

Nicholas's "better half," Alexandra, actually amounted to his "two-thirds" insofar as intelligence and will were concerned. She seemed to realize this and, on occasion, would upbraid her husband for not showing enough of either quality. After one such tongue-lashing, delivered in the form of a letter, Nicholas, after conceding that Alexandra was correct on all major points, signed off as "Your poor, weak-willed little hubby." Yet, for all of her resolve, Alexandra was, in many ways, unsure of herself. She was of German background and, even before the war, this had caused some people within and outside of the court to view her with suspicion. With the coming of the war, moreover, one that was not going all that well, this feeling quite naturally intensified. Also, over time, many came to believe that *Tsarina* Alexandra had far too much to say about running things. Her German background, as well as Russian misogyny, had much to do with this. Of at least equal importance, however, was the feeling that Alexandra was quite daft. This was in large measure due to the ways in which she attempted to deal with her sense of insecurity, and, more importantly, a gnawing family problem.

Nicholas and Alexandra had five children, four daughters and a son. The daughters were healthy enough, but, the boy, Alexei, who, as *"Tsarevich,"* was heir apparent, suffered from hemophilia. For reasons political and personal, this was a source of much anguish for his parents. Both often called upon divine aid; but, Alexandra was particularly persistent in this regard. Born a Protestant, her marriage to Nicholas necessitated her conversion to Russian Orthodoxy, a faith to which she adhered with that fanaticism often shown by converts. Such was reinforced by the belief that her new faith would help her in becoming closer to the Russian people, whose very soul (at least as Alexandra saw it) was embodied in Orthodoxy. Thus, as Nicholas—himself, of course, a true believer—looked on with a mixture of admiration and perplexed *ennui,* she surrounded herself with a variety of mystics and self-proclaimed holy men, whose advice and prayers were made all the more urgent due to Alexei's illness. One of these was not merely influential; but, would play an important role in accelerating the demise of the imperial family.

Grigori Efimovich Rasputin was born in far-off Siberia. He grew up almost totally uneducated and remained semi-literate throughout his life. Yet, this mysterious (and usually filthy) individual, possessed of both extraordinary physical strength and seemingly limitless sensual energies, could be amazingly shrewd, and it is entirely possible that he possessed certain psychic powers. Also, and this was of particular importance for Alexandra, he offered himself as a self-educated holy man, and there can be little doubt that he believed himself to be one.

In 1907, Rasputin (his name can be translated as "debauched one") managed to have himself presented at the imperial court. Nicholas and Alexandra—but, the latter in particular—were greatly impressed by a man who, in his appearance and apparent piety, seemed to embody the soul of Mother Russia. As matters turned out, Rasputin had a somewhat unique "take" on certain crucial theological issues. If, he reasoned, one did not sin, then one would never know the joy of God's forgiveness. Thus, in order to be able to live in a state of grace, one *had* to sin. Words such as these were poured into the ears of seemingly numberless women, some of them members of the court, and, in a curious reversal of the sacrament of transubstantiation, that which was sacred attained mundane form. Within a very short period of time, Rasputin's sexual exploits became the talk of Petrograd. In due course, they were the talk of Russia.

While the self-proclaimed holy man never approached Alexandra for sexual favors, his impact on her was enormous. For, not only was he a consistent purveyor of down-home wisdom; but, through apparently genuine hypnotic powers, he could ease the suffering of young Alexei. Indeed, it appeared that he could even control the hemophiliac's terrible bleeding. With reason, the spiritually-tormented *Tsarina* came to rely on Rasputin for advice in all areas, including political ones. At times, her husband was constrained to take it. In due course, men who the Siberian monk could manipulate or control were appointed to important positions. That these were often individuals totally unqualified to hold the posts to which they had been appointed seemed to be of little consequence. For a government which, even before military disaster supervened, was widely perceived of as being corrupt and incompetent, Rasputin's appearance on the scene constituted a disaster.

During the war, for many Russians of all classes, Nicholas, Alexandra, and Rasputin came to represent a kind of unholy trinity. An, at times, astonishingly shallow representative of God on earth manipulated by a scheming "foreigner" who, in turn, was under the hypnotic influence of an unwashed lecher mouthing self-justifying platitudes—so matters appeared to be. As platitudinous as Rasputin often was, however, he made one prediction to which the usually attentive imperial pair should have attended more closely. As Russia prepared to enter World War I, he predicted that the conflict would bring about the fall of the Romanov Dynasty. To be sure, as mentioned earlier, the excesses of this man played no small role in helping to bring this situation about. Yet, as slavish as Rasputin could be in his relationships with Nicholas and Alexandra, he seemed to recognize that these last representatives of a debased autocracy had been condemned by history.

Russian State, Society, and Army in 1917

The state which led the Russian people into war in 1914 was a singular blend of Orthodox piety, incompetence, and corruption. In a country in which nothing ever seemed to go quite right, it was perhaps fitting that an act informed by the most pious of motives would have disastrous results. About three weeks after Russia's entrance into the war, Nicholas II declared that the government vodka monopoly would be closed down "for the duration." The vodka monopoly was the government's greatest single source of revenue. Thus, a poor country which, under normal fiscal circumstances, would be hard pressed to finance a war such as that now underway, was essentially cutting its own throat. In any case, Russia's wartime prohibition (at least so far as vodka was concerned) was about as successful as the American variant would be. Those able to do so simply switched to other alcoholic beverages, and peasants simply hoarded more grain than usual for purposes of bootlegging. The sometimes ghastly results of these efforts often found their way to the front as the government was left to ponder the problems created when Orthodox principle confronted fiscal realities posed by modern warfare.

Unhappily for the early Russian war effort, incompetence and corruption were artfully blended together in the porcine form of Vladimir Sukhomlinov (1848–1926), between 1908 and 1915, the country's Minister of War. Like Rasputin, with whom he always managed to be on very good terms, he could be described as "a man of parts," but, most of them private. Unhappily, this indolent warrior-of-the-bedroom was hardly fit to direct any war effort whatsoever, much less the one upon which his unhappy country embarked in August, 1914.

Having served in the cavalry during the successful 1877–1878 war against Turkey, Sukhomlinov seemed to have concluded that all future wars would pretty much resemble the one just concluded. The phrase "modern war" infuriated him and, even after Russian embarrassment in the Russo-Japanese War, he continued to believe in the superiority of the bayonet. He spoke and acted as if technological innovations such as the machine gun and quick-firing artillery had been introduced for the sole purpose of annoying him. " 'As war was,' " he once declared, " 'so it has remained . . . all these things are merely vicious innovations. Look at me for instance: I have not read a military manual for the last twenty-five years.' "[1] Obviously proud of that fact, he did next to nothing to prepare the Russian military, to say nothing of Russian industry, for possible substantive challenges in the future.

Sukhomlinov's incompetence was complemented by corruption, and thousands of rubles provided him for "official" uses were squandered for ones of a decidedly personal nature. At the same time, it was well-known in governmental circles that he was on good terms with a number of foreign officers, including an Austrian one who, shortly before the war, was unmasked as an espionage agent. All in the name of good fellowship, he had been invited to observe Russian Army maneuvers. A subordinate of Sukhomlinov, more directly linked to such improprieties, was actually tried for treason. Due, however, to his boss's intervention, he was released and, in fact, was allowed to assume his previous post. Sukhomlinov himself escaped any form of punishment, even censure, due to his tie to Rasputin.

In June, 1915, after staggering military reserves, Sukhomlinov was dismissed. Nicholas II, who was quite fond the man, sent him a warm letter, thanking him for his services. In view of the fact that the now disgraced former Minister of War was one of the most loathed men in the country, this tells us much about "weak-willed hubby's" sense of political judgement. Sukhomlinov's successor, General A. A. Polivanov, was a thoroughly competent man who made strenuous efforts to improve conditions in the army, while helping to put Russian industry on a far more realistic war-footing. Yet, by the time of Sukhomlinov's dismissal, over 300,000 Russian soldiers had paid for his incompetence with their lives, and resentment over this, as well as with the Tsar's favoring of him, never died. In any event, another scandal of staggering proportions was on the way.

B. V. Sturmer was another man much favored by Rasputin (and thus, of course, by Nicholas and Alexandra as well). Early in 1916, this individual, widely viewed—and not only due to his name—as being pro-German, was appointed to the extremely important post of President of the Council of Ministers. It was widely believed that Alexandra and Rasputin were responsible for this, and there was a storm of protest in the *Duma* in particular, and the country in general. Sturmer, even the *Tsarina,* were accused of treason. While there now can be no doubt of Alexandra's loyalty to the war effort, the Sturmer connection, engineered, of course, by Rasputin, points to a lack of political judgement about on par with her husband's. In any event, in November, 1916, Sturmer was dismissed from his post. Alexandra, despite much public muttering, remained at hers, at least for the time being, and Rasputin at his quite unofficial but important one. So far as the latter was concerned, however, things would change very soon.

On a typically cold Petrograd night, the holy man was invited to the home of a nobleman where, he was told, food, drink, gypsy music, and possibly sex awaited him. Once there, Rasputin was plied with cakes and wine laced with cyanide. To the dismay of his hosts, he showed no effects other than to become somewhat depressed. It was necessary to shoot him. This seemed to work; but, as the assassins prepared to dispose of the presumably now dead Rasputin, he suddenly revived and rose to his feet. Thus, the now thoroughly terrified noblemen—convinced that they were dealing with some sort of superhuman being—had to shoot him again. Rasputin's body was then tossed into the icy River Neva. When later recovered by divers, it was discovered (at least according to rumor) that the lungs contained water, indicating that he was still alive when thrown into the river. Convinced that their country had been freed from the most corrupting of influences,

Russians of all classes rejoiced upon hearing the news of Rasputin's demise. Nicholas and Alexandra went into mourning. In due course, Alexandra had a chapel built in his memory and often went there to pray. Perhaps, on occasion, she prayed for herself and her family, remembering that Rasputin had once declared that, if he were to die, so would the Romanovs.

The elimination of Rasputin of course had little real impact on the general course of events. Far more important were Russia's very basic structural deficiencies of which his admittedly important role in national affairs was merely symptomatic. Between the 1890s and the outbreak of the war, the country had undergone rapid industrialization and, while many in the traditionally landed nobility had in fact played roles in this process, the class was in somewhat of an economic decline relative to a growing bourgeoisie. Yet, socially and politically, its influence remained strong and, despite efforts at reform, major posts in the government and the army often went to noblemen utterly unfit to hold them. While, by war's outbreak, Russia was on its way to becoming a major industrial power—by 1914, it was third in the world in the production of pig iron—most of its people still lived on the land. In the only comprehensive census ever taken in Imperial Russia, that of 1897, it was revealed that 87 percent of Russians lived in rural areas. By 1914, of course, this number had diminished somewhat. Yet, although precise figures are uncertain, it is plain that the majority of Russians, and the vast majority of these peasants, still lived on the land, and generally in conditions which were extremely backward.

One of results of social backwardness is illiteracy, and the 1897 census found 79 percent of the population to be illiterate. Authorities at all levels certainly attempted to deal with the problem and notable advances were made in primary and secondary education. This was revealed in surveys of men drafted into the Russian Army. In 1894, the illiteracy rate was 62 percent, in 1904, 44 percent, and in 1913, 32 percent. Yet, as pointed out by the historian, Michael T. Florinsky, these figures were deceptive. Many of the young men who were recorded as "literate," though having attended school while children, had not read a word since then and, in point of fact, could barely sign their names.[2] By far, illiteracy was most prevalent in rural areas. Most who lived in cities and worked in rapidly expanding industries (at least most males) held jobs which required some level of literacy. Hence, the ever-growing industrial proletariat was, on the whole, literate. In some ways, this was unfortunate for their employers in particular, and Imperial Russia in general.

Though a not inconsiderable proportion of the Russian industrial work force retained rural roots and lived in cities on a seasonal basis, there certainly was a growing number of folk who could be classified as "proletarian," with interests traditional to their class. These naturally included such things as wages, working hours, and working conditions and these, even by standards of the time, were mostly atrocious. There were no real unions to represent working class interests. Not unexpectedly, then, representatives of radical political organizations and radical literature had very strong impacts upon Russian workers and were at least partially responsible for a wave of strikes just before the war. In 1914, during the initial flush of patriotic enthusiasm, there were very few strikes. In 1915, there were over one thousand strikes involving over 500,000 workers; the following year, 1,400, which idled over one million. As 1917 dawned, it was plain that matters could be, from the points of view of management and the government, even worse.[3] The reasons for all of this labor unrest were obvious. Also obvious was that, wartime conditions being what they were, little could be done about them.

As mentioned earlier, after a slow start, Russian industry did a good job with regard to the manufacturing of war materials. As the military sector of the economy expanded, however, that concerned with the production of consumer goods contracted. Quite early in 1915, then, there were shortages and rising prices. While, on the whole, Russian workers, particularly those involved in the armaments industry, saw their wages increase during the war, they could not keep pace with the cost of living. Ominously, government efforts, through controls, to strike a balance between assuring Russian peasants a fair price for their grain and workers affordable bread failed miserably. The peasants simply hoarded much of their harvest, some, as noted earlier, for the purpose of turning it into bootleg liquor. Thus, in the cities, there were food shortages and, ironically, in part *due* to government efforts to control prices, what was available was often more expensive than ever.

While peasants were often reluctant to place their grain on the market, what grain as was made available often never made it to the increasingly hungry cities. This was due to the ghastly state of the Russian railways. Even before the war, the system barely served the needs of the country. Track and equipment maintenance was notoriously poor, and, just before the outbreak of war, the number of locomotives in working order totalled 20,000—not really all that many for a country the size of Russia. In 1914, there were around 540,000 railway cars—again, not a particularly impressive number. Furthermore, despite its very considerable expansion between 1890 and 1910, the Russian rail "net" was very thin in places, particularly in the eastern regions of the country. All of these factors, taken together, spelled disaster in wartime conditions.

Naturally, the demands of the military came first and this logically meant that equipment available for transporting civilian goods—to say nothing of civilians themselves—fell off sharply. Under the strains imposed by overuse and worse maintenance than ever before, the number of locomotives in working order dropped dramatically. By 1917, there were only 9,000 of these and only 174,000 cars to pull.[4] Under these conditions, it was well-nigh impossible to supply even the army adequately, to say nothing of the civilian portion of the population. Thus it was that, while workers and their families increasingly lacked very basic necessities, a large portion of the impressive output of Russian war industries either never made it to the front, or got there too late to be of value. This leads us to a consideration of the state of the army itself.

In 1916, the Russian Army had performed extremely well. As described earlier, the "Brusilov Offensive" would be the most successful one mounted by any of the Allies until that which brought the war to an end. When it finally ground to a halt, however, one million men had been lost. The morale of the survivors was not high. Due largely to transportation problems described above, there were shortages of just about everything. Though not as often as before, soldiers going into battle sometimes would have to wait for a comrade to be killed or wounded in order to use his rifle, and often there would be precious few bullets with which to load it. Artillery, always a specialty of the Russian Army, was, with regard to design and the quality of those who serviced the guns, often on par with German counterparts. Very often, however, it fell silent at crucial moments due to a lack of shells. While, as a rule, soldiers ate better than workers in the cities, rations were often inadequate, as were medical supplies. Indeed, there were occasional cases of men being operated on without benefit of anesthesia.

Gaps between officers and men remained wide throughout the war; a fact underscored by the rule that an ordinary soldier address his superior by the term "your excellency." Ordinary soldiers might not have come to resent this as much as they did had their officers been paragons of competence which, in many, perhaps most, cases they were not. It was not that Russian officers lacked courage. In fact, in a way, they were perhaps *too* brave. Wanting to set examples for their men while showing that behavior which could be deemed servile was beneath them, Russian officers often refused to "duck down," much less get on their bellies, while leading assaults, or even, on occasion, while being on the receiving end of an artillery bombardment. By 1917, most of their poorly-supplied, often indifferently trained charges were not especially impressed by such behavior. In any case, the bravest and the best (not always, of course, one and the same) were now gone, many killed during Russia's most successful military operation.

As ill-informed as the average Russian soldier was, he knew that the overall leadership of state and army was of poor quality. There were almost always floating about numberless rumors regarding incompetence and corruption at high levels and, more often than not, these rumors proved to have been true. As mentioned earlier, in August, 1915, out of a misplaced sense of God-sanctified duty, the greatest leader of all, Nicholas II, assumed personal command of the army. So far as is known, the morale of the average Russian soldier did not leap up at his hearing about this and, considering the always parlous state of the army, this was a very unwise move, the sort of one upon which the Tsar could be counted to make in political or military areas. Now, in the eyes of soldiers and Russians in general the Tsar could be held personally responsible for military reverses, staggering casualties, and general mismanagement if not outright blundering, in the pursuance of a cause whose meaning and purpose was becoming increasingly obscure.

By the beginning of 1917, the Russian Army (at least hypothetically, better equipped than ever before) was in a condition of physical and, more importantly, spiritual exhaustion. For about a year and a half, it had been headed—although hardly led—by a man whose character and deportment seemed to underscore the veracity of that old Russian expression, "God and the Tsar are far away." At the same time, in seeming to preside over unparalleled suffering and disaster at a time in which God seemed to be further away than ever, he increasingly could be held accountable for both. As time went on, however, as more and more people, common and not so common, began to reflect upon the war experience and the incompetence, corruption, and just plain rot revealed by it, it became plain to many that an entire system had to be held responsible for this noxious situation. As Leon Trotsky, who would soon play a rather large role in what was to come, put it when describing Europe before the outbreak of World War I, "History's soldier's boot was poised above the ant-heap."

THE MARCH REVOLUTION AND THE PROVISIONAL GOVERNMENT

During the first few months of 1917, Russia experienced the harshest winter in recent memory. As now often hungry citizens struggled to obtain increasingly expensive heating fuel, the transportation system, dependent as it was upon overworked and badly maintained locomotives, collapsed. Shipments of foodstuffs to the cities virtually ceased, and the same held true with regard to shipments to the front. To be sure, less of the latter were needed since soldiers were now deserting in the thousands.

By late February, protests and food riots had broken out in several cities. By early March, strikes had taken place, and a munitions works in Petrograd "locked out" its protesting employees. Most of those working in the armaments industries were male. By this time however, with over 13 million men having been called up for military service (though, as we have seen, the number of those actually at the front was declining somewhat), most of the total labor force was female. This was the primary reason why women's labor organizations wished to demonstrate on March 8, "Women's Day." The legions of female workers, nurses, and others involved in the war effort would be honored while, at the same time, they, or at least their representatives would be able to call for better pay and working conditions. This had been planned for some time, with the government giving reluctant approval for the event to take place.

March 8 saw thousands of women, most of them textile workers, take to the streets in massive demonstrations. They were soon joined by the male comrades who had been striking the munitions works. The demonstrations increased in intensity. At times, they were close to being riots, and there was some looting of food stores. Police efforts to break them up resulted in several hundred casualties, and this served to further infuriate the demonstrators. Troops were called out; but, it soon became plain that almost all of the Petrograd garrison was sympathetic to them. Even the Cossacks, who earlier could have been counted upon to squelch disorders of this nature with ferocity, showed little zest on this occasion. Some of them were observed fraternizing with the protesting workers. The government finally called upon what it thought were more reliable front-line soldiers to deal with the situation. Upon leaving the lines, however, most "voted with their feet" and went home.

While all this was going on, the Tsar was at military headquarters at a town called Mogilev. He received messages from government officials in Petrograd insisting that he return to the city. While reflecting upon them, he received another message. This one, from the now revivified *Duma,* urged him to abdicate. Nicholas II responded by ordering the *Duma* dissolved. Instead, twelve of its members formed what became known as the "Provisional Committee." This took place on March 13, 1917. Two days later, this committee became the "Provisional Government." On March 14, however, there appeared probably one of the most extraordinary military orders of all time—"Order Number One." It was issued by a hastily formed council of workers and soldiers called the *"Soviet,"* an entity which, in turn, was modelled after an organization that had first appeared in the 1905 Revolution. This time, however, the Petrograd *Soviet,* which claimed to represent the true interests of Russian workers and soldiers, would be of greater permanence and significance than its predecessor. Initially, it agreed to support the Provisional Government, and the two organizations joined in planning for general elections for a constituent assembly to take place later in the year. There was one significant difference, however, between the Provisional Government and the *Soviet.* While the former had urged the Tsar to abdicate, it insisted that the war had to go on, so long as the enemy threatened Russian soil. The *Soviet,* on the other hand, called for an end to the war. This position informed "Order Number One," which virtually abolished discipline of any kind in the Russian Army. There were now two sources of executive authority in Russia, and time would tell which was a better judge of political and social realities.

The Tsar, hoping to set things aright, or at least see for himself what was going on, set out on the opulent imperial train for Petrograd. The train got as far as Pskov, a town about two hundred miles southwest of Petrograd, and went no further. For a while, the "Tsar of All The Russias," brooded on a magnificently outfitted train (one of the very few running at the time, of course), stranded many miles from his destination. It was a fitting metaphor for his pathetic reign in particular, and the state of Imperial Russia in general. Soon, his somber reveries were interrupted by the appearance of representatives of the new Provisional Government. Politely, but firmly, they requested his abdication. With that peculiar combination of condescension and weak-willed indifference characteristic of him when not bolstered by the presence of his wife, he complied. Fearing to be separated from his physically-enfeebled son, Nicholas refused to abdicate in favor of him. So, he asked his brother Mikhail to take it over. He refused. Even if he had accepted, it probably would not have meant much since, by this time, both the Provisional Government and the Petrograd *Soviet* (which was quite strident in its demands) were calling for a republic. On March 15, 1917, exactly a week after the Women's Day demonstrations, Nicholas II signed the abdication papers. On the same day, an unusually liberal nobleman, Prince Lvov, was declared "prime minister" of a new-born Russian republic. Unfortunately, it was one lacking a significant number of republicans.

At first, the Western Allies welcomed the establishment of a republican Russia. While depicted in their propaganda as a stalwart foe of German autocracy and militarism, just about everyone in the Allied camp had to admit, if only to themselves, that Tsarist Russia was far more autocratic than Wilhelmine Germany. Now, with the overthrow of this most retrograde of governments, a kind of social embarrassment had been brought to an end. At the same time, a new, seemingly republican oriented, government, was determined to keep Russia in the war. To be sure, it was well known in Western military circles that desertions in the Russian Army were continuing at an alarming rate. Yet, the revolution seemed to augur a time of renewed hope for the Russian people in general and the army in particular. In any event, the new regime, one striving to become as Western as possible in the shortest time possible, could not help but set things aright in the near future.

Most in Allied government and military circles were either naive with regard to conditions in Russia and the attitudes engendered by them, or they simply saw what they chose to see. The new Provisional Government might very well have viewed it as its sacred task to keep Russia in the war so long as Russian soil was threatened. The overwhelming majority of the Russian people, however, had had enough of a war whose purposes had become increasingly obscure as casualties soared and home-front suffering increased in direct proportion. Over time, it became plain that the Petrograd *Soviet* represented the wishes of the Russian people far more than did the Provisional Government. In any case, whether or not they knew of that "Order Number One" issued by the latter, Russian soldiers, sometimes after murdering their officers, streamed away from the lines in increasingly large numbers. Far to the rear, their peasant brothers were grabbing land for themselves and, for men starved of supplies and often hating their officers more than the declared enemy, the temptation was too much to resist. Yet, most of the Russian Army was still intact, at least physically, and was certainly capable of standing on the defensive. At the same time, as we have seen, the new government was determined to keep Russia in the war, no matter what. The German General Staff cast about for a way in which, from its perspective, events in Russia could be pushed through to their logical conclusion. In Zurich, an exiled Russian of considerable notoriety, was convinced that he could utilize the concerns of the German military establishment for his own purposes.

In 1903, the Marxist Russian Social Democratic Labor Party, of course, in exile at the time, split over the issue of how Marxist doctrine was to be applied to Russia. The founder and leader of the party, Georgi Plekhanov (1857–1918), adhering to orthodox Marxist principles, believed that, while the party certainly should offer advice and leadership to the working masses, a real revolution would result only from concerted mass action. Grounded in knowledge of the laws of history, the party could point the way. It could not, however, undertake revolutionary action on its own. Besides, in the Russian case, action in the near future seemed beside the point. Even in 1903, while industrial growth was proceeding at a rapid pace, Russia was far from the industrialized country in which Marx saw history's last revolution taking place. While hardly denigrating the role of action, Plekhanov saw it as occurring in conformity with inviolate laws of history. These same laws would see to it that, in due, course, workers in an industrialized Russia, complete with ruling bourgeois class, would become aware of their oppression. Then, and only then, would there be a true *proletarian* revolution in Russia.

For V.I. Lenin (1870–1924), however, whose brother had been hanged for participating in a plot against Alexander III (1881–1894), father of Nicholas II, Plekhanov's attempts to apply orthodox Marxist principles to Russia were absurd. While adhering to certain basic Marxist principles, most importantly, the emphases upon history as class struggle and the inherently unjust nature of the class-dominated state, Lenin thought it necessary to adjust Marxist doctrine to Russian realities.

In the past, efforts by idealistic young revolutionaries to go to the people and arouse them to acting in their own self-interest (as seen, of course, from the revolutionaries' perspective) had failed miserably. Either they were ignored or turned over to the authorities as agents of the anti-Christ. Once, in a somewhat petulant mood, Marx had referred to "the idiocy of rural life." As many revolutionaries came to see it, the vast majority of Russia's population was awash in bucolic idiocy. Thus, those seeking to act in its best interest had to organize themselves into tightly-knit, ruthlessly disciplined conspiratorial organizations. During the 1880s, there emerged a phenomenon consonant with Russian social backwardness—the professional revolutionary, fanatically committed to a cause for which he/she was willing to kill or be killed; all, of course, "in the name of the people."

Lenin's martyred brother had been a member of just such an organization. Lenin, convinced that Russian conditions did not allow for those approaches perhaps applicable in Central and Western Europe, where better educated workers could be counted on to recognize what was in their interests (and he was even skeptical about them), thought that the Social Democratic Labor Party ought to be organized along the lines of Russian revolutionary organizations such as the one to which his brother had belonged. Also, unlike Plekhanov, Lenin, perhaps because of his brother's experience, had little faith in laws of history. Rather, he placed much emphasis upon the role of individual action. To be sure, Russia was industrializing, but, it would be some time before it was a truly industrialized power. In the interim, a tightly-knit conspiratorial organization ready and willing to undertake action if circumstances called for it was necessary.

In 1903, meeting in exile, the Social Democratic Labor Party split apart. The precipitating factor was the editorial policy of the party newspaper. The real reasons, however, were differences regarding ideology and party organization between Plekhanov and Lenin. Those who had more faith in history and the masses—and thus followed Plekhanov—outnumbered those who supported Lenin who, as he saw it, had more of an appreciation for Russian conditions and thus had faith in neither. Lenin succeeded, however, in getting more of his followers elected to the editorial board of the party newspaper. Hence, his followers assumed the name *"Bolshevik,"* or "majority." For a variety of reasons, the most important of which remain obscure, Plekhanov's supporters seemed to be content with being covered by the term *"Menshevik,"* which means "minority," even though there were more of them than those who supported Lenin.

When the war came, Lenin was in exile. He participated in several Socialist conferences held to protest the war. His, however, was not exactly a message of peace. In fact, it was plain to many of his fellow delegates that he rather favored the war, seeing in it a means by which many millions of embittered soldiers and workers could be rallied against their respective imperialist governments. A war of nations, he declared, had to be turned into a war of classes. He was as mocking of pacifism as any general.

By early 1917, this *pro forma* humanist who didn't seem to like people all that much had grown discouraged. Despite several years of unprecedented slaughter, and military and governmental incompetence on all sides, upon which *Bolshevik* propaganda hardly needed to embellish, there was little sign that the war of nations was about to transform itself into a war of classes. In despair, Lenin commented that he and his followers could not count upon seeing great revolutionary battles fought in their lifetimes. Then, there came the news of the March Revolution and the fall of the Tsar. There then followed reports that, even as most of the Russian people wanted their country to quit the war, the Provisional Government was determined to see it through, so long as Russian soil was threatened. From his home-in-exile in Zurich, Lenin, with the aid of Swiss Socialists, was able to make contact with the German General Staff. If, he argued, they would allow him to travel across the lines and enter Russia, he would do his utmost to bring down the Provisional Government and get his country out of the war. After some reflection, the German military agreed to Lenin's proposal. A special car would be attached to a train leaving Zurich for points east. Lenin and friends would have it all to themselves. Neither soldiers nor German civil authorities would board the car, and Lenin promised that neither he nor any of his companions would leave it before it reached its destination, which was Petrograd.

Word of these arrangements soon got out and Russians at home, and even some non-*Bolshevik* ones in exile abroad, accused Lenin of taking German bribes, of committing treason. Allied governments were equally condemnatory. Lenin, however, didn't give a damn for personal popularity when matters of principle were at stake and, on April 9, 1917, the soon-to-be-legendary "sealed train" pulled out of Zurich. After a journey much slowed by wartime conditions, the train arrived in Petrograd on April 16. The Provisional Government could have had the train stopped at the frontier. Vastly underestimating their single-minded opponent, however, and convinced that his dealings with the German military had served to discredit him, they allowed it to proceed.

As the train entered Petrograd's Finland Station, Lenin was greeted with roses, cheers, and a band playing that eternal anthem of revolution, the *Marseillaise.* He was also greeted by the leader of the Petrograd *Soviet* who declared, among other things, that it was necessary for Russians to defend the gains of revolution against enemies foreign and domestic. Lenin, of course, realized that use of the term "foreign" meant that at least this particular *Soviet* official was saying that Russia must stay in the war, even as reform took place back home. The man who had used the German military for his own purposes while defying public opinion in his country, indeed, that in the Allied countries in general, would have none of it. Ignoring the call upon patriotism, Lenin declared that he had arrived as representative of international proletarian revolution. He was taking a chance in making this statement. It was, however, greeted with a thunderous roar of approval. It had been made, it seems, at a time when the Provisional Government was in serious trouble.

In the face of increasing popular concern that Russia withdraw from the war, the Provisional Government seemed more determined than ever to see things through to the end. In a crucial vote, the Petrograd *Soviet* voiced its confidence in the "official" government by the barest of margins. There were resignations, and cabinet reshufflings. In one of the latter, the former minister of justice, Alexander Kerensky (1881–1971), became the new minister of war. Kerensky was a member of the Labor Party, a non-marxist socialist organization. To his governmental colleagues, most of whom were middle class in background and interests, he was a radical. Yet, like them, he was in favor of keeping Russia in the war.

By late May, 1917, *Bolshevik* influence in the Petrograd *Soviet,* while growing somewhat, was still quite limited. Yet, Lenin, with his keen political instincts recognized that gaining control of this organization was what really mattered. "All power to the *Soviet!*" became a leading slogan of the *Bolsheviks.* Over time, as *Soviets* were formed in places other than Petrograd, it had, to government ears, a particularly ominous ring. Another *Bolshevik* slogan was perhaps of greater importance, however. "Peace, land, bread!" spoke to the most crucial concerns of the vast majority of Russians. And it was the increasing belief of many Russians, particularly those in the urban working class, that Lenin and his followers offered the greatest possibility of obtaining all three, that caused *Bolshevik* influence in the Petrograd *Soviet* (and later, some others as well) to grow substantially over time. By the end of May, Lenin had been joined by Leon Trotsky (1879–1940). At the time of the original *Menshevik/Bolshevik* split, Trotsky had tended more to the *Menshevik* point of view. He had played an active role in the 1905 Revolution, displaying excellent leadership and organizational abilities, while Lenin's role had been negligible. By 1917, however, Trotsky, in exile in the United States at the time, saw Russia's future as best served by the *Bolsheviks.* Thus it was that he returned to the Motherland to put these extraordinary abilities at Lenin's disposal. The latter would make good use of them.

Trotsky and Kerensky shared a quality in common—they were both excellent orators. Trotsky's speeches and proclamations, however, seemed to illumine or explicate realities, while often showing the way towards a better future. Kerensky, on the other hand, often came across as a self-promoting windbag, utterly divorced from such crucial issues as the needs and desires of the Russian people, and the true condition of the Russian Army. With regards to the latter concern, certainly if he *had* allowed himself to know of its state by the summer of 1917, he would not have imagined that it could have undertaken sustained offensive operations.

By June, 1917, desertions numbered in the hundreds of thousands. Those soldiers who chose to remain in their units, in keeping with the principles enunciated in the famed "Order Number One," often formed themselves into committees which, besides championing the rights and interests of soldiers, sometimes elected officers from amongst their ranks. In any event, even units in which more traditional chains of command existed, the hatred of men for their officers sometimes assumed homicidal proportions. As ever, supplies were short, and tempers increasingly so. An officer attempting to assert his authority was often putting himself at risk. It was this army, one virtually decaying on its feet, that Kerensky ordered to undertake an offensive. Such it did, in July, 1917, in Galicia. Surprisingly, under the command of the now widely-respected General Brusilov, it did gain some initial successes. Then, the men simply lost the will to advance further and, when hit by a strong Austro-German counterattack, they took off for home in large numbers. A later attempt to undertake an offensive in the same general area never got off the ground. After retiring quite rapidly to new positions, what was left of the Russian Army in the region managed to hold on the defensive, as, at the moment, their opponents did not have enough men to press their advantage.

Minister of War Alexander Kerensky had been responsible for ordering the disastrous offensive of July, 1917. As it was winding down to its disastrous conclusion, the Lvov government collapsed. Replacing the thoroughly shaken and discouraged prince proved to be difficult. In the end, it was Kerensky who, while retaining the post of minister of war, became prime minister. After presiding over a horrendous military disaster, he was about to preside over a political one. Initially, though, he enjoyed a success against the *Bolsheviks*. On July 17, 1917, encouraged by the failed July offensive and by signs of ever-increasing disaffection in the military and the public at large, they took part in an uprising against the government. It proved to be premature. Somehow, Kerensky was able to find enough loyal troops in Petrograd to put down the badly coordinated revolt and, while a loyal cadre, including Trotsky, stayed on in the capital to sustain the cause, Lenin fled into Finland. Some of Lenin's followers, Trotsky included, were arrested. By the end of July, 1917, Kerensky appeared to be pretty much in control of the situation. This would change.

In September, the general who, after the collapse of the July offensive, had succeeded General Brusilov as commander of the Russian

Army, Lavr Kornilov, attempted to stage a *coup* against the Kerensky government. While at first a supporter of the March Revolution, he saw the Kerensky government as going nowhere, while not being severe enough on *Bolshevik* agitators. Kornilov's march on Petrograd failed, and large numbers of Lenin's followers, even with their leader in exile and Trotsky in prison, played a crucial role in bringing this about. A group of relatively well-armed and well-disciplined workers, the "Red Guard," joined in digging trenches in and around the capital, while at least some of those *Bolshevik* agitators so hated by Kornilov now showed up amongst his own troops.

Kerensky was, at this point, at wit's end. His regime had been saved, but, this was in large part due to the activities of a political organization he feared and hated. His government fell, and now he was ruling as a kind of semi-dictator. Still very unsure of himself, however, he sought to make peace with the *Bolsheviks,* obviously a, if not the, party of the future. *Bolshevik* prisoners were released and, in due course, Lenin deemed it safe enough to return from Finland. By the time he joined his colleague Trotsky in Petrograd in October, 1917, matters were going very well from their perspective. In part because of their important role in putting down the Kornilov Revolt, in part because of the infuriating stasis of a government which, while seemingly not doing very much, insisted that Russia would remain in the war, the *Bolsheviks* were gaining an increasing amount of support. By early October, those who were promising "peace, land, and bread" had achieved majorities in both the Petrograd *Soviet* (headed by Trotsky), and the one in Moscow as well. Peasant Soviets had been forming in the countryside, increasing numbers of soldiers and sailors, even if not formally joining the *Soviets,* were sympathetic to the *Bolsheviks,* and the Red Guard stood ready for action. As Kerensky nervously met with his ministers in the former home of the Tsar, the Winter Palace, "history's soldier's boot" was about to descend again.

THE BOLSHEVIK SEIZURE OF POWER

By early November, 1917, Lenin had decided that the time had come for a *Bolshevik* seizure of power. Large numbers of Red Guardsmen had been gathered together in Petrograd, and they were promised support by a contingent of mutinous sailors. Army regiments stationed in the city had declared that they no longer recognized the Provisional Government and henceforth would take orders only from the Petrograd *Soviet.* On the night of November 6, Alexander Kerensky, recognizing how precarious the situation had become, held an emergency meeting of his cabinet in the Winter Palace. Not a great deal came of it and, early the next morning, he set out to try and find troops which might be loyal to the government. At 10:00 A.M., Trotsky issued a proclamation declaring that the government had fallen. It had not, of course—not yet, anyway. It was, however, a masterpiece of propaganda showmanship which showed the inhabitants of Petrograd just how confident the *Bolsheviks* were of themselves while, at the same time, shaking what little confidence Kerensky's forlorn ministers still had.

Throughout the day of November 7, 1917, gangs of Red Guardsmen and heavily armed sailors seized government buildings throughout the city. They encountered no resistance. By nightfall, only the Winter Palace itself remained in the hands of the Provisional Government. The huge building was defended by a force numbering around one thousand, including a contingent of cadets and about 150 women soldiers. After the guns of the cruiser *Aurora* and those of the Peter and Paul Fortress fired blank rounds to signal that the time for assaulting the palace had arrived, a general bombardment of the palace began. Some of the defenders, including almost all of the women, surrendered at that point. Then, small numbers of Red Guardsmen and sailors began infiltrating the Winter Palace. In due course, revolutionary troops flooded in in large numbers, many of them heading straight for the wine cellar. Kerensky's ministers who, with great courage, had remained at their posts, were arrested. As for Kerensky himself, he was, as we have seen, away, looking in vain for support. In due course, his travels took him out of the country altogether. Later, he settled in the United States and, until his death in 1971, he was a frequent speaker on college campuses throughout the country. Described by some as if he were a kind of footnote to history, he certainly didn't act as if he were aware of this.

By the early morning of November 8, all of the Winter Palace had been taken. There had been little resistance and few casualties on either side. In view of all the drama preceding and surrounding it, the storming of the Winter Palace was almost anti-climactic. Russia did, however, now have a new government. Later that day, at a meeting of the Petrograd *Soviet,* Lenin showed that it was quite serious about fulfilling at least one of its promises. To thunderous applause, he announced that his government was going to take Russia out of the war. On November 21, an order was issued that Russian soldiers were to fraternize with the enemy. This in fact began, and, much to the discomfiture of German officers, Russians and Germans met in no-man's land, shaking hands, embracing and, in some cases, even dancing. On November 26, Foreign Commissar Leon Trotsky sent a message to the German High Command, requesting peace negotiations. On December 2, 1917, a delegation representing the new *Bolshevik* government passed through the German lines. It was on its way to the city of Brest Litovsk, the city where, for three months, negotiations would take place. Russia's soon-to-be former Allies were both angered and horrified at what was going on. If Russia dropped out of the war, Germany would be able to concentrate on the Western Front and, for the first time, achieve strategic supremacy there. On top of that, there was a new government which, besides betraying the alliance, was soon talking about the need for world revolution. Who knew what could become of this? Somehow, heads of governments began to think, the *Bolshevik* regime had to be overthrown and, if at all possible, Russia kept in the war. As 1917 approached its end, at least the first undertaking seemed possible. At the time, the government conducting peace negotiations with the German High Command controlled Petrograd, but not much else. Fairly soon, however, it would begin to assert its authority over the rest of Russia. The circumstances in which this took place would add a new dimension of horror to that conflict which played so crucial a role in bringing Lenin to power. During the course of it all, unfortunate precedents would be set.

In fact, an unfortunate precedent was set rather early. In November, 1917, the elections for a constituent assembly took place. The Bolsheviks captured 9.8 million votes, or 24 percent of those voting. Certainly, this was a respectable showing. The big winners, however, were the peasant-oriented Socialist Revolutionaries, who received 20.8 million votes—58 percent of votes cast. Of course, when the formal Constituent Assembly first met, on January 18, 1918, its composition reflected the vote. Parliamentary niceties held little charm for Lenin. The only force of any significance around consisted of Red Guardsmen and pro-Bolshevik sailors. It was used to disperse the Assembly, and, the following day, January 19, the Executive Committee of the Congress of Soviets declared that it would not meet again. There was little in the way of meaningful public protest, and thus the new regime could claim a victory of sorts. It would not fare so well in dealing with the German military at Brest Litovsk.

14

Diplomatic Games and American Entry into the War

"BUSINESS AS USUAL" DIPLOMACY AND RESULTANT DIFFICULTIES

As seen earlier, Italy, which had in effect left the Triple Alliance upon the outbreak of war, had been persuaded to join the Allies through promises of territorial gain. Throughout the war, diplomatic dealings, some of them of a rather dubious nature, would be an important weapon, and, at times, one side or the other would show consummate skill in playing the old games, albeit in circumstances which were somewhat more strained than usual. Occasionally, impressive tactical triumphs would be registered. More often than not, though, these triumphs contained within them the seeds of strategic disasters, although, to be sure, most of these would not become apparent until the end of the war.

Sigmund Freud, in a moment of petulance, once declared that more lunacy had come out of the Middle East than anywhere else. He was referring in this instance to the Jewish, Christian, and Muslim religions. If one shares Freud's view that religions are varieties of infantilism this viewpoint can be seen as having merit. At the same time, however, outside powers, striving for gain in the region, have often engaged in varieties of diplomacy suggestive of psychological dysfunctionalism.

As we have seen, Turkey's entrance into the war created a number of problems for the Allies. There were threats posed to Allied oil supplies, and to the Suez Canal, and, with the Dardanelles remaining in Turkish hands, Russia was largely cut off from her Western partners. As we have seen earlier, while Allied efforts to gain control over the

Dardanelles resulted in disaster, the initial threat to the Suez Canal faded fairly rapidly. Yet, the Turkish threat to the oil fields remained, and a new attack on Suez was possible. There were still large Turkish forces about and, due to the Allies' understandable fixation with the Western Front, their manpower commitments to the Middle East had to be limited. There was an answer to this dilemma, however, and British diplomats were quick to seize upon it.

It was well-known that, while Turks and Arabs shared the same religion, that was just about all they shared. Ethnically, they were different peoples and, on the local level, one or the other group of Arabs felt far more loyalty to a family of prominence than to the Turkish government. While the Turks, when irritated by Arab subjects, never dealt with them as they would with the Armenians (even if a shared religion did not count for much, then demographic considerations made this impossible), Arabs throughout the Ottoman Empire had reason to feel oppressed, at times, exploited. In 1915, British diplomats in Cairo contacted a very prominent Arab leader, Sherif Hussein of Mecca. He was told that the British would support an Arab independence movement in exchange, of course, for Arab support of the Allied war effort. Obviously, the latter would have to come in the form of rebellion against Turkey.

As we have seen, in April, 1916, a British army suffered disaster at Kut-al-Amara. In June, there was some recompense when a force commanded by Sherif Hussein attacked and captured Medina, in western Arabia (now Saudi Arabia). By December, 1916, his position had become strong enough so that the British could recognize him as king of Arabia. To the west, apparent British support for Arab independence was responsible for even more excitement. Colonel T.E. Lawrence (1888—1935), in peacetime, an archaeologist, was undertaking activities which, in due course, would cause him to be referred to as "Lawrence of Arabia." Leading what amounted to an Arab guerrilla army, he lent invaluable support to a British offensive which drove the Turks out of Egypt completely, thus ending the threat to the Suez Canal. Eventually, this offensive would carry the British into Palestine, and, for the public, the best-known of its aspects were the exploits of Lawrence, the English champion of Arab independence. By the end of 1916, the Turkish hold on the more western portions of the Empire was either ended altogether or at least badly shaken. Those British diplomats in Cairo who had struck a deal with Sherif Hussein must have been very pleased with themselves. Even before the attack on Medina, however, an extraordinary diplomatic deal was struck by diplomats who acted as if they were completely unaware of the earlier one concluded between the British government and Hussein. It is more likely, of course, that they knew of it, but did not hold it to be of much importance.

In March, 1916, an English diplomat, Sir Mark Sykes, joined his French counterpart and signed what became known as the "Sykes-Picot Agreement." A little more than a month later, a representative of Russia would sign it. What this agreement did was to provide for the post-war division of the Ottoman Empire between the presumably victorious Allied powers. In view of the fact that, up to that point, the Allied military effort in the Middle East had not been crowned with much success (around the time that Russia was signing on to it, Townshend would surrender at Kut-al-Amara), the Sykes-Picot Agreement seemed to beg a few questions. Of far greater significance for the long term, however, was the fact that it could be seen as contradicting at least the spirit, if not the letter, of the agreement concluded with Sherif Hussein in 1915 and various promises given the Arabs by T. E. Lawrence.

The terms of Sykes-Picot provided that, after the war, Syria would be given over to the French, while Mesopotamia (now Iraq) would fall under British control. Due to its importance to three religions (the ones deemed loony by Freud), Palestine would fall under some form of international administration. Russia was to receive Turkish territory adjacent to her. Later, an ancillary treaty between France, Great Britain, and Italy would provide that the recent addition to the Allied camp would receive a large chunk of southwestern Turkey.

The arrangements with Russia and Italy, involving as they did Turkey proper, did not fly in the face of agreements concluded with the Arabs. Those, however, involving France and Great Britain were extremely problematic in this regard. To be sure, a large chunk of Ottoman territory, most of what is now Saudi Arabia, was reserved for the Arabs. Earlier arrangements, however, did not call for a strong British and French presence in *any* of the Arab territories, while the thought of placing Palestine under some form of international control was anathema to Arab public opinion. After all, besides religious considerations, the vast majority of its inhabitants were Arabs. For the present, the terms of the Sykes-Picot agreement remained secret. In due course, however, they would be revealed. Even if they had remained secret until a more convenient time for their unveiling, however, the Sykes-Picot Agreement in general pointed to the problems created when short-term wartime exigencies compelled a power with imperial interests of its own to make promises which had to have long-term consequences. The agreements concluded between Great Britain and Arab leaders contributed to a heightening of Arab nationalism. This would now be frustrated by arrangements made to ensure traditional imperialist interests in the Middle East. The situation was made far worse by another British effort to deal with short-term exigencies by obtaining the support of another group of nationalists with an interest in the region.

Ever since the 1880s, with rising anti-Semitism throughout Europe—and, in Eastern Europe, this was assuming increasingly violent forms—a growing number of Jews were interested in obtaining some sort of Jewish homeland. For many, the Biblical home of the Jews, now Palestine, came to mind. Most of these early advocates of what would become known as "Zionism" were strongly religious. The Austrian Jew, Theodor Herzl (1860—1904), however, knew little about the tenets of Judaism. For him, what he saw as the worsening political and social situations for Jews all over the world necessitated the establishment of a sovereign Jewish state. In 1896, he published a book entitled *The Jewish State.* The proposed location for such a state was Palestine. The book brought him instant publicity, and, a year later, Herzl presided over the First Zionist Congress, in Basel, Switzerland.

In the years following this congress, the Zionist movement grew in strength, particularly among the Jews of Eastern Europe. At one point, the British government suggested Uganda as a possibility for a Jewish homeland. The vast majority of Zionists, however, were emotionally committed to Palestine. Indeed, since the 1880s—but, particularly after the founding of a formal Zionist movement in 1897—there had been a growing Jewish emigration to this Turkish-held territory. By 1914, there were close to 90,000 Jews, most of them residing in Jerusalem, Haifa, the newly-created city of Tel Aviv, and a number of agricultural settlements. They were, however, vastly outnumbered by the Arab population which, at the time, totalled some 700,000.

In 1917, the Allied military situation in the Middle East had improved markedly. In March, after heavy fighting, Baghdad fell to the British, and, in September, another British army, commanded by General Edmund Allenby (1861—1936) was assaulting the Turks at Gaza. Soon, Allenby's army, greatly assisted by T. E. Lawrence's irregulars, was advancing through Palestine. It was obvious that Turkish rule in that area was soon to end and that it would now pass, at least for awhile, under British control. Having succeeded in obtaining Arab support for its war effort in the Middle East, Allenby's successes now made it possible for the British government to seek to obtain that of another party with interests in the region.

On November 2, 1917, the British foreign secretary, Arthur J. Balfour (1848—1930), announced that his government viewed "with favor" the establishment of a Jewish "homeland" in Palestine. Such, of course, would have to be done without infringing upon the "civil and religious rights of the non-Jewish communities," i.e., the Arabs and the relatively small number of Christians living there. What would become known as the "Balfour Declaration" was announced not because the British government was sympathetically disposed towards Zionism; but, rather, to strengthen—and, in some cases, gain—Jewish support for the war effort. That of particularly wealthy Jews was, of course, especially welcome. The Jews of Great Britain, of all classes, had strongly supported their country in its hour of need. What was crucial was securing the enthusiastic support of Jews in other parts of the world. British government leaders knew very well that the Jewish communities in the United States, which had come into the war in April, and Russia, which, at the time, was at least nominally still in it, had somewhat mixed opinions about the war. Memories of bitter persecution in Tsarist Russia made it difficult for many Jews to support—or, in some cases, even favor—the Allied cause. Now, the Tsar had been overthrown, but bad memories died hard.

Evidence would suggest that the Balfour Declaration did play an important role in causing Jews to lend support to the Allied war effort. To that extent, one could say that this diplomatic move was successful. Once again, however, an approach to dealing with short-term concerns helped to lay the groundwork for future difficulties.

It was not at all surprising that Arabs, both in and outside of Palestine, saw the Balfour Declaration as clashing with promises made by Great Britain to them. Thus, as most Jews, upon learning of it, rejoiced, most Arabs reacted in a somewhat different fashion. As they saw it, Great Britain had betrayed them. Worse was to come.

In December, 1917, the newly-established *Bolshevik* government, in an effort to gain world-wide support by showing just how perfidious the old regime, and those to which it was allied, could be, released the full text of the Sykes-Picot agreement; at the same time, of course, declaring that it would never pursue the sort of imperialistic course of which such a document was representative. The French and British governments were both outraged and embarrassed. Arab public opinion was mainly outraged.

To be sure, if one examined the promises made by the British to the Arabs with those made to the Jews, and then compared both to the post-war arrangements envisaged in the Sykes-Picot agreement, they did not, in a strictly logical sense, have to cancel each other out. If one were to be *rational* about it, however, particularly when competing nationalistic claims in the area were brought into the picture, they certainly did. Feeling the strains engendered by short-term exigencies, the British government had attempted to tap into two nationalistic movements for support. In so doing, of course, it had heightened nationalistic feelings on both sides. Why it thought that it could succeed in getting away with this was perhaps revealed in the Sykes-Picot Agreement. After the war was over, the document seemed to suggest, it would be "business as usual" again, and the areas in the Middle East formerly controlled by Turkey would be apportioned amongst the victorious powers. Such a time-honored approach had worked before, hadn't it? Even after Balfour's extraordinary "declaration," it would appear that the British government gave little thought as to what the consequences of its actions might be. In any event, out of needs generated by the most terrible war Europe had ever seen, there arose long-ranging problems with which we appear to be doomed to live for some time. Later, when he did have time to reflect on British diplomatic adventures during the Great War, Arthur Balfour remarked that, as he saw it, in wartime situations one sometimes has to make promises which probably would not have been made in times of peace. Bearing in mind what eventually resulted from those made by some of his colleagues, and by him, it was a rather bland assessment of the problem.

Questionable diplomatic moods in pursuit of short-term objectives were not the exclusive preserve of the Allies. In September, 1915, the Germans and Austro-Hungarians promised support for Bulgaria's territorial claims in Macedonia if the country would enter the war on their side. As seen earlier, Bulgaria did such and it was the Bulgarian Army which played the greatest role in penning-up a large Allied expeditionary force in Salonika. Thus, one could maintain that this particular diplomatic move on the part of the Central Powers was crowned with success. Certainly, this was true in the short-term. Long-term results, however, of outsiders meddling in tragically confused Balkan circumstances were not particularly pleasant.

Until the 17th Century, Poland had been a state of considerable power. By the end of the 18th Century, a combination of increasing backwardness relative to neighboring powers, diplomatic ineptitude, and corruption of an extraordinarily high order had been responsible for the country's disappearing from the map—partitioned between

Russia, Austria, and Prussia. Over time, there grew up a strong sense of Polish nationalism. Occasionally, for power-political reasons, one or another outside power would encourage it, usually to embarrass or frighten Russia, whose policies in her portion of Poland were seen as particularly odious. In November, 1916, the German and Austro-Hungarian governments declared that they would recognize an independent Poland if the Polish people would get behind their war effort. In some respects, this was a logical move. Foreign occupation, unsuccessful revolts against it, social backwardness, and a gnawing state of generalized unhappiness had left the Poles hosting strong resentments against a great variety of peoples in the area. Of the partitioning powers, however, the Russians were hated the most. In the end, most Poles came to support the Central Powers, and some even fought on their side.

Naturally, recognition of an independent Poland by Germany and Austria-Hungary would be meaningful only in the event of their winning the war. Of course they did not; but, as it was, Polish independence was assured by the victorious Allies. In the interim, however, the Central Powers had done much to help inflame Polish nationalism, something which would have results which, in future, many would find disquieting.

As in the case of British and French policies with regard to the Middle East, those of Germany and Austria-Hungary concerning Eastern Europe were often responsible for short-term successes. Yet, over the long-term, the consequences were decidedly negative. In yet another way, there was a crucial similarity between some of the diplomatic moves of the two enemy camps. Both the Allies and the Central Powers acted as if they thought that nationalisms, aroused in the service of their respective immediate concerns, could be "put on the back-burner" once matters had died down a bit; or, at the very least, they could be controlled. In a word, the diplomatic efforts of the major warring powers were informed by the infuriatingly arrogant notion that, even as they were engaged in the most destructive war in the history of the Western world—and several varieties of nationalism were playing no small role in sustaining respective military efforts—traditional power-political concerns, the only ones, of course, which really mattered, could be advanced. As for promises and assurances which might have the effect of encouraging the national of concern of less important folk, these were of little consequence. It was "business as usual," with all but the most immediate concerns surrendered to a God of history which each of the major combatants assumed to be on its side.

Francis Joseph I, Emperor of Austria and King of Hungary, had come to the throne in 1848 as the result of a revolution. Thus, some saw his regime as beginning under a cloud. Indeed, the new, eighteen-year-old ruler of a polyglot, at times, seemingly held together only by mutual hatreds which obviated the possibility of unified action against it, would be haunted by dark clouds throughout his reign. In 1889, his son Rudolf either committed suicide—which was generally suspected at the time—or was murdered. Since his mistress was found lying dead beside him, tragedy was spiced with scandal. In 1898, Francis Joseph's wife, Elizabeth, was assassinated by an anarchist while on vacation in Switzerland. It turned out that he had nothing against her personally. Being an anarchist, though, he was kind of duty-bound to kill the first ruler who happened to come along. In June, 1914, the assassination of his nephew, Franz Ferdinand, after Rudolf's death, now heir to the throne, and his wife in Sarajevo was the proximate cause of the current war. Now, increasingly bitter and remote, this most tragic of rulers was forced to watch hundreds of thousands of his subjects die in a war which, increasingly, seemed to be fought on German terms and for German goals. As 1916 was drawing to a close, at the age of eighty-six, death mercifully claimed the ravaged soul of Francis Joseph. The coming to the throne of his grand-nephew Charles would make possible one of the few diplomatic efforts which showed much of a departure from "business as usual" approaches.

Charles was furious over the continuously growing control exercised by the German General Staff over the Austrian Army—and, in the eyes of some, even the government as well. As time went on, he became increasingly aware of the fact that the duo which, in August, 1916, had replaced Erich von Falkenhayn as commander-in-chief of the German Army, Hindenburg and Ludendorff, were really running the show in Germany. He was especially suspicious of Ludendorff. Furthermore, Charles' wife, the Empress Zita, of French background, absolutely loathed the Germans.

Naturally, both Hindenburg and Ludendorff knew that the new royal couple did not exactly view them with affection, and, particularly in the case of Ludendorff, surely one of history's great haters, negative feelings were returned with a vengeance. Of greater genuine *concern* for Germany's new dictators, however, was that the new Austro-Hungarian foreign minister, Ottokar Czernin, shared Charles' suspicions of them. He was particularly untrusting of Ludendorff who, with some accuracy, he saw as the true master of Germany. Czernin, as desirous of peace as were Charles and Zita, was eager to establish contact with the Allies.

In the last months of 1917, contact was indeed made with the empress's brother, Prince Sixte de Bourbon. Because he was of the old French royal house, he was not allowed to serve in the French armed forces. He was, however, an officer in the Belgian Army. Thus, in making contact with Prince Sixte, who, in due course, paid a visit to Charles, the rulers of Austria-Hungary were in fact committing treason. It is possible that this thought occurred to them; but, nonetheless, arrangements were made for representatives of the British and Austro-Hungarian governments to meet in Switzerland. It soon became plain that, as the Allies saw it, Austria-Hungary could obtain peace only as part of a general settlement involving all of the warring parties. The Allied representatives declared that only if Germany would make it plain that she was willing to make some territorial compromises—say, returning Alsace-Lorraine to France—only then, could there be a general peace settlement. With some trepidation, Count Czernin asked Ludendorff if Germany, i.e., Ludendorff, would be willing to consider a compromise of this nature. Not now, not ever, was his reply, and peace plans were quietly shelved for the moment.

The Allies had a reason for standing firm during the secret negotiations in Switzerland—the same reason why it ill-served General Ludendorff to be so truculent. Since April of that year, the United States was in the war. How that situation came about will be the subject of the next section.

"THE YANKS ARE COMING": AMERICA ENTERS THE WAR

While American entry into World War I on the Allied side was hardly inevitable, there were a several factors which made it likely. Of considerable importance, of course, were shared political and cultural affinities with Great Britain. Certain nationality groups in the United States, such as the Irish, did not exactly celebrate them, but, most Anglo-Saxon folk did, and the "movers and the shakers" at the upper levels of the American political scene were of this group. Then, there was the question of German behavior.

It is highly doubtful that the behavior of German soldiers was worse than that of Russian ones, particularly if one bears in mind such uncongenial sorts as Cossacks. Oft-times, though, particularly during the campaign in Belgium, it, as we have seen, had been bad enough, and public relations had never been the German government's strong suite. A good example of this had been provided by Chancellor Bethmann-

Hollweg himself. Upon learning that Great Britain was entering the war, in part because of German violation of Belgian neutrality, something that had been guaranteed by the 1839 Treaty of London, he expressed amazement that the British would go to war over "a scrap of paper." It was a phrase which would haunt him, and Germany as a whole, for some time.

As we have seen, submarine warfare was just about a strategic necessity for Germany; but, again, in the public relations department, it had its drawbacks, and the sinking of the *Lusitania,* in May, 1915, demonstrated this rather well. Over 100 of the close to 1,200 lives lost were American and, as mentioned earlier, there was a storm of protest, public and diplomatic, over the incident. Germany did not want to risk breaking off diplomatic relations with the United States and, as mentioned before, after several other, less horrific incidents, the German government gave pledges that, in future, there would be restrictions placed on the activities of German U-boat captains. No longer would they be allowed to attack passenger ships without warning. The last of these pledges, the one dubbed *"Sussex,"* was still holding as of the beginning of 1917. It was, however, serving to put the German submarine campaign at a severe disadvantage, and there were enormous pressures upon the German government to, once again, allow for unrestricted submarine warfare.

One of the reasons why submarine warfare was so crucial to the German war effort was that American firms were supplying the Allies with raw materials and even artillery shells (the poor quality of at least some of the early shipments of these had provoked a scandal on both sides of the Atlantic). Individual American citizens of means were also advancing loans to the Allies. Little could be done about the loans. Ships carrying materials whose sole purpose was to kill German soldiers could be—and, from the German perspective, should be—sunk. To be sure, some American munitions makers had declared that they would sell their wares to anybody able to come and pick them up. With the British fleet ruling at least the surface of the Atlantic, however, it was plain that only Allied merchantmen would be loading up in eastern ports. As the German government saw it, American neutrality, despite occasional official condemnations of Allied actions—such as the brutal crushing of the Easter Monday Uprising in Ireland—was a cruel hoax.

As seen earlier, what became known as the British "Hunger Blockade" of Germany was far more destructive of human life; but, it lacked the drama attendant upon the torpedoing of passenger ships. And there was no lack of genuine atrocities committed by the German Army. Of course, in this regard, there was much exaggeration on the part of Allied propagandists and, since the major wire services were all in Allied hands, reportage tended to be somewhat one-sided. Then, there was the matter of the "Bryce Report."

About a week after the *Lusitania* went down, the well-known—and, in American academic circles, well-liked—British historian, Lord Bryce, produced a document which purported to be an accurate cataloguing of atrocities committed by the German Army in Belgium. A good number of the events described in Bryce's latest contribution to historical scholarship would turn out to be grossly exaggerated or, in some cases, wholly fictive. For large numbers of Americans, still stunned by the *Lusitania* incident, the Bryce report was an accurate portrayal of Huns in action.

By early 1917, then, American public opinion was, for the most part, squarely in support of the Allies. Some American young men, anticipating their country's entrance into the war, were undergoing military training at various camps, the best known of them being the one near Plattsburgh, New York. Indeed, there were a scattering of Americans who already were fighting for the Allies. Some, usually using Canada as an entry point, joined the British forces. Probably the most famed group of Americans, however, was known as the "Lafayette Escadrille"—an all-American squadron attached to the French Air Force. Besides public opinion however, there was the crucial factor of that of the government and, by late 1916, despite the fact that President Wilson had been elected for his second term (albeit narrowly) in part because of the slogan "He kept us out of war," some of its most important representatives had come to the conclusion that American interests would best be served by an Allied victory. Since it was plain that a stalemate now prevailed, and that such a victory seemed to be in doubt (the effects of the "Starvation Blockade" on the German homefront were not really appreciated at the time), American intervention came to be seen as necessary.

William Jennings Bryan (1860—1925), who had made several unsuccessful tries at the presidency, served as President Wilson's secretary of state until about mid-1915. A fervent supporter of American neutrality, he resigned in protest after his boss sent the German government a very sharp note following the sinking of the *Lusitania.* Bryan was succeeded at his post by Robert Lansing (1864—1928). It soon became obvious that, unlike his predecessor, Lansing was a champion of the Allied cause and, this being the case, sought to convince Wilson that America had to play a stronger role in supporting it. Over time, actual intervention came to be seen as the only meaningful alternative. It is probable that Wilson was headed in this direction in any case. Although he declared that the United States had to be neutral "in thought, word, and deed," it was pretty obvious to all that he favored the Allied cause. Also, over time, he became convinced that his country would play, in fact, ought to play, a greater role in the world. The first crucial role Wilson saw for it was assuring that, once the current war was over, there would be a arrangements in place to assure that this most terrible of conflicts would be the last. If the United States—in truth, as the somewhat messianic Wilson probably saw it, he himself—was to be able to lead the world towards a better future, it had to play a major role in winning a just peace. The only way this could come about, of course, was if the United States entered the war on the side of the Allies. Thus, it is entirely possible that, even without Lansing's influence, Wilson would have sought to lead America into the war. Whatever the case, certain German actions made a decision to enter the war far easier than it otherwise might have been.

In August, 1915, a high-ranking German intelligence officer carelessly left his briefcase behind when getting off a New York streetcar. In due course, it was in the hands of the American secret service. Among other things, it contained documents pretty well establishing the fact that German agents in the country were involved in acts of sabotage directed—and understandably so—against munition works supplying war materials to the Allies. Two diplomats were implicated and booted out of the country. In 1916, a gigantic explosion in Jersey City, New Jersey completely destroyed a pier piled high with munitions. While it was never completely established that German agents were responsible for the blast, most people, in and out of government, believed that they were, and such was probably the case. Certainly, in view of the fact that the United States, or at least quite a few American firms, were playing a one-sided role in the war, actions such as this are understandable. Understandable or not however, they are generally not conducive to the maintenance of good diplomatic relations.

Early in January, 1917, the German government—in truth, the German military, which was actually running things—decided that strategic realities dictated that Germany had to commence, once again, with unrestricted submarine warfare. Naturally, all knew that this might bring the United States into the conflict. As the German government saw it, however, America was neutral in name only, anyway. Also, it would be some time before a large American Army would be ready for combat. In the meantime, a ruthless U-boat campaign could well bring the Allies, Great Britain in particular, to their knees. It was a gamble in any case; but, military realities being what they were, Germany's leaders thought that they had no real choice in the matter. On January 31, 1917, the German government announced the commencement of unrestricted submarine warfare. On February 3, President Wilson informed the Congress that he had severed diplomatic relations with Germany.

Although, as mentioned earlier, most Americans were pro-Ally, it is probable that, even with the reintroduction of unrestricted submarine warfare, the country as a whole was not in favor of entering the war. After probably one of the greatest diplomatic blunders of all time, however, the American mood had changed considerably. What was primarily responsible for this was not German action on the high seas, but German efforts "south of the border."

Since 1911, Mexico had been torn by revolution and civil war. In 1913, the revolutionary regime of Francisco Madero was overthrown by Victoriano Huerta. A representative of the wealthy, land-owning class, he was obviously opposed to any meaningful reform. He was also anti-American. After an incident involving American sailors and Mexican authorities at Tampico, in April, 1914, American sailors and marines attacked, captured, and, for awhile, occupied the coastal city of Veracruz. Arbitration soon settled the problem; but, even Mexicans who loathed Huerta were infuriated at the forceful American action. At the same time, the American government lifted an arms embargo against Mexico, thus allowing Huerta's opponents to obtain valuable weaponry. In July, 1914, as Europe headed into war, Huerta's forces were defeated and he fled to Spain. One of those who shared in the victory over him was Mexico's next president, Venustiano Carranza. An important ally of his was Francisco ("Pancho") Villa (1877?—1923). Within a year or so, it was plain that Carranza was losing interest in meaningful reforms, and his former lieutenant, Villa, turned on him. Once again, Mexico was inflamed in civil war.

The man who soon became known as "Pancho Villa" was a colorful, if mostly loathsome, individual who, while something of a genuine reformer, seemed most of all to enjoy killing. In January, 1916, his forces slaughtered a party of American mining engineers in northern Mexico. In March, he raided across the border and attacked Columbus, New Mexico. Seventeen Americans died in the incident. An infuriated American government ordered General John J. Pershing (1860—1948) to take a cavalry force (it eventually totalled around

12,000 men) into Mexico and destroy Villa's army. At first, the Carranza government gave cautious approval to the American intervention. But, as Pershing, in vain efforts to even find his opponent, pressed ever deeper into Mexico, Carranza—indeed, probably most Mexicans—became increasingly hostile to the expedition. Pershing's soldiers never clashed with those of Villa. They did, however, clash with regular Mexican troops. Eventually, with things falling apart with Germany, Pershing was ordered to take his men home and, in February, 1917, the American military embarrassment came to an end. It had contributed to growing Mexican resentment against what they saw as a bullying northern neighbor. To be sure, once America found itself at war with Germany, some would say that Pershing's Mexican expedition had provided at least one group of soldiers with excellent preparation, and this would certainly have been the case if the war in Europe were carried out mainly on horse-back. The expedition did provide the background for the aforementioned diplomatic blunder; and we must now consider it.

Friction between the United States and Mexico did not go unnoticed in Berlin and, with the policy of unrestricted submarine warfare about to be announced, the German government was determined to take advantage of it. On January 16, 1917, German Foreign Secretary Arthur Zimmermann (1864–1940) cabled a most imaginative message to the German ambassador in Mexico City. If, as anticipated, war should break out between Germany and the United States, he—the ambassador—should attempt to put together a Mexican-German alliance. The Mexican government should be told that, as a reward for joining on with Germany—and provided, of course, that America was defeated in the war to come—Mexico would receive those territories taken from her in the 1846–1848 war with the United States. These consisted of Texas, New Mexico, and Arizona. Furthermore, Zimmermann went on, Japan, now in the Allied camp, but resentful of American racism, should, if possible, be persuaded to join the proposed alliance.

This extraordinary missive was intercepted by British intelligence, decoded, and the results turned over to the American government. Soon, it was released to the press, and, on March 1, 1917, the American public teamed of this daring foray on the part of Germany's foreign minister. The uproar was tremendous, and the upsurge of anti-German sentiment helped to contribute to support for President Wilson in his efforts to get the approval of the American Congress for the arming of American merchant ships. After much heated debate on the issue, the president prevailed. But, the four American merchant ships sunk by U-boats during the month of March were all unarmed, and loss of life had been considerable. It was plain that a strong American response would be forthcoming.

President Wilson, as suggested earlier, certainly was pro-Ally in sentiment, and some historians have suggested that, bearing in mind his vision of a post-war world and the role in expected to have the United States play in it, he eventually would have had to take the country into the war. This might well have been the case. Wilson was, however, hardly a war-like individual. In fact, more blood-thirsty types such as the former President, Theodore Roosevelt (who was eager to raise his own division and leap into the fray), viewed him as a kind of sissy. It was not a joyful Wilson who, on April 2, 1917, stood with bowed head before a joint session of Congress. There was no radio, to say nothing of television, in 1917; but, all of America seemed to know what was going to happen. Outside the Capitol Building, squads of cavalrymen battled to keep surging crowds under control. Inside, after providing a litany of justifications for declaring war, the American president requested that Congress act accordingly. On April 4, 1917, the Senate passed the war resolution overwhelmingly. On April 6, it cleared the House, although there was considerable opposition amongst Midwestern Congressmen, some of whom represented constituents who were either very isolationist in sentiment, of German background, or both. The United States was about to enter the first "overseas" war in its history, and neither it nor the world as a whole would ever be the same.

15

Nineteen Seventeen: America Mobilizes; Europe Bleeds On

MOBILIZATION, INDOCTRINATION, AND MASS HYSTERIA

By the end of the first week of April, 1917, the United States was in the war. At first, however, the Congress was reluctant to go along with President Wilson's demand that there be general conscription. The last time there had been a draft was in the middle of the Civil War and its introduction had occasioned some of the worst civil unrest the country had ever seen. Now, especially with significant portions of the population, such as German-Americans, either luke-warm about or opposed to American involvement in the war, there was the possibility, it was feared, of more of the same, and on a far larger scale. To be sure, a recruitment agency, the Selective Service, was set up almost immediately. At first, though, it was literally quite selective, and only slightly more than 500,000 men were called into service. This was not enough for Wilson, who demanded that all able-bodied men between the ages of twenty-one and thirty-one should be registered. In mid-May, the Congress somewhat grudgingly agreed to pass a general conscription law, and it provided that, on June 5, nine and a half million men would be registered at conscription booths all over the country.

To the surprise and relief of many in the government, there were no civil disturbances of any consequence. Instead, the registrants seemed to be possessed of an excitement, even an enthusiasm, which the war-weary world had not seen since the heady "August Days" of 1914. Americans, both in and out of uniform, were seized with an extraordinary optimism. There was not doubt that American manpower would turn the tide; that "we" would win the war.

The commander of those troops to be sent overseas, the "American Expeditionary Force" (AEF), was none other than John J. Pershing. His recent failure to even *find,* much less capture, Pancho Villa, rankled some. But, he was the only high-ranking officer with any real military experience at all, at least from a command perspective, and he wanted the job very badly. By the end of May, with a staff which, by today's standards, was positively minuscule, he was off to France to begin the process of coordinating the American war effort with that of the Allies.

As Pershing was on his way, the building of barracks and manufacturing of combat gear—knapsacks, boots, mess tins, uniforms, gas masks, etc.—was proceeding at a frantic pace. As for actual weapons, production was undertaken on the "Model 1917" Springfield rifle, and on an especially cumbersome automatic rifle. Some machine guns were also turned out. Shell production in factories which had been providing such for the Allies for some time naturally increased. Yet, while the Congress set aside millions of dollars for the manufacturing and testing of aircraft and tanks, it was soon plain that, with regards to just about everything but small arms, the AEF would have to be equipped by the Allies. American industry simply could not "retool" quickly enough and the relatively few tanks and planes of American manufacture which actually turned up in Europe did so after the fighting had ended. American forces overseas would receive all of their artillery pieces and tanks from the French and the British, while pilots of the small, but growing, "American Air Service" would fly in Allied, mainly French, planes. At times, there were even shortages with regard to small arms as well, and American soldiers had to rely on British Enfield rifles and French and British machine guns. It was obvious that the American contribution to the war effort would be in the form of some millions of men who, in a war long since surrendered over to attrition, would, quite literally, constitute "fresh blood." Perhaps of equal importance was the enormous morale boost given the near exhausted Allies by America's entrance into the war. Unlike the British and the French, the United States had not gone through massive blood-lettings, and the first young men who arrived in Great Britain and France in the summer of 1917 were, in terms of physical appearance, most impressive. It would be awhile, however, before enough troops would be present on the continent to enable American forces to play a crucial role in the fighting. In due course, there would indeed be enough; this, despite the fact that leading German naval strategists had declared that U-boats would be able to present this from happening. From the German perspective what went wrong?

In March, 1917, German submariners sent 500,000 tons of Allied shipping to the bottom. In April, what turned out to be the record for one month, 800,000 tons, were destroyed. After that, however, shipping losses began to decline, and fairly dramatically at that. This was due to several reasons. First of all, the American and British naval commands put together what became known as the "convoy system." Instead of travelling singly, or in very small groups, ships were brought together in large groups, presided over by squadrons of destroyers. In World War II, German submariners would be able, up to a point, to deal with guarded convoys. In World War I, however, there was neither the technology nor the tactical refinement necessary for Germany's submarine fleet to be able to respond adequately to this new challenge. The second factor responsible for dooming the German submarine campaign was the so-called "North Sea mine barrage." British and American warships laid down what amounted to underwater minefields in the North Sea, a critical area with regard to submarine operations. Mines, up to then deadly to surface ships, now assured that hundreds of German sailors would die horrible deaths fathoms beneath the waves. As Allied shipping losses declined, German submarine losses rose sharply. By the end of summer, 1917, it was plain to both the Allies and the Germans that U-boats could not prevent the landing of a large American force on the continent.

Throughout the summer and fall of 1917, American troops arrived in France. After further training, in the course of which British and French instructors played crucial roles in exposing the newcomers to some of the wrinkles of trench warfare, they were gradually filtered into the line. On November 2, 1917, three American soldiers were killed in a German raid on their trench, eleven others taken away as prisoners. This being a war, one could have expected that, sooner or later, something like this might happen. When, however, America was apprised of the first combat deaths of three of its sons, there was an indignant outcry. "Huns Kill Three Pershing Men!"—so read one newspaper headline. It pointed to a home-front mood in which confidence in ultimate victory was rapidly being complemented by hysteria.

To be sure, in his speech calling for the declaration of war against Germany President Wilson had been careful to point out that the United States was not waging war on the German people. In fact, he drew a sharp line between the German people and the autocratic regime which, without any concern about whether or not those over which it ruled approved of its decisions, had taken the country into war. Indeed, as Wilson saw it, the war was a kind of crusade against autocracy.

"The world," he declared, "must be made safe for democracy." In order that the American people were properly informed—perhaps "indoctrinated" would be a better word—as to the reasons the country was now at war, a "Committee of Public Information," headed by a Colorado journalist named George Creel, was established. Very soon, it was known simply as the "Creel Committee." Under its direction, an enormous variety of posters and pamphlets was turned out and the relatively new film industry was put to work producing movies of a decidedly propagandistic nature. Under Creel's direction, the "Four Minute Men" phenomenon put in an appearance. These were zealots in the cause of Wilsonian idealism whose job it was to be able, in four minutes, to explain to any audience anywhere in the country the reasons why the United States was sending vast armies overseas for the first time in its history.

Apologists for Creel have pointed out that, while his committee did engage in a certain degree of censorship, it never used the "big lie" to stir up hatred for Germans, much less German-Americans. Yet, the, at times, extremely strident tone of at least some of the propaganda produced by his committee certainly contributed to a growing war hysteria. Whatever the role played in it by the Creel Committee might have been, many, perhaps most, Americans were soon off on a nationalistic toot which, in sheer lunacy, rivaled analogous phenomena on the other side of the Atlantic. Some of the results of this were, to be sure, useful for the war effort. The super-patriotic vaudevillian, George M. Cohan produced one of the most stirring calls-to-battle imaginable, "Over There," while movie stars such as Douglas Fairbanks, Mary Pickford, and Charlie Chaplin lent their efforts to extremely successful "Liberty Loan" war bond drives. Nationalistic fervor, however, often went hand-in-hand (as it usually does in wartime situations) with hatred of an enemy perceived of as demonic, one whose nefarious representatives were obviously everywhere. In the eyes of a great many Americans, in view of the gravity of the situation, very serious measures had to be undertaken.

German *"Kultur"* had now been revealed as the kind which would inculcate people with values consonant with such activities as crucifying captured Canadian soldiers, raping nuns, and torturing small children. Thus, in various parts of the country, war was declared upon it. In some colleges and universities, the teaching of the German language came to an end. Some symphony orchestras would no longer play music composed by Germans and, with regard to at least several of the recognized musical periods, that effectively eliminated just about everything. More mundane areas of life could not be ignored, of course, and thus it was that sauerkraut was renewed "liberty cabbage," the frankfurter, "liberty sausage," and the humble dachshund, the "liberty hound." A statue of Goethe, in Chicago's Lincoln Park, was vandalized, and, in various places around the country, individual German-Americans were physically assaulted. There were even several cases, in the American West, of farmers of German extraction losing their land. A veritable spy-mania swept the country and citizens who, from a strictly clinical standpoint, would be adjudged sane, seriously believed that enemy agents ensconced on hill-tops, signalled one another with mirrors, and that others busied themselves slipping particles of ground glass into bandages destined for military use. When the deadly Spanish Influenza arrived in the United States in 1918, some citizens would blame it on the Germans, and several crack-brained souls claimed to have seen a German submarine surface, release a dark, obviously pestilential, cloud, and then submerge. In the heady atmosphere engendered by the country's first large-scale overseas adventure, many Americans seemed willing, even eager, to believe just about anything. While, as suggested above, the Creel Commission has been seen as generally not going in for hate propaganda, a very famous poster put out under its auspices both reflected and contributed to a growing hysteria. It showed New York City under attack from German submarines and aircraft. The Statue of Liberty was in headless shambles, buildings of the city's skyline blasted into rubble. Just about everyone viewing the preposterous piece must have known that, at the time, no airplane in the world had the range and performance-capacity to fly the Atlantic, level New York City, and return home. Yet, while perhaps not believing *literally* in the poster's grim message, many who saw it were both moved and angered by it. The combination of nationalistic pride, hatred of an enemy perceived of as inhuman, and general fear, at times bordering on paranoia, was responsible for an ugliness in public life which would not disappear with the end of the war. Indeed, it would blend in well with more traditional fears and prejudices to produce a period dominated by paranoid fears and race-hatred not seen in the United States since the Civil War.

The average American, even if occasionally troubled by evidence of nationalistic excess, wholly supported the war effort. Some radical voices were raised in protest—and, in turn, some of these were jailed. Yet, as the newly-created War Industries Board organized the resources of the most economically-powerful country on earth (while imposing ration schemes on a civilian population quite willing to accept them), few were deeply disturbed by sporadic infringements on civil liberties. Most Americans were inspired by the spectacle of a mighty nation committed to war in the name of principles identified—at least by the government—as being at the very core of national life. Less concerned over the role of idealism in American entrance into the war, the Allies waited with decreasing patience for the United States to play a significant role in military operations. There were, as we shall see, very palpable reasons for this concern.

EUROPE BLEEDS ON

THE NIVELLE OFFENSIVE: BLOOD PURGE AND MUTINY

As we have seen, one of the heroes of Verdun, General Robert Nivelle, replaced General Joffre as head of the French Army. Initially, he seemed to have been an excellent choice. Whereas Joffre was a remote, secretive soul who rarely shared his views with anyone other than a few carefully chosen military confidants, Nivelle was an affable, seemingly friendly sort, who simply radiated confidence. In his retaking of Fort Douaumont during the later stage of the Verdun battle, he had succeeded, in attacking along a very narrow front, in achieving a very sudden concentration of forces. These, after a short, but intensive, preliminary bombardment, had attained a notable success. Now, in charge of all of the French Army, Nivelle thought that he could apply what he called the "Nivelle System" in a much grander way.

What limited ebb-and-flow there was on the Western Front had resulted in there being a ten-to-twenty mile German "bulge" in the Allied lines between Arras in the north and Soissons to the south. In January, 1917, shortly after he was appointed commander-in-chief of the French Army, Nivelle came up with what he said was a fool-proof scheme of destroying the German armies and thus completely rupturing the enemy lines. Allied armies, British ones to the north, French to the south, would attack at the flanks of the "bulge," rapidly penetrating behind it. Thus, the trapped German troops would either be taken prisoner or annihilated. So pleased was Nivelle with his plan, so confident was he of its success (after all, it had worked at Fort Douaumont), that he made many copies of it so that as many Allied generals and assorted political big-wigs as possible could be apprised of it.

Some of Nivelle's French colleagues were very skeptical over a plan which assumed that methods involved in an attack on a very limited front could be successfully applied on one of over 100 kilometres. British Prime Minister Lloyd-George, however, disgusted over the murderous follies of his own generals, Haig in particular, was enchanted by it. And Nivelle did enjoy support from at least some of his French colleagues. Thus, by the end of January, 1917, over 1,200,000 French troops were moving into positions along the Aisne River in preparation for an assault on what had become known as the "Oise Salient."

Nivelle's eagerness to share his brain-storm with as many relevant folk as possible had allowed the Germans to obtain a pretty good idea of what he had in mind. The massive troop movements in preparation for the anticipated assault—somehow, Nivelle thought, the operation would remain something of a secret—left them with no doubts whatsoever on that score. Generals Ludendorff and Hindenburg decided that if the German armies threatened with attack would pull out of the Oise Salient "bulge," not only would they be taken out of a somewhat exposed position, but, withdrawn to one which would be much stronger. At the same time, the line would be shortened to a significant degree, and thus the German defense could be more concentrated.

Early in February, 1917, German troops began withdrawing out of that salient, the pinching off of which had been the initial goal of Nivelle's anticipated attack. As they withdrew to what they would call the "Siegfried Line" (the Allies referred to it as the "Hindenburg Line"), they carried out what was called "Operation Alberich." Alberich was the name of the malicious dwarf in the Nibelungen Saga (at this point, the spirit of Richard Wagner would appear to have been abroad at the German GHQ), and it was an appropriate designation for what was carried out. As the Germans withdrew, they created a desert—homes were demolished by the thousands, orchard trees cut down, forests set on fire, wells poisoned, railways and roads wrecked. Some German soldiers, having gotten to know French families, wept when telling their shocked neighbors what they had been ordered to do. Orders were orders, however, and they were carried out with impressive thoroughness.

With the German line now both straightened and shortened, whatever rationale there had been for Nivelle's offensive had, in reality, vanished. Yet, as had happened with actual battles in the Great War, his anticipated offensive had gained an inertial momentum in the general's mind, and he insisted that he would precede with it. When protests were raised against the attack, the usually affable Nivelle, exploding in towering rage, threatened to resign. Since there was nobody around at the time either willing or able to fill his—as matters turned out, rather small—shoes, colleagues, political and military, backed off, and agreed that the offensive would take place. British and French commanders, determined, however, that there would be a slight delay while British troops undertook a somewhat more limited offensive of their own, designed to draw off as much German troops as possible from the French portion of the front.

On April 9, 1917, the British struck out from Arras, the town which, as we have seen, was on the northern flank of the now-vanished salient. At first, the attack was, by Western Front standards, a success. Most of Vimy Ridge was taken by a Canadian corps, and, in some areas, there was an advance of almost a mile. By mid-April, the British lines had been pushed forward for four miles in some places. Yet, although, in terms of ground gained, the attack around Arras was more successful than previous British ventures, it was, in the end, a disappointment. Outside of the capture of most of Vimy Ridge, little of consequence had been taken. The attack had been contained well-short of the Hindenburg Line proper, and the Germans had been able to accomplish this without having to draw troops away from their front facing the French. While losses sustained by the British were thus out of proportion in comparison with results achieved, the Arras disappointment was not, except for the families of those lost in the campaign, a disaster. Nivelle's grand adventure, of which the Arras operation was the opening act, was, and it would shake not just the army, but all of France.

By the end of March, 1917, General Nivelle knew that, with German abandonment of the old "Oise Salient," their defensive positions had been much improved. Furthermore, these positions had been heavily reinforced. As he saw it, however, it didn't matter. The greater the number of Germans there, he blandly proclaimed, the greater his victory would be. The initial goal of Nivelle's troops was the capture of a heavily-defended ridge known as the Chemin des Dames, most of which was several miles from the French lines. After that, the French Army, in a flurry of offensive enthusiasm, would breach the Hindenburg Line. The offensive would commence on April 16. To soften things up, the French artillery began a bombardment on April 2.

If we bear in mind the main aspects of what was called the "Nivelle System," it is plain that, with regard to the operation under way, it no longer existed. In place of the intense, but brief, surprise bombardment, there was that long-term shelling that had become something of a tradition on the Western Front. There had been no sudden—and, by the enemy, unforeseen—concentration of forces. Rather, the German High Command, fully aware of what Nivelle was up to, had made certain, both through shortening their line and by reinforcing the new one, that the French numerical advantage was minimal. When Nivelle had first broached the subject—and, as we have seen, to just about anyone who would stand still long enough to listen to it—his supposedly new approach to the Western Front deadlock was presented as tailor-made for the task of pinching off an enemy salient. Now, the salient was, itself, gone. In truth, as we have seen, by the time the French Army first struck out along the Aisne River, on April 16, 1917, there *was* no "Nivelle System" of any kind—only a Nivelle ego in the service of which tens of thousands of Frenchmen would pay a bitter price.

As had been so often the case with regard to previous Allied offensives, the preliminary bombardment had left now greatly-strengthened German defensive positions almost intact. Thus it was that, when French soldiers left their trenches on the morning of April 16, they stepped into the most heavily-concentrated machine gun and artillery fire imaginable. On the very first day, what would become known as the "Chemin des Dames Offensive" cost the French around 40,000 casualties. Almost no ground at all had been taken and, even without a bad turn in the weather (there were now periods of rain, sleet, and snow, and it had long been determined that, at least on the Western Front, such conditions generally favored armies fighting on the defensive), it was plain that little more could be accomplished by continuing the attack. It was continued, nonetheless, for close to two terrible weeks. Around 250,000 Frenchmen were killed, wounded, or missing. German losses were around a quarter of this. Incredibly enough, Nivelle had demonstrated an ability to expend lives at a pace more rapid than that set by Douglas Haig. Not since August, 1914, had the French Army suffered losses so high in so brief a period of time.

By April, 1917, however, the average French soldier had had enough. On April 29, 1917, a French infantry regiment mutinied. Within days, there were incidents of indiscipline throughout the army. There were desertions. In most cases, however, men simply refused to move forward or got so drunk on *pinard,* the rough, red army wine, that they couldn't move in any case. In some instances, those soldiers who did go into the line bleated as if they were sheep being led to slaughter. One way or another the whole world would learn of the wanton manner in which their lives were being expended. By mid-May, it was estimated that, out of the French Army's 112 divisions, only 44 had not been affected by the mutiny, and even some of these units were viewed with suspicion by their generals. The mood of this thoroughly dispirited army was best captured by the frequently-repeated declaration that thosc in rebellion would defend their trenches if attacked. They were, however, "'not so stupid as to march against undamaged machine guns!'"[1]

It seems almost an impossibility, but the German High Command did not learn about the mutiny until much later, by which time such knowledge didn't mean a great deal. No matter what the Germans knew or didn't know about it, there was no question but that Nivelle had to be replaced as head of the French Army. At a meeting of generals in May, 1917, Nivelle was subjected to a merciless attack. Under a steady barrage of insults, he tried, without much success, to shift blame for the failure to his subordinates. Thoroughly discredited, an object of contempt throughout France, the once cocky purveyor of the "Nivelle System" was sent away to serve at a meaningless post in North Africa. He was replaced as commander in chief of the French Army, by Philippe Pétain, another hero of Verdun. As mentioned earlier, he was, unlike so many other French generals, a somewhat cautious soul. It was his task to convince the average French soldier that the French High Command would take his life seriously; seriously enough so that it would not be thrown away in some mindless offensive. At the same time, though, at least some of the mutineers had to be punished. About 2,900 were under arrest. Between 50 and 60 of them were shot, over 1,300 sentenced to hard labor, while the rest received relatively light sentences.

Even as sentencing of the mutineers was being carried out, Pétain was undertaking a campaign which, in its own way, was as serious as that carried out at Verdun. He personally visited a number of units, talking to individual soldiers, inspecting food and medical services, and making certain that all officers at all levels of the chain of command became aware that, from now on, French soldiers would have faith in the fundamental fairness of the system. Above all, Pétain made it plain that, for the time being, the French Army would stand on the defensive. As for any substantive offensive venture in the future, well, Pétain declared, he was "waiting for the Americans and the tanks."

HAIG ON A FIELD OF HIS OWN CHOOSING: FLANDERS, 1917

While, as we have seen earlier, Douglas Haig undertook the campaign on the Somme with enthusiasm once he was committed to it, he originally wanted the BEF to attack in Flanders. He had had much support for this. The Admiralty in particular, convinced (wrongly, as matters turned out) that many, if not most, German U-boats were based at various points on the Belgian coast, were particularly keen on an offensive which would result in its capture. After the Nivelle debacle, Haig—who never had much respect for anything French in any case—was convinced (or argued as if he was) that, unless a substantial offensive operation was undertaken, the French Army might well collapse altogether. In this case, many of his colleagues and some civilian higher-ups agreed with him. Thus, despite the suspicions of his nemesis, Lloyd-George, Haig proceeded with his plan to launch a major offensive in Flanders, its ultimate object being the capture of the Belgian coast. The success, admittedly limited, of a preparatory operation was seen by some as auguring well for the more substantive enterprise being prepared by the BEF's commander in chief.

must off far French army

The first objective of Haig's anticipated Flanders offensive was Passchendaele Ridge. Though less than two hundred feet high, it was the *only* "high ground" in the neighborhood of Ypres and the Germans who were entrenched upon it had put their advantage to good use. The southernmost portion of Passchendaele Ridge was Messines Ridge. It stuck out as a kind of "bulge" in the British line, a kind of salient within the Ypres Salient. The British were determined to take it, and, early in June, 1917, did so, and in an unusually ingenious, if horrific, way. For some months, British sappers had been running tunnels under no-man's land, and thence, under the German positions. In all, nineteen tunnels were dug, and they were packed with 500 tons of explosives. The Germans were aware that something untoward was going on; but, for once, their fabled technical ingenuity failed them, and the British operation went on undetected.

Passchendale

tunnelled mines

At 3:10 A.M., on June 7, 1917, what amounted to nineteen gigantic mines went off all at once. Lloyd-George, at work at his study, heard the dull rumble and the room shook as if struck by a mild earthquake. British troops bracing for the advance upon Messines Ridge were, in some cases, blown to the back of their trench. Just about all were awestruck at the sight of the hated ridge being blown skyward. Within seconds, over 20,000 German soldiers were killed or badly wounded. The survivors were either stupefied or hysterical and, as British troops entered what was left of their positions, many of the former, weeping uncontrollably, grasped at their ankles or tried to embrace them. Without much trouble, 7,500 prisoners were taken. While, as happened so often, the Germans soon rallied, the British attackers succeeded, for once, in reaching their prescribed objective on time, and counterattacks were largely unsuccessful. In due course, hopefully quite soon, all of Passchendaele Ridge would be in British hands.

As in the case of the Somme battle, Haig anticipated a breakthrough and thought that his beloved cavalry might play a role in it. Of course, if a breakthrough did not occur, the battle-to-come could then be viewed as one of the "wearing out" variety. As preparations were underway, Haig's staff received unwelcome bits of information from several quarters. Some of this came from Belgian geographical and meteorological experts. They pointed out that if, as was almost always the case, the assault was to be preceded by a massive artillery bombardment, low-lying fields would be turned into veritable swamps by water released from smashed dikes and drainage canals. Also, the attack, scheduled to take place towards the end of July, would be underway around the beginning of the Flanders' rainy season. Haig and colleagues were allowed to draw their own conclusions. Cautionary admonitions came from a quarter closer to home—the Tank Corps. Obviously very sensitive to questions of terrain, its own geographical and weather experts sent off a variety of geological maps to Haig's headquarters. Coming to much the same conclusion as their Belgian counterparts, the tankmen pointed out that, in the anticipated quagmire, tank operations would be difficult, if not impossible. This was bad news indeed, and Haig and staff did not wish to hear about it. The Tank Corps was told not to bother them with their "ridiculous maps."

On July 22, 1917, 3,000 British artillery pieces commenced a ferocious bombardment which, in nine day's time, resulted in three million shells being hurled into and around the German lines. On average, each yard of the front received four and three-fourths tons of shells. On July 31, shortly before dawn, the soldiers of Hubert Gough's (1870–1963) 5th Army left their trenches and, under a rolling barrage, began their advance towards the German lines.

While the British preliminary bombardment obviously caused both casualties and damage, the German positions, which consisted, in large part, of lines of machine gun nests with interlocking fields of fire, were mostly intact. As Gough's men advanced into withering fire, a light rain began. By evening, it had developed into a steady downpour. The first day of what would become known as "Third Ypres" saw an average gain of 1,000 yards in exchange for over 31,000 casualties. The first objective of Haig's long-yearned-for Flanders Offensive, Passchendaele Ridge, loomed off in distant, smoky mists.

It was now a "wearing out" battle, and, as in the case of the Somme, Commander in Chief Haig was determined to see it through to the end. As the rains continued, the Belgian experts and British tankmen were proved correct. The Flanders battlefield was turned into a vast sea of mud in which tanks stalled as infantrymen floundered forward in attacks which gained very little. When, around the middle of August, the skies cleared for a bit, the British assault, pressed with greater-than-ever determination, was rewarded with greater territorial gain. Soon, however, the rains began again and these, plus the usual determined German defense, slowed the Fifth Army's advance down to its previous crawl. To make matters worse, it was during Third Ypres that the Germans introduced a new gas, *"Gelbkreuz"* ("yellow cross"), known in the Allied camp as "mustard gas." Besides having the usual asphyxiating qualities, it produced hideous burns. By September, it was plain that Gough's troops had been pretty much played-out.

At this point, the attack was pressed by the British Second Army, commanded by General Herbert Plumer (1857–1932). This was the army that had triumphed at Messines in June and, for awhile, it seemed as if it would do the same in September, and on a far broader scale. In due course, however, the attritional effects of rain, mud, and the determined German defense brought Plumer's assaults to a near stand-still. In October, the rains were worse than ever, but Haig continued to press the offensive, this despite the fact that his very loyal subordinates, Gough and Plumer, requested that he call it off. Finally, on November 4, 1917, Canadian troops succeeded in capturing the village of Passchendaele (or, rather, where the village once was; there was almost nothing whatsoever left of it), which crowned the ridge bearing its name. After this "success," the battle was declared over and, of course, a British victory.

For some time afterward, controversy raged over how much of the BEF had been sacrificed in Third Ypres. It is probable that British losses totalled around 300,000, while there were 260,000 German casualties. The maximum advance was about five miles. Shortly after the somber end of the 1917 Flanders campaign, Chief of Staff Launcelot Kiggell (1862–1954) paid a visit—his first and, so far as is known, only one—to the front line. As his staff car churned forward in the clinging mud, he showed increasing signs of distress. Finally, it is said, he burst into tears. "Good God," he sobbed, "did we really send men to fight in that?" All that his guide could say in response was that it was worse further up the line.

Haig justified pressing Third Ypres in several ways. First of all, he said, with the French Army in so miserable a state after the failure of the Nivelle Offensive and all that flowed from it, it was necessary to keep the Germans preoccupied. Otherwise, the French Army could be destroyed. Also, even if the hoped-for breakthrough had not occurred, it was necessary to keep the pressure on in order that the German Army be worn down in an attritional battle. The first motive mentioned has been called into question. With regard to the second, however, there was a mad sort of logic attaching to it, and this we will consider later. Unfortunately, however, while Haig's bludgeoning assaults did indeed wear down the German Army to a considerable degree, they also had the effect of wearing down his own as well. He had no significant reserves left. This, from the British perspective, was too bad, because, later in November they would have been of great value.

On November 20, 1917, there occurred what was, up to that time, the most successful tank attack of the war. Advancing on dry ground ideal for the use of armor, the British Third Army, spearheaded by over 300 tanks, broke through the Hindenburg Line near the French city of Cambrai. In one day, the two defending German divisions in the area were completely destroyed, and more than 8,000 prisoners taken. By the following day, more ground had been gained than in the four months of Third Ypres, and for relatively small losses. Unfortunately, the latter engagement had so drained Haig's army that there were precious few men available to exploit what amounted to a very successful attack. Within days, the Germans, at first fearing a major breakthrough, realized that the British were not in a position to really affect one and began counterattacks which, in due course, won back almost all of the ground lost during the first two days of what became known as the "Battle of Cambrai." While Third Ypres was the primary reason why there weren't enough troops left to turn Cambrai into a truly decisive victory, there was a secondary one. Late October had seen a disaster in Italy, and what meager British troops as were available had to be off for more southern climes.

THE CAPORETTO DISASTER

Between June, 1915 and September, 1917, the Italian Army launched a total of eleven major offensives on the Isonzo River line. The sixth of them saw it capture the city of Gorizia ("Graz" to the Austrians); other than that, there had been no gains of any significance. Of the almost 500,000 men sacrificed by Italy in 1916 alone, the overwhelming majority of them were lost in attacks on the Isonzo Front. By October, 1917, troops in that area were exhausted, bitter, and, in some cases, near mutinous. The German and Austro-Hungarian generals knew of conditions on the Italian side of the line and were determined to take advantage of them. Crack German mountain divisions were dispatched to bolster the Austro-Hungarian legions on the Isonzo Front and, on October 24, 1917, there was mounted a ferocious assault on the Italian line which, almost everywhere, gave way immediately. Between day one of the attack and November 12, when, with the help of British and French troops, the Italians finally held on the Piave River, about ninety miles from their original line, 330,000 men had been lost, 300,000 of them as prisoners. The commander of the army, General Cadorna, was sacked and his replacement, General Armando Diaz (1861–1928) wisely determined that, for the present, the Italian Army ought best to forgo offensive operations. The Italian nationalistic press demanded that the new line be held at all costs; that soon the shame of Caporetto would be revenged. One of the loudest of these voices was that of a man recently invalided out of the army, the Socialist turned nationalist newspaper editor, Benito Mussolini. Of course, much more would be heard from him later.

Some Reflections on Field Marshal Sir Douglas Haig

Even during the war, there were those, Prime Minister Lloyd-George being most prominent among them, who viewed Douglas Haig as a blundering, soulless butcher. After the war, this judgement came to be shared by a large number of historians as well as no small number of military men. There can be no question that, in his offensives on the Somme and in Flanders, Haig, after deceiving himself as to the possibility of rapid breakthroughs (he was greatly aided in this deception by a fawning staff which had learned to tell him only what he wanted to hear), stubbornly persisted in costly, grinding attacks which gained very little at the cost of hundreds of thousands of casualties. In the end, his primary justification for these hideous, "wearing out" battles, was that they were indeed wearing down the German Army. It was of particular importance for the BEF to participate in such bloodbaths, he reasoned, because of problems confronting the French, at Verdun in 1916, and after the Nivelle disaster in 1917. After the Caporetto disaster, it became more plain to him than ever that, if the war was to be won, it had to be on the Western Front, and this would occur through an attritional wearing down of the German Army. After the war, Haig responded to all criticisms by declaring that the entire war on the Western Front had to be perceived as one great battle and that, in the end, he had won it.

As indicated before, Haig's arguments concerning French problems seem specious. At the time, he did not make too much of them and, in any case, he disliked the French and was not all that much distressed by what disasters as might befall them. We can say for certain, though, that, with regard to his claim that the wearing, grinding attacks served to wear down the German Army, he must be seen as having a point. After all, while his losses on the Somme and in the Flanders operation were always higher than those of the enemy, the Germans had fewer men to lose. In point of fact, the German General Staff was well aware of this and it is plain, from reading situational reports and memoirs, that folk such as General Ludendorff appreciated the terrible effects that Haig's attritional approach was having on the army. Also, while Haig was probably being disingenuous when he claimed that concerns for the French caused him to press his often seemingly pointless offensives, it is plain that, particularly with regard to the attack in Flanders, this argument, albeit retrospectively, was probably correct. Certainly it was plain that, after Caporetto, the war would not be won on the Italian Front.

Field Marshal Haig was able to keep at his task in large measure because he would not allow himself to hear or see anything that would cause him to seriously consider other approaches. What psychologists call "dissonant" information would be ignored or rejected. Haig rarely visited hospitals for fear that what he saw might cause him to have second thoughts about what he was doing, even though he was convinced that he was enjoying divine guidance. In a very real sense, we can say that a person who chooses not to deal with dissonant information or consistently engages in what is called "denial" is suffering from a variety of psychological dysfunctionalism.

The Great War, World War I—whatever one chooses to call it—was an attritional war *par excellence.* Victory, however empty or sparse it might have been, would be gained by the side which, in the end, could bring to bear masses of men and material and wear down its enemy. Grinding, remorseless battles, in all conditions, was what would do it over time. Douglas Haig, who, personally, was not a cruel man, was, from a psychological perspective, probably not quite "all there." He heard and saw only what he wanted to hear and to see. Utilizing massive defense mechanisms, he shielded himself from anything that might cause him to waver from his determined course. Certainly, it is obvious that, outside of the Starvation Blockade, the wearing down of the German Army, a process in which Haig's bludgeoning, soulless approach played a crucial role, was the key to victory. From the Allied perspective, if not from that of the God of history, it was fortunate that Haig was, in key ways, dysfunctional as a human being. By standards of the Great War, this made him the ideal soldier. In retrospect, if a war in which, particularly in Flanders, wounded soldiers literally drowned in mud, were to be seen through to a "victorious" conclusion, the last thing needed was a strong dose of mental health.

16

Nineteen Eighteen: Russian Agonies/German Failures

RUSSIA: FROM BREST LITOVSK TO CIVIL WAR

As we have seen, in the first days of December, 1917, the new Bolshevik government in Russia dispatched a delegation to negotiate a peace with the German High Command. On December 12, it was announced that terms for an armistice had been agreed upon and this went into effect three days later. The armistice was to last for a month. A week after the armistice terms had been announced, a meeting took place between the two High Command chiefs, Hindenburg and Ludendorff, and the leading civilian representatives of the German government. A touch of imperial dignity was added by the presence of Wilhelm II, by this time, a largely superfluous figure with regard to decision-making of any real importance. The current chancellor, Georg von Hertling (1843–1919), was also present. He was, however, an aging nonentity whose contributions to the proceedings were limited. The really important civilian present at this crucial meeting was Foreign Secretary Richard von Kuhlmann (1873–1948). He was for a peace of conciliation. He knew full well that the military people present were out for conquest. Their spirit was best captured by Hindenburg. When, after awakening from one of his frequent naps, he was asked by Kuhlmann why he thought Germany should lay claim to Russia's Baltic territories, he replied, "'for the basing of my left wing in the next war.'"[1] It was a somewhat disquieting response, though no doubt an honest one.

The conference, which had taken place in the German city of Kreuznach, ended with no clear winner. It was plain to Kuhlmann, however, as he headed back to Brest Litovsk, that the hard terms laid down by the High Command duo would have to prevail. When the foreign minister reached his destination, he informed the leading German military figure there, Max von Hoffmann, of the approach demanded by Ludendorff and Hindenburg. Hoffmann was hardly a shrinking violet himself; but, he thought that Germany's interests would best be served if a more moderate approach, such as that of Kuhlmann's, were taken. Yet, he, like Kuhlmann, soon realized that, for the moment at least, the High Command held all the cards.

It was perhaps fortunate that, hypothetically at least, good Bolsheviks were principled non-believers in Christmas. It was just about at Christmas-time that the obviously uncomfortable Hoffmann presented the Russian delegation with Ludendorff's holiday-season surprise. The new regime would be able to obtain peace at the price of surrendering to Germany all of Russian Poland and the Baltic territories—eighteen provinces in all. Both stupefied and enraged, the Russian delegation threatened to leave the conference. At that point, the Austro-Hungarian delegation informed its German counterpart that, if the conference dissolved, Vienna would be willing to sign a separate peace with the Russians. When Hoffmann told the delegation that such a move would cause Germany to withdraw vital support from the Austro-Hungarian front, it quickly backed down.

Negotiations at Brest Litovsk did stall for a bit over the annexations issue. Russia, however, did not dare to end them. Instead, when negotiations resumed in January, 1918, their delegation was headed by Leon Trotsky, noted for his eloquence and power as a speaker. His oratorical skills left the Germans unmoved. The only party in the neighborhood moved in any significant direction by unfolding events was a party of Ukrainian nationalists. Wishing independence from what they perceived to be a supine Bolshevik Russia, they requested that Germany recognize such while providing the new Ukrainian regime with protection. Desperate to feed their hungry populations with Ukrainian grain, Germany and Austria-Hungary signed the requested treaty. The Bolshevik regime was seeing things go from bad to worse, and very rapidly at that.

Grasping at straws, Trotsky made a move which, in the history of diplomacy, was unique, to say the least. Russia could not make peace with Germany unless it was one without annexations. At the same time, Russia did not wish to continue the war. So, Russia, while not signing a peace treaty, would simply demobilize and drop out. It was a kind of "declaration of peace." Almost unhinged by this extraordinary maneuver, the German delegation was, for awhile, reduced to a gibbering stupor. It didn't stay in this condition very long, for, as the Russians headed home, convinced that Germany would not attack a country which, while not formally at peace with her, was not at war either, Hoffmann revealed that he had been ordered to open up a massive assault on the country should negotiations fail. After declaring the armistice null-and-void, German troops began moving east on February 18, 1918.

There was nothing to stop them. Town after town fell without a struggle. Some in the German High Command declared that the massive assault was designed to rid Europe of the menace of Bolshevism. Hoffmann and those under him knew better. They were going to grab as much land and resources as possible in order to strengthen the German war effort. In desperation, the Russian government declared that it would sign any treaty the Germans wished them to sign if only the advance were halted. It pressed grimly on. Finally, the Germans agreed to meet a Russian delegation at Brest Litovsk again and, on March 3, 1918, the treaty which came to bear the name of that town was signed. By virtue of it, Russia had to give up 34% of her population, 32% of her arable land, 50% of her industrial plant, and 90% of her coal resources. As a furious Trotsky put pen to paper, he declared, "'This is a peace that Russia, grinding her teeth, is forced to accept.'"[2] Later, when confronted with an admittedly unjust peace, few Germans, in their understandable self-pity, would remember the then wildly-hailed Peace of Brest Litovsk, in comparison to which that of Versailles was mild indeed.

With all of Russian Poland, the Baltic region, and the most valuable portions of western Russia in their hands, and with what amounted to a puppet independent Ukrainian government at their beck-and-call, the Germans at first appeared to be "sitting pretty." Yet, in due course, it became plain that occupying such vast amounts of territory, with an underdeveloped transportation system guaranteeing the thinnest of supply lines, would be more difficult than initially anticipated. Thus, while some grain shipments were sent west, these never amounted to the floods of rye and wheat envisaged by the German government. In point of fact, German military personnel soon found themselves involved in more-or-less "traditional" pursuits.

First of all, while anti-Russian sentiments were strong in places such as the Ukraine, local peasants were not particularly pleased at having to surrender large portions of their harvests to the Germans. Sullen compliance eventually yielded to resistance. Perhaps of greater importance, though, was the fact that German occupation troops soon found themselves caught up in a full-fledged civil war. In the spring of 1918, the new Bolshevik government was in control of Petrograd, Moscow, attaching territories, and very little else. What became known as the "White Armies," i.e., legions comprised of supporters of the Romanov Dynasty, with some disgruntled Mensheviks and Social Revolutionaries thrown in, menaced the new regime from several different directions. The Ukraine itself was home to probably one of the oddest armies of all times, as oxymoronic as it might sound, one of anarchists. Depending on geographical circumstances and/or the whim of its leader, Nestor Makhno (1889–1935), it fought Whites, Reds, and Ukrainian nationalists. Somewhere in the midst of all of this, were about one million German troops, often having to defend themselves from attack either from outraged peasants, or from one army or another even as their officers tried to shield them from increasingly effective Bolshevik propaganda.

The upshot of it all, was that when, in 1918, German armies in the west needed reinforcements, much fewer than expected could be withdrawn from the former Eastern Front. Now, what turned out to be the crack-brained scheme of Ludendorff and Hindenburg had been responsible for tying-down hundreds of thousands of German soldiers on what, in effect, turned out to be a *variety* of "fronts." In the meantime, Germans on the home-front continued to go hungry from want of bread.

As for the Russian people themselves, the civil war now under way would be responsible for the loss of approximately 15 million lives, about five million more than those claimed, on all fronts, by the war that had made so catastrophic an event possible in the first place. In no small way, the Allies as well bore much responsibility for it. For a variety of reasons, the most crucial of which were the securing of arms shipped to Russia when the country was still in the war and, because as time went on, they increasingly perceived the Bolsheviks as a menace, the Allies supported efforts to overthrow the besieged regime. Relatively small, and, in the end, useless, detachments of British, French, and American troops were sent into the fray while the Japanese—whose military contributions to the Great War itself had been minimal—sent an army of over 75,000 men into eastern regions in a quite unideological old-fashioned attempt at simple land-grabbing.

In the end, the only foreign army that accomplished much of anything in Russia was the so-called "Czechoslovak Legion." Consisting of Czech and Slovak soldiers captured while serving with Austro-Hungarian forces, they had thrown in their lot with the Russians, hoping to fight for the freedom of their Bohemian homeland from the Habsburgs. Now, with Russia out of the war, they wanted to go to one of the still several active fronts to continue the struggle there. To get to the west, though, the Legion had first to go east, towards the port of Vladivostok. Ships there would then bring them west. In due course, as chaos (for much of which the Legion was responsible) flared up all around, the Czech and Slovak soldiers, on captured trains, headed east on the Trans-Siberian Railway, fighting off usually feeble efforts to stop them. After some months of travel, with just enough fighting to qualify the extraordinary adventure as a military one, the Legion arrived in Vladivostok, boarded ships, and arrived in the west after the war there had ended. The soldiers were in time, though, to witness the founding of the new state of Czechoslovakia, something which, of course, would set in train consequences which are being felt to this day.

The successful journey of the Czechoslovak Legion spelled doom for the most important political prisoners in Russia. The former Tsar, Nicholas, and his family were being held captive in the town of Ekaterinburg, located in the Ural Mountains. In July, 1918, as the Czechoslovak Legion was on the move, it was rumored that it would soon be in the vicinity. On the night of July 16, the family was told not to go to bed because they were to be moved to a different location. After awhile, they were ordered to go down into the cellar of the house in which they were being held. Once there, the current head of the guard detail, a Captain Yurovsky, came into the room with what turned out to be a firing squad. He read a statement in which it was explained why political necessity dictated that the imperial family could not be allowed to survive. "Thus," Yurovsky concluded, staring coldly at Nicholas, "your life is ended." Perhaps hoping to set an example for his forlorn and terrified family, Nicholas replied, with dignity, "I am ready." Yurovsky then shot him, and the last of Russia's Tsars died, no doubt still unaware of how what he had done or neglected to do had been responsible for his, and his family's, terrible fate.

Alexandra and the five children were then gunned down, as was the family dog, a spaniel. Several of the sisters did not die at once, so it was necessary to use the bayonet on them. As if to underscore the hideous misfortune that had attended the family, the women had sought to keep their guards from stealing some especially-treasured pieces of jewelry by concealing them in their corsets. These proved to be close to impervious to bayonet thrusts and thus these unfortunate souls had to be stuck again and again before they died. All the bodies were then taken away to a mine shaft. After being further mutilated, they were dropped into it and set afire. When the Czech force finally did arrive, on July 25, no trace of the Tsar and his family could be found. Recently, though, what are thought to be some remains have been discovered.

At first, the *Bolshevik* leadership denied having ordered the executions, blaming them instead on the overly zealous local *Soviet,* several of whose members were in fact later executed for acting without orders from above. Now, however, it has become plain that the gruesome deed was carried out on orders from the highest authorities. This action, the new government's denial of responsibility for it, and then its executing some of those who had carried it out in efforts to cover itself served to define its character. This received amplification in the doctrine of "War Communism," by virtue of which people and resources were ruthlessly husbanded in the name of the people, and in the establishment of a new secret police force, the *Cheka* (later on, this organization would be known as the GPU, then the NKVD, finally, the KGB), in order to be certain that all decrees would be enforced. Of course, White opponents, while not as well organized, could be equally as merciless. Between 1918 and 1922, while between 100,000 and 200,000 soldiers died in battle (the clashing armies were relatively small), many thousands more were executed, close to 200,000 Jews slaughtered in pogroms, while millions perished from hunger and disease. In the end, the formation of a 5 million-man Red Army, brought together by now Commissar of War Trotsky's organizational and oratorical brilliance, plus ruthless recruitment policies, decided the issue. Lack of coordination between the several White Armies, and Allied uncertainties as to goals and how to go about obtaining them also played roles in the *Bolshevik* victory.

In 1922, Russia officially became the Union of Soviet Socialist Republics. With the hideous Great War still a recent memory, millions all over the world, who either did not know of the terrible circumstances attending its birth, chose not to learn of them, or fell back upon rationalizations to justify such excesses, saw the new country as offering hope for a better world. As many saw it, it could, indeed would offer an example of social justice while helping to end the injustices of capitalism and its byproduct, imperialism, phenomena which, in the eyes of no small number of people, had been responsible for the recently-ended conflict, indeed, war in general. Perhaps if Lenin who, while ruthless in war, was never megalomaniacal, had lived on for awhile, at least some of the hopes nurtured both inside of the country and abroad might have been realized. Exhausted by ceaseless labors, and suffering from lingering side-effects of a 1918 assassination attempt, he died of a stroke in 1924. He was succeeded by a man who Lenin never really trusted. Born in Georgia, in the Caucasus, a one-time student of theology, Joseph Vissarionovich Djugashvili (1879–1953) dropped his singularly un-Russian last name for the very Russian, "Stalin," meaning "of steel." By 1928, having disposed of every possible opponent—including Trotsky, the man most responsible for the Bolshevik victory, but now a "non-person"—this monstrous being, one who combined megalomania and the most casuistic use of ideology imaginable, was sole ruler of what was now usually called the "Soviet Union." The man "of steel" would be just that, and millions would suffer for it.

NEW WORLD IDEALISM TO THE FORE: WILSON'S FOURTEEN POINTS

As Secretary of State Robert Lansing saw it, the United States was entering the war to protect what he perceived to be American interests. President Wilson certainly agreed with him. At the same time, however, simple power-political considerations were not enough for him. They smacked too much of the tawdry motives behind the actions of the Old World powers. No, there had to be some sort of higher purpose animating American entrance into the war. In his April, 1917 speech before the Congress, the president had declared that "The world must be made safe for democracy." Obviously, if conditions favoring democracy were to prevail, it was plain that the peace that would follow the presumed Allied victory had to be one informed by fundamental justice. On January 8, 1918, before a rather sparse gathering in the halls of Congress, President Wilson presented the world with his famous "Fourteen Points," implementation of which, he thought, would provide the framework for a just peace. They were as follows:

1. Abolition of secret diplomacy.
2. Freedom to navigate the high seas in peace and war.
3. Removal of economic barriers among nations.
4. Reduction of armaments.

5. Adjustment of colonial claims in the interest of both the inhabitants and the powers concerned.
6. Restoration of Russia and a welcome for her in the society of nations.
7. The return of Belgium to her people.
8. Evacuation and restoration of French territory, including Alsace-Lorraine.
9. Readjustment of Italian frontiers "'along clearly recognizable lines of nationality.'"
10. Free opportunity for "'autonomous development'" for [the] people[s] of Austria-Hungary.
11. Restoration of the Balkan nations and freer access to the sea for Serbia.
12. Protection for minorities in Turkey.
13. An independent Poland.
14. "'A general association of nations'" to secure "'mutual guarantees of political independence and territorial integrity to great and small states alike.'"[3]

Of the world leaders, only Lenin, it appeared, received the Fourteen Points with enthusiasm (ironically enough, in due course his country would be receiving several thousand American troops, part of the above-mentioned Allied effort to overthrow his government). Point number six was, of course, particularly appealing to him. The general tone, though, of the proposals was suggestive of some sort of new world order that he found rather more pleasing than the old one. Naturally, points seven through twelve did not especially please the governments of Germany, Austria-Hungary, and Turkey. But then, the United States was on the side of the Allies, in any case. Wilson must have known, however, that Great Britain and France would also not be altogether pleased with his attempt to gild the Allied cause with a gloss of New World idealism.

Great Britain, whose blockade was gradually starving Germany to death, was not exactly enthralled with point number two. And neither Great Britain or France was greatly excited over point five. Point number one was an object of general mirth which transcended battle lines, while the idea of some sort of "'general association of nations,'" though deemed admirable in the abstract, struck many as utopian. Alas, it was in the end, the point which Woodrow Wilson took most seriously, and this would have results both ironic and catastrophic. For the present, however, the Allies, grateful for American entrance into the war, were in no position to go too far in challenging what traditional Old World leaderships saw as a noble but naive effort to right wrongs seemingly sewn into the very fabric of human affairs.

AN ATTEMPT TO END ATTRITIONAL WAR: LUDENDORFF AND HIS "STORM SECTIONS"

As might be expected, General Ludendorff was not very impressed with Wilsonian idealism. Besides, during the winter days of 1917/1918 he was preoccupied not with what the shape of the post-war world would be, but with devising a means by which the war could be won before America had much of a role to play in it. While loathing his former boss, Falkenhayn, he did share his belief that Germany, even without the entrance of the United States, could not win a war of attrition. Thus, a means had to be found to end the suffocating deadlock on the Western Front.

Allied offensives, while serving to wear down the German Army, had succeeded in gaining very little ground at enormous cost. Perhaps, with their superior manpower reserves, the British and French commands could afford such blood-baths. As Ludendorff saw it, if Germany was to win the war, her armies would have to achieve a rapid, decisive, *strategic* victory, and this translated into "break-through." With trench systems firmly in place, however, how could this be achieved?

In due course, it dawned on Ludendorff that, precisely because the war on the Western Front had devolved into an essentially static one of attrition, commanders had become accustomed to viewing it in these terms.

As a result, the approach, particularly that of the Allies, to offensive warfare had become extremely rigid. After massive artillery bombardments, which generally left crucial defensive positions essentially intact, masses of infantry would be hurled against dug-in machine guns, supported by artillery that had been little damaged by the pre-assault fireworks. After some months of seesawing back and forth, the offensive would come to an end, with some thousands of shell-torn yards of ground in the hands of the attackers. Nobody, at least on the Allied side, seemed to be able to imagine going about things any differently. Germany *had* to. A way had to be found to break the

a need for off failure artillery left defense intact

stalemate, and soon. Furthermore, Ludendorff reasoned, if a truly substantial break-through could be affected, it was entirely possible that the Allies who, since 1914 had become unaccustomed to any sort of "war of movement," would be thrown into a complete dither by it, and thus would not be able to offer any coordinated response.

Some recent engagements provided Ludendorff with clues as to how a strategically-significant breakthrough might be achieved. In some of the last significant fighting on the Eastern Front, near the city of Riga, a relatively unknown general named Oskar von Hutier had succeeded in breaking the Russian lines through what amounted to the use of infiltration. Enemy strong-points would be ignored as heavily-armed units, virtually self-supporting, probed for weak points. The same approach, only on a much larger scale, had been employed by Austro-German armies at Caporetto, and, at one point, during the German counterattack after the initially successful British tank attack at Cambrai. Now, Ludendorff reasoned, this new tactical approach had to be used on the grandest scale imaginable.

General von Hutier was brought west to help plan what came to be called "Operation Michael." Emphasis would be placed, as in the past, on massive use of artillery, and 6,000 pieces were made available for this. The bombardment, however, which would involve an ingenious mixture of high explosive and gas shells, was not supposed to last all that long. It was to have a shock, rather than "wearing down," effect. In the meantime, under cover of the artillery, units of heavily-armed, self-supporting soldiers—especially self-reliant and aggressive souls had been culled from the German divisions—would move forward, probing for weak spots in the enemy defenses, ignoring strong-points. If these were isolated, they could be dealt with in due course. The specially-trained and equipped German infantrymen were organized into what became known as *"Sturmabteilungen,"* or "storm sections." Later, shortly after the war was over, the term would become known in a slightly different context.

While Ludendorff envisaged a series of blows to be delivered against both British and French forces, the first of them, "Operation Michael," as we have seen, was to be directed against the British alone. The force targeted was General Gough's Fifth Army, battered from the fighting in Third Ypres. Also, as General Ludendorff knew very well, it had not been substantially reinforced. This was due to Lloyd George's understandable unwillingness to supply Haig with masses of troops out of fear of what the stodgy plodder might do with them. Also held back—and perhaps this was of greater significance—

were construction troops. Fifth Army defensive positions were in terrible shape, and it is entirely possible that even the traditional mass attack, which Ludendorff sought to avoid, might have achieved a break-through. To make matters worse for Gough, who was beginning to suspect that his army would soon be hit with a devastating assault, Lloyd George had promised the French, still thought to be severely shaken since the terrible events of April, 1917, that the British would take over about thirty miles of their line. The Fifth Army was the one adjacent to the French forces, so it was called upon to undertake this task. Stretched thin, undermanned, and ensconced in ill-prepared positions, this force was an ideal target for one about to embark on a new adventure in applied military science.

The early morning of March 21, 1918 saw conditions which were ideal for the type of infiltrating attack ordered by Ludendorff. The battlefield was heavily-shrouded in fog. Just before 5:00 A.M., 6,000 guns, preparing the way for an assault by three full-strength German armies, opened up. At first, though, the fire was directed not against the forward British positions. Rather—and here, Ludendorff showed that he had learned much from Allied disasters—the British artillery was targeted. Unlike hapless Allied soldiers in earlier attacks, assaulting German infantrymen would not have be torn apart by fire from virtually undisturbed cannons. Only later was the fire directed against British infantry positions.

At 9:40 A.M., the German storm units began their assault. Armed with light machine guns, flamethrowers, and light mortars, they probed for weak spots, found them, and prepared the way for larger units. Soon, Fifth Army's front had been breached all along the line, while the link between it and the Third Army, on Fifth's left flank, was in the process of being shattered. Gough, fearing encirclement, fell back. Within a few days, the Third Army was forced to do the same. As a stunned British High Command confronted what was amounting to military disaster, Ludendorff scented victory. Of perhaps much greater importance, so did many of his men.

As we have seen earlier, Ernst Jünger, a very aggressive young man by any standard, had adjusted to war better than most. Indeed, in his testimony to the joys of bayonet fighting, he gave the impression that he came close to enjoying it. Yet, having to fight on the defensive almost all of the time frustrated him. Ludendorff's massive March assault revivified him, convincing this oft-decorated hero that, once again, life was worth living. He described the action of his storm unit in a manner suggestive of rape: "'We approach as conquerers, armed with all the means of power. We will force open the closed door and enter by force into the forbidden land . . . We will demolish the dikes and break like a storm flood into the broad, untouched regions.' "[4] For Jünger, many thousands of German soldiers like him, and, of course, for their commander, Ludendorff, it was now or never.

The British and French governments recognized that they were facing the prospects of defeat before the Americans arrived in strength. On March 26, 1918, the commanders of the Allied armies, joined by high-ranking representatives of the two governments, held a somber meeting in Doullens, France. Very quickly, it was decided that the crisis called for a unity of command hitherto lacking. General Haig, for once seeing a situation for what it was, knew full well that he could not assume that he would be called upon to provide it. After some discussion, it was decided that the French general, Ferdinand Foch (1851–1929), since May, 1917, Pétain's chief of staff, would assume supreme command over the Allied armies including that of the newly-arriving Americans.

As the Allies were striving for unity, the German offensive ground on, pushing the British back, until they were well-behind the Somme, a region of very painful recent memory. By early April, however, the German soldiers were running out of ammunition and, in no small measure due to the successful British blockade of their country, food as well. Furthermore, while tens of thousands of British prisoners had been taken, anticipated massive encirclements had not taken place. The reason was plain: Ludendorff lacked the reserves to carry them out. This was, of course, in part due to the wearing-down of the German Army accomplished by Haig's unimaginative, and hideously costly, offensives. Ludendorff could certainly not be held accountable for this, of course. If, however, he had allowed for a reasonable peace with Bolshevik Russia, now embroiled in civil war, it probably would not have been necessary to keep close to a million troops in the east. As grain was shipped to Germany and Austria-Hungary in very disappointing quantities, troops which might have provided enough reserves to ensure strategic victory for "Operation Michael" were engaged in frustrating, and often dangerous efforts, to take as much rye and wheat from an increasingly outraged peasantry. From time to time, of course, as mentioned earlier, they would have to defend themselves against attacks which could come from one of several directions.

Ludendorff, like so many hard-boiled military types who believe that, in order to attain success, one must always apply the most severe measures imaginable, had outwitted himself. If he had not been so insistent on grinding Russia down at Brest Litovsk, he might well have had one million extra men to bring to bear in "Operation Michael." To be sure, by the time the offensive had been called off, on April 5, 1918, his armies had captured 90,000 men, more than 1,000 artillery pieces, and overrun around 1,250 miles of French landscape. Yet, while gaining far more territory in about two weeks than had all of the Allied Western Front offensives in three years, he had not achieved a strategic victory. This being the case, he had to strike elsewhere.

On April 9, 1918, after an unusually intensive bombardment of mustard gas, German troops struck out against the Allied line north of Armentieres, on the River Lys. The nine divisions in the German assault fell upon a portion of the front manned by four Portuguese brigades. Portugal enjoyed the reputation of being Britain's oldest ally; in these circumstances, however, its palpable representatives turned out to be the most useless ones imaginable. Pausing only long enough to remove their boots, they took off for the rear at almost Olympic-quality speed. In their only successful engagement, they overwhelmed the men of a British battalion speeding towards the front on bicycles. Thus equipped, some hundreds of Portuguese became a kind of negative vanguard for more numerous comrades fleeing on foot. Some of them did not feel assured of safety until they had managed to reach the port of Le Havre.

The assault now underway was dubbed "Operation Georgette," and it was being directed against the British First and Second Armies. Unlike "Michael," it was not characterized by attempts at infiltration. Local conditions did not allow for such, and thus what resulted was the sort of unsubtle, head-on variety of attack reminiscent of the Allied approach. By this time, one must note, Ludendorff was falling back upon an approach which—even if not quite as long-term as that of Haig—has to be described as "attritional." As had been so often the case before, circumstances generic to World War I had defeated an attempt to transcend them, and, with the attack in the Somme region, "Michael," having failed, Ludendorff saw no other possibility than to press on with a more-or-less conventional Western Front onslaught.

Conventional or not, "Georgette" came very close to succeeding in breaking through the British lines. Gradually, the First and Second Armies were pressed back. Fighting furiously, they were nonetheless forced to abandon Messines Ridge, Polygon Wood, and yes, Passchendaele, all those monuments to Haig's obstinacy won at such terrible cost. Yet, by the end of April, the German offensive had spent itself. Besides the extraordinary stubbornness shown by the

British, there was the factor of German exhaustion, and hunger played a very large role in this. Often, it was noted, initially successful German attacks were not pressed home with as much vigor as they ought to have been. Quite simply, men, in desperate efforts to supplement meager rations, were scouring the farms and fields of Flanders for food. Even more so than in Ludendorff's earlier offensive, the unheroic, indeed, rather sordid, British "Starvation Blockade" was obviously paying strategic dividends. On April 29, 1917, "Georgette" was brought to a close. As in the case of "Michael," it had gained far more territory than any and all of the previous Allied offensives; yet, in the end, it, like its predecessor, was a strategic failure.

Again, either or both of Ludendorff's attempts to knock the BEF out of the war might have succeeded if he had had greater reserves at his disposal. As we have seen, however, losses sustained in containing Haig's offensives of the previous two years, plus the commander in chief's harsh Russian policy had prevented such from being available. Ludendorff's efforts to gain a strategic victory before the arrival of the Americans in force had been frustrated by the deadly combination of Haig/Ludendorff. Between March 21 and April 29, 1918, Allied losses, the lion's share of them British, totalled over 490,000, and 290,000 of these were prisoners or missing. German losses were reckoned at over 375,000, of which 40,000 were prisoners or missing. Never before had the Germans claimed as many Allied prisoners in so brief a period of time. Yet, British and French legions were about to be reinforced with ones from the United States. Thus, however terribly it rings upon the ear, their losses could be "made good." The loss of 375,000 German soldiers could not. Furthermore, despite the fact that such losses perhaps had the immediate effect of allowing survivors to enjoy a temporary increase in their rations, it was plain that, over time, the British blockade was starting to have effects upon the army's combat abilities. For the time-being, however, it was, despite the strategic disappointments of March–April, 1918, still capable of making quite impressive offensive efforts.

Around the middle of April, while the operation along the Lys was still underway, General Ludendorff ordered that an offensive against the French be undertaken in the region of Chemin des Dames (the site of Nivelle's disaster of about a year earlier). This portion of the front, the domain of the French Sixth Army, had been quiet for awhile. In fact, several British divisions which had been badly mauled in earlier fights had been sent to the area for purposes of recuperation. Soon to arrive in the area were young men who, in their optimism and eagerness for combat, were reminiscent of naive French and English youths of times past. They were the Americans of the Second and Third Divisions, and soon their longing for excitement would be fulfilled.

The commander of the Sixth Army was Denis Auguste Duchesne, arguably the worst general in the French Army at that time. Like Nivelle, he was possessed of a violent temper and an ability to ignore information which he did not wish to hear. By the beginning of the third week in May, it had become plain to American intelligence that General Ludendorff was about to launch a major assault against the Sixth Army. Apprised of this alarming piece of news, French intelligence officers brought it to General Duchesne's attention. He dismissed it with contempt. There were no signs, he declared, that there was to be a major German offensive in the Chemin des Dames area. At the time, eighteen fresh German divisions were moving into the German front lines with seven more behind them as reserves. Over three thousand artillery pieces were being manhandled into place. How Duschesne managed not to notice all of this activity is hard to imagine.

To make matters even worse, the tactical dispositions in which the six French and five British divisions were placed bordered on the criminal. In view of the initial successes enjoyed by German troops using the new storm tactics, it had become plain that those facing them ought to be echeloned in depth. Duchesne, however, had jam-packed his luckless soldiers in the front line trenches. And, since he did not believe that any major engagement was in the offing, these were in no shape whatsoever to withstand a concentrated bombardment. Such had been planned for some time by Colonel Georg von Bruchmüller, probably the best artillerymen in any army.

Between 12:45 and 1:00 A.M. on May 27, 1918, thousands of gas shells rained down on the Allied positions. This had the effect of penning the French and British soldiers in their dugouts, trapping them like rats for what was to come. Almost immediately after the short, but extremely intense, gas bombardment was over, Bruchmüller's more than three thousand cannon unleashed one of high explosive shells which, in its fury, had not been seen since the first day at Verdun. Half-suffocated in the dugouts, men of the Sixth Army were soon being shredded, crushed to death, or buried alive. As the bombardment raged on, some, tormented beyond endurance, went mad, and either raced out into the open to certain death or committed suicide. When, after two-and-a-half hours of this, the German storm units commenced their assault, there was virtually nothing left to oppose them. In one day, they gained almost twelve miles, the greatest single-day's advance since the introduction of trench warfare.

As astonished as the Allies at the amazing breakthrough, General Ludendorff hurled every available man into the breach. This turned out to be a mistake, although of the sort that most people become aware of only in retrospect. For in plunging relentlessly ahead, the now victory-seasoned German troops were not providing that broad, *strategic* advance which was the ultimate purpose of Ludendorff's tactical innovations. Rather, they were creating what would amount to a dangerous bulge in their own lines, while, of course, assuring that, in future, problems of lengthening supply lines would obtain.

At the time, however, all that Ludendorff and his frantic Allied counterparts knew was that, at the current rate of advance, German soldiers would soon be on the Marne River, which was in fact reached by them on May 30. Paris was but fifty miles distant. It was in these circumstances, that American soldiers were, for the first time, called upon to play roles which were of great importance for the now seemingly lost Allied cause.

American soldiers had seen some fighting earlier. On April 20, 1918, a German assault had driven some of the newcomers out of the village of Seicheprey, on the eastern end of the line. While the Americans had been able to retake it, the results of the engagement were not flattering. On May 28, American troops succeeded in capturing the village of Cantigny, on the western portion of the line, and holding it against powerful German counter-attacks. While this engagement cost the First Division over 1,600 casualties, it was the first clear American victory "over there," and thus a morale-booster for the "Yanks" and their allies as well. Nonetheless, neither Seicheprey nor Cantigny was of any real importance (except, of course, for those killed and wounded and their families). Americans would play truly crucial roles in two critical engagements engendered by Duchesne's incompetence.

On June 1, 1918, German troops were about to cross the Marne near the town of Chateau-Thierry. Machine gunners of the American Third Division managed to hold them off until an important bridge could be blown up by French engineers. While a relatively minor engagement, it played an important role in slowing the German advance. Also, it was of immense value with regard to Allied morale. To make matters even better, Third Division's losses had been very light. This was not to be the case with regard to the second crucial encounter involving American troops. Before considering this engagement, however, it is necessary to devote some attention to the psychological state of German soldiery. For, while this is a subjective factor the ultimate importance of which can never be known for certain, there is no question but that the soldiers taking part in what was the next-to-last major German offensive of the war were not in the same state as those of a year earlier.

As seen earlier, the effectiveness of "Georgette" had been blunted to some extent by hungry soldiers taking valuable time to forage for food. As German troops participating in the at-first astonishingly successful Chemin des Dames offensive overran towns such as Soissons in the Champagne, they found cellars full of the product named after that region. Thus, the day it fell to the Germans, May 29, 1918, saw Soissons overrun with drunken soldiers. Not only, for the moment at least, could there be no thought of pressing the offensive further; but, supply transports were blocked by hordes of reeling men who jammed the roads. When the men paused from their revels, it was to augment their rations through looting. While these actions did not amount to a mutiny, and there was little in the way of desertion, for the first time in the war indiscipline on a large scale was seriously affecting German Army operations. Furthermore, this was not occurring in an army facing defeat, but one enjoying, in this case literally, the full flush of victory. Far more than in the case of "Georgette," the results of privation engendered by the Allied blockade of Germany were made plain in the drunken pillage of Soissons.

The soldiers of the American Second Division who were about to take part in the first crucial (and costly) show of strength between the new arrivals and the Germans did not suffer from want of much of anything. All that they lacked was experience, and, while this could prove costly, it had its positive side as well. The well-provisioned Americans had not had to endure months, if not years, of grinding, soul-eroding combat. Thus, even if having to endure heavy casualties, this did not have to be perceived as simply "more of the same" in a bloodbath seemingly without end. While, over time, naive optimism might well wear away, a basic confidence in a positive outcome to things would remain. This confidence which, in due course, would be strained to some extent, helped to sustain American troops in action, while serving to bolster Allied morale in general, in the crucial days when the German advance was being brought to a halt.

Close by Chateau-Thierry, where American troops had halted a German advance with relatively light casualties, was a forest called Belleau Wood. Overrun by the Germans, it was not really of much strategic value to anybody. Yet, as in the case of Verdun, it was, at the time, perceived as being of importance. This being the case, what was seen as the best body of American troops in the area, a Marine brigade attached to the Second Division, was ordered to take it. On June 6, 1918, after what turned out to be a very ineffectual artillery barrage, the Marines left their trenches and began to advance on the wood. In order to get there, it was necessary to advance through a wheat-field, and thus the attackers were "wide-open" to the scores of machine guns sited in rows throughout the forest. What resulted, albeit on a smaller scale, was the sort of slaughter endured by the British on the first day of the Somme attack. The assault was a failure. With extraordinary courage the Marines came back and, in successive attacks, succeeded in taking portions of the wood. Always, though, they were stopped short of their goal of taking the forest altogether.

While the Marines, who, on the whole, were excellent marksmen, repulsed German efforts to win back those bits of territory they had lost, it became plain that, for all their mettle, Belleau Wood would not be taken by rifle and bayonet alone. On three separate occasions, the Marines were pulled back from their positions and the wood blasted with artillery. Finally, on June 25, after the most sustained bombardment yet, the Marines, now supported by other elements of the Second Division, succeeded in taking the thoroughly shredded forest. By that time, over 5,700 of them, i.e., about 60% of the Marine Brigade, had been killed or wounded.

While there can be no question that, without massive artillery support, Belleau Wood could not have been taken by the Americans, the sturdiness of them in the assault impressed friend and foe alike. In the end, the taking of the wood was not of much tactical significance. The willingness of Americans to sustain an assault, even in the face of enormous losses, was, however, a fillip to morale. For those who bothered to examine closely what actually had occurred at Belleau Wood, it must have been plain that, excellent Marine marksmanship to the side, the battle there had been a kind of microcosm of the war as a whole. In an attritional conflict, the German enemy (furthermore, one which was suffering from deficiencies of all kinds) had been worn down by a force which could afford to absorb higher losses. With hundreds of thousands of young, healthy, and enthusiastic Americans heading into the line, victory-through-attrition was all but assured.

Before this came about, the Allies had to deal with Ludendorff's final offensive effort. With unintended irony, it was dubbed *"Friedensturm"* ("peace offensive"), and its obvious purpose was to be successful enough so that Germany would be able to conclude the war on its terms. Part of the attack would be in eastern Champagne, just west of Verdun. In this case though, French intelligence, which, in the recent past, had been so deficient, was very much on the mark both as to where and when the assault would take place. It had determined that the enemy bombardment would begin at a little after noon, on July 15. One hour before this was to occur, the French artillery opened up a ferocious one of its own. The Germans were thrown completely off-guard. More surprises awaited them. The commander of the French Fourth Army—the troops immediately affected by the German attack—General Henri Gouraud, had learned from Duchesne's disaster. He had arranged a defense-in-depth designed to strain any attack to the utmost, while allowing for counterattacks when warranted. With the assistance of an American division, Gouraud succeeded in containing the attack in one day.

The Germans also struck further to the west, near Chateau-Thierry, and here some initial success was registered against the French Fifth Army, whose commander, unlike Gouraud, had not learned much from recent events. In what would come to be called the "Second Battle of the Marne," the German Seventh Army crashed through the French defenses. The American unit in the vicinity, the Third Division, was at first driven back. Its front never broke, however, and it soon rallied and pushed back the German attackers. By day's end, they were back on the north bank of the Marne. In due course, attacks against the French were also contained. At this point, Ludendorff recognized that, for the moment, the German Army was spent so far as offensive operations were concerned. Probably not recognizing that such would be its strategic posture for the remainder of the war, he ordered that his exhausted soldiers assume a defensive one. Now, it was the turn of the Allies to go on the offensive, and, beginning on July 18, there commenced a series of attacks which would wear down a valiant, but now greatly outnumbered and under-supplied enemy. And, again, in this most attritional wars, numbers and supplies were all that really mattered.

WAR OF MOVEMENT (RELATIVELY SPEAKING) RETURNS FOR THE ALLIES

With the containment and then rolling back of Ludendorff's 1918 offensives, it was plain to all that soon the Allies would be undertaking ones of their own. In retrospect, it is also plain that they had to succeed. Between March 21 and mid-July, 1918, Ludendorff had lost over 700,000 men. Allied casualties had also been severe, but, especially with the arrival of the Americans, they could better afford them. Also, as seen earlier, by this time German soldiers were suffering from shortages of all kinds, perhaps most importantly, of food. Declines in morale were becoming more common. German soldiers would still be able to offer stiff resistance and exact a heavy toll from their enemies. Yet, while Ludendorff would, or perhaps could, not recognize the situation for what it was, many of his soldiers did. They would go on fighting, but, without much hope.

To be sure, as in the next world war, the Germans came out with some technological wrinkles as the end approached. By 1918, they had produced the world's first all-metal fighter aircraft. There is no record, however, of their ever having put in an appearance in combat. In March, 1918, the citizens of Paris learned that their ingenious foe had in its possession an artillery piece capable of hitting the city from 75 miles away. On Good Friday, one of its shells struck the church of Saint Gervais, then packed with worshippers. Falling masonry crushed to death 88 of them, injuring scores more. Shortly thereafter, however, French front line artillery began raining shells on the area where what was known as the "Paris Gun" (there were actually several of them) was housed. By the beginning of May, after having fired around two hundred rounds, it was withdrawn. While adding a bit of gratuitous horror to the already dismal picture, it had been of no military significance whatsoever. In any case, by July, 1918, as would be the case 37 years later, it was far too late for technological innovations such as those just described to reverse a deteriorating strategic situation.

Ludendorff, as we have seen, launched offensives utilizing new tactics because he knew that Germany could never win a war of attrition. Determined to avoid such, his assaults nonetheless assumed, over time, the character of those associated with his opponents. In a word, they became attritional, and, far less than the Allies, could he afford them. Those realities generic to the Great War, particularly to the Western Front, had defeated probably the most tactically-gifted practitioner of what he—along with quite a few others—liked to call "the art of war." While the Allies would soon be on the move, and their "war of movement" would be sustained until the end, it amounted to an attritional wearing-down of their enemy. Ludendorff, in greatly weakening the German Army through his bold, but, in the end, wasteful offensives, can be seen as having as much to do with Allied success, however grisly, as anything else.

The first of the great Allied offensives took place along the Marne, in an area roughly between Soissons and Chateau-Thierry, and it was a Franco-American affair. Underway on July 18, 1918, it ground forward in extremely heavy fighting. On August 3, Soissons fell and, three days later, with French and American troops having reached the Vesle and Aisne Rivers—it was declared ended. On average, the advance had been about seventeen miles and, by Western Front standards, this amounted to an enormous gain. The Americans alone had lost 50,000 men, the French, somewhat more than that. Though German losses in killed and wounded had been less than those of their opponents, they surrendered 30,000 prisoners and much material of war. To this day, argument rages over how strategically-significant was the massive Allied attack which brought "The Second Battle of the Marne" to a successful conclusion. This was not what really mattered, however. Its main impact was on Allied morale, which positively soared as a result of this.

General Ludendorff, while not exactly pleased with the Allied success (whatever its strategic significance) was not unduly perturbed by it either. He was working on a surprise of his own—an anticipated offensive in Flanders. Very soon, however, his plans—as usual, very bold, indeed, under the circumstances, downright imaginative—had to be shelved. A British offensive had supervened and, unlike previous efforts from that quarter, it was both unanticipated and very successful.

Henry Rawlinson (1864–1925), commander of the British Fourth Army, was greatly impressed with the potentials of the tank. He was also impressed with the value of surprise, thus far not exactly a characteristic of British offensive efforts. He began planning an attack in which tanks would play a greater role than ever before; moreover, one which would catch the enemy completely off-balance. With the approval of his commander, Haig, and overall commander of the Allied forces, Foch, he arrived at a scheme in which his army—in a later modification, two French armies were added on, with heavy use of tanks, would attack from positions east of the city of Amiens. This was in the area of the old Somme battlefield. Unlike the situation in 1916, this offensive effort would catch the German enemy completely by surprise.

The noise of 450 tanks being moved into position was drowned out by Royal Air Force planes, which flew continuously over the area. Artillery was moved into place only at night and, by daybreak, the 2,000 or so pieces were under camouflage. Just so there could be no "leaks" from overly talkative personnel, soldiers were not informed about what was afoot until one day before the assault was to begin. This took place at 4:20 A.M., August 8, 1918. Taken completely by surprise, the Germans fell back and, in some places, retreat turned into rout. For the first few days, the Allied armies, with Canadian and Australian troops spearheading the British effort, rolled forward at an astonishing pace. In due course, however, the German army stricken by the attack, the Eighteenth, began to rally, and further efforts to press the operation proved costly. On August 21, it was brought to an end.

While, eventually, the attack before Amiens was brought to a halt, there could be no question that it had been a success. There had been some 46,000 Allied casualties, while total German losses were estimated at 75,000. Of these, almost 30,000 were known to have been captured, 21,000 by Rawlinson's Fourth Army. By Western Front bloodbath standards, what became known as the "Battle of Amiens" was not considered costly. There had been an, by standards of the time, amazing advance of twelve miles. The territory lost, however, was not of crucial importance to the Germans. Yet, according to General Ludendorff, the engagement was the turning point of the war. Why was this the case?

General Ludendorff never had the reputation as being a good-humored soul. Every picture taken of him catches the man with what seems to be the severest of frowns. He appears to have been the sort of person who would smile only when passing gas. Yet, the confidence he had in his soldiers was virtually boundless. They could, he thought, do just about anything, particularly when placed at the disposal of a military genius such as himself. What upset Ludendorff about the Allied success at Amiens was that, for the first time (or at least it was the first time *he* was aware of it) German soldiers not only displayed a lack of morale, but showed that they could be just as panic-stricken as ones of other countries. On August 13, as the battle was still underway, Ludendorff informed his Emperor that the war could no longer be won, and that some sort of diplomatic solution was needed. When Ludendorff's words became known in Vienna, concerns for Austro-Hungarian withdrawal from the conflict increased markedly. In Sofia, capital of Germany's ally, Bulgaria, they were responsible for the fall of the pro-German Radoslavov Ministry, and its replacement by one deemed hostile to German interests. The country remained in the war, at least for the moment. Few, however, were willing to count on Bulgarian participation in it for much longer.

Later, when writing memoirs which, by any standard, were unusually self-justifying, Ludendorff declared that "'August 8 was the Black

Day of the German Army . . . It put the decline of our fighting powers beyond all doubt. The Army had ceased to be a perfect fighting instrument.' "[5] Of course, no army is "a perfect fighting instrument." In a sense, though, Ludendorff had a point. If Germany were to be able to win a war in which every strategic circumstance militated against such an outcome, the army had to be just about "perfect." As it was, it was still a very good one, in fact better than Ludendorff was willing to appreciate. The vanity of the man compelled him to believe that he was being let down by his sorely-tried men rather than to admit that he had played a major role in weakening the army to the point that disasters such as the one before Amiens could befall it.

Throughout August, German soldiers, at times, fighting with the courage of desperation, were pressed back all along the line. As yet, however, the American Army had yet to undertake a totally independent major operation of its own. Units of it had always been engaged in joint ventures with British and French troops. For Pershing, for whom holding the army together as a single entity was almost a fetish, this was unacceptable. Sooner-or-later, and better sooner, the troops of the AEF would have to undertake a massive offensive operation, and all on its own. In due course, he saw an opportunity for this.

East of Verdun, there was a German bulge in the Allied line. Since the southernmost town in this protuberance was St. Mihiel, it was called the "St. Mihiel Salient." A pinching-off of the salient was called for, and Pershing saw American troops as the ones to do it. After conversations, sometimes heated, with Foch, who wished to retain as much control as possible over all of the Allied armies, he received permission to proceed with the operation. The American First Army, totalling some 665,000 men, was selected for the attack, and Pershing assumed direct command of it. The French would play a role in the battle, but this would be confined to a Colonial corps.

Relatively few tanks were available for the anticipated operation. The British could not afford to provide any of theirs; while the French could supply less than 300. Some of these, though, would be taken into battle by men of the newly-formed American Tank Corps. Their performance in what was to come would be far from spectacular. Even the bombast of their commander, Colonel George S. Patton (1885–1945), who would be known for much more of the same in the next world go-around, could not compensate for lack of experience. There was, however, lots of artillery—over 3,000 pieces—to provide cover. And, of greater interest, the largest concentration of aircraft ever. More than 1,500 planes would provide for a degree of aerial support unknown up to that point.

The German High Command recognized that the soldiers in the St. Mihiel Salient were in a dangerous tactical situation and began to make plans for pulling them out. The withdrawal in fact began on September 10, 1918, two days before the American First Army and the French II Colonial Corps struck the salient from both sides. Thus, the attackers struck the Germans as they were engaged in the process of withdrawing, and this made it very difficult for them to offer strong resistance all along the line. An army in retreat is rarely in the position to put up much of a fight. Thus it was that the St. Mihiel Salient was essentially eliminated in one day and, by standards of the time, with very small losses. There were around 7,000 American casualties, while the Germans lost 15,000 men in prisoners alone. Almost 7,000 more Americans, however, would be killed or wounded by artillery fire which, once the German fall-back position had been attained, became very heavy.

Because the Germans had been caught while pulling out of the salient anyway, the St. Mihiel engagement became known as "the battle in which the Americans relieved the Germans." Nonetheless, it had been most successful. Indeed, General Pershing believed that, if Foch had allowed him to press the operation further, he might have broken the Hindenburg line and pressed on to the fortress city of Metz. This was, and is, a very debatable point. What is not debatable is the fact that, in an almost entirely independent operation of its own, an American army had attained a success which, if not spectacular in view of the circumstances in which it was achieved, was at least notable. Certainly, it contributed to a further strengthening of Allied morale. In view of the massive assault, all along the line envisaged by the overall Allied commander, Foch, such would be needed in the days ahead.

German morale was, of course, very much on the decline. Certainly, this was due largely to the series of setbacks sustained by German soldiers since the middle of July and to increasing hunger as rations became ever more lean. There was, however, another reason for the decline in German morale. This was due to news from back home, where near-starvation had become something of a way of life, and in many cases, death, for quite awhile. Before focusing attention on the battles which brought World War I to a close, we must spend some time considering the impact of the "Starvation Blockade" upon the German home front.

GERMANY 1915–1918: STARVATION AND UNREST

Quite understandably, the German government was concerned that total support be thrown behind the war effort. Unlike those of the Allies, however, it never appreciated the need to make certain that civilian needs were met to the point where adequate morale could be maintained on the home front. Probably much of this was due to the fact that, in contrast to what prevailed in the lands of the Allies, where governments remained in civilian hands, what amounted to a military dictatorship prevailed in Germany for a good part of the war. Only occasionally sensitive to the suffering of soldiers, "military men" such as Hindenburg and Ludendorff could hardly have been expected to have devoted much thought to problems faced by the civilian population.

In an earlier chapter, we devoted some time to the failure of the German wartime economy. As industrialists prospered, the real wages of workers declined. Fearful of raising taxes, the German government relied almost entirely on loans, in the form of bonds. The wartime inflation created by this practice, bad enough at the time, would have positively devastating effects well after the war was over.

There can be little doubt, though, that the aspect of the failed German wartime economy that would have the greatest impact upon home front morale was the failure to implement an adequate rationing system. Certainly, even if one were in place, the ruthless blockade initiated by the British in 1915 would still have had a terrible impact on the German population. Yet, the failure of the government to provide for a workable system of price controls for food (something which led to its hoarding by German farmers whose supposedly unselfish and folksy qualities had been extolled by generations of Romantics), and its seeming insensitivity to the enormous suffering that this created, especially in the large cities, engendered both despair and anger.

By 1916, a variety of goods could be obtained only on the black market. Food riots, which Germany had not seen since the 1840s, broke out, and the winter of 1916–1917 was dubbed the "Turnip Winter." This was due to the fact that, because of a bad harvest, one of the food items grown in abundance in Germany, potatoes, were in extremely short supply; something made worse yet by the inadequate rationing system mentioned earlier. Turnips were available as a substitute of sorts, and, for many Germans, this was just about their sole source of sustenance. Even what was supposed to amount to "coffee" was made from them.

An average adult needs about 2,000 calories a day to keep going, and the pre-war German diet usually provided considerably more than that. During the terrible "Turnip Winter" mentioned above—as some farmers and hoarders prospered—most Germans subsisted on 1,000 calories or less. In these terrible circumstances, children suffered the most. Even in peacetime, especially for working class families, fresh fruit was hard to come by. During the blockade years, it was usually not available at all. Other foodstuffs so necessary for growth and good health such as fresh vegetables, milk, and meat were always in extremely short supply and often also not available. With husbands away, many of them forever, mothers, often weak from hunger, worked long hours in the factories. Afterwards, they would wait in long lines for rationed foodstuffs that never appeared. They then returned home where, hungry and exhausted, they would attempt to undertake "normal" mothering functions. The most basic of these, however, providing nourishment, was often beyond them. At the same time, of course, they often had to assume functions identified with fathers. Shortly after the war ended (but with the Allied blockade still in place; an unspeakable atrocity which will be examined in due course), an observer described a district where "'90 percent of the children were ricketty and where children of three years are only beginning to walk.'" Upon seeing such wretched beings, one might believe that he or she was gazing upon kindergarten youngsters. Sadly, they were children seven or eight years old. "'Tiny faces, with large dull eyes, overshadowed by huge puffed, ricketty foreheads, their small arms just skin and bone, and above the crooked legs with their dislocated joints the swollen, pointed stomachs of the hunger oedema.'"[6] How many Germans, the majority being old people and children, actually died as a result of the Starvation Blockade and their government's inability to deal with it is uncertain. Estimates range between 350,000 and 750,000. If the higher figure can be accepted, then more Germans died as a result of the Starvation Blockade of World War I than from air raids in World War II.

A distinguished psychohistorian, Peter Loewenberg, has offered the hypothesis that those infants and small children deprived of adequate parenting and often even of food would come, when older, to see Hitler as a kind of father figure and grand nurturer. Hence, he has suggested, the Starvation Blockade which, in the eyes of many, was the primary reason for the Allied victory in World War I, was a very crucial reason why the National Socialist movement was able to tap into a well-spring of youthful enthusiasm, in the end, virtually assuring that there would be a World War II. This writer basically accepts the Loewenberg hypothesis.

As Germans starved, working people soon appreciated that, even as their real wages had been declining at the rate of about 10% a year, large scale entrepreneurs were waxing fat as a result of needs generated by the German war economy. There was an increasing number of strikes, the most crucial, that affecting the armaments industry, in January, 1918. Such was condemned by the leadership of the Social Democratic Party, which by-and-large bought the argument that Germany was fighting in self-defense, and thus the war effort deserved to be supported by the working class. By this time, however, substantial numbers of Social Democrats, some of whom had never really supported the war effort, *all* of whom had become fed up with working class suffering as a result of it, had broken away from the mother party and founded political organizations of their own.

The first to leave was a group which called itself "Spartacists." They named themselves after a Roman slave who, in 73 B.C., led a revolt of gladiators against the Roman Republic (the masochism in this defies belief; after some initial successes, Spartacus and several thousand of his followers were captured and crucified). Adhering to more-or-less orthodox Marxist beliefs (at the end of December, 1918, the Spartacists would declare themselves to be the Communist Party of Germany), this group called for an end to the war of nations, and for the overthrow of international capitalism, which they blamed for the war in the first place. In other words, the Spartacists stood foursquare for class war and a dictatorship of the proletariat.

In 1917, another group broke away from the Social Democratic Party. Calling themselves the "Independent Socialists of Germany," these people also called for an end to the war and the eventual establishment of a German Socialist republic. They were, however, not as radical as the Spartacists, and did not come out in favor of class war, nor did they stand for that dictatorship of the proletariat hallowed by Marxist orthodoxy. Independent Socialists joined with Spartacists, however, in supporting such actions as the munitions strike of January, 1918.

The strike was soon brought to an end. The anger and frustration responsible for it, however, did not go away. Neither did hunger, perhaps the single most important "fact" in German life at the time. The emotional and physical conditions of folks on the home front would have enormous consequences in the short run, and, without doubt, in the long run as well. So would the splintering of the left. As unrest continued to grow in Germany, the country's army, itself suffering from the effects of the terrible blockade, steeled itself for the massive Allied offensives all knew had to be on the way.

17

Nineteen Eighteen: Finale and Collapse

By the end of August, Marshal Ferdinand Foch had arrived at a general strategical approach by which the war would be brought to an end. On the far northwestern end of the line, British forces, with Belgian support, and with whatever French assistance as might be available, would strike out along the coast down to the already-blood-drenched Ypres Salient. On their right flank, the main portion of the BEF, with whatever American support possible, would attack in the direction of Cambrai, its eventual goal being the cracking of what the Allies called the "Hindenburg Line" (for those Germans who manned it, the *"Siegfried Stellung")*. In approximately the center of the front, a French Army would advance in Champagne, striking across the Aisne River. On the right wing of this force, the American Army's task was to clear the Argonne area, including the forest bearing that name, and breach the Hindenburg line (the portion facing the Americans was known as the *"Kriemhilde Stellung")*. On the far right, i.e., southeastern portion of the front, another substantial French force was to hold the line down to the Vosges Mountains. It would function as a kind of strategic reserve.

Plan to crack H.L.

Foch called for British and American troops to spearhead the assault, with the French Army in the center pacing their advance. Hopefully, British and American forces would be able to achieve decisive breakthroughs, while the French force, advancing in the center (albeit, at a more measured pace) would demolish the now-trapped German Army. Some historians have maintained that Foch's calling for a more leisurely advance on the part of French forces was due to his unwillingness, so soon after recent disasters, to exert them all that much. Whether or not this was indeed the case, the American and British forces were probably in better shape to undertake aggressive offensive action. And, to be sure, the role envisaged for the French armies in the center of the line was crucial enough. In any event, Foch's rallying call, "Tout le monde a la bataille!" ("Everyone to battle!") pretty much described what was to happen. In the mightiest offensive of the war, 3,900,000 men were to attack all along the line. There would be extensive armored support, and the Allies enjoyed superiority in artillery and overall command of the air.

The German force confronting them totalled around 2,300,000 men. While this was significant in terms of numbers (there would have been lots more men available if Ludendorff had not staged his, what in the end, turned out to be extravagantly wasteful offensives), it was by now, under-supplied, hungry, and exhausted. Almost every German soldier knew of the terrible conditions which prevailed on the home front, and this contributed greatly to falling morale. Yet, while Foch hoped for a break-through, nobody expected the German Army to fold. It would either be destroyed, or worn down—a process which, as we have seen, had in fact been underway for some time.

At 2:30 A.M., September 26, 1918, 2,700 French and American artillery pieces opened up in advance of the American assault in the Argonne. In a most intensive three-hour bombardment, more ammunition was expended than during the entire American Civil War. Then, at 5:30 A.M., troops of the American First Army—some of whose units already had been "blooded" at Saint Mihiel—left their trenches in what was, up to that point, the largest (and, when it was all over, costliest) campaign in American history. Eventually, close to 1,200,000 American troops would take part in it.

The Germans in the area were outnumbered by about eight-to-one. And, the shock of the attack (the German High Command had expected it to take place further to the east), as well as this vast American numerical supremacy, led to a fairly successful first day's advance, though it fell short of what Pershing had planned on. Then, however, as the Germans, as they had done so often in the past, recovered, and offered increasingly stiff resistance, the very size of the American force began to work against it. Particularly in the Argonne Forest proper, where the left wing of this force was attacking, roads were few, and these became badly jammed. Supplies could not move and, while some soldiers had taken part in earlier actions, most had not. While eager, they were very "green," as, for that matter, were their officers. Not being able to follow maps of the broken and partially-wooded country in which they were fighting, no small number of them got lost. Also, and somewhat pathetically, many American neophytes, advancing through wooded areas, sought to maintain contact by calling out to one another. Within a few days, the great drive had stalled, and, now in the process of being reenforced, the Germans were staging counter attacks, in places driving back more advanced American units. Desperately trying to keep the pressure on, Pershing, after the briefest of pauses, commenced another assault on October 4. Gains were minimal, losses heavy.

Both their Allies and the German enemy were impressed by the offensive spirit of the young Americans. Allied observers, however, were appalled, even saddened, at the reckless manner in which they were hurled into assaults. Attacking straight up, regulation-number-of-paces apart, they were mowed down by the score and then often lay in neat rows, as if struck down while on parade. It could have been the French at any time between August, 1914 and May, 1917; or, the British between spring, 1915 and the first weeks of Haig's 1917 Flanders Offensive.

When Americans were initially engaged, they had gained reputations as being self-reliant and, somewhat like the British soldiers of 1914, crack shots. And, to be sure, the dismal Argonne operation did produce the heroics of Sergeant Alvin York, a sharpshooter from Tennessee, who, after picking off any number of Germans, accepted the surrender of more than one hundred of them. Most of the Americans in what came to be called the "Meuse-Argonne Offensive" were not exactly in this league. Indeed, many of them had never before fired a gun. It is plain that, in fact, the newly-arrived Americans (as already had been demonstrated on a smaller scale in Belleau Wood) were falling into a familiar pattern. Naively eager for action, astonishingly brave in the attack, they were being fed into an attritional massacre revoltingly similar to all those that had taken place before it. Although never going into the issue in his memoirs, Pershing had taken the same road as Joffre, Haig, Nivelle, and, in the end, Ludendorff. Now, however, with hundreds of thousands of new, expendable young lives available, and with the German enemy worn down as never before—and, on top of that, hungry—chances for a victorious conclusion were greater than ever.

The French troops on the American left flank had endured attritional massacre variety offensives up to and including the Nivelle disaster. Very recently, large numbers had been slaughtered while on the defensive in the Chemin des Dames. Now, according to plan, they began a relatively cautious advance. If and when the Americans and the British were to break through the German defenses, they would seal the victory by attacking with vigor in the center.

Unlike the Americans, who had to cover considerable ground before reaching the main German defensive positions, the British, attacking in the Artois (they were assisted by two American divisions), were very close to the Hindenburg line. Probably, this was a source of scant comfort for the men of the three armies involved in the assault. This began on September 28, 1918 and, at first, progress was very slow. The British-Belgian attack further north, in Flanders (there was, as anticipated, some French support), immediately encountered those difficulties generic to the region. Rain and mud were at least as important as enemy resistance in slowing the anticipated advance to a crawl.

The German situation on the Western Front, on September 28, 1918, was not as bad as it might have been. Everywhere, Allied advances had either been slowed down or brought to a halt. On the other hand, Germany's overall military situation was not favorable. The hitherto almost comically-inactive Allied force in Salonika was suddenly on the offensive, cutting through a Bulgarian Army much weakened by typhus. A German army sent to support the Bulgarians was forced to retreat. It was plain that, within a very brief period of time, Bulgaria would be out of the war. When this occurred, Vienna could be taken from the south by the Allies. Between September 18 and September 21, at Megiddo, where Joshua had once fought, General Allenby destroyed an entire Turkish army. Now, the road to the strategically-vital city of Damascus was open, and it was plain that, very soon, Turkey would be following the Bulgarian example. Furthermore, all knew that Austria-Hungary was waiting upon any appropriate event to leave the war. Also, it was plain that, while the Allied offensive had, thus far, been contained, all strategic advantage rested on their side, and some hundreds of thousands of American troops had yet to be committed. All of these factors weighed heavily upon the mind of General Ludendorff. On the afternoon of September 28, during the course of a staff conference at his headquarters in Spa, Belgium, he began railing against all who he saw as having betrayed him. That amounted to just about everyone, including Wilhelm. Everywhere, there had been weakness, indecision, or misjudgment. Eventually, by some accounts, foaming at the mouth, he suffered a nervous collapse. Later, barely recovered, he visited Hindenburg. All was lost, he said; Germany had to call for an armistice before the front was shattered and the Fatherland itself overrun. Within hours, the Emperor and the at least *de jure* government in Berlin were notified of Ludendorff's dire appraisal. In truth, as seen earlier, Ludendorff and Hindenburg, but especially the former, had been the *de facto* government up to this point. Now, Ludendorff, perceiving that all was lost, was calling upon the official, i.e., civilian, government to make peace. In the not-too-distant-future, angry super-patriots, including, of course, Ludendorff himself, would be able to disassociate the German military from the plaintive call for peace, first voiced by Ludendorff.

It was decided that President Wilson ought to be the one approached by the German government. After all, as espouser of the Fourteen Points, he might be inclined to be more sensitive to German concerns. Also, as leader of a country which had not been in the war for very long, and one whose soil had not been ravaged beyond belief, lack of personal malice might make Wilson less vengeful with regards to conditions for an armistice, to say nothing of the terms of a future peace agreement. Around the beginning of October, 1918, the antediluvian Hertling was replaced as chancellor by Prince Max von Baden. Despite his noble title, he was internationally-known for his pacific and liberal attitudes. Such would make him, it was thought, more acceptable to a New World idealist who, despite his obvious naivete, seemed to hold all the cards with regard to Germany's future fate. At the same time, the *Reichstag* was informed of Germany's true military situation. Up to that point, censorship imposed by the military had been so effective that few really knew how grave matters had become. Now, even though the High Command itself was owning up to conditions as they really were, some delegates refused to believe it.

Soon, press censorship was lifted, and, over time, the German people were able to learn about the real state of affairs. Unrest due to terrible conditions on the home front now was complemented by a sense of betrayal. So, all of the massive sacrifices endured by the common folk had been for nothing. A rising chorus of voices began calling for peace. Soon, Wilson had in his hands Germany's first peace note.

Actually, between September 28 and October 4, the German armies in the West had succeeded in pretty much holding the Allies at bay. To be sure, Passchendaele had been retaken by the British on September 29. This, however, was more of symbolic significance than anything else. On October 5, the British succeeded in cracking the Hindenburg line, and now most of the BEF was in open country, but in too exhausted a state to undertake a vigorous pursuit. Furthermore, as for the American prong of the pincer attack; it was still held fast in the wastes of the Argonne.

By October 7, Ludendorff, to the horror of all but the most hard-line military types, had recovered his nerve. The German Army now seemed to be in far better shape than he had assumed a little more than a week before. He began calling for all-out resistance. The German government, which had accepted Wilson's Fourteen Points as a basis for negotiations, was much embarrassed by this outburst of bellicosity on Ludendorff's part. Such would harden Wilson's resolve. From the German perspective, the situation was made all the more desperate by the sinking of the passenger ship, *Leinster* by a U-boat. Over five hundred civilians, mostly women and children, perished as a result of this ill-timed attack. On October 23, the German government received a note in which the American president demanded that the current military leadership be replaced before peace negotiations could begin. Otherwise, Wilson declared, the issue would be pressed until total German surrender. On October 26, Emperor Wilhelm formally dismissed Ludendorff. Soon, the man who once saw himself as representing a rock of certitude in a sea of weakness and indecision donned false whiskers and dark glasses and headed off for neutral Sweden.

Ludendorff had a fine sense of timing. On October 24, 1918, the rested and reequipped Italian Army, under better leadership, launched a massive offensive against the Austro-Hungarians near the town of Vittorio Veneto. Within a few days, it was plain that a rout as under-way. While not wishing to take anything away from the newly-inspired Italian Army, which certainly showed both courage and prowess, they were up against a foe which, by this time, pretty much knew that the war was over. In any event, the Vittorio Veneto engagement ended with the total collapse of the Austro-Hungarian Army on the Italian Front on November 2. The following day, the Austro-Hungarian government requested an armistice. Four days earlier, Turkey had left the war. Germany was on its own.

Mid-October had found the German Army giving ground very slowly and, all things considered, fighting well. The British, having broken through the Hindenburg Line, were strained by exhaustion. The French, as planned, were moving ahead with what commanders like to call "deliberate speed." The bulk of the American Army was engaged in heavy fighting in the Meuse-Argonne. By this time, it was plain to one and all that the battle was being terribly mismanaged. Pershing, who had insisted on directing the First Army's offensive personally, had been severely, some thought viciously, criticized by Clemenceau. While never really owning up to it, it was plain that the man, affectionately known as "Black Jack," had bitten off far more than he could chew. He turned over immediate command of the attacking army to General Hunter Liggett. Wisely, he recognized that his battered soldiers needed to rest while a better means of pressing the attack was discovered. Pershing, as had Allied commanders in the past, had shown a predilection to select a point of attack and then, once the engagement had begun, to press on, even in the face of ever-stiffening resistance. Liggett shifted the main point of the assault more to the center, where he perceived a weakness in the German line. On November 1, the Americans were on the offensive again.

Initially, there was heavy resistance. But, Liggett had been right, and soon the Germans were being pressed back at an ever-quickening pace. On the left of the First Army, the French picked up the pace of their advance somewhat. Perhaps most decisively, the British armies in Flanders and northern France began to roll forward. On November 4, between the Scarpe and Sambre Rivers, they shattered the German rear guard. It was plain that, within a few days, all German troops on the British portion of the front would be driven out of France. For General Wilhelm Groener (1867–1939), who had succeeded Ludendorff, this was the last straw. Come what may, there had to be peace. In Germany itself, no small number of folk had come to the same conclusion.

The German fleet had been largely inactive since Jutland. Confined to port, German sailors had plenty of time to reflect upon matters, among other things, the extraordinary disparities between officers and men. In the German Army, discipline could be harsh. Yet, while it would be naive to exaggerate it, shared dangers were responsible for a certain degree of camaraderie between officers and men. The former certainly enjoyed privileges with regard to food and accommodations. But, in battle, hardship, agonizing wounds, and death were their lot, too. In the idled ships of the High Seas Fleet, sailors, whose rations were, as the result of growing food shortages, increasingly cut, saw officers living rather well, even sumptuously, at least by their standards. With no danger serving as a tie that bound, resentment grew. In any case, by late October, 1918, these were not men to be ordered out on some sort of do-or-die mission. Yet, in a kind of frustration-grounded last gasp, this is precisely what the German Admiralty did.

The sailors learned of the order on November 3, 1918. Within a day, the fleet was rocked by mutiny. In Kiel, sailors murdered their officers and soon red flags were being displayed on capital ships. While it was true that the mutineers had been targets of radical propaganda for some time, the "Reds" did not have to rely much on exaggeration. Conditions pretty much spoke for themselves, and this explains the fury, at times of homicidal proportions, of the sailors' response to the idiotic demand that they, in effect, commit suicide. The government rushed in speakers to deal with the situation. Several were, in fact Socialists. To be sure, these were of the more conservative variety, ones who still supported the war effort. Yet, they could recognize things for what they were even as their presence might help to calm matters. Such did occur, but not before hundreds of revolutionary sailors had spread disorder throughout portions of northern Germany. In Berlin, there was Spartacist agitation and, on all sides, cries for Wilhelm's abdication.

Throughout the war, Bavarians had nurtured resentment against the German High Command. Proportionally, more Bavarians had been killed or wounded than had other Germans, and the phrase, "Prussian war, Bavarian fight" was frequently articulated. In the chaotic atmosphere of early November, many expressed the opinion that Bavaria ought to secede from Germany. Acting on this belief, an Independent Socialist by the name of Kurt Eisner (1867–1919) declared Bavaria independent. With the establishment of a Bavarian Socialist republic, the ruling Wittelsbach Dynasty would naturally have to go. Eisner's own variety of Socialism was informed by the philosophy of Immanuel Kant, which had been undergoing a kind of revival before the war. Thus it was that this well-intentioned soul declared that the new Bavaria would be ruled according to the dictates of the Kantian "categorical imperative." Only in the power vacuum created by impending collapse could so bizarre a state of affairs prevail, and it would not prevail for long. In due course, Eisner would be assassinated, in part because he was Jewish. And, for a while afterwards, there would be an even more bizarre state of affairs, albeit even more short lived than that following from Eisner's pathetic attempt to translate leading elements of German Idealism into political reality.

While all this was going on, Wilhelm was at German GHQ at the Spa. In a stormy confrontation with him, General Greener declared that the army would no longer support him; that he had no choice but to abdicate. When Hindenburg, the most monarchical of generals, reluctantly went along with these harsh judgements, Wilhelm agreed to abandon the throne. He also agreed with Hindenburg's opinion that he seek asylum in the Netherlands. On November 9, 1918, Wilhelm II signed the document of abdication, and the Crown Prince was constrained to do the same. On the same day, in Berlin, a republic was declared, as was a Provisional Government under the leadership of the Social Democratic Party chief, Friedrich Ebert (1871–1925). After ordering the posting of placards announcing the imperial abdication, Prince Max von Baden surrendered what authority he had to Ebert, who found himself having to confront chaos not seen in Berlin since the Revolution of 1848.

On the morning of November 10, 1918, the ex-Emperor, Wilhelm, sat in stupefied silence on the imperial train as it headed for the Dutch frontier. Once there, he proceeded to the chateau of Count Godard Bentinck. Wilhelm and Bentinck were brothers in a fraternal organization called Knights of the Order of Saint John of Malta, and it was required that, in times of trouble, brothers provide sanctuary for each other. Confronted with Wilhelm and imperial retinue, the count was, understandably, somewhat startled. Asylum was granted, however, and, this being done, the former ruler of what had once been the strongest power in Europe asked for a cup of English tea. Wilhelm II, unlike his unfortunate cousin-by-marriage, Nicholas II, was a man of considerable intelligence. Like the last Tsar of Russia, however, he was basically a weak, vacillating individual. Unfortunately, while Nicholas rarely postured or pretended to be stronger than he was, Wilhelm often did both. Thus, in his blustering poses and hyperbolic language, he came to stand for what many saw or came to see as everything that was wrong with Germany. Of course, from 1916 on, he reigned rather than ruled. The pathetic state of the man becomes plain when we realize that, in his own mind, he probably never perceived this.

As Wilhelm was settling down to his first day in exile, a German armistice delegation was facing Marshal Foch in a railroad carriage in the forest of Compiègne. It was headed by a civilian, Matthias Erzberger (1875–1921) of the Catholic Center Party, and this was unfortunate. Later on, leading German military figures, and ex-soldiers and civilians unwilling to accept defeat, would be able to claim that the German military *per se* had never really surrendered; that the army had been betrayed. Such folk either did not know about Ludendorff's September 28 descent into hysteria, or, in marvelous examples of denial, chose *not* to know about it. Hyper-nationalists came to despise Erzberger for his important role in obtaining the armistice. Three years after the end of the war, several such people assassinated him.

army could blame Erzberger

The members of the German delegation knew that, even with Wilson's Fourteen Points hovering vaguely in the background, the terms of the armistice would be severe. Nothing, however, prepared them for what was demanded of their defeated country. The terms read out by Foch's aide, Maxim Weygand, would result in rendering Germany virtually defenseless. Not only were German armies to vacate all occupied territories, including Alsace-Lorraine, but German territory west of the Rhine as well. The Germans were given six days to move out of the occupied territories, an impossibly short period of time, especially in view of the half-starved state of the army. The armistice terms provided that the Allies would set up "bridgeheads" in crucial Rhenish cities. Germany was called upon to surrender 5,000 artillery pieces, 25,000 machine guns, 3,000 trench mortars, and 1,700 aircraft. All submarines were to be turned over to the Allies, and almost all of the fleet's capital ships, plus fifty destroyers, were to be interned in British ports. For the time being, the Allied blockade of Germany would not be lifted. With reason, Germans learning of the harsh armistice terms expected that a formal peace treaty would not be informed by the spirit of the Fourteen Points.

The armistice was agreed to on November 10, and the German delegates requested that fighting end on that day. The Allies had decided, however, that, for the sake of symbolism, hostilities would cease at 11:00 A.M., November 11, 1918—the "eleventh" hour of the eleventh day of the eleventh month. This rare military concession to poetic usage was, of course, responsible for loss of life even more meaningless than the toll thus far exacted.

After the guns fell silent on a day which, in future, would come to represent lost hopes as much as anything else, a, to many, eerie silence prevailed. Some soldiers broke into cheers and embraced one another, some wept, others lay down in the mud and went to sleep. Soon, very cautiously at first, parties of men left the trenches and former enemies met in no-man's land. Souvenirs were exchanged. Hungry and exhausted German soldiers were quite willing to surrender weaponry (Luger pistols were an important item here) in exchange for soap, cigarettes, and food items. In due course, however, there came the inevitable orders forbidding fraternization. After all, maybe the armistice would break down, and it would be too much to bear if so magnificent a victory were undone by a large-scale version of the 1914 Christmas truce.

What the Allies "won" exactly was uncertain; but, there could be no question that Germany had lost. Thus, victory, if by default, could be claimed. Certainly, on that day when, after years of the most concentrated slaughter the world had ever seen, peace reigned at last, none of the Allied soldiers on now silent fields could have imagined that, in what would amount to a historical moment, all of their heroism, suffering, and ability to endure the unendurable—all would be rendered vain, indeed, in the eyes of pitiless history, tragically absurd. Perhaps someone recalled lines penned by the eleventh century Persian poet, Omar Khayyam, as his commentary upon those human acts which, taken together, constitute historical experience:

The moving finger writes, and having writ,
Moves on. Nor all your piety or wit shall
Lure it back to cancel half a line, nor
All your tears wash out a word of it.

18

War's Triumph Over Peace

THE TOLL

It has been estimated that, in dollar values of the time, the Great War cost those who participated in it $337,000,000,000. Today, that would work out to be somewhat in the range of 9 trillion dollars. The toll taken of those who fought in the conflict was equal to around twice the number of lives lost in all the wars fought in the Western World between 1790 and 1914. Even today, as remains are still occasionally unearthed, especially around areas of sustained, maximum activity such as Verdun, a precise accounting remains uncertain. It is plain, though, that between nine and ten million participants in the great adventure of 1914 were killed or died of wounds. Since the number of men mobilized totalled around 72 million, taking the minimum approximate estimate of those slain, one out of eight called to service died.

In terms of raw numbers of those slain, Germany topped the list with slightly over 2,000,000 combat-related deaths. Russia, with 1,700,000 was second. Of the major powers, however, France, with over 1,300,000 dead, suffered the highest proportional losses, more than four times the number the country would lose in World War II. British and Imperial military deaths totalled 940,000, close to three times more than those to be sustained in the future world conflict. Austria-Hungary, in the war which brought the existence of the vexed political entity to an end, lost 1,200,000 of its people. Turkey, in losing its empire, lost 750,000 in combat, or as a result of it, and perhaps this was a factor in determining that it would not enter World War II. Italy, with 680,000 combat-related deaths, lost almost four times as many combatants in World War I than it would in World War II. That crucial late-comer, the United States, sustained 116,000 dead, altogether. Of these, however, "only" 55,000 were combat-related fatalities. A slight majority of those Americans who died in service were victims of disease, particularly of the influenza pandemic about which more will be said later. Of all of the major participants in the First World War, the United States was the only one which lost more of its combatants to disease than in combat. But, then again, American troops had been involved in sustained fighting only since May, 1918. Losses sustained by "minor" players, such as Serbia, Belgium, and Romania, served to push military deaths to over nine million. About five million civilians died as a direct result of the war, among these, perhaps around one million Armenians, victims of what many have called the century's first fling at genocide. Some have maintained, however, that the estimate of five million civilian deaths is far too low. Perhaps the number was closer to ten million . . .

In any event, in the years 1918-1919, nature gave an impressive demonstration in which it became plain that, in ways impervious to sentiments—national, class, or pacific—it could outdo human artifices of any kind, however sophisticated they might be. In the world-wide Spanish Influenza pandemic of that time, well over 20,000,000 people died. In Germany and in Austro-Hungarian lands in states of disintegration, its work was made easier, it must be said, by the debilitating effects of hunger, the result of a very human blockade. For many a soul unfortunate enough to live just about anywhere in these now-blighted lands, that mind-numbing combination of starvation, defeat, collapse, chaos, and pestilence must have been enough to make it seem as if the world had come to an end.

THE GERMAN PROVISIONAL GOVERNMENT/A WAR THAT WOULD NOT DIE

For many, perhaps most, Germans *a* world had indeed come to an end. Imperial Germany was no more. To be sure, Allied pressure—behind which, some hoped, lurked the spirit of the Fourteen Points—had much to do with this. Certainly, there had been a collapse rather than a revolution. But, with radicals taking to the streets, army officers beaten-up, and sloganeering everywhere, there were signs of monstrous things to come. And there was, after all, the Provisional Government, embodied in the Council of Peoples' Representatives, consisting of three "Majority Socialists" (those who had stuck by a party leadership that had remained loyal to the war effort) and three Independent Socialists. Could one expect radical moves from this body? Since its tone was generally set by Friedrich Ebert, certainly not.

Ebert was a Socialist, to be sure, and he was in favor of reforms—a truly meaningful *Reichstag,* for example. He was not, however, by any stretch of the imagination, radical. Indeed, he once declared that he "hated revolution like sin." Like many of those who led the Social Democratic Party, he had not only become rather accustomed to that bourgeois society that had taken shape within Imperial contours, but, in some ways, had something of a stake in it. Thus, in the seemingly halcyon days before the war, his adherence to Marxist precepts of any kind had become rather attenuated. Perhaps, someday, in God's good time, Germany would become Socialist. Now, as ground-work was being laid for a Constituent Assembly which would determine the fate of that beloved country for which two of his sons had died, it was up to this new leader to preserve order.

In a telephone conversation, Ebert and Groener struck a deal. The Provisional Government would take measures to make certain that radical leftists would be unable to tamper with traditional military usages such as discipline, rank, and the authority attaching to it. In return, the army would not interfere with the implementation of measures which probably would result in Germany's becoming a republic. For the moment, Ebert was not worried as much about the army as he was about those infuriating renegades who recently had bolted the party, and now, on street corners all over Berlin, were calling for truly radical measures, in some cases, class war. In a word, the at-least-technically left-wing Provisional Government needed protection from those further on the left. While both Ebert and Groener had been concerned to protect the integrity of the army, there wasn't much of one left, at least for the time being. As soon as units arrived home, they melted away. It was in welcoming one such unit home, to what he called "a new Germany," that Ebert, without question proud of an army in which two sons, gone forever, had served, made a rhetorical flourish which would have grave consequences. After declaring that a new government had brought the war to an end, he trumpeted, "'I salute you, who return unvanquished from the field of battle.'"[1] Very soon, there would be many who would see this declaration as a confession of treason. Such was hardly on Ebert's mind. He needed a force to protect the Provisional Government and to preserve order.

It was almost providential, but, personnel for such a force were almost immediately available. For thousands of demobilized soldiers, homeland was home no longer. The strife-torn, starving, disease-ridden republic-in-the-making was really not “their” country any more, and they felt as if they had no place in it. Furthermore, many of them quite simply could not accept the reality of defeat. They had, in fact, internalized the war and it raged on within them. Watching a group of soldiers return to Berlin, on December 11, 1918, a young man declared, approvingly, that “ ‘They would always carry the front in their blood; the approaching death, the glorious suspense, the suffering, the smoke, the cold steel . . . The war is ended but the warriors still march!’ ”[2] In an earlier chapter, we considered Ernst Jünger’s glorification of war in all of its horrors. For him, those in whom the war would not end were not cursed, but privileged. “ ‘Hardened as scarcely another generation ever was in fire and flame, we could go into life as though from the anvil; into friendship, love, politics, professions, into all that destiny had in store. It is not every generation that is so favored.’ ”[3] Many of this “favored” group would be marching again, some, sooner than they could have dreamed.

These men would enter an organization known as the “Free Corps,” which, secretly funded by the Provisional Government, was, at least in part, to fill the gap left by the largely-demobilized regular army. This group, consisting of probably the most battle-hardened, alienated, and thus, most ruthless collection of fighting men in the Western World, was to protect the embryonic new republic, primarily against internal enemies, such as left-wing radicals, but also against foreign foes—forces of the newly-established states of Poland, Latvia, and Lithuania which were pressing claims on German-held territory. Within a little more than a month after the armistice, the Free Corps, ranks swollen with those in whom war had become not merely a way of life, but life itself, and youths who had been too young to serve in the Great War (and resented it), was in action everywhere.

With regard to domestic problems, the Free Corps first put in a major appearance in January, 1919. There was a major left-wing uprising in Berlin. Out of a sense of duty, the new Communist Party (before December 31, 1918, the Spartacists) joined in this effort to overthrow what those on the far left saw as a government that had betrayed Socialist principles. Some who participated in the revolt also wanted to prevent elections for the Constituent Assembly, scheduled for January 19, 1919, from taking place. The German people was simply too naively conservative—even the so-called “Workers and Soldiers Councils,” modelled after the Russian *Soviet,* had proved unwilling to assert themselves and seize power. Thus, it was argued, the Constituent Assembly would serve simply to represent traditional bourgeois interests.

Nobody was more critical of Ebert and colleagues than Rosa Luxemburg (1870–1919). She and Karl Liebknecht (1871–1919), son of one of the founders of the Social Democratic Party, led the Spartacists, and later, the Communist Party which came out of it. Far more eloquent and theoretically rigorous than Liebknecht (in fact, Luxemburg was one of the most brilliant Marxists ever), she had come to appreciate the fact that the dazed, starving, and spiritually-traumatized German people were not up for a mass uprising. Also, she was opposed to any effort to block the elections of January 19. Dictatorial-type *coups* were not to her liking, and, in this regard, she had deep suspicions about Lenin. Yet, as she saw it, the newly-established Communist Party could not stand by while workers battled for their rights. Thus it was that the Communists joined in the January uprising which, because of this, became somewhat-inaccurately known as the "Spartacist Revolt."

The indifferently-led and badly-armed rebels really had no chance at all against the forces which the Provisional Government threw against them. These consisted of some regular army troops and Free Corps units who, displaying an at times pathological enthusiasm, crushed the revolt in one week's time. Luxemburg and Liebknecht were arrested, beaten with rifle-butts, and shot; though, to be as fair as possible to the Free Corps, "regular" military folk were responsible for this. Ebert and other members of the Provisional Government expressed shock over the incident. This, however, did not outweigh their appreciation of the Free Corps' effectiveness, and when another left-wing revolt broke out in Berlin in March, 1919, they did not hesitate to call for its services. In the first major left- wing uprising in Berlin, several hundred had died. In the March revolt, over a thousand. The Free Corps had become one of the most important players in German political life.

It, of course, did not confine its involvement in domestic political turmoil—to which, of course, it made its own modest contributions—to Berlin. In February, 1919, after his ill-defined party lost a crucial election, the Bavarian Kurt Eisner was shot dead on his way to hand in his resignation to the Bavarian parliament. A Social Democratic government which followed was soon overthrown by anarchists who, in turn, were overthrown by much more ruthless Communists, some of whom were of Russian origin. During their short-lived rule in Munich, the Communists proved that they could be harsh indeed. There were confiscations of property and a number of hostages were executed. There was much worse to come. At the end of April, 1919, Free Corps units attacked Red-held Munich which, ironically enough, fell on May Day. Well over a thousand died, almost all of them at the hands of the Free Corps. Prisoners were beaten, shot, and trampled to death. There was at least one case of a leading representative of the left being sliced into small pieces.

The Free Corps had been called into existence mainly in order to deal with threats from the left. It had proved to be most efficient in that capacity. Of course, those who joined the Free Corps were not animated by enthusiasm for republican usages. Indeed, they were, almost all of them, either monarchists or right-wing nihilists. As indicated above, they fought in order to fight—to keep the war alive, especially in themselves. This would rage on until that time in which the German nation as a whole would once again be strong enough to regain that glory due to it. Portly, dull Friedrich Ebert and his pettifogging cronies were, as the average Free Corps man saw it, representative of a new Germany which, as soon as possible, had to be overthrown. Indeed, within an astonishingly short period of time, probably all Free Corps men—and quite a few outside of the organization as well—came to believe that Ebert and followers (along, of course, with Communists, Socialists, Jews, Pacifists, and maybe Freemasons) had betrayed the country by ending the war. After all, had not the Social Democratic leader greeted home-coming soldiers as returning "unvanquished from the field of battle?"

Friedrich Ebert, who uttered these words, probably amongst the most ill-chosen in modern history, was not unintelligent; nor did he lack personal and political courage. He was not known, however, for boundless flights of imagination. Hence, at least initially, he probably could not have suspected that the group formed in order to protect the Provisional Government and assure order, would someday turn against the republic of which he would be the first president. In time, the Free Corps would fade away, many of its members going into other right-wing organizations which, in the early years of what became known as the "Weimar Republic," sprouted like poisonous mushrooms. One of these groups was headed by an honored veteran who, like so many others of his ilk, found defeat impossible to assimilate. Unlike most, however, he would show an astonishing aptitude for politics.

In 1919, the Hitler phenomenon lay ahead in a future seemingly shrouded in crepe. As Free Corps units fought to restore order throughout Germany, Allied diplomats were gathering, initially in Paris, later in nearby Versailles. Revenge was on the minds of many of them, and this would assume the form of national humiliation—good "growing weather" for the pathological nationalism of which the Free Corps and Hitler were representative.

"BLESSED ARE THE PEACE-MAKERS"?: THE POLITICS OF NATIONAL HUMILIATION

When Woodrow Wilson arrived in Europe, on December 13, 1918, in order to attend the peace conference, he was the man of the hour. For many, he had come to represent a new order replete with new possibilities. Some kind of "new world order" seemed to be at hand, and Wilson was its prophet. The savior-like aspect of Wilson, which he did little to dispel, was not appreciated by everyone. Clemenceau remarked that he found it very difficult to deal with somebody who "talks like the Lord-God one day, and Lloyd George the next." Quite a bit before the peace conference began, it became plain that Wilsonian idealism—which, as we have seen, did not in any way inform the armistice negotiations—and crude, often cruel, power-political concerns did not lend themselves to easy synthesis. Here too, Clemenceau had a word to say; in many respects, as matters turned out, the last one. "God gave us Ten Commandments," he snickered, "and we broke them. Wilson gave us Fourteen Points. We shall see."

In the old days, peace treaties were drawn up with the defeated party(ies) having roles to play in the proceedings. The recently ended war was of such a nature that this was precluded. In the first modern mass war, mass death had engendered mass bitterness, a deadly complement to mass nationalism. Passions were too high for governments to even consider conducting the peace conference along decorous lines hallowed by tradition. No, the Allies would draw up a treaty; then it would be shown to the German enemy. Since the blockade was being maintained and Allied troops could explode out of the Rhineland bridgeheads, he would be in no position to refuse to sign the treaty, no matter how harsh it might be. "We'll squeeze the lemon until the pips squeak," Lloyd George told delighted countrymen. As vengeful as Lloyd George sounded, far worse could be expected of Clemenceau. Germany was not only going to "pay" for losing what was seen as an aggressive war, commenced by that country. The nation was going to be humiliated. Would the representative of New World idealism be able to do anything at all about it?

Wilson certainly was not as concerned with revenge as were Lloyd George and Clemenceau. But, as high as American casualties had been during our relatively brief period of participation in the war, they were as nothing compared to those of Great Britain and France. Also, in the French (and, for that matter, Belgian) case, there was the question of destruction which, up to that time, could not even have been imagined. Some villages had been so thoroughly destroyed that, where they once had been, had to be marked by the name of the (former) place mounted on a placard. In their final retreat in the summer and autumn of 1918, the Germans committed acts of gratuitous vandalism on a mass scale. In some places, it was worse than the "Alberich" action of April, 1917. Clemenceau thought that Wilson ought to see some of the destruction for himself. Maybe then he could gain an appreciation of why the French felt as they did. Wilson refused to take the proposed tour. He did not want to lose any of his objectivity. While the man's position is understandable, it did not in any way please Clemenceau.

Well, even if President Wilson made something of a gaffe in refusing to view examples of the war's destruction, it perhaps pointed to a person who, extremely sensitive in nature, really did fear about having his objectivity marred. Over time, however, it became plain that there was something abstract, almost cold, about the man. For example, many Americans present at the conference thought that a visit to the Meuse-Argonne was in order. After all, some tens of thousands of the president's countrymen had been killed or wounded there. It could well have been argued that, without this enormous sacrifice, the conference might not have been taking place at all. Wilson showed no inclination whatsoever to getting his hands soiled in that blood-soaked wasteland. He did, however, attend a round of diplomatic functions and soirees. As in most heavily-wooded areas in Europe, the Argonne Forest is home to wild boars. This summons forth the image of President Wilson dining on fancy hors d'oeuvres in Paris as boars dine on what was left of some of the scores of his countrymen listed as "missing" in the Argonne. In many ways, despite his obvious belief in the principles embodied in the Fourteen Points, it was hard to know what to expect from such a person once diplomatic horse-trading set in. There could be no doubt, however, that he soon would be on a collision course with other Allied leaders.

The first day of the Paris Peace Conference was January 18, 1919, and the choice of that particular day foreshadowed what was to come. On that day, in 1871, the founding of the German Empire had been declared. The 1919 action was part of a conscientiously-applied effort at national humiliation. Such was possible because Clemenceau, and to a lesser extent, Lloyd George, largely set the tone of the conference. They were able to do so because President Wilson, as outraged as he sometimes was over their pressures and demands, was obsessed with seeing Point Fourteen of his "program" translated into reality. This point called for the establishment of some sort of international body to ensure the preservation of peace—a league of nations.

Neither Clemenceau nor Lloyd George was particularly keen about such an organization. Very soon, though, it became plain that, in order to get their support for it, Wilson was willing, however grudgingly at times, to sacrifice both spirit and letter of virtually all of his other "points." It didn't take long before this tendency was obvious to one and all, and delegations from a number of the states represented at the conference (there were thirty-two in all) were quick to take advantage of it in pressing claims of their own. What resulted from some of these will be considered later. We are concerned, for now, about the fate of Germany.

By March, after dealing with a variety of issues attendant upon the collapse of the Austro-Hungarian Empire, the conference turned its attention to Germany. There was general agreement that the German Army had to be reduced in size, and a 100,000 man limit was set for it. Also, Germany was to have no heavy artillery, tanks, or military aircraft, and new naval vessels could not displace more than 15,000 tons.

Territorial arrangements were more vexed. The French wanted the Rhineland broken off and formed into an independent republic under strong influence from Paris. The British and Americans opposed the idea, and the French backed off. To assuage French fears, however, it was agreed that the Rhineland area would be demilitarized, i.e., no German troops were to be allowed there. Alsace-Lorraine, with all of its coal resources, would be returned to France, and plebiscites would determine whether Germany or the newly-formed Polish state (which was showing some very aggressive tendencies with regard to frontier issues) would obtain Upper Silesia and, by virtue of a "corridor," which separated East Prussia from the rest of Germany, access to the sea. The German port city of Danzig would be declared a "free city." The industry-rich Saar Basin would go to France for fifteen years as mandate to the new "League of Nations." Then, a plebiscite would determine its fate. Since almost all of its inhabitants were German, this flew in the face of Wilsonian "self-determination." Furious, he threatened to go home. Then, more concerned than ever with the fate of his "league," he gave in.

Of course, Germany had to surrender all of her colonies to the Allies, i.e., Great Britain and France. As in the case of the Saar, they would be held as mandates to the League of Nations. While the German colonies had never been profitable for the mother country, indeed, constituting something of a financial drain, this represented another humiliation for many Germans. An even greater humiliation was the Allied demand that Germany turn over the ex-Kaiser and a number of other national leaders for trial as war criminals. Faced with more urgent post- war concerns, the Allied governments would not press this issue.

One issue, however, embodied in the infamous Article 231, was pressed. Germany and her Allies were declared to have been solely responsible for the war and thus would be required to pay for all damages sustained by her opponents. The first payment, totalling approximately five billion dollars, would be due on May 1, 1921. How much more Germany would have to pay up in the form of reparation payments would be determined at that time. It was very plain that the total ultimately agreed upon would be burdensome; that the German lemon would indeed be "squeeze[d] until the pips squeaked." Of the handsome total to be collected, 52% was to go to France, 22% to Great Britain, 10% to Italy, and 8% to Belgium.

Around the middle of April, a German delegation was summoned to Versailles to learn of what the Allies had in store for them. Once there, these somber people, hoping against hope that Wilson had been able to be a moderating influence, were deposited in a building surrounded by barbed wire. They were being treated as prisoners-of-war—another slap in the face to German national pride. Every bit as concerned with symbolism as those who had determined that the war would end at the "eleventh hour," the Allies presented their guests with the peace terms on May 7, 1919, the fourth anniversary of the sinking of the *Lusitania.* Insult was piled upon insult. Late in March, the blockade had been partially lifted; but, the Allies made it plain that if Germany showed any defiance in the face of them, to say nothing of refusing to accept the harsh peace terms, it would be reimposed.

Confronted with the terms, the head of the German delegation, Ulrich von Brockdorff-Rantzau, was furious. When it came to reparations, he declared, the Allies ought to remember an important fact: "'The hundreds of thousands of noncombatants who have perished since November 11 by reason of the blockade were killed with cold deliberation after our adversaries had conquered and victory had been assured to them.'" Then, after a pause, "'Think of that when you speak of guilt and punishment.'" President Wilson who, in his monomaniacal concern for the "league" and his reputation had momentarily lost track of the humanitarian principles supposedly informing both, called the foreign minister's words "'tactless.'"[4] In any event, Brockdorff-Rantzau would not sign the peace treaty until his government—and the German public—heard of it. As the German delegation left the room in the Trianon Palace in which the terms had been presented, one of its members turned to Clemenceau and posed what was meant to be a rhetorical question: "What will history say of this?" Clemenceau's retort was instantaneous: "It will not say that Belgium invaded Germany."

When Germans learned of the peace terms, there were mass protests everywhere, and the first chancellor of the new republic resigned. Amongst the Allies, Lloyd George was having troubled second thoughts. Clemenceau, however, stood firm. And by now, Wilson was as intransigent as anybody. He coldly rejected Lloyd George's suggestion—whatever it was worth at this point—that Germany at least be allowed to join the League of Nations so that the country would not be driven into isolation. No, the American president said; Germany did not merit the privilege of membership in the august international-body-to-be. As the peace conference was drawing to a close, Wilson, who, Clemenceau once declared, "spoke like the Lord God one day and Lloyd George the next," was sounding more like Clemenceau and God rolled up into one.

German outrage was futile. The Allies held their bridgeheads at Cologne, Koblenz, and Mainz—where, according to the treaty, they were to remain for five, ten, and fifteen years, respectively—and these could serve as springboards for an invasion of Germany as a whole. Also, of course, the blockade could be reimposed at any time. On June 28, 1919, representatives of what was supposed to be a "new" Germany signed what became known as the "Treaty of Versailles." The choice of the date for the signing was another insult. As we recall, June 28 was the anniversary of the assassination of Archduke Franz Ferdinand and his wife. The place chosen for the signing was a further humiliation. The delegations gathered in the Hall of Mirrors of the main palace of Versailles. When the German Empire had been declared, on January 18, 1871, it had been in that room.

It has been said that, in their outrage over the treaty imposed on them, Germans forgot the far harsher Peace of Brest-Litovsk imposed upon a then supine Russia. Of course, there is some truth to this. The Peace of Versailles, however, was harsh enough. Through plebiscites and simple annexation, Germany lost around 25,000 square miles of territory and 6.5 million people, at least half of whom were German-speaking. Confronted with the need to pay staggering reparations, the country's economy was hobbled through the loss of the resource and industry-rich territories of Alsace-Lorraine, the Saar, and Upper Silesia. In having to surrender these regions, Germany gave up 75% of her iron-ore, 68% of her zinc, and 26% of her coal. Of perhaps greater concern for the future, however, was that enormous loss of pride, something that was seemingly deliberately engendered not only by the treaty itself, but in the manner in which it was imposed on the country. This is a subject to which we will return at the end of this chapter.

While Germany was harshly punished at Versailles, the Austro-Hungarian Empire disappeared altogether. The completely new state of Czechoslovakia was formed from remnants of it. While it had a democratic form of government (indeed, it would be the only country so ruled in East-Central Europe), substantial problems between Czechs and Slovaks were evident almost from the time of the new nation's inception. Just how critical these problems could become would become plain in due course. Czechoslovakia's neighbor to the north-east was Poland, a sovereign state for the first time since 1795. This country immediately put in a claim for the important mining district of Teschen, also claimed by Czechoslovakia, but containing a significant Polish minority population. The Poles pressed their claim by invading the place; but, after considerable discussion, it was decided that it should go to Czechoslovakia, and Poland sullenly withdrew its troops. Land taken from the new state of Lithuania and from what would become the Soviet Union, however, was kept, and this left Poland with large minority populations within its frontiers, none of them particularly happy.

Romania had been recognized as an independent state since 1878. For being on the winning side, however, it doubled its size, the most important addition being Transylvania, taken from Hungary, now independent. Besides a presumably large collection of beings "who go bump in the night," this brought in several million quite palpable Hungarians, almost none of whom were exactly enthused about being placed under Romanian rule. Later, like Poland, flexing its muscles, Romania took advantage of Russian weaknesses to grab Bessarabia. Thus, as was also the case with Poland, Romania came to have large minority populations in the country. As a source of tensions, it would serve to fuel Romanian nationalistic paranoia, in due course becoming the source of a pernicious variety of Fascism.

Serbia had not bothered to wait for a peace conference to reap rewards for her being on the winning side in World War I. In December, 1918, it was announced that there was a new entity called "The Kingdom of Serbs, Croats, and Slovenes." Some years later, this rather cumbersome name was replaced by the word "Yugoslavia," which means "kingdom of the south Slavs." It consisted of the former Serbia with Croatia, Slovenia, and Bosnia, all formerly parts of the old Austro-Hungarian Empire, added on to it. Croatians and Slovenes were Catholic, somewhat more economically sophisticated, and more Western-oriented than the largely rural and Orthodox Serbs. Bosnia, the most backward portion of the new state, was largely Muslim. A Serbian dynasty ruled over what became Yugoslavia and, within a very short period of time, it became obvious that many Croatians, Slovenes, and Bosnians were not at all pleased with this arrangement. Generally, the Serb-dominated government could count on support only from Montenegro. Previously independent, this tiny region on the Adriatic also was annexed by Serbia, albeit with little protest on the part of its inhabitants. Versailles, and later treaties as well, put stamps of approval on the new south Slav state, little appreciating what would lie ahead for a land generally united by language, but vexed by cultural, social, and religious differences.

As indicated earlier, Austria and Hungary were separated. Many, perhaps most, Austrians would have preferred to have united with Germany, the arrangements at Versailles having separated the now-truncated and landlocked country both from markets for her products and, obviously, seaports. The Treaty of Versailles specifically forbade this, however. Furthermore, a region known as the Sudetenland, home to about three million Austrians, went to Czechoslovakia, and this would be the source of future troubles. In fact, as a result of such, Czechoslovakia would be the first true victim of Nazi German aggression. Some 250,000 Austrians in the South Tyrol were now citizens of Italy, and this did not sit well with most of them. As seen earlier, Hungary lost Transylvania to Romania, and this became a source of much nationalistic rancor. As in the case of Romania, which saw the rise of a Fascist movement due, in part, to tensions arising from her obtaining Transylvania, a Fascism would arise in Hungary as well; only, in this case, it came into being in large measure because of the *loss* of Transylvania.

None of the developments mentioned above, almost all of which resulted from the break-up of the Austro-Hungarian Empire, augured well for the future. Indeed, at least emotionally, one cannot help, at times, to agree with Winston Churchill, who once described the Empire's demise as one of the greatest tragedies of the Twentieth Century. "National self-determination"—an ingredient crucial to the potpourri comprising Wilsonian idealism—probably has rationalized more outright butchery as any other phrase in any language.

Austria, shorn of land, prestige, and, above all, hope, sent a delegation to Saint-Germain-en-Laye, just outside of Paris, in September, 1919, to sign a treaty the contents of which had been, in most aspects, a forgone conclusion for some time. Bulgaria, which, for all of the suffering endured by its soldiers, was still a minor player in the overall scheme of things, dispatched its delegation to Neuilly, also near Paris, in November. Territorial losses to Greece and Romania had been agreed upon at Versailles, and the unhappy defenders of Bulgarian interests put pens to paper confirming these. Representatives of Turkey met Allied counterparts at Sevres, France early in June, 1920. There, it was agreed that, on top of surrendering what was left of the old Ottoman Empire to Great Britain and France as mandates to the League of Nations, spheres of influence in Anatolia, i.e., Turkey itself, would be distributed amongst the Allies. Resistance on the part of a Turkey reinvigorated by a new leader, Kemal Ataturk (1881–1938) rendered the spheres of influence scheme null and void. Syria and Lebanon, however, did go to France, Mesopotamia, i.e., Iraq, as well as Palestine, to Great Britain.

As mentioned earlier, Middle Eastern issues had been greatly complicated by British encouragement of Arab nationalism, while more-or-less traditional colonial arrangements between Great Britain and France had been arrived at through the Sykes-Picot Agreement. When, on top of this already contradictory amalgam, one added British encouragement, through the Balfour Declaration, of Zionism, then troubles unimagined and perhaps unimaginable loomed on the horizon. The festering Israeli-Arab conflict thus came directly out of World War I concerns.

We have been considering problems arising from territorial arrangements concerning, with the exception of Romania, the losers in the Great War. Representatives of one of the winners left Versailles greatly disappointed and this would have extraordinary consequences very shortly. In order to entice Italy to enter the war, the country had been promised a great deal. And indeed, as we have seen, she did receive the South Tyrol, much to the displeasure of Austrians living there. Italy also obtained the Trentino, the Dodecanese Islands and the island of Rhodes (from Turkey), and the port of Trieste. The Allies, however, had also stated that they would support Italian claims in Albania and with regard to islands off of the Dalmatian coast. New power-political concerns, however, especially those surrounding the emergence of what would become Yugoslavia, now rendered these particular promises null-and-void. Italians felt betrayed and there was much bitterness. In September, 1919, the Italian poet and war hero, Gabriele D'Annunzio (1865-1938) led a group of around one thousand adventurers in seizing the Dalmatian port city of Fiume, designated to go to Yugoslavia. While the Italian government declared official embarrassment and disowned the action, the Italian public, for the most part, was delighted with it. When, under international pressure, the Italian government dispatched forces which expelled D'Annunzio, bitterness developed into fury.

Italian foreign policy disappointments came on top of a massive war-time debt. There was unemployment, and hundreds of thousands of discharged soldiers could not find work. Strikes abounded and there was a pervasive fear of Communism. Italian frustrations and bitterness—the feeling that 680,000 men had died in vain—provided the background for the rise to power of a man who had done all that he could to involve Italy in the war. To some extent taking his cue from D'Annunzio, Benito Mussolini would lead his Fascist movement to power in October, 1922. While elements that can be seen as Fascistic in nature had been around before World War I in Italy and elsewhere, it is difficult, if not impossible, to imagine Fascist movements taking hold to any significant degree—to say nothing of actually seizing power—without the frustrations, fears, disappointments, and bitterness generated both by the war itself and by the treaties which brought the conflict to an end, all the while, of course, serving "to make the world safe for democracy."

In fact, of course, the botched peace-making of 1919, and the legacy of fear, disappointment, hatred, and brutalization left by the conflict, revealed clearly that, in the end, the war had triumphed over what Abraham Lincoln had once called "the better angels of our nature." For their part, the Allies had demonstrated this at Versailles. In Germany, this most terrible of triumphs doomed the country's first experiment in democracy while pointing the way to horrors unimagined.

NATIONAL SHAME AND A TAINTED REPUBLIC

Historians offer a variety of reasons why the Weimar Republic failed. The fact that Germans simply weren't accustomed to republican usages, most importantly, pluralism, is often cited as being of paramount importance. Mention is usually made of the fact that the system of "proportional representation," by virtue of which political parties would be represented in the now-powerful *Reichstag* in direct proportion to votes received, allowed for legislative confusion while making it very difficult to form working governmental coalitions. In view of the fact that there were almost a score of political parties in Germany, each representing a particular class or interest group, proportional representation certainly did create many problems. As a sort of

unemployment

Compre

war had won

failure

counterweight to what some constitutional planners saw as the "over-democratization" embodied in proportional representation, there was Article 48. This allowed the president of the republic—who, unlike the chancellor, was not much involved in its day-to-day concerns—to suspend civil liberties and rule by decree in times of national emergency. To be sure, such an order would have to be counter-signed by the chancellor. Those who drew up the Weimar constitution, however, were not very precise in determining the *Reichstag's* role in this process, and this would certainly create difficulties.

The old German Empire, while authoritarian in nature, was a rather loose confederation. Individual states, such as Bavaria, Prussia, or Saxony, retained a good deal of power. For example, there was no really meaningful national tax. Each state collected taxes on its own and donated a portion of the funds thus obtained to the central government in Berlin. Unlike in neighboring France, where education had become highly centralized, the nature and quality of German schools varied widely from region to region. There was no true national railway system. Ironically enough, it was a republican Germany in which, with the exception of education, a high degree of centralization took place. In some areas, most notably Bavaria, the loss of considerable local autonomy became a major source of resentment. Not surprisingly, Adolf Hitler was able to make much use of Bavarian separatism for his own purposes although, of course, he was ultimately concerned not with breaking free from the Weimar state, but taking it over.

The army, which Groener had committed to the defense of the republic, became, as an all-volunteer outfit, more of a state-within-a-state than it ever had been in the days of the Empire, and the *Reichstag* had little real control over it even though such was supposedly assured by the Weimar constitution. It was no friend of the republic, much less a defender of it, and this would become plain on several occasions. On top of this, most bureaucrats, jurists, teachers, and professors were, at best, very coolly-disposed to republicanism. In many ways, the claim goes, the high percentages gained in the January 19, 1919 Constituent Assembly elections by identifiably republican-oriented parties was due to the fact that the German people thought that if they accepted a form of government foisted on them by the Allies, things might go better for them at the peace table. Such, of course, had not occurred and, over time, Weimar Germany became a republic increasingly bereft of republicans.

Finally, a country economically-weakened through having to surrender up territories rich in natural resources was being compelled to pay burdensome reparations. The precise total, arrived at in May, 1921, amounted to about 32 billion dollars, and the government ruling at the time was so traumatized by the Allied claim that it resigned. In a word, the Allies, in need of funds for reconstruction and/or to pay back hefty American loans, were placing terrible burdens on a republican government which was both unprecedented and largely unwanted. That at least some of Germany's financial difficulties were due to massive war-time expenditures, and hence had little to do with the new republic, was something often overlooked by disgruntled Germans beset by an inflation which would reach unimaginable proportions in 1923.

Certainly, all of these factors were important in hobbling, perhaps fatally crippling, the Weimar experiment almost from its inception. Yet, it is probable that the most crucial reason that the German people never really "took" to the Weimar Republic was psychological. Here, two crucial dates are of importance. As we recall, the Versailles Treaty was signed on June 28, 1919. On July 31, 1919, a little more than a month after representatives of the republic-in-formation signed a treaty which, in the eyes of many, did everything but strip Germany of its sovereignty, the Weimar Republic officially came into being. For many, probably most, Germans, this was a fateful association. The Weimar Republic was born in despair and soon became not merely a symbol of national humiliation, but its embodiment.

For those Germans who simply could not accept defeat, for those who comforted themselves with the thought that, rather than the army failing, the country had been "stabbed in the back" by a coterie of leftists and Jews, the republic was a monument not only to national shame, but treason. And the fact that a Jew, the famous legal expert, Hugo Preuss (1860–1925), played a leading role in drawing up the Weimar constitution, was taken as evidence that, not only was the republic a political travesty, but a cultural abomination as well. November, 1918, which saw the abdication of Wilhelm II and the coming to power of the Council of Peoples' Representatives headed by the colorless Ebert, came to viewed as a time in which treason assured German national humiliation. Psychologically burdened with the terrible legacy of two million war dead and hundreds of thousands dead of hunger on the home front, many Germans would be most receptive to a politician who made much use of the term "November Criminals."

After the ghastly inflation of 1923, itself a terrible psychological, as well as an economic, shock to the German people, things seemed to be better for the country. Left and right-wing coup attempts, such as Hitler's November, 1923 effort, appeared to be things of the past. Reparation payments continued, but in modified forms which put less of a strain upon the country. Germany became internationally-respectable again, in fact, joining the League of Nations in 1926. Yet, the association of Weimar with national shame remained and this was clearly revealed in the 1925 presidential elections made necessary by the death of Friedrich Ebert, first president of the republic. In a runoff election, the German people elected Paul von Hindenburg, a very palpable representative of an old Germany, redolent with military glory, as their president. While certainly an honorable individual, he detested the republican political system and everybody knew it.

It can be argued that, if Germany had not been staggered by the world depression of 1929, the republic might well have survived. "What if" historical questions generally are impossible to resolve. What can be said, however, is that the association of the republic with defeat, humiliation, and immense spiritual loss was probably the single most important factor in determining that, in times of stress, people would turn away from it. Furthermore, Germans on both battle and home fronts had been brutalized by the war and its bitter consequences. A movement which, seemingly more religious than political, was willing to use violence in its efforts to come to power; a movement which called for revenge against those perceived as betraying the Fatherland—such a movement would attract enormous support from a population so conditioned by war-time associations and bitterness that many could accept, indeed rejoice, in seeing national idealism articulated in the idiom of brutality. The mounded corpses on shell-ravaged fields, the desiccated bodies of children starved by a pitiless blockade—in themselves, almost impossible for the mind to assimilate—foreshadowed scenes which would have been impossible without the Great War and the resultant humiliation of the German people.

Throughout this book, the terms "Great War," "World War I," and "First World War" have been used interchangeably. In terms of what resulted from it with regard to the traumatization and brutalization of Europe in general, and, more pointedly, Germany in particular, I think that the first designation is to be preferred. For, with regard to war and what comes from it, a certain threshold had been passed. No reasonably well-balanced person in Europe emerged from the conflict in favor of mass death, but, Europeans had become accustomed to it and, depending on who would be victimized, would now accept it as having a role to play in national politics. Thus, words such as the following, which appeared in the June 28, 1919 issue of the conservative *Deutsche Zeitung,* were informed by a willingness that "vengeance" assume forms unimaginable before 1914: "Vengeance! German nation! Today in the Hall of Mirrors at Versailles a disgraceful treaty is being signed . . . Never forget it! The German people, with unceasing labor, will push forward to reconquer that place among the nations of the world to which they are entitled. There will be vengeance for the shame of 1919."[5]

19

Epilogue

From a non-European perspective, the Great War was a downright positive event—even if inordinate numbers of non-European peoples were sacrificed in a white man's war—because the European imperial powers were greatly weakened by it. Indeed, most historians see it as the beginning of the end for European imperialism. While this is no doubt true, it is too bad that the cost had to be so high. And, even bearing in mind those technical advances which often occur as a result of wartime demands, one is hard-pressed to find anything of positive value coming out of it. Not only did the war, and the so-called "peace" built upon the ruins, ensure that there would be another go-around; it prepared the way for the most systematic attempt at mass extermination ever seen. Verdun and the Somme hardened people, while the slaughter of the Armenians showed that even a rather primitive country could carry it off and, further, essentially get away with it. Mass murder in the name of Soviet idealism would not have occurred without the most terrible of revolutions, in turn, unthinkable without the Great War.

Even after the terrible truths about the Great War became plain, they could, through sentimentalization, trivialization, and political chicanery, be ignored, modified to suit nationalistic usages, or even twisted into their opposite. Most Europeans emerged from the war with strengthened nationalistic feelings. Also, with the breakup of Empires, there were more varieties of nationalism than ever before. And this brings us to another crucial point.

Power-political arrangements during the war and at the peace table assured that there would be varieties of conflict which would continue on even after a second great global conflict. The current conflicts in

Eastern Europe and the Middle East were made, if not inevitable, than certainly highly probable by the Great War and what followed hard upon it. Ironically enough, traditional imperial interests, at least insofar as the Middle East was concerned, laid the foundation for problems which have persisted long after the Empires themselves faded into oblivion.

Finally, one can consider the fate of Wilsonian idealism. When the American president returned to the United States, he found that the country, beset with pressing domestic issues such as labor troubles, increasing racial tensions, and a rising hysteria about Bolshevism, had lost considerable interest in international issues. Certainly, the Congress had, in any case. In September, after a summer of race-rioting which served to make 1919 the bloodiest single non-wartime year in American history, he travelled about the country attempting to garner public support for America's signing of the Peace of Versailles and the country's joining the League of Nations. If America did not join the League, he had declared before Congress, it would "break the heart of the world." During the course of a grueling journey, Wilson had a stroke which incapacitated him. Later, he was coherent enough to assimilate the news that Congress had determined that the United States would neither sign the Versailles treaty nor join the League. There was no vast public outcry of indignation, and the only heart of note broken was the president's own. A virtual recluse, he died in 1924. Under his political tutelage, America had become a true world power, even if its citizenry did not wish to assume those responsibilities attaching to such a status.

When asking Congress to declare war on Germany, Woodrow Wilson had declared that "the world must be made safe for democracy." Alas, what the Great War had done was to clear the way for political leaders and movements which would pose the greatest threats to democracy the world had ever seen. Obviously, as this writer sees it, nothing of lasting good came of the Great War. Millions indeed died in vain. Yet, the war tells us much about human beings and human nature while, at the same time, being an experience of a rather singular sort. For these reasons we must remember it, even if, over time, the turning of "Armistice Day" into "Veterans' Day" already has served to trivialize it to some degree.

If one visits Pearl Harbor, one can observe oil still leaking from the sunken battleship *Arizona.* According to the person who guided a group of us on a tour, some believe that when the last bubble of oil escapes the ruined hull, in which over a thousand men are entombed, there will be peace. Some day, the last live shell fired in anger over seventy-five years ago will be exploded. Unlike what seems to prevail in the case of the *Arizona,* however, there appears to be no general agreement as to what this might mean . . .

Notes

[Chapters 1, 10, 14, 17, and 19 do not have any notes.]

Chapter 2

1. S.L.A. Marshall, *The American Heritage History of World War I,* New York, American Heritage Publishing Co., Inc., 1964, p. 9.

2. Friedrich von Bernhardi, *Germany and the Next War.* Translated by Allen H. Powles, New York, Chas. A. Eron, 1914, pp. 173–174. (Emphasis is Bernhardi's.)

Chapter 3

1. William Craig Wade, *The Titanic: End of a Dream,* New York, Penguin Books, 1980, p. 102.

2. Ibid., p. 383.

3. Walter Lord, *A Night to Remember,* New York, Holt, Rinehardt & Winston, 1955, p. 113.

4. Barbara W. Tuchman, *The Proud Tower: A Portrait of the World Before the War: 1890–1914,* New York, Macmillan, 1966, p. 382.

5. Brian Bond, *War and Society in Europe, 1870–1970,* Oxford and New York, Oxford University Press, 1984, p. 75.

6. Ibid., p. 76.

7. Paul Fussell, *The Great War and Modern Memory,* Oxford and New York, Oxford University Press, 1975, p. 231.

8. Bond, op. cit., p. 76.

9. Ibid., p. 98.

10. Michael C. C. Adams, *The Great Adventure: Male Desire and the Coming of World War I,* Bloomington, Indiana, Indiana University Press, 1990, p. 91.

Chapter 4

1. Immanuel Geiss (ed.), *July 1914. The Outbreak of the First World War: Selected Documents,* New York, The Norton Library, 1967, p. 332.

2. Ibid., p. 333.

3. Michael Balfour, *The Kaiser and His Times,* New York, The Norton Library, 1972, p. 355.

4. J. M. Winter, *The Experience of World War I,* Oxford and New York, Oxford University Press, 1989, p. 115, p. 165.

5. S. L. A. Marshall, *The American Heritage History of World War I,* New York, The American Heritage Publishing Co., Inc., 1964, p. 9; Winter, ibid., p. 165.

6. Brian Bond, *War and Society in Europe, 1870–1970,* Oxford and New York, Oxford University Press, 1984, p. 96.

7. Paul Fussell, *The Great War and Modern Memory,* Oxford and New York, Oxford University Press, 1975, p. 19.

Chapter 5

1. Barbara Tuchman, *The Guns of August,* New York, Dell Publishing Co., Inc., 1969, p. 199.

2. Ibid., p. 68.

3. Ibid., p. 342.

Chapter 6

1. George L. Mosse, *Fallen Soldiers: Reshaping the Memory of the World Wars.* New York: Oxford University Press, 1989, pp. 70–71.

2. Robert Graves, *Goodbye to All That.* Garden City and New York, Anchor Books, 1957, p. 113.

3. Alistair Horne, *The Price of Glory. Verdun, 1916.* New York, MacFadden-Bartell, 1964, pp. 72–73.

4. Oscar Williams (ed.), *A Little Treasury of Modern Poetry: English and American.* New York, Charles Scribner's Sons, 1946, p. 235.

Chapter 7

1. Alan Clark, *The Donkeys.* London: Hutchinson, 1961, p. 126.

2. Ibid., p. 173.

Chapter 8

1. Charles Fair, *From the Jaws of Victory,* New York, Simon and Schuster, 1971, p. 323.

2. Ibid., p. 329.

3. S. L. A. Marshall, *The American Heritage History of World War I,* New York, Simon and Schuster, 1964.

4. Robert Melson, "Provocation or Nationalism: A Critical Inquiry into the Armenian Genocide of 1915," in Frank Chalk and Kurt Jonassohn (eds.), *The History and Sociology of Genocide: Analyses and Case Studies,* New Haven & London, Yale University Press, 1990, p. 283.

Chapter 9

1. S. L. A. Marshall, *The American Heritage History of World War I,* New York, Simon and Schuster, 1964, p. 142.

2. Tomes A. Bailey, *A Diplomatic History of the American People,* Eighth Edition, New York, Appleton-Century-Crofts, 1969, p. 578.

Chapter 11

1. General Erich von Falkenhayn, *General Headquarters 1914–1916 and its Critical Decisions,* London, Hutchinson, 1920, p. 214.

2. Ibid., p. 217.

3. Ibid., pp. 217–218.

4. Alistair Horne, *The Price of Glory: Verdun 1916,* New York, MacFadden-Bartell, 1964, p. 48.

5. Falkenhayn, op. cit., p. 237.

6. Horne, op. cit., p. 237.

7. Ibid., p. 327.

8. John Keegan, *The Face of Battle,* New York, Viking Press, 1976, p. 258.

9. S. L. A. Marshall, *The American Heritage History of World War I,* New York, American Heritage Publishing Company, Inc., 1964, p. 180.

10. Lyn MacDonald, *Somme,* London, Atheneum, 1983, p. 178.

11. *Sir Douglas Haig's Despatches December 1915–April 1919,* edited by Lt. Colonel J.W. Boraston, London, Dent; New York, Dutton, 1920, p. 51.

12. Marshall, op. cit.

13. Captain B.H. Liddell Hart, *The Real War: 1914–1918,* Boston and Toronto, Little, Brown and Company, 1930, p. 279.

14. Ibid., p. 292.

Chapter 12

1. S. L. A. Marshall, *The American Heritage History of World War I,* New York, American Heritage Publishing Company, p. 234.

2. J. M. Winter, *The Experience of World War I,* Oxford and New York, Oxford University Press, 1989, p. 141.

3. Erich Maria Remarque, *All Quiet on the Western Front,* translated from the German by A. W. Wheen, New York, Fawcett Crest, 1982, p. 111.

4. Edwin Campion Vaughn, *Some Desperate Glory: The World War I Diary of a British Officer, 1917,* with an Introduction by Robert Cowley, New York, Henry Holt and Company, 1988, p. 232.

5. Ernst Jünger, *Storm of Steel,* translated from the German by Basil Creighton, with an Introduction by R. H. Mottram, Garden City and New York, Doubleday, Doran, and Co., 1929, p. 211.

6. Diana Candell and Jean Liddiard, *Working for Victory? Images of Women in the First World War, 1914-1918,* London, Routledge and Kegan Paul, 1987, p. 7.

7. Helen Zenna Smith, *Not So Quiet . . . ,* Afterword by Jane Marcus, New York, The Feminist Press, 1989, p. 59.

8. Carl Zuckmayer, *Als wär's ein Stuck von Mir: Erinnerungen,* Frankfurt-am-Main, Fischer Taschenbuch Verlag, 1977, p. 175.

9. Joachim Remak, *The Origins of World War I,* New York, Holt, Rinehart and Winston, 1967, p. 82.

10. Winter, op. cit., p. 169.

11. A description of the pope legend is to be found in Stanley Weintraub, *A Stillness Heard Round the World: The End of the Great War, November, 1918,* New York and Oxford, Oxford University Press, 1985, p. 6.

Chapter 13

1. Barbara Tuchman, *The Guns of August,* New York, Dell, 1969, p. 80.

2. Michael T. Florinsky, *Russia: A History and an Interpretation,* Volume II, New York, Macmillan, 1960, pp. 1256-1257.

3. Ibid., pp. 1375-1376.

4. Ibid., p. 1356.

Chapter 15

1. Captain B.H. Liddell Hart, *The Real War: 1914-1918,* Boston: Little, Brown and Company, 1930, p. 301.

Chapter 16

1. S.L.A. Marshall, *The American Heritage History of World War I,* New York, American Heritage Publishing Company, Inc., 1964, p. 225.

2. Ibid., p. 228.

3. Thomas A. Bailey, *A Diplomatic History of the American People,* eighth edition, New York, Appleton-Century-Crofts, 1969, p. 598.

4. Jünger, *Feuer und Blut,* cited in Eric J. Leed, *No Man's Land: Combat and Identity in World War I,* London, New York, Melbourne, Cambridge University Press, 1979, pp. 158-159.

5. Barrie Pitt, *1918: The Last Act,* New York, Ballantine Books, 1963, pp. 223-224.

6. Peter Loewenberg, "The Psychohistorical Origins of the Nazi Youth Cohort," in Peter Loewenberg, *Decoding the Past: The Psychohistorical Approach,* New York, Alfred A. Knopf, 1983, p. 258.

Chapter 18

1. Stanley Weintraub, *A Stillness Heard Round the World. The End of the Great War: November 1919,* New York/Oxford, Oxford University Press, 1985, p. 406.

2. Ibid.

3. Ernst Jünger, *Storm of Steel,* translated by Basil Creighton, with an introduction by R. H. Mottran, Garden City, New York, Doubleday, Doran and Co., 1929, p. 280.

4. Weintraub, op. cit., p. 156.

5. Louis L. Snyder, *The Weimar Republic. A History of Germany from Ebert to Hitler,* Princeton, New Jersey, D. Van Nostrand Company, Inc., 1966, p. 136.

Index